Desert Imaginations

Desert Imaginations

A HISTORY OF SAHARANISM AND ITS RADICAL CONSEQUENCES

Brahim El Guabli

UNIVERSITY OF CALIFORNIA PRESS

University of California Press
Oakland, California

Library of Congress Cataloging-in-Publication Data

Names: Guabli, Brahim El, author.
Title: Desert imaginations : a history of Saharanism and its radical consequences / Brahim El Guabli.
Description: Oakland, California : University of California Press, [2025] | Includes bibliographical references and index.
Identifiers: LCCN 2025015450 (print) | LCCN 2025015451 (ebook) | ISBN 9780520401785 (hardback) | ISBN 9780520401792 (paperback) | ISBN 9780520401808 (ebook)
Subjects: LCSH: Deserts—Social aspects. | Desert ecology. | Deserts—Environmental aspects.
Classification: LCC GF55 .G83 2026 (print) | LCC GF55 (ebook) | DDC 304.20966—dc23/eng/20250615
LC record available at https://lccn.loc.gov/2025015450
LC ebook record available at https://lccn.loc.gov/2025015451

Manufactured in the United States of America

GPSR Authorized Representative: Easy Access System Europe, Mustamäe tee 50, 10621 Tallinn, Estonia, gpsr.requests@easproject.com

34 33 32 31 30 29 28 27 26 25
10 9 8 7 6 5 4 3 2 1

For my family.
For the memory of both my maternal and paternal grandparents, who lived and survived some of this history.

For Hawad in trans-Amazigh and trans-Saharan tag^{w}*mat.*

CONTENTS

PREFACE

My family are desert people. My father is Sahrawi, and my mother is Black and Amazigh, and both of their trajectories include histories of journeys, crossings, nomadism, and movement in and across deserts. The arid land where I grew up and spent most of my life is full of people and places that have deep emotional and mnemonic significance for me. This desert is nothing short of home. However, the phenomenon that I define as Saharanism has created a universalized image of deserts as empty, uninhabited, sandy, and unowned lands; such notions have reduced a rich universe and its biome to a set of clichés and superficial images that, for the critical observer, fail to do justice to these places. In conceptualizing Saharanism, *Desert Imaginations* aims to offer both a vocabulary and a novel theoretical framework that can help explain the sources of ready-made ideas that people almost automatically associate with deserts. Understanding Saharanism as the ideational apparatus undergirding and justifying the myriad enterprises that have taken place in deserts shifts attention from these desert-focused undertakings per se to their intellectual origins in Saharanism—that is, from the material actions to the ideology that fosters or even incentivizes the treatment of deserts as spaces available for and suited to all manner of exploitative, inhumane, and ecocidal endeavors.

My work on *Desert Imaginations* over the past seven years has taught me that Saharanism is closer to home than I had imagined. When I started conducting research for this book in 2018, it had never occurred to me just how profoundly it has impacted my own pre-Saharan hometown of Ouarzazate. A well-known destination for Hollywood filmmakers seeking desert landscapes for movies set in premodern periods or war-torn Middle Eastern countries, Ouarzazate, also called the Hollywood of Africa, has since 2016 added the largest solar farm in the world to its catalogue of landmarks. In fact, it has become a solar energy "sacrifice zone" that generates clean energy for other parts of the country or even potentially for European countries at the expense of the transformed Ouarzazi environment.[1] This sprawling power plant, called Noor-Ouarzazate, is the clearest example of Saharanism's ability to transform space and change a place's topography forever—along the way, revealing the invisible toll that clean energy projects take on desert dwellers and their environments.

Although I was aware that the Noor-Ouarzazate project had been approved in 2010, one year after I moved to the US, nothing prepared me for the first time I saw its transformative impact on the city of Ouarzazate and its vicinity. That was in December 2022. The COVID-19 pandemic had prevented me from visiting Morocco for more than three years, but, ironically, it had not impeded the construction of a gargantuan structure that so changed my hometown's visual identity. As my bus arrived from the direction of Marrakesh at sunset, I noticed a powerful light on top of a high tower that looked like an oddly incandescent lighthouse behind Tikniwin, or "the twin hills." At first sight, the column evoked the tower that France had built in 1960 at the Hammoudia testing site for carrying out its atmospheric nuclear experiments in the Reggane region of the Sahara. Luckily, the Noor-Ouarzazate tower has nothing to do with atomic testing. Nevertheless, it is representative of Saharanism's experimental dimension and the enduring colonization of desert spaces. Similar to the toxic legacy of "nuclear colonialism," which Danielle Endres, inspired by the work of Ward Churchill and Winona LaDuke,[2] defines as "a system of domination through which governments and corporations target indigenous peoples and their lands to maintain the nuclear production process,"[3] Noor-Ouarzazate has forever changed Ouarzazate's identity. The age of solar energy, which this city and its surrounding areas have been forced to enter, has ushered in a series of Saharanism-underlain transformations that will leave their ecological imprint on the region for generations.

Ṭṭāqa (energy) is the local name for this phallic structure. I immediately understood that the residents have added a neologism to their lexicon to refer to the newest landmark in their topography, but I was more interested in learning how this foreboding edifice had shifted their relationship to their environment. I learned that *ṭṭāqa* is polysemic and refers simultaneously to the solar energy farm, the tower, and the energy it produces. *Ṭṭāqa* specifically refers to the Noor-Ouarzazate solar project but also indirectly evokes a national renewable energies project run by the Moroccan Agency for Sustainable Energy (Masen) that has high-stakes, transnational ramifications, and embodies a top-down statal choice. Masen, which was created in 2010 to harness all renewable energies across Morocco, is a private but publicly funded company that seeks to produce fifty-two percent of Morocco's electricity from renewable sources by 2030.[4] From the perspective of the Global North, where the impact of global warming is threatening economic prosperity and citizens' comfort, this goal is commendable, since it dovetails completely with the UN-led move toward using renewable energies to mitigate the effects of climate change on Earth. Morocco, as a country that has no proven oil or gas reserves in commercial quantities, has real economic reasons to harvest sun and wind energy to achieve both energy security and self-sufficiency. However, there is always a difference between official discourse, which is mindful of the UN's benchmarks and fully attuned to international clean energy strategies, and the way projects like *ṭṭāqa* have reshaped the lives of ordinary people in whose backyards these lofty goals play out. Masen's glossy literature about the benefits of clean energy clearly overlooks the fact that eight thousand villagers no longer have access to three thousand acres (twelve square miles) of what had previously served as pasture lands.[5] This literature also ignores the fate of El Mansour Eddahbi, a reservoir constructed in 1971 that was once one of Morocco's fullest lakes but that has dried up because, among other factors, its water has been used to wash and cool down the solar-panel mirrors amid the severe drought that has been ongoing for five years.[6] According to the online newspaper *Alyaoum 24*, Noor-Ouarzazate uses up one percent of the water stored in the lake, the equivalent of 2.2 million cubic meters annually—a significant amount of this vital commodity of which farmers in the Draa Valley are deprived and which is given to Masen for free.[7] Even worse, local residents have reported that since the advent of *ṭṭāqa*, temperatures have risen and there has been a total absence of afternoon summer rains that used to cool down the inclement weather.

Ṭṭāqa is a contemporary example of Saharanism's brutal commodification of desert lands in an area where people never needed to treat their land as a commodity. Land is inherited and passed down from one generation to the next, and woe to the person who sells it, whether it is built up or not. After all, land is Mother Earth, and the connection to it should be one of nurturing and respect that observes a strict balance between need and desire rather than exploitation and extraction. Because land was not commodified, communal landownership practices in Ouarzazate and its surrounding villages, for instance, ensured that almost everyone had a parcel of land on which to build a home. This wise use of land resources meant that homelessness was unheard of in this region until recently. Starting in 2000, however, the ancestral wisdom that privileged shelter and the well-being of community members succumbed to capitalist pressures on these desert communities. Schemes characterized by the "develop-to-own" style designed in Rabat and Casablanca have brought investors who have no qualms about upending the local value system and dispossessing people in southeastern Morocco of their lands. Ranging from growing watermelons to running hotels, their development projects require significant amounts of water and further jeopardize a dry area that relies on very scarce rain waters. These investors' landgrabbing practices represent a local embodiment of Saharanism's long history of exploitative attitudes vis-à-vis arid lands, their people, and their resources.

Ṭṭāqa's over-the-top presence has colonized my hometown's identity. The solar-power tower is the first thing you see, regardless of the means of transportation or the direction you come from. During the day, this panoptic structure, which my wife likened to the "Eye of Sauron" in the *Lord of the Rings*, appears as an omnipresent, all-seeing eye with a 360-degree field of vision. The tower stands exuberantly tall, occupying the once-open space between villages and the giant, blue Atlas Mountains. However, there is even more to this colonization of desertic space. The sea of solar panels, built with exquisite Moroccan engineering know-how combined with cutting-edge European technology and multinational venture capitalist investments, has swallowed up thousands of acres of communal land. What once served as terrain for pastures and held potential for farming and construction is now occupied by a colossal technostructure that transforms sun rays into electricity around the clock. Funded through public money and exploited by a subsidiary of the Saudi Akwa Power, *ṭṭāqa*, in its larger significance, is just one iteration of a great number of desert-focused projects that connect deserts across the globe. From California, where the US Bureau of Land Management has developed a Desert Renewable Energy Conservation Plan to generate electricity, to western Saudi Arabia, where Mohammed Bin Salman is building the desert city of Neom, variations of *ṭṭāqa* and "solar sacrifice zones" have appeared,[8] underlain by the same conceptualization of deserts as places that invite extractive and experimental projects.

In the eyes of Masen's experts, the construction of their Noor stations endowed useless land with value. Masen's promotional video states that prior to their expropriation and exploitation by Masen and the National Office for Electricity, "these barren lands were devoid of any activity. The wind blew on the mountains without turning any turbines and the water flowed in the rivers without being stored in dams."[9] Masen's head of technical design repeated the same platitudes when she took pride in "transforming a bare, sterile, and unusable land into something green and flamboyant that will enlighten the lives of many households."[10] These statements would shock anyone who grew up in Ouarzazate. However, the shock dissipates when these misconceptions are read as classic tropes from the book of Saharanism. Notions of nonuse actively wipe out centuries-long histories of pastoralism, farming, and nomadism on the land. Pursuant to this thinking, desert lands can only claim a right to existence when and if they surrender to development or capitalistic ventures. The fact that these statements were made by Moroccans reveals that Saharanism—as a desert imagination—is an ideology that has been internalized both locally and globally.

There is no doubt that sustainability will benefit greatly from decreased reliance on fossil fuels. Likewise, humanity at large will also benefit from reducing individuals' carbon footprint and contributions to the greenhouse effect. Eerily, deserts are again posited as areas that have to be sacrificed for humanity's rescue. In the 1930s, when oil was discovered in commercial amounts in the Gulf and other areas, deserts were depicted as saviors because their sediments contained hundreds of years of consumable energy. Now that pollution from fossil fuels is understood to be unsustainable, deserts are coveted for their potential to extract solar energy and mineral resources like lithium to, again, resolve human need for energy. The Noor-Ouarzazate project is an example of this global trend of returning to deserts for newer, albeit less lethal, extractive energy endeavors, which still sacrifice desert lands and biodiversity to better life conditions elsewhere. Thus, the function of deserts as humanity's saviors has not changed after one hundred years, but neither has their image. They remain places to be feared, monitored, taken from, and most of all offered on the altar of human whims whenever necessary. *Desert Imaginations* draws connections between past and present discourses about and enterprises in deserts in order to show historical continuities between the ideas underlying the extractive and experimental uses that have been made of arid spaces across different deserts.

Saharanism's impact becomes even more dangerous when it meets authoritarianism. As a general rule, dictators tend to care more about impressing the world in order to boost their legitimacy than heeding their local image.

Despots doggedly adhere to any international benchmarks except those protecting human rights, and the promotion of green energy is one of the areas in which several Tamazghan (broader North African) and Middle Eastern dictators are demonstrating their prowess. However, this dictatorial zeal, which does indeed impress UN bodies and is met with praise from the Global North, hides the realities of their subjugated desert people. Rather than devising creative, sustainable solutions to the dispossessed inhabitants' problems, the Moroccan state privileged the easier option of securing the solar plant. Fenced and surveilled, the site of Noor-Ouarzazate looks like a fortress of blue solar panels. Through this militarization, the state killed two birds with one stone: it protects extraction and makes its presence known to the inhabitants of an area in which such an intrusive presence was not needed.

As demonstrated by this example from my hometown, Saharanism is at work on many levels and in many places. My hope is that *Desert Imaginations* will carve out a space for other scholars to push its boundaries and examine its manifestations across different deserts, languages, and cultures. My interdisciplinary methodology, combined with a historical approach and close reading of various types of sources, has allowed me to present a bird's-eye view of Saharanism as well as a microhistory of its enduring impacts in the Sahara and other deserts. I am hopeful that other scholars will draw on their intimate knowledge of specific deserts to further theorize and particularize this wide-ranging articulation of Saharanism. Now that Saharanism has been named and some of its aspects defined, it should no longer elude the critical attention of desert scholars. *Desert Imaginations* will hopefully reverse the recurrent trope of "unveiling deserts" by removing the veil of Saharanism, the ideology that for so long has determined how deserts have been (mis)treated and made into objects of transformation.

Desert Imaginations is divided into a preface, an introduction, five chapters, and an epilogue. The preface sheds light on Saharanism through the politics of solar energy in my own hometown and furnishes a summary of the book's overarching argument. The introduction provides the conceptualization of Saharanism and its evolution over time through a historical approach. Using the Sahara as a case study, the introduction defines Saharanism as a universalizing, trans-desert ideology that operates in deserts regardless of their specific location. It also demonstrates that the grammar of racialization, exploitation, extraction, and environmental mayhem is the common trait of Saharanism-inspired policies and projects that continue to shape literature, film, and other cultural media that consciously or inadvertently sustain Saharanism. Covering precolonial, colonial, and postcolonial periods, the introduction furnishes a broad but historically grounded articulation of Saharanism and its manifestations across deserts.

Chapter 1 is entitled "Spiritual Saharanism: The Desert as a Fanatical, Racialized Space." In this chapter, I draw on the history of specific religious experiences in the Sahara—particularly in the writings of Cardinal Lavigerie, Charles de Foucauld, Isabelle Eberhardt, Carlo Carretto, and Ernest Psichari, among others—to define "spiritual Saharanism" as the intersection of spirituality, conquest, and colonialism as they played out in the Sahara since France's colonization of Algeria in the nineteenth century. The chapter reveals how the Sahara emerged in the eyes of spiritual Saharanism as a place infested by brutal enslavers and godless criminals who had to be fought and subdued through the re-Christianization of the Sahara. Whether its proponents preached humanitarian causes or explicit colonialism, spiritual Saharanism, the chapter demonstrates, was violent, racist, and deeply embedded in Islamophobia, which keeps poking its head into discussions about immigration in Europe today.

Chapter 2, "Extractive Saharanism: Everything in Deserts Is Extractable!," reconstructs Saharanism's extractive nature and its manifestations in post–World War II French discourses about the Sahara. In the past, Saharanism's extraction took the form of slavery, whereby people were dislocated from their desert homes and sold to enslavers, but nowadays it has taken various forms, including—but not limited to—exploitation of oil reserves, minerals, wind, solar energy, aquifer water, and workers' labor. The chapter reveals how the colonially constructed notion of *mise en valeur* (extractive development) is still at work in discourses about and attitudes vis-à-vis resources deposited in deserts.

Chapter 3, "Experimental Saharanism: Deserts as a Testing Ground," examines Saharanism's justification of turning the Sahara and other deserts into spaces for scientific experimentation. Between the early 1900s and 1965, France, like the US and the Soviet Union, among others, attempted many experimental projects in the desert under its control. Ranging from the failed 1874 project to create an internal sea in the Sahara to the arrival of André Citroën's cars in the early twentieth century, these endeavors included testing trains, trucks, helicopters, missiles, chemical weapons, and atomic bombs. Interweaving several histories of experimentation in deserts, this chapter tells the story of "experimental Saharanism" and its weaponization of the supposed emptiness of the desert to the point of making that emptiness a reality at the expense of desert biomes.

Chapter 4, entitled "Sexual Saharanism: Transgression and Impunity in the Desert," contends that in tandem with the development of spiritual and experimental Saharanism, there developed a sex-obsessed dimension, which I have called "sexual Saharanism." Those engaged in sexual Saharanism have portrayed deserts as places where social, ethical, and legal norms surrounding sexual behaviors can be transgressed and contravened with total impunity. Best represented by the phrase "what happens in Vegas stays in Vegas," sexual Saharanism took the form of colonial pedophilia and prostitution in the colonial Sahara and has manifested in current US counterculture. I examine André Gide and Oscar Wilde's pedophilic practices in Algeria and the myth of Ouled Naïl prostitution in the Sahara. Beyond the Sahara, I articulate the place sexuality and transgression occupy in the annual Burning Man festival in Nevada and the HBO series *Westworld*, in which deserts function as locations for self-liberation.

Chapter 5, "'Unity of Creatures': Saharanism Meets Desert Ecocare," defines and deploys the concept of ecological care (ecocare) to demonstrate that Saharanism's reductive attitudes toward deserts have not gone unaddressed by Indigenous cultural producers. I use the works of Abdelrahman Munif, Ibrahim al-Koni, Omar Al Ansari, and Hocine Hacene, who all hail from desert societies, to construct ecocare as a form of desert environmentalism. Desert ecocare, as I conceptualize it, is a proactive form of both resistance and statement of existence against Saharanism's proponents' disregard for all desert lives.

Finally, in lieu of a conclusion, the epilogue, "Desert Legalese, Art, and the Path Forward," draws some crucial conclusions regarding Saharanism and opens up its horizons to applications as a trans-desert ideology. From the ongoing devasting war on Palestinians in Gaza to the transnational schemes to develop or swap ownership of deserts, this trans-desertic logic has been clearly apparent in the way arid lands are not only talked about but also actively desertified to conform to preconceived visions of Saharanism's proponents. The epilogue also highlights the myriad artistic, legal, and activist counter-imaginaries and resistances that have emerged from desert spaces and which continuously unsettle Saharanism and its impactful legacies.

ABBREVIATIONS

BBC	British Broadcasting Corporation
BIA	Bureau d'organisation des ensembles industriels africains
CBD	Center for Biological Diversity
CBP	US Customs and Border Protection
CEA	Commissariat à l'énergie atomique
CEMO	Centre d'expérimentations militaires des oasis
CGEM	Confédération générale des entreprises du Maroc
CIEES	Centre interarmées d'essais d'engins spéciaux
CREPS	Compagnie de recherches et d'exploitation de pétrole au Sahara
CSEM	Centre saharien d'expérimentations militaires
DAM	Direction des applications militaires
DTC	Desert Training Center
FAO	Food and Agriculture Organization
Frontex	European Border and Coast Guard Agency
IAEA	International Atomic Energy Agency
Masen	Moroccan Agency for Sustainable Energy
NATO	North Atlantic Treaty Organization
NPR	National Public Radio
NTS	Nevada Test Site

OCRS	Organisation commune des régions sahariennes
SCS	Soil Conservation Service
SIC	Saharan Industrial Complex
SW	Special Weapons
UNESCO	United Nations Educational, Scientific, and Cultural Organization
USSR	Union of Soviet Socialist Republics
ZOIA	Zone d'organisation industrielle africaine

NOTE ON TRANSLITERATION AND TRANSLATION

I have used a vocalized and shortened version of the IJMES transliteration system. Because vocalization counts in Arabic, I opted for a transliteration version that reflects this grammatical feature of the language.

Unless otherwise specified, all the translations from the Arabic, French, and Tamazight are mine.

Introduction

GENEALOGIES AND MANIFESTATIONS OF SAHARANISM

THIS IS NOT A BOOK about the history of deserts. It is rather a history of ideas about deserts. The book aims to articulate a conceptual framework that can help explain why what happens in deserts is almost expected to take place in them. Deserts are among the most marginalized and overlooked spaces on earth. This marginalization is due not to a dearth of deserts but is instead the consequence of their abundance, coupled with a long imaginative history that has portrayed them as exploitable, hostile, and dangerous spaces. The imaginaries underlying the way deserts are perceived encompass legacies of communities, individuals, and entities as varied as the ancient Greeks, Leo Africanus (1494–1554), Jacques Lebaudy (1868–1919), André Gide (1869–1951), Paul Bowles (1910–1999), *Star Wars*, UNESCO, the Burning Man festival, the European Border and Coast Guard Agency (Frontex), and US Customs and Border Protection (CBP), among others.[1] Both cultural producers and state bureaucrats have participated in the invention, deployment, perpetuation, reinvention, and dissemination of the particularly powerful desert imaginary, which I propose to call "Saharanism."[2]

Saharanism is not a recent phenomenon. Even though it reached its height in the context of colonial enterprises in the nineteenth and twentieth centuries, Saharanism is a well-established practice with roots extending back to the Greeks' encounters with Ethiopians and the Romans' conception of desert spaces beyond the North African coastline as *solitudines*. Ancient Greeks drew the earliest maps of the Sahara, and Leo Africanus's *History and Description of Africa* shaped European perceptions of sub-Saharan Africa for centuries. Gide and Bowles, among others, entrenched the Sahara in their readers' imaginations as a space for liberation and impunity. The actions of Lebaudy, a descendent of a wealthy French family whose own history connects financial success with colonialism, Napoleonian politics, and the end of the sugar plantation industry in the Caribbean, embodies the bizarrerie that played out in the Sahara. *Star Wars* invented the Tatooine, Jakku, and Er'Kit deserts, captivating the attention of generations of viewers and shaping their views of the landscape. UNESCO built on the legacy of colonial Saharanism and disseminated it through its Arid Zones Program.[3] The Burning Man festival is now a brand that has had a home in Black Rock City, in northwestern Nevada, since 1991. Similar to the CBP's mission in the Sonoran Desert, Frontex's aim has been to police the African desert, thereby transferring European borders to the Sahara.[4] These desert-focused obsessions have ecological and human costs that have never been linked, let alone theorized, in a more holistic and interdisciplinary way.[5]

Saharanism is a globalizing desert imaginary that undergirds the way deserts are perceived and acted upon globally; in other words, it is a mode of knowledge and a blueprint for various actionable endeavors that play out in deserts. Or, to paraphrase geographer Mike Heffernan's claim, things that are inconceivable in "ordinary" places are not only incentivized but also considered inherent to deserts.[6] The outcome of an extensive history of treasure-hunting, racialization, adventurous enterprises, and imperialistic intervention in desert spaces, Saharanism has legitimized the transformation of arid landscapes into loci for both material and immaterial extraction. Furthermore, deserts have long been focal points for experimenting with large-scale industrial projects as well as testing lethal military equipment.[7] In conceptualizing Saharanism, I am less interested in what Edward Said called the "apparent ontological inequality of Occident and Orient" than I am in understanding the ways that theoretical knowledge of deserts and subsequent actions within them have worked to exploit real or imagined existential conditions of the landscape.[8] Deserts are expansive ecological spaces that make up thirty-three percent of Earth's surface and are transformed by Saharanism into powerful imaginaries of emptiness, solitude, death, and danger, all of which coalesce to remove them from the purview of ethics, law, and normative understandings of both life and humanity.

Although Saharanism evokes the word *ṣaḥrāʾ* (desert) in Arabic, the notion of *khālāʾ* (wilderness, emptiness) best suits its multilayered meaning and implications. Therefore, I propose the Arabic *istikhlāʾ*, which means, among other things, making into a desert or wilderness, and the English word *desertism*, which implies the notions of both desertification and desertion, as equivalents to Saharanism. Both *istikhlāʾ* and desertism capture the discursive and practical creation of deserts and the desertion of ethical and legal considerations when it comes to doing things to or in deserts. Even though the concept refers to the Arabic word *ṣaḥrāʾ*, its theoretical implications apply to all deserts, both hot and cold, since the ideational framework around which Saharanism is constructed exists within an interconnected web of deserts around the globe,[9] a reality that Michel Roux brings up in his attribution of the sandy desert's invasion of public imagination in France to "a network of complex esthetic, philosophical, and historical associations."[10] This network of ideas forms the backbone of this powerful imaginary, which, whether we call it Saharanism, *istikhlāʾ*, or desertism, is an ideology that has been at work, consciously or unconsciously, in the many questionable enterprises that have unfolded and continue to unfold in deserts.

Said defined Orientalism as "a field of learned study" of the Orient, and he demonstrated the various forms of contrived authority that Orientalists derived from their engagement with this invented space.[11] By virtue of this artificial scholarly authority, Orientalists can and must distance themselves from the physical Orient.[12] Whereas Orientalists have to place themselves outside the Orient to gain control over it, the *Saharien* (Saharanist), or the practitioner of Saharanism, is expected to have immediate contact with the desert or even to "go native" in order to gain "firsthand" practical knowledge of it. Despite the overlaps between Orientalism and Saharanism, particularly in the nineteenth century, Saharanism as I conceptualize it is a transcontinental, transnational imaginary that focuses on the distinctively desertic ecological space regardless of its location or the racial and ethnic affiliations of its populations. It examines the historical trajectory of misrepresentation driven by racialized encounters between ancient Greeks, Romans, Arabs, Asians, Westerners, and the inhabitants of desert environments. Saharanism is not the province of one culture, language, or group of people, and its practice has shifted with changes in power dynamics and zones of influence, as evidenced by Ibn Battuta's *riḥla* (travel) in the thirteenth century and Taiwanese author Sanmao's writings about the Spanish Sahara in the 1970s.[13] Saharanists draw on a complex and seemingly immutable matrix of ideas to inform and justify their endeavors in deserts. Nevertheless, there is a difference between those who practice Saharanism as an ideological attitude toward deserts and desert enthusiasts, or what Reynar Banham calls "desert freaks,"[14] who are generally drawn to deserts for personal reasons that are devoid of ideology. By conceptualizing Saharanism and delineating its intellectual genealogies and manifestations, it becomes possible to perceive how it has morphed over time into a powerful system of ideas that justify extraction, experimentation, racialization, and sexual exploitation in desert environments. Its diverse manifestations range from the most mundane activities (like taking pictures with camels and sand dunes) to industrial and security projects carried out by ideologically informed Saharanists.[15] Saharanism's increasing banality is embodied in desert literature, art, film, and tourism, all of which have been amplified in conjunction with the phenomenal consolidation of this ancient ideology, beginning in the nineteenth century. The American expansion west and the Anglo-French colonization of the Sahara in the nineteenth century enmeshed deserts into conversations about conservation and development. This brought deserts closer to larger audiences and gave Saharanism the power to potentially reach every home and permeate the daily life of all societies. In telling a story of ambassadorship, exploration, missionary action, cartography, indigeneity, and military conquest, *Desert Imaginations* theorizes Saharanism as it has evolved and changed, specifically during dramatic encounters between deserts and those who planted or perpetuated the seeds of Saharanism.

The Romans described the desert as *terra incognita* (unknown land). They also used *solitudines* to refer to the desert beyond the recognizable places they had colonized in North Africa.[16] In their imagination, the desert separated the familiar world of civilization (the city) from the world of "barbarians" who had to be fended off. According to French archaeologist André Berthier, "Rome had divided North Africa into provinces, which it enriched thanks to Mediterranean trade, but which it meticulously separated from the Sahara by a trench, a limit, guarded by legionnaires and Syrian guards."[17] Before the Romans, the Greeks had depicted the Egyptian dwellers of the desert as "Ethiopian," which means "burned face."[18] By doing so, the Greeks committed one of the first recorded acts of racialization that would continue to be inherent to Saharanism. More recently, French political scientists and legal scholars have drawn on the notion of *terra nullius* (no-man's land) either to diminish the importance of Indigenous Saharans or to simply deny their existence in order to claim sovereignty over the Sahara. *Terra nullius*, as Heffernan rightly suggests, has allowed "forms of innovation and experimentation unimaginable elsewhere [to be] deemed not only possible but necessary" in the desert.[19] Hence, by virtue of being itself, the desert invites this Saharan imaginary that seeks to mold it to the expectations and desires of Saharanism's proponents.

Because of Saharanism, deserts have become "national sacrifice zones."[20] According to Steve Lerner, this concept is an "Orwellian term coined by government officials [during the Cold War] to designate areas dangerously contaminated as a result of the mining and processing of uranium into nuclear weapons."[21] Sacrifice zones are towns, corridors, and areas, located particularly in the Global South or in poor or remote areas in industrialized societies, that are delivered to toxic and deadly undertakings in order to enhance national defense or create prosperity in other, more important, areas. Mining writer Christopher Pollon states in his book *Pitfall: The Race to Mine the World's Most Vulnerable Place,* "Sacrifice zones are landscapes destroyed for the sake of benefits delivered somewhere else."[22] Deserts come easily to mind as the primary spaces whose people as well as flora and fauna have been constantly sacrificed as their territories have been associated with extraction and experimentation. Even Lerner, who is so rightly concerned as anyone should be about the implantation of these industries in inhabited low-income areas, mentions higher expenses as the reason companies prefer to implant their polluting industries in low-income areas instead of deserts. Hence, of all sacrifice zones, deserts are the most likely to draw less contestation because Saharanism has already desertified them. However, the sacrifices that deserts have been forced to make go beyond anthropogenic ecocides to include the deliberate assassination of migrants, the uprooting of populations, and the myriad forms of sexual predation that are now lost to history. Even though there has been growing awareness of the destructive effects of anthropogenic pollution in other areas, deserts have remained the default sacrifice zones—a situation that can only change when Saharanism is theorized, understood, and actively deconstructed.

GENEALOGIES OF SAHARANISM: AFRICA, EUROPE, AND THE AMERICAS

A constellation of fortuitous events and circumstances set the development and propagation of Saharanism into motion. By the twelfth century, the Sahara was closed to non-Muslims, particularly European Christians, and everything the latter knew about it was mediated through Muslim travelers, merchants, and pilgrims who crossed the desert through Egypt on their pilgrimage to Mecca. Ibn Battuta (1304–1369), the famed Moroccan explorer, was in Cairo in 1326, only two years after Mansa Musa, the king of Mali, made his historic passage through the city. This ruler, who reigned over a large kingdom that included modern-day Senegal, Mauritania, Gambia,

Guinea, and Mali, made a lasting impression on the Egyptians and the historical records for the amount of gold and the number of slaves he brought with him.[23] Some sources argue that in the wake of Mansa Musa's voyage, the price of the precious metal plummeted for two decades or, according to other accounts, even a century.[24] Although the city of Timbuktu was not the capital of the Kingdom of Mali, it somehow became associated with Mansa Musa's wealth and golden treasures.

Coincidentally, Prince John of Aragon (1350–1396) had commissioned the Spanish cartographer Abraham Cresques (1325–1387), together with his son Jehudà Cresques (1350–1427), to draw the map of the then-known world. The resulting 1375 Catalan Atlas (Fig. 1) reflects their interpretation of the news of Mansa Musa's trip. Cresques and his son depicted the desert, racialized Mansa Musa, and fed the image of his kingdom as a land of gold: "This Negro lord is called Musa Mali, Lord of the Negroes of Guinea. So abundant is the gold which is found in his country that he is the richest and most noble king in the land."[25] The golden imaginary of the Sahara was born, and the seeds for exploratory and gold-hunting Saharanism were planted through the Cresques' cartography. As historian Christoph Strobel has noted, the trip created an image of Mali as "a place of splendor, wealth, and sophistication."[26] General Yves de Boisboissel of the Académie des sciences coloniales evoked the centrality of Timbuktu in this imagination, writing that the city "had long captured the dream of seekers of adventure or merely material profit."[27] However, the physical Sahara remained elusive, even impenetrable to non-Muslim Europeans, since its Indigenous inhabitants, backed by powerful Muslim states, refused entry to those who did not share their Islamic faith.

Granada-born ambassador Hassan al-Wazzān al-Fāsī (1494–1554), also known as Leo Africanus, would later entrench the image of Timbuktu as a city of gold and Islamic learning. Kidnapped in 1516 while in Tunisia on his way back from a trip to Egypt, al-Wazzān was sold to the court of Pope Leo X in Italy, where he published *The History and Description of Africa* in Italian in 1550.[28] *Waṣfu ifrīqīyya*, as it came to be known in Arabic, shaped European knowledge about the Sahara for centuries, thanks to the frenzy of translations and the lack of comparable works.[29] Within a very short period of time, the book was translated into Latin (1556), French (1556), English (1600/1896), and Dutch (1665). German was the last influential European language into which the book was translated, in 1805. It has also been translated into Arabic in Morocco, Egypt, and Saudi Arabia. Thus, over the centuries, al-Wazzān's Saharanism became an object of a multilingual enterprise.

FIGURE 1. "The King of Mali as represented in the Catalan Atlas." Photo courtesy of the Bibliothèque nationale de France.

The History and Description of Africa draws on the previous knowledge of Arab and Roman geographers to divide the region into different areas and describe their peoples. In his account of Black Africa, or *Bilād al-Sudān*, al-Wazzān describes Timbuktu as having a bustling commercial life, with Amazigh merchants selling European fabric in the city.[30] He recounts that the city's inhabitants were so rich that they used pieces of gold and cowry shells to acquire "trivial things."[31] Foreigners were particularly wealthy, to the extent that two of them were even married to daughters of the king.[32] This provided confirmation of Timbuktu as a golden locale. Faithful to the racialization and Othering inherent to Saharanism, al-Wazzān describes Numidians as being anarchic, ignorant, and treacherous killers. He portrays the people south of the Sahara as "ferocious, lacking reason, intelligence, and experience."[33] In addition, al-Wazzān emphasized the image of a golden city offering an abundance of slaves and concubines in a land that had no laws—a concept that would later be picked up by colonial scholars, both civilian and military, who turned it into a ubiquitous trait of their literature.

Both Ibn Battuta and al-Wazzān initiated a Saharanism that was Arab-Islamic, exploratory, and ambassadorial. In both cases, travel through the desert was subsidiary to a main mission—namely, a pilgrimage in Ibn

Battuta's case and ambassadorship in al-Wazzān's. Unlike European explorers who were attempting to "discover" the Sahara, Muslim travelers had access to it merely by virtue of being Muslim, thus it did not evoke the same curiosity or fascination. Nevertheless, Ibn Battuta and al-Wazzān inscribed what they saw and experienced with authorial expertise, establishing the building blocks for a Hispano-Islamic Saharan imagination (reflected in the Cresques' cartography) that would persist with Timbuktu as its center of gravity until 1828, when twenty-six-year-old French explorer René Caillié reached Timbuktu and wrote his *Journal d'un voyage à Temboctou et à Jenné, dans l'Afrique centrale,* which destroyed the myth of the golden city.[34] Scottish citizen Gordon Laing had entered Timbuktu two years before Caillié, in 1826, but his murder deprived him of the opportunity to publish his observations.[35]

Between al-Wazzān's ambassadorial travels in the sixteenth century and Caillié's arrival in Timbuktu in 1828,[36] much had changed in the Mediterranean and Atlantic worlds. European commercial and technological advancements had slowly chipped away at both the power of the North African pirates at sea and the Muslim monopoly on trade routes through the Sahara.[37] The Atlantic Ocean diminished the desert's commercial importance, although it did not detract from the magic of its allure for a different type of adventurer-explorer. The debate in Britain about the legitimacy of the slave trade from the Gold Coast (modern-day Ghana) to the West Indies was raging, pushing the African Company to write, publish, and promote the dubious story of an American citizen named Robert Adams, who claimed to have been enslaved in Timbuktu. Released in 1816, *The Narrative of Robert Adams: A Barbary Captive* was a story that powerful people made "their own for the sake of power of various kinds: personal, economic, scientific, and imperial."[38] The result is a fascination with the desert through a story of white slavery that features "shipwreck, slavery, exotic cities, and strange people, a resourceful determined hero, spiritual struggle, sexual transgression, and so much more."[39] The transcontinental reception of Adams's narrative coincided with European competition over control in Africa. It was at this juncture that Saharanism shifted from its "heroic era" to become an institutionalized European enterprise with ramifications that intertwined with erstwhile golden imaginaries, colonial conquest, and imperialistic endeavors to apportion Africa into colonial dominions among France, England, and other European nations.[40]

Funded by professional associations and business interests, such as the African Association and the African Institution in London, as well as the

Société de géographie de Paris, which paid Caillié 10,000 francs for being the first European to reach Timbuktu, this explorer-adventurer conceptualization of Saharanism focused on maps and cartography.[41] Its implicit goal was to open new markets and increase European knowledge of "unknown" places for the sake of later imperialistic conquest. The generosity of lobbying societies combined with imperialistic interests, which also undergirded Orientalism, supported this brand of Saharanism as it developed the knowledge needed to penetrate the desert and connect different parts of Africa, despite Caillié's demystification of Timbuktu. Adventurer-explorer Saharanism was not, however, limited to interest in the Sahara alone. Many of the commissioned explorers made detours via Syria, Palestine, or Arabia. For instance, German explorer Ulrich Jasper Seetzen spent a long time in modern-day Syria and Palestine before going to Mecca and then Yemen, where he was murdered in 1811 on his way to the Sahara.[42] Nineteenth-century French geographer Vivien de Saint-Martin wrote that Seetzen was the first European to have reached Mecca and Medina since Ludovico di Varthema in 1503.[43] By the end of the nineteenth century, imperialistic Saharanism created its own corpus of works that portrayed the desert purely as a security threat.[44] Saharanism was overtaken by the European self-referentiality theorized by Said, principally as a result of the profusion of the Sahara-focused literature, which would later serve as proof of European sovereignty.[45]

French colonization of Algeria in 1830 replaced Saharanism's amateur explorer-adventurer with an imperialist army. Sharing borders with the desert, France felt compelled to control this *terre* usually described as "mysterious"[46] and "unknown,"[47] endowing Saharanism with the systematically violent, mythicized, racializing, and militaristic character that both connects to and diverges from Orientalism. After 1830, the people of the desert are represented as treacherous, rebellious, and untrustworthy, their pacification requiring the use of force. On December 4, 1852, General Aimable Pélissier led an army of six thousand to take the city of Laghouat (located 249 miles south of Algiers), adding another massacre to the one the army had already committed in Zaʿatsha (Zaatcha) while pursuing this Saharanist vision.[48] The famous painter Eugène Fromentin visited Laghouat shortly afterward, writing that he "enter[ed] a half-dead city."[49] To justify the slaughter, the French officer accompanying Fromentin evoked the story of a saint who supposedly said, "Listen, I condemn you to devour each other like lions who are forced to live in the same cage until the day the Christians [I believe that he even said the French], these lion tamers, come to take all of you together and muzzle you."[50] According to this line of thinking, the French soldiers carried out the will of a Muslim saint by killing a bunch of ferocious animals.

The massacres in Zaʿatsha and Laghouat demonstrated Saharanism's disregard for the environment as well, establishing the blueprint for the irradiation of the Sahara during the French nuclear experiments in the 1960s. Along with unconfirmed reports of the use of chemical weapons,[51] the French army used water wells as burial grounds for hundreds of human and animal corpses. The lieutenant accompanying him confessed to Fromentin that the army heaped the dead wherever they could.[52] To appease Fromentin's anxiety about the pollution of the aquifer, the lieutenant emphasized that the desert drought was capable of getting rid of any infestation or infection, revealing an early weaponization of the extreme environment to erase the consequences of the massacre.

Fromentin's book does not recount everything he saw. Swedish historian Sven Lindqvist found this long passage in Fromentin's notes: "We literally waded in blood, and for two days it was impossible to get anywhere for the heaps of corpses. Not only hundreds of men, shot or with bayonet wounds all over them, but also—why not say it as it is?—the bodies of huge numbers of women, children, horses, donkeys, camels, yes, even dogs . . . a terrible book could be written about [it]."[53] Lindqvist does not comment on the environmental mayhem in the desert town, but he remarks on how Fromentin "deleted the passage [from the book]. He blamed the silence in Laghouat on the climate. It became romanticism."[54] Saharanism forgets, manipulates, and even disavows the witnessed truth. Lindqvist links the massacre in Laghouat to the birth of modern racism, particularly when the French realized their need for water and conscripted Black Saharans to dig up the corpses the soldiers had buried in the wells. Through this act, the French racialized the clean-up labor.[55]

The figure of the *Saharien* arose in conjunction with the desire to subdue the Sahara and its inhabitants. Unlike their predecessors, *Sahariens* were the civilians and army officers who spent a long time in the Sahara, learned its languages, and were more or less possessed by a sort of Saharan mystique, a sense of self formed through their purportedly intimate knowledge of both people and place. Saharanists sought to achieve what Valentine Mudimbe later established as the imbrication of territorial organization, economic annexation, and natives' mental reformation by colonialism.[56] Henri Duveyrier, a young Saint-Simonian who authored the classic *Les Touareg du nord*,[57] is the quintessential Saharanist: young, adventurous, authoritative, and linked to the state. Saint-Simonians combined a religious belief with the conviction that harnessing science and technology could improve people's condition.[58] Duveyrier would later commit suicide as a result either of personal guilt or underhanded accusations of his writings as being the cause of the massacre of Lieutenant Flatters's reconnaissance mission to the Hoggar in 1881,[59] but he continued to be seen as a model Saharanist.[60] Starting in 1875, the French business community was heavily invested in the project of a trans-Saharan railway that would link the metropole to its sub-Saharan African colonies via Algeria, and several military and civilian missions were assigned to scout places where it could pass. Flatters was given one of these scouting missions, but only a few members of his party were able to return alive and tell the story of the violent murder of their associates by the Tuaregs.[61] The Pères blancs (White Fathers) also experienced the Tuaregs' rejection of foreigners in their land.[62] After several murders, Cardinal Lavigerie limited the Pères blancs' work in the Sahara to Ouargla, Ghardaïa, and El Goléa.[63] The loss of missionaries transformed the image of the Sahara from "a land of legends, populated by chivalrous nomads, to . . . a fabulous region defended by ferocious hordes who severely prohibit access to it."[64]

The Senusiyya Sufi order quickly became the French colonialists' white whale to justify all the resistance they faced in the Sahara.[65] Jean-Louis Triaud rightly summarizes this unique situation, writing, "No other Muslim brotherhood has been subject to such lasting surveillance and hostility by the French administration and publicists. The haunting obsession with the Senusiyya, the denunciation of this brotherhood, then the open struggle against it, hold a separate place in the colonial gesture."[66] In fact, this situation helped create and sustain the image of the Sahara as an unsafe place infested by bloodthirsty multitudes. The construction of this violent image gave French authorities an excuse for the twenty years they abandoned any action in the Sahara.[67] Notably, the Tuareg resistance to French penetration of the Sahara led to the profusion of military literature whose authors tried to embody Saharanism's ideological principles. After 1881, the Sahara was entirely conceptualized through French martyrology, which focused on the figures of Lieutenant Flatters and priest Charles de Foucauld, who exemplified sacrifice for empire.

In *Sahara et Soudan: Les régiments de dromadaires,* Captain Wolff and Lieutenant Blachère offered a theoretical and methodological conception of the Saharanist.[68] The authors posited that the pacification of the desert was the best way to avenge France's honor after Flatters's death. In this context, the Tuareg (who inhabited the still-unsubdued parts of the Sahara) were the new

Garamantes, whose ancestors had been defeated by the Romans eighteen centuries before. According to this logic, Algeria was Italy's bread basket because Rome had secured its southern borders, in turn monopolizing trade with the Sudan through the pacification of the Sahara.[69] It is well known that the Romans built stone *limites* to separate their civilization from the world of the barbarians in the desert.[70] Wolff and Blachère argued that the desert, this uninhabited land, provided refuge to "all those who did not have to bend to the yoke of the victorious, those of inferior status, fugitive criminals, and bandits of all races, and those banished from all countries."[71] To put an end to lawlessness, the desert had to be policed and disciplined. This thought continued to circulate well into the middle of the twentieth century. Émile Bélime, the famous director of the Office of Niger and a governor of colonies, wrote in 1951 that "Black Africa" would be happy to see the Sahara annexed to the metropole because "throughout time, the desert had only spewed forth killers and pillagers."[72] Others, like Colonel d'Eu, the man who occupied In Salah and authored *In-Salah et le Tidikelt: Journal des opérations*, focused on the unknown-ness and virginity of the land, linking its domination to both gaining more knowledge of the landscape and becoming masters of it.[73] The ideas and practical expertise that Saharanists acquired over many years of service in the Sahara enabled them to present plans for its control and the exploitation of its resources, but also to disagree with the government's approach to its security.

Wolff and Blachère clearly defined the character and the mission of the Saharanist in *Sahara et Soudan*.[74] The authors wedded desert romanticism to strategies of military conquest to advocate for the creation of a camel-mounted force that would be adapted to the desert conditions. Special financial incentives and adequate equipment would ensure the efficiency of these mixed troops. Their descriptions of the clothing and look of the Saharanist is textbook romanticism.[75] In Sudan and Egypt, Britain set up a Camel Corps of the Sudan Defence Force in 1883. In 1934, the force was highlighted as a position that brought the interested officer into "contact with a people who by their simplicity, humour and primitive manly qualities, are a delightful study. It holds increased responsibilities of command and unequalled opportunities for trek and the nomad life of the desert."[76] In other words, it was a dreamy lifestyle in which the British or French officer leads a group of native soldiers while enjoying the plenitude of desert life. In 1902, theory was put into practice, and France officialized the creation of the Compagnies méharistes sahariennes. The Saharanist became an idealized connoisseur of the desert and its way of life, even better than its Indigenous natives.[77]

The US created its own camel corps even before France and Britain, reflecting an exploitative attitude vis-à-vis desert animals.[78] As Odie Faulk and Forrest B. Johnson have shown, the US government sent emissaries to buy camels from North Africa and the Middle East just as routes, communications, and transportation became pressing issues for its expansion westward.[79] Johnson details the history of the US Army's decision to import camels and to use them in the American Southwest at a time when the country was torn apart by war against Native Americans and the Mormons in Utah.[80] Although it is unclear how the idea originated, the notion that "camels were a practical solution to the army's transportation problems in the American desert" may have arisen as early as 1836, though it did not truly gain purchase until the 1850s.[81] Similar to the Saharanism-infused schemes that unfolded in other deserts, the media and public-facing venues were instrumental in selling the idea to the American public, further allowing the Saharan imaginary in which this scheme participated to reach a wider public. As Johnson notes, "some of the most brilliant men of the country" participated in the campaign to bring over the camels.[82] The evocative language and metaphors used by the American officials to get the public excited about buying $30,000 worth of camels "stimulated the reader's imagination."[83] A "rider with 'rifle and revolver,' for example, painted a picture in one's mind of Beale [the army officer in charge of the mission] and his team moving through the Wild West, ready for action."[84] Further consolidating Saharanism's inter-desert nature, a former soldier from French Algeria named Hadj Ali, American officers, and camels from different deserts were conjoined in the mission to conquer the American West.[85] Around the same time, Australia also imported about two thousand Muslim cameleers alongside the twenty thousand camels Australian entrepreneurs brought into the country between 1860 and 1920.[86]

The novelistic genre participated in the perfection of the heroic image of the Saharanist. Roger Frison-Roche's *La piste oubliée*, which Paul Bowles translated into English as *The Lost Trail of the Sahara*, represents the pinnacle of Saharanism.[87] Taking place in In Salah, the Hoggar, and Tanezrouft, the narrative follows Lieutenant Beaufort's first mission in the desert, which focused on capturing a Tuareg who had murdered a French officer in 1928. Originally from Savoy, the lieutenant moves to the desert after his wife, Dominique, dies tragically in a ski accident. Aptly named, the twenty-six-year-old officer is fit, strong, and handsome.[88] However, he has no experience of the desert, a place where he is compelled to lead and assert his authority over a racially stratified group consisting of two French citizens, several Chaamba (the French-friendly Arab nomadic tribes of the north), Tuaregs, and Black individuals. Beaufort lives up to expectations—the man who starts out as a *boujadi* (naif and inexperienced) gains maturity as the novel progresses, becoming an expert Saharanist who stops at nothing to penetrate and master the Sahara.

Notably, the novel's complex plot shows the interconnections between military and scientific missions in the desert, specifically with Lignac's paleontological mission serving as cover for the army's search for the murderer of a French military officer. At its core, however, the novel is about the gradual process through which the Sahara inhabits the Saharanist. Beaufort travels the desert, acquiring skills and even becoming unrecognizable to Lignac. Beaufort "had [acquired] the jumpy and rapid gait of the nomad . . . . None would have recognized the athletic officer of the chasseurs of the beginning of the year in this skinny, ascetic figure."[89] Writing to his superior officer in Tamanrasset, Beaufort embraces his Saharanist identity, emphasizing that the "desert, once again, was shaping me as it pleased."[90] The desert takes possession of Beaufort, turning him into a quasi-prophetic figure and trailblazer—Beaufort "felt an imperious force pushing him toward the south."[91] As a result, Lignac ends up finding "the trail of the Garamantes, the route of emeralds, gold, and slaves; the secret route—so secret that we forgot about its itinerary."[92] The desert mystique that many Saharanists discuss in their writing had brought Beaufort to the point of knowing the desert better than its native inhabitants.[93]

Graphic novels also reflected this military Saharanism. Following in the footsteps of the French cinema's dissemination of the "myth of the immense and mysterious Sahara with its intrepid meharists and besieged forts," as Philippe Delisle has argued, the colonized Maghreb became a popular setting for works of art.[94] Specifically, Belgian cartoonist Hergé's *Le crabe aux pinces d'or* has a section that takes place in the desert.[95] Published in 1941 and then again 1946, this story features an investigation that leads Tintin and Captain Haddock to the desert after their plane crashes on the way to Spain. *Tintin au pays de l'or noir* is also set in the desert.[96] Published in 1950, at a time when French society was concerned with oil (or "black gold"), this story popularizes the idea of the desert as a source of petrol. Independently of their plots, the desert itself emerges in these graphic novels as a land of thirst, mirages, ergs (sand dunes), sabotage, bones, bandits and brigands, and disorder. In *Le crabe*, the appearance of the meharist saves Tintin and Haddock from death. Delcourt, the French Saharanist officer commanding the post of Afghar, offers them wine in the middle of the desert, and his actions reveal his knowledge about everything that happened in this expansive space. Not only did Delcourt and his meharists notice the plane crash, but he also sent his soldiers to check what happened. The anarchic desert depicted in these stories is always subdued by the appearance of a white person who defeats the Saharan evil represented by bandits, saboteurs, and pillagers. A similar image of the desert is likewise depicted in Pierre Straiteur's *Chez les Touaregs au litham bleu*, published in 1946 by the Catholic Collection cœurs vaillants.[97] *Chez les Touaregs* tells the story of the conquest of the Sahara and the Sudan in a condescending tone that asserts France's supremacy over the tattered, uncivilized, and violent people of the desert. The ways that connections among the army, the church, and literature coalesced in the creation and perpetuation of French Saharanism are, in retrospect, very obvious.

The interwar period brought even more celebrations of the meharists and legionnaires working in the Sahara. General Laperrine said that they were exhausted people who gave more than their bodies predisposed them to give.[98] *Mon légionnaire*, a 1937 Edith Piaf song, recounts the story of a young woman who has a one-night stand with a legionnaire whose name she does not even learn, pairing unrequited love with an idealizing picture of the soldiers in the desert. Piaf toured the US in 1939, and it is not difficult to surmise that this song resonated with American women and families whose members were about to be sent to participate in World War II. Antoine de Saint-Exupéry, in turn, popularized the desert as a space of innocence in the children's book *Le petit prince*, but it is his book *Terre des hommes*, which he published about the same time as Piaf's tour, that brought Saharanism to the skies and oceans.[99] In this book, the ocean, desert, and sky all emerge as spaces for growth by fostering reflections on the fragility of human life. To further confirm his Saharanist vocation, Saint-Exupéry called Captain Bonnafous, a meharist in charge of the Adrar region in Mauritania, an "archangel" and a man whose "step rings in the heart of the desert."[100] Hence, Saharanism has the ability to infiltrate all manner of literature in both subtle and overt ways.

This profusion of literature was part of the larger edifice of Saharanism. Conceiving of the desert as a *vide absolu* (absolute void) and a dangerous space, Saharanism and its advocates legitimized French ownership through repeated references to martyrology.[101] French ambassador Gabriel Puaux reported that Émile-Félix Gautier, the famous geographer, asserted his country's ownership of the Sahara because General Laperrine and Charles de Foucauld gave it to France through their deaths.[102] Others would add more names to the list, but the underlying idea is that French blood was spilled to dominate the desert and, by virtue of this bloodshed, France had acquired ownership of the territory. This martyrology was very powerful during colonial times, infiltrating all levels of authority and state institutions. Foucauld's assassination by the Tuaregs in 1916 not only confirmed the (constructed) ferocious reputation of these desert dwellers, but it also gave France an iconic Saharan martyr who has occupied a high place in Christian martyrology ever since. Evoking the power of the "Saharan literature" produced in the colonial period, anthropologist André Bourgeot stresses how it participated in the sustenance and performance of these myths.[103]

The emergence of Saharanism in the US was contemporaneous to the development of its Franco-Anglophone counterpart in Africa. In *Desert Passages: Encounters with American Deserts*, Patricia Nelson Limerick makes the fascinating argument that Frederick Jackson Turner's notion of the frontier missed the importance of water—and desert by extension—in his establishment of the connection between "democracy and the American character."[104] Limerick uses this oversight to examine the underrated place the desert occupied in American historiography, which mainly associated it with a myth.[105] Through this process and a sustained engagement with the harshness of the desert as an environment, Limerick captures the shift in American imagination from the desert simply being a place to cross to one that defied American ideals of confidence and development, agrarian and extractive.[106] For instance, the discovery of mines in 1850 "gave deserts a new value, but it was the transitory value appropriate to extraction. From a place to get across, the desert had become a place to get things out of, a meaning that hardly encouraged feelings of responsibility or attachment in new arrivals."[107] An important aspect of the American encounter with the desert, in addition to the extermination of Native Americans, was the widespread idea that civilization was the equivalent of making the desert recede.[108] George P. Marsh, whom geographer Diana Davis credits with conveying European ideas about deserts to his American readers,[109] described the desert as a "formidable enemy," which had to be combated and stabilized to make it useful for human use.[110] The predominance of the extractivist approach did not, however, mean that all stakeholders agreed on a shared vision. As Limerick articulates, there were "reclamationists," whose views dovetail with my definition of Saharanism, and "conservationists," who saw value in keeping the desert intact[111]—a discourse reminiscent of the first generation of French Saharanists, who found themselves in conflict with the technocratic and exploitative approaches to the Sahara. There is no doubt that the discursive and practical strategies of American Saharanism made their way back to the Sahara via Europe, particularly in the grand designs of explorers and businessmen like the entrepreneurial Marquis de Morès (b. 1858), who lived in the Dakota Territory and rubbed shoulders with Theodore Roosevelt before returning to the Sahara,[112] where he was killed in 1896 on his way to Sudan to incite tribes to rise up against Britain.[113] Quentin Crewe best rendered this connection between the American West and the Sahara, writing, the "Sahara was for [de Morès] the perfect place to demonstrate his deepest beliefs and his physical prowess. It was in some degree another wild west, but it had so much more to appeal to de Morès' misguided imagination." [114] More concretely, however, as Davis has demonstrated, American anti-desert policies and practices were disseminated through British and French officials' visits to the Soil Conservation Service (SCS), as well as the visits the American employees affiliated with the SCS paid to British and French colonies.[115] In Britain, Ritchie Calder's Saharanism-infused, serialized articles "Men against Desert," which cover his two-month journey from Algeria to Palestine/Israel, were integrated into the curriculum in fifteen thousand schools across the country, in addition to the simultaneous publication of his dispatches in more than forty news outlets worldwide.[116]

THE DESERT AS SPACE FOR IMPUNITY AND BIZARRERIE

Once it took hold of the public imagination, Saharanism became a transnational and transdisciplinary phenomenon, placing the Sahara and other deserts at the heart of conversations about locusts, "black gold," and nuclear technologies. Saharanism assumed several manifestations in carceral states' projects as well as in literature and industrial thinking to legitimize actions that would not ordinarily have been condoned in inhabited urban spaces. Owing to the powerful literature underlying it, Saharanism has placed deserts, writ large, outside normative ethics, creating the possibility for criminalized behaviors to be not only imaginable but desirable in deserts. Saharanism legitimized the desertion of ethics and morality when it comes to what happens in desertic areas.

The predominance of a carceral imagination that has weaponized deserts' harsh conditions for punishment is just one manifestation of Saharanism's ethical desertion. Without being anachronistic, it is important to note that there is a long tradition of sending criminals and outcasts to oases, even dating back to the ancient Greeks and Egyptians. Accordingly, while the desert was considered harsh, the green space within it—the oasis—was used for "exiling, far away from the river, relatives and criminals, and as a burial ground for them after their death."[117] But the weaponization of deserts against humans reached a different level in the twentieth century. Nation-state policies gave rise to practices that erected deserts—not oases—as spaces of punishment par excellence. From the US internment of 125,284 Japanese Americans in different camps, including in desertic areas, to France's establishment of its own Nazi-style labor camps in the Sahara during World War II, deserts became part of a punitive logic that sought to preemptively protect the state or execute its vision of a hierarchized humanity. As Jason De León has shown in *The Land of Open Graves: Living and Dying on the Migrant Trail*, this punitive aspect has increasingly taken a systematic, necro-inducing form in pushing migrants to take paths that would lead to their demise.[118] Rémi Carayol and Laurent Gagnol, two journalists in *Le Monde diplomatique*, have shown how this "wallization" of deserts operates in the Sahara to curb migration and other supposed security threats, impacting along the way Saharans' lifestyle and contributing to the "externalization" of the European Union's borders into Africa (Map 1).[119] Aomar Boum and Najib Berber have aptly called the mass of humans sent to labor camps in the Sahara during the Vichy era "undesirables."[120] After all, the sub-Saharan African and Latin American migrants, the prisoners of war, and the Japanese American citizens were and are still considered excess populations that could be dispensed with, and deserts offer the expansive secretive space needed to strip them of their humanity to which the normative ethics cease to apply. Nonetheless, even as much scholarship produced about these internments has focused on the human tragedies they have caused and the internal political machinations that continue to motivate them in the first place, Saharanism, per se, has eluded scholars' attention.

One might expect that desert societies would be less inclined to weaponize their deserts, but Tamazghan and Middle Eastern states, for instance, are not innocent of using Saharanism-inspired methods to punish their opponents. States in these areas have mobilized their deserts' unforgiving weather to terrorize their enemies. The prison camps of al-Kharga in Egypt, Tazmamart in Morocco, and Tadmur in Syria attest to the use of desert jails to isolate, severely punish, and slowly murder opponents.[121] Some of these prisons, like the Tazmamart military garrison and other internment camps

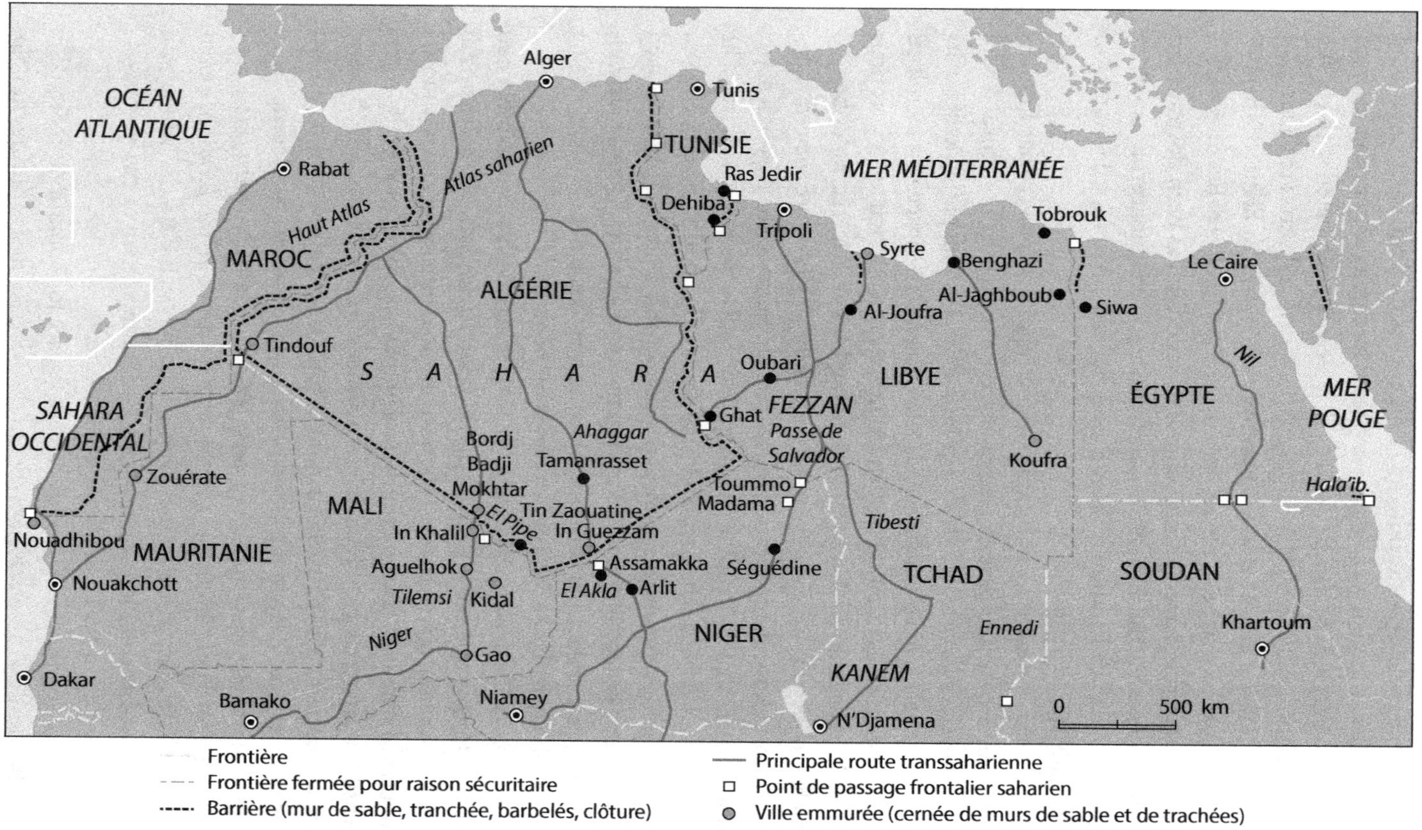

MAP 1. Walls (*barrières*) in the Sahara. At different times, Morocco, Algeria, Tunisia, and Egypt all built walls on their desert borders to control mobility in the desert. Redrawn from map courtesy of Agnès Stienne, *Le Monde diplomatique*, October 2021.

in the Algerian desert, were inherited from the colonial era. In the 1990s, and in the midst of its civil war, Algeria deported hundreds, if not thousands, of its citizens accused of Islamism to sites that were contaminated with residue from radiation and chemical weapons.[122] The idea that deserts are remote and secluded grants jailers a sense of impunity that is more difficult for them to have in spaces that are closely monitored or likely to be discovered. Nevertheless, this carceral dimension of Saharanism has been documented in many memoirs and novelistic works, including the pioneering novels of Saudi thinker Abdelrahman Munif, who has captured the inhumanity of these jails and their custodians.[123]

The legal and moral ramifications of this godlike power that humans acquire over others in deserts are portrayed in Saharanist literature. André Gide's novel *L'immoraliste*, which accommodates the pedophilic desires of its main character named Michel, depicts the Sahara as a space to which legal norms and notions of moral outrage do not apply. Gide, who was notorious for seeking sexual relationships with young boys in Algeria, hides behind Michel to recount his own experiences in Biskra. When interviewed about this history, Australian literary critic Robert Dessaix told the Algerian newspaper *Liberté* that to "fulfill his destiny, Gide had to go overseas. In 1893, he embarked in Algeria, the mythical homeland of his healing and liberation. He treated his tuberculosis there and went beyond taboos."[124] When asked about Gide's pedophilic practices in Algeria and the Sahara, Dessaix, defending Gide, responded that this kind of thing was possible at the time, adding that "nobody had ever complained about his behavior."[125]

L'immoraliste depicts the desert as a place where both accountability and moral outrage are absent. Michel can regain his health as he abuses the Arab children without fear. Although the novel is about other issues, we are mostly concerned here with the way the Sahara figures as a space for morally reprehensible transgressions, which, in the manner of the early massacre, have no consequences for the perpetrator. Saharanism has established the desert as a lawless land, and individuals like Michel are able to draw on that image to reproduce their own massacres on a smaller scale. Novelist Henry de Montherlant would later represent this sexual predation in *L'histoire d'amour de la rose de sable*, depicting the love triangle between Captain Auligny, his famous artist friend Pierre de Guiscart, and Rahma (Ram), a twelve-year-old Moroccan girl, in the desert town of Birbatine.[126]

The same construction of the desert as a space for impunity is repeated in Paul Bowles's *The Sheltering Sky*. Set in the Algerian desert during the colonial period, *The Sheltering Sky* tells the story of an upper middle-class American couple, Port and Kit Moresby, who travel to the desert to resolve their marital issues. As they travel, their relationship becomes increasingly complicated. Port becomes obsessed with going deeper into the desert, seeking more isolation and solitude, while Kit cheats on her husband with their friend Tunner. In both *L'immoraliste* and *The Sheltering Sky* the main characters are a man and a woman, with the male character being nursed or attended to by the female character. In this case, Port suffers from peritonitis. Michel and Kit share a disturbing interest in and fantasy of Arab boys. However, desert impunity manifests itself in *The Sheltering Sky* not in the abuse of children, but when Kit locks her moribund husband in a room in the French garrison of El Goléa and disappears into the oasis, leaving him to die. When the US consulate repatriates Kit to Algiers, her role in Port's death is simply ignored and the story of Port's death is forever confined to the desert, his final resting place. Essentially, what happens in the desert stays in the desert, a concept popularly evoked for the city of Las Vegas in the US.

The Sheltering Sky recycles Saharanist fantasies by romanticizing the desert, exaggerating its dangers, and fetishizing young Black/Brown bodies. Kit's abduction by two Arab caravanners, who take turns having intercourse with her, along with her introduction into a harem in the desert, are titillating elements of Saharanism that Bernardo Bertolucci's film rendition brought to wider audiences in 1990. In fact, this is representative of the cross-pollination of American and European Saharanisms during World War II, particularly through encounters between soldiers and civilian populations as well as through American films set in North Africa. Although *Casablanca* was the cinematographic work that defined the coordinates of North Africa in the American imagination during the war, *Sahara* (1943), which was filmed in California but set in the Libyan desert, depicts the quintessential traits of cinematic Saharanism. Not only was the Sahara recreated in the California desert to fill in for North Africa,[127] but everything about the way the story treats the desert as a hostile land to be survived and dominated draws on Saharanist tropes. The desert emerges in the film as a hierarchized and racialized space where the Black Sudanese character named Timbo takes care of the needs of his white peers. Through and through, the desert is constructed as a space of death, a site where mayhem can ultimately serve to prove heroism. The film also gestures to notions of development or *mise en valeur*, which Albert Sarraut, the French minister of the colonies in the 1920s, proposed to enhance investment in order to accelerate extraction in the colonies.[128] For Williams, a character in *Sahara*, "planning on how to irrigate this desert" to "make it bloom" is both a "problem" and a "project" that he is willing to undertake even as the German troops surround the small unit he was with.[129]

Anthropologist Judith Scheele and historian James McDougall have written that for Euro-Americans, the Sahara is "an overly familiar symbol of the unknown, an empty stage to display our courage and fears."[130] Courage and prowess manifest in the form of bizarre and grandiose undertakings in the desert, which also took the form of searches for an inland sea in Australia and the construction of one in the Sahara in nineteenth century. Until his death, Captain Charles Sturt believed that God had ordained him to find the inland sea, "a large body of water [that] exists in the interior," although his 1844 expedition to find it almost ended in tragedy.[131] Similarly, some French colonial administrators in Algeria thought that it was possible to bring the Mediterranean from Tunisia into the Sahara to create what they called an inland sea. The difference, however, is that Sturt acted alone, whereas sections of the French colonial army were behind the project in Algeria. The various discussions and feasibility studies that were generated by this idea of a vast internal sea that could pass through the depressions of the Algerian chott with Tunisia show a true embedding of Saharanism's transformative ideology. What mattered in this case was the existence of the will and the mobilization of resources to make the belief that anything can happen in a desert into a reality, although in the end, no French institution could afford its stupendous costs.

However, the twentieth century witnessed its own bizarreries, which are exemplified by the actions of Jacques Lebaudy and Jack Mortimer Sheppard. Lebaudy made many failed attempts to convince the French government to allow him to undertake both investments and expeditions in the Sahara. Fed up with the French government's disregard, Lebaudy sailed aboard a little ship with a small group of mercenaries to invade and claim Cape Juby in southern Morocco. Making a caricature of himself, Lebaudy declared himself emperor of the Sahara and "informed the French authorities that he was henceforth to be addressed as Jacques I, Najin-al-Den, Emperor of the Sahara, Commander of the Faithful, King of Tarfaia, Duke of Arleuf and Prince of Chal-Huin."[132] The self-declared emperor decided to build two cities to be named Troy and Polis, respectively. The narrator of *Moi, empereur du Sahara*, a novelized version of Lebaudy's story, reveals that Lebaudy "wanted to restore his country's greatness as Napoleon had in the past. . . . An Empire! That was Jacques Lebaudy's dream: a country that he would build and from which he would shine on the entire world, a country in which the traditions of liberty would not be violated, an Empire for which he himself would make the laws."[133] Scholarship has yet to examine the significance of his endeavor, particularly how his tale creates associations among deserts, wealth, and foolish actions. Lebaudy was, in reality, another probable connector between Saharanism in Africa and its reception in America, where William Ernest Walker had already created a precedent by "set[ting] himself up as president of what he called the 'Republic of Lower California'" in the Mexican desert.[134] Like Walker, Lebaudy was wealthy and extravagant, and his shocking murder by his wife in their New York mansion in 1919 made his Saharan endeavors a topic of interest for many newspapers of the time.

Similarly grandiose and outlandish was Jack Mortimer Sheppard's plan to sail the Sahara. An American adventurer-photojournalist-entrepreneur, Sheppard's endeavor was born of his encounter with a Texan engineer who complained to him about the difficulties of transportation in the desert. The Texan dismissed Sheppard's solutions but he piqued his interest when he put forward his imaginative idea about sailing the Sahara. Sheppard proceeded to tell the Texan: "If the Sahara and other great deserts will hold up a loaded camel, they ought to hold up a set of inflated tyres. What's more, the wind is free and a wheeled yacht doesn't need fuel, food, or water."[135] What follows is a most ambitious project that takes Sheppard from Morocco to Senegal through Algeria and numerous other African countries. Sheppard's narrative commemorates his athletic prowess, offers racist comments about the people and places he encounters, and tells of heroic fights against fictitious terrorists, which reproduce fixtures of Saharanist adventurism and its racialization of desert peoples.

Although they lack the ideological sophistication and complexity of their predecessors, Lebaudy's and Sheppard's endeavors set the stage for the more experimental desert ventures to come. Their outlandish pursuits, as entirely futile as they may seem, pale in comparison to state discourses about deserts and their imagined futures. Theirs were individual enterprises that could be dismissed as signs of mental illness, in Lebaudy's case, and a manifestation of unbridled hubris and entrepreneurship, in Sheppard's. However, a much more plausible explanation for these actions is their embeddedness in a long tradition of both discourses and practices in which arid lands have been reduced to the space par excellence for big dreams that no one would dare consider in an urban setting. Thus, even small individual undertakings in desert spaces should not be divorced from the larger systems of ideas transforming arid spaces into something other than what their harsh ecological conditions are meant to be.

SAHARANISM AND DEVELOPMENTAL DREAMS

The Sahara has also served as a site for the projection of dreams of an industrial and experimental nature. These dreams had nothing to do with the interests of local, colonized populations, but rather have everything to do with French colonial interests. Saharanism in this regard took the form of a robust exploitative ideology that portrayed the desert as a land inviting extractions of all kinds. Accordingly, this desert's wind, water, sand, mineral, soil, oil, and people (labor) were all up for grabs. When France turned to the Sahara both as a source of wealth and a space for the continuation of its dying colonial empire in the 1950s,[136] there was a profusion of Saharanist literature, conferences, and media presence that gave Saharanism a public face. As the literary and journalistic relics of this time show, blurring boundaries between Saharanism and state policy benefited the latter's attempts to reach every French home as France became an oil-producing country.[137]

The goal of reinforcing France's grip on the now-resource-rich Sahara triggered a variety of projects, including some that reversed older colonial beliefs. This new brand of strategic and economic interest in the midst of decolonization and the Cold War shifted Saharanists' discourse from trans-Saharan exchanges to intra-Saharan development schemes, aimed at benefiting Europe and the colonial Eurafrique. Nineteenth-century Saharanism fought to incorporate the Sahara into French Algeria, but the looming Algerian independence required more of a "separatist" approach. Thus, the heirs of this same Saharanism endeavored to remap Algeria without the Sahara. France established the Organisation commune des régions sahariennes (OCRS, 1957–63), which redrew the map of the Sahara, creating a de facto desert state annexed to France under the name "Afrique saharienne française" (French Saharan Africa).[138] A response to the belated realization that the personal competition between different French officers at the turn of the century had created a geopolitical reality in which the Sahara was under different politico-military and administrative regimes divided among Algeria, French Equatorial Africa, and French West Africa,[139] the OCRS was established to create administrative unity and carry out development projects in the reunified Sahara by investing in the areas of "energy, mining, water, industry, and agriculture."[140] Its founding document incited the OCRS to "initiate the installation of extractive and transformation industries, and to create, when the circumstances allow it, industrial complexes."[141] The OCRS had the grand mission of undeserting and industrializing the Sahara, supposedly for the benefit of both the native Saharans and their larger chimeral Eurafrique community, which, in the midst of decolonization in Africa and globally, was hailed by some as "France's last chance."[142]

Algerian architectural historian Samia Henni used the phrase "extractive infrastructure" to describe the measures taken by French authorities at this juncture.[143] In Henni's analysis, all these initiatives were geared toward amputating the desert from Algeria on the eve of independence. However, the grand scale and the Saharanism-infused ideology underlying this infrastructure would be lost when the focus turned only to the built infrastructure itself. In reality, French officials and technocrats spurred a decade-long cultural, political, and social engagement with the Sahara. Therefore, it would be more accurate to refer to an interconnected set of infrastructures that extended from legal reforms to business codes, the territorial reorganization of the Sahara, and economic incentives to global finance.[144] These measures aimed to facilitate the exploitation of the Sahara's increasingly discoverable riches, but also, and most importantly, implemented French Saharanism's vision of the desert as a space for its myriad extractive colonial enterprises.

Reflecting the spirit of the time, Louis Armand, the general director of the Société nationale des chemins de fer (SNCF) as well as the president of the Bureau d'organisation des ensembles industriels africains (BIA), invited French people to replace their vision of the Sahara of caravans with an industrialized one.[145] It was time for the desert's *mise en valeur*, following development models in the US and the USSR.[146] Emptiness and the presumed "virginity" of the land drove the conception of space and land ownership in these discourses, which urged France to forsake its outdated economic formula that had proved inadequate for the Sahara.[147] Per Armand's vision, the Sahara became "a new country" with wind, sun, and minerals that were all extractable.[148] The Indigenous populations, referred to as *peuplades* (tribes, which diminishes their complex organization as societies), only appeared in these discourses when it was necessary to show their numerical insignificance, like in geographer André Allix's allegation that "in such a territory, we cannot even talk about population. The people, despite the relative diversity of their races and appearances, are more scattered than the tufts of hard grass on these dusty beaches called camel pastures."[149] The same concept is at work when commentators stated that only two million people inhabited an area nine times larger than France.[150]

In a 1959 speech to the Ambassadors' Seminar, Jacques Soustelle, deputy minister in charge of the Sahara and atomic energy, declared that "since May of last year [1958], France has started to hope again," adding that "France is turning its face toward the future."[151] Strikingly, the desert was now a source of optimism, challenging the Heideggerian argument that humanity, after civilization, would become a desert.[152] The discovery of gas and oil was the source of hope for a country that was becoming desperate.[153] Soustelle, an anthropologist of Mayan civilization by training, was a staunch believer in French Algeria and leveraged every possible media and publication outlet to get his message across, contributing to Saharanism's extractivism during the five years before Algeria's independence in 1962.

At the same time, work was underway to build a nuclear weapon. Mastering nuclear technology on the sands of the Sahara was only the culmination of the myriad technological experiments that different French industrialists, including carmaker Citroën, had been undertaking in the desert since the 1920s. In order to implement its 1956 decision to join the world nuclear club, the government established the Centre saharien d'expérimentations militaires (CSEM) de Reggane and the Centre d'expérimentations militaires des oasis (CEMO) in 1958. Historian Benjamin Stora has highlighted how, starting in 1959, the Sahara became "the main site of the French army's experimentation in chemical weapons, rockets, and nuclear tests."[154] Gerboise bleue (Blue Jerboa) was the first in a series of seventeen nuclear experiments that were carried out in the Tanezrouft and the Hoggar starting on February 13, 1960.[155] It would not be unreasonable to wonder if all the talk about the Sahara's *mise en valeur* in tandem with the public fascination with the Saharanists' musings about desert development was simply a cover-up to deflect attention from the nuclear tests. Whether this is the case or not, one thing is certain: French Saharanism bequeathed us a very rich legacy that is important to examine in dialogue with its counterparts that unfolded in other arid lands.

COUNTERVISIONS TO FRENCH SAHARANISM

These designs were not met with accolades from other actors and stakeholders whose sovereignty over the Sahara and its resources stood opposite to the French state's. Although the French were acting as though there was no decolonial movement opposing their projects to carve out a Saharan entity under the bogus OCRS, literature from this period shows that French Saharanism was not entirely lost on Tamazghan leaders in both northern and sub-Saharan parts of the Sahara. Dey Sidi Baba, a Mauritanian-Moroccan politician, wrote in 1958 that France's endeavor to detach the Sahara from Africa was utopic.[156] It could even be said that much of France's endeavor to entrench its presence in the Algerian Sahara was motivated by its fear of Allal al-Fassi's agenda to oust them from what he constructed as precolonial Morocco's territories, which included the Adrar region in Algeria, parts of the Sudan, and the totality of today's Mauritania. Al-Fassi believed that Morocco's independence of 1956 was incomplete, and declared that "as long as the Spanish Sahara, as long as the desert from Tindouf to Attar, and as long as the outer reaches of the Algerian-Moroccan borders are not freed from their [French] tutelage, our independence will remain lame and our first obligation will be to continue the struggle in order to free and unify [our] homeland."[157] Concurrently, al-Fassi understood the importance of knowledge production to counter French Saharanism's projects. He founded *Perspectives sahariennes*, a monthly journal that was entirely dedicated to Saharan issues, in 1958 and published a significant number of contributions that took to task most of the salient French schemes for the future of the Sahara. In his first editorial, al-Fassi clearly discarded any approach to the question of the Sahara as solely economic and scientific, acknowledging it rather as a political, social, and human question that could not be answered without the participation of the Saharans themselves.[158] Retrospectively, many articles featured in *Perspectives sahariennes* could be said to contain an *avant-l'heure* critique of the ideology that I now define as Saharanism.[159]

Algerian leaders were also placing the Sahara at the center of their political struggle. The Sahara was a fixture of the articles published in *El Moujahid*, the newspaper of Jabhat al-Taḥrīr al-Waṭanī (the National Liberation Front, FLN), during the Algerian War of Independence (1954–62). Commenting on the 1960 reform that granted the OCRS autonomy from the Ministry of the Sahara, a result of a power grab between different ministers in the French government, *El Moujahid* considered this nebulous organization's new status an additional step toward French imperialism's machinations against Algeria's "independence and African unity."[160] The anonymous author of the article also critiqued the positions of the "integrationists," who, against the Algerian struggle for independence, espoused France's annexation of the Sahara as expressed in Soustelle's claim that there would be "no Saharan petrol for France without the French Sahara."[161] This attitude represented what the article called "nationalisme-petrolisme" (petrol nationalism), which, again, disregarded the status of territories and their people to ensure markets for oil extracted from the Sahara and inject its revenues in hard currencies into the French budget.[162] In another article titled "Le Sahara algérien," published in 1961, *El Moujahid* articulated the FLN's policy vis-à-vis the French precursor of a neoliberal strategy to consolidate the grip of international, particularly Anglophone, companies on Algerian natural resources in the Sahara.[163] This nationalist vision rejected France's designs to carve out a Saharan entity for itself and spelled out four principles that independent Algeria defined for its postindependence Sahara policy. These were Algeria's territorial unity, including the Sahara; the Sahara as a connector between different African stakeholders; a model of development using the resources of the Sahara primarily for the benefit of its people and neighboring countries; and finally, international cooperation, all of which privileged genuine independence in the face of foreign intervention in Algerian sovereignty over under- and aboveground resources.

THE DESERTS' ABSENTED DIMENSION: SAHARANISM AGAINST INDIGENOUS PEOPLE

Saharanism has always had a blind spot about desert peoples, if it even acknowledges their existence in the first place. Emptying the deserts of their inhabitants served to justify their exploitation and domination by the powerful. That said, discursive emptiness was not enough to actually empty deserts. Oftentimes, discourse was accompanied by genocidal wars or displacements, as was the case during the Conquest of the Desert in Patagonia (Argentina) and during Australian and American conquests of the lands occupied by Indigenous peoples.[164] The Soviet Union also displaced Indigenous populations from their permafrost homelands in order to exploit and industrialize their desert territories and turn them into "industrial deserts," in Paul Josephson's wording.[165] The "cult of violence,"[166] which historian Benjamin Brower has already demonstrated in his work about the French conquest of the Sahara, is consubstantial with Saharanism, especially when manipulation fails to fully obscure and deny the obvious existence of peoples who call deserts home.

This violence and its Saharanist origins have not gone unarticulated by desert Indigenous peoples. It is true that the colonial system closed all the avenues to a critical consciousness that would dispute and resist its legitimacy. However, it only took a few decades for local elites, who realized the noxious and inherently destructive nature of Saharanism, to rise up and challenge its premises and reveal its long-term effects on local societies and their murdered ecologies. Contrasting local imaginaries of the desert with Saharanism's universalizing extractive imaginary allows us to see another facet of deserts that geographers and anthropologists know too well, because, for a long while, only they perceived the gap Saharanism created between the lived desert, where life exists and evolves in difficult ecological and environmental conditions, and the ideologized desert, which was constructed to serve colonial practices.

Indigenous peoples' insurgency against Saharanism and its impact took several critical forms—both artistic and literary—that all coalesced to consecrate deserts' function as home. In the Sahara, Tuareg writers Ibrahim al-Koni and Omar Al Ansari have published novels that depict the environmental and human impact that extraction and testing have wreaked on their homeland. Al-Koni's novel *al-Waram* (*The Tumor*) depicts how oil turned a Saharan society into an authoritarian community, incriminating the discovery of oil as the source of every social ailment.[167] However, it is his first novel, *Nazīf al-ḥajar* (*The Bleeding of the Stone*) that reveals the environmental damage caused by the combination of flaunting desert laws and the introduction of lethal machinery into the Saharan space.[168] Amitav Ghosh has critiqued Western novels' focus on human agency, underlining the fact that their "Cartesian dualism . . . arrogates all intelligence and agency to the human while denying them to every other kind of beings."[169] Al-Koni does exactly the opposite by revealing how the desert and its animals are sentient beings who have agency in the habitat they share with humans. This literary choice does not just represent a counter-imaginary to Saharanism's focus on emptiness and death—it also shows the existence of an implicit, and sometimes explicit, pact between all the elements of desert life. It is this possibility of human and nonhuman cooperation that Saharanism has not been able to capture in its projection of its own biases onto the nature of desert existence.

Saharanism's sinister dimensions emerge even more strongly when we examine the literary and cinematic depictions of its transformative impact upon societies and ecologies. *Mudun al-milḥ* (*Cities of Salt*), Abdelrahman Munif's five-book series, depicts the transformation of a desert society into an urbanized state with a central authoritarian regime after the American discovery of oil.[170] As the petrol-modernity depicted in *Cities of Salt* demonstrates, extractive Saharanism does not merely bring mayhem to nature but also transforms the future of societies exposed to its actions. Similar to the chain of relentless transformations unleashed by the discovery of oil, nuclear testing and its legacies of radiation have colonized not only the past and present of societies where these tests took place, but it has also irrevocably influenced their future. Al Ansari has best depicted the deadly impact of French nuclear experiments in the Sahara in his novel *Ṭabīb tinbuktū* (*The Physician of Timbuktu*), in which the insurgency against Saharanism functions as a historical recording of the latter's crimes against the desert's people as well as its flora and fauna. This literary engagement with Saharanism is further developed in Elisabeth Leuvrey's film *At(h)ome*,[171] which revisits the French nuclear experiments in the Algerian desert. Leuvrey's film demystifies Saharanism's construction of the desert's emptiness and shows that actual people who lived in the Sahara experienced France's racialized nuclear bomb. The viewer can easily see that the bombs were tested amid Black Tuaregs of Tan Afella in the Hoggar. The Tuaregs were the ones who delayed France's conquest of the Sahara for two decades after the murder of Flatters, and one wonders if the nuclear testing among their descendants was the French military's way to settle their gory historical accounts with them.[172]

Literature is evidently not the only locus where a counter-Saharanist imagination has been articulated. Critical essays have also served as a space for the publication of Indigeneity-informed views of deserts. Both al-Koni and Munif wrote essays on the environmental transformation that the discovery of oil wrought upon desert societies. In a moving essay in his collection *Waṭanī saḥrāʾ kubrā* (*My Homeland Is a Great Desert*), al-Koni writes:

> The oil wells have become, for the people of the Sahara, a bottomless abyss since the day they brought their paralysis upon the people of this virgin homeland. The paralysis of the soul before that of the body. The blessing [of oil] turned quickly into a curse because of lassitude, which not only killed their innate love of work but also shook their moral values. The bleeding of the earth, which is called oil, has managed to bring a curse on the people of the land, because this liquid was really never petrol. In fact, it was the blood of our mother earth. Drilling it is a violation of the belly of this mother and a defiling of its sacred soul.[173]

In al-Koni's understanding, the drilling of oil is nothing but bloodshed that strikes at the womb of Mother Earth. This violation of the sanctity of life turns into a curse, since it leads to a variety of woes informed by the loss of a petrol society's core values. Likewise, Munif stresses the fact that the discovery of oil in the Gulf destroyed the tenets of these societies' cultural and economic production, leading to subservience to global capitalism. Contrasting al-Koni's and Munif's conclusions with those of French Saharanism regarding oil in the 1950s reveals how this commodity was an affliction for desert natives. The differences between these critical and environmentally aware analyses and those informed by Saharanism simply cannot be bridged, because they represent antithetical positions vis-à-vis desert ecologies.

This introduction has traced the development of Saharanism from the search for the fabled city of Timbuktu in the thirteenth century to the twentieth-century French nuclear tests in the Algerian Sahara, showing how Saharanism developed, changed, transformed, and manifested in different guises over time. If anything, this long history and the intellectual genealogies underlying it reveal that Saharanism is dynamic and syncretic, possessing the capacity to mobilize different modes of knowledge and power structures. A wide array of historical, literary, cartographic, and military sources have helped me theorize Saharanism's maturation into a powerful system of interconnected ideas that encompass the mystical, the sublime, and the horrific all at once. The next chapters demonstrate how hundreds of years of discursive and actionable endeavors have created many deserts whose common trait is being a haven for terrorists, a threat to civilized societies, and a space for all manner of extraction, experimentation, and wild imaginings.

Nothing captures better the evolving nature of Saharanism than the home page of the Burning Man festival website, which drills into the minds of participants that "the mind-altering experience of Burning Man is its own drug."[174] Thanks to Saharanism, the desert is now a modern drug for postdigital age Silicon Valley entrepreneurs to experience in Black Rock City—391 miles from the nuclear Ground Zero still haunting the Nevada desert.

ONE

Spiritual Saharanism

THE DESERT AS A FANATICAL, RACIALIZED SPACE

DURING THE COVID-19 PANDEMIC, Pope Francis, unbeknownst to the general public, declared Charles de Foucauld (1858–1916) a saint on May 15, 2022, in St. Peter's Square. This canonization of the French officer-turned -priest was the culmination of a century-long process that had begun in 1916.[1] Through his sanctification of Foucauld, Pope Francis conferred ecclesiastic legitimacy on the legacy of a prominent proponent of "spiritual Saharanism," which this chapter defines as a practice that deploys the ideals of charity, spirituality, and universal brotherhood toward the greater goal of forever entrenching the colonization of the Sahara and evangelizing its Indigenous people. The hagiographic practices that followed Foucauld's murder in the Hoggar in the Algerian Sahara on December 1, 1916, had a lasting impact on the afterlife of spiritual Saharanism and the way that religiosity and spirituality have been imagined in and through this African desert. As a result, the Sahara was conceptualized and presented to both church and lay audiences as a space that invited religious antagonism, conversion, racism, and colonial violence, which today continue to undergird postcolonial Islamophobia. Foucauld's sainthood is a testament to the endurance of spiritual Saharanism as a composite of multifaceted theoretical and practical endeavors shaped by religious figures, including hagiographers, politicians, scholars, military officers, and churchgoers, who successfully established a spiritual "ideational ecosystem" centered on the Sahara. Along with Cardinal Lavigerie (1825–1892), the archbishop of Algiers and apostolic delegate of the Sahara and the Sudan between 1867 and 1892, Foucauld was one of many individuals who were involved in the desert business since the late nineteenth century for exploratory, espionage, military, or spiritual pursuits (or even all of these at once).[2] Foucauld's life story, which his sanctification will further amplify, has been pivotal in shaping the contemporary experience of desert spirituality across the globe.

Lavigerie and Foucauld used their prominent positions to solidify spiritual Saharanism into a household presence in the nineteenth and twentieth centuries.[3] They were the two most important figures who established spiritual Saharanism's "ideational ecosystem," by which I mean the set of beliefs that fosters the production of this thought and its transmission across temporalities and spaces through various networks. Thus, the ideational ecosystems they created and navigated helped disseminate their ideas and those of their network members underlying the imbrication of spirituality, military authority, and their dehumanizing consequences in the desert. The influential networks that proponents of spiritual Saharanism mobilized enabled their ideas to infiltrate a wide array of social and cultural environments. This chapter recounts how Lavigerie, aided by a powerful institutional streak of spiritual Saharanism, undertook multiple initiatives to both dominate and evangelize the Sahara, and how Foucauld and his network of civilian and military intimates individualized spiritual Saharanism. Tracing both continuities and discontinuities within spiritual Saharanism since the nineteenth century, the chapter attends to the myriad ways in which spiritual Saharanism served as a launchpad for the Islamophobia and violent racialization vis-à-vis the Indigenous inhabitants of the Sahara.

In its broadest significance, spiritual Saharanism's ideational ecosystem is the ensemble of institutional and community-based resources that helped (or continue to help) generate, implement, produce, and inform spiritual discourses and actions that unfold in deserts. In this specific context, it is made up of church institutions, faith-based congregations, circles of friendship, intellectual affinity groups, and publication outlets that placed the Sahara at the core of a large, transnational spiritual enterprise that surpassed the desert's physical borders. Although the ideational ecosystem of spiritual Saharanism resulted in the dissemination of faith-based prejudices about the Saharan peoples, there is a crucial difference between the reception of powerful players around whom these ideational ecosystems revolved and the degree of acceptance they enjoyed across the social spectrum. Lavigerie's spiritual Saharanism was institutional, and the Catholic Church's networks and publication outlets were integral to his ecosystem, whereas the one represented by Foucauld was more self-directed. Nevertheless, the strong ties between the religious, cultural, and military establishments in both France and Algeria allowed Foucauld to bridge the divide that separated secular and religious networks at the turn of the century, making any pigeonholing of his multifaceted person to only his religious aspect reductive, as anthropologist André Bourget has argued.[4] By addressing how Lavigerie, Foucauld, and a coterie of other spiritual Saharanists integrated the desert space of the Sahara into their ideational ecosystems, this chapter theorizes a phenomenon that has eluded the attention of prior scholarship on the story of Christianity in the colonial Sahara since the nineteenth century. Saharanism has been a game changer in the way Christianity was disseminated throughout Africa.

THE PARAMETERS OF SPIRITUAL SAHARANISM

Spiritual Saharanism should not be confused with the adjacent spiritual practices for which desert spaces have been known for millennia.[5] "Desert Fathers" were present in the deserts of Palestine, Syria, and Egypt even before Christianity became Rome's dominant religion. Christianity placed value on "detachment from selfish concerns,"[6] fostering monks' and other ordinary people's withdrawal from the mundane affairs of the world.[7] The Desert Fathers' values of simplicity, poverty, and a life of constant hardship reinforced monasticism in their solitude in the desert and won them both admiration and a reputation for holiness among their contemporaries.[8] Davis has highlighted how the popularity of desert monasticism even pushed Bible exegetes to revise their previously negative depictions of deserts, depicting them as the "most perfect locations for Christian withdrawal from the world."[9] Algerian polymath Malek Bennabi has written that these Christian *ḥunafāʾ* were "men of very rare mettle. They left the idolatry of their time in order to confine themselves to the worship of the one God."[10] These recluses observed no specific rituals and had no designated places for their worship.[11] Likewise, jurist Muhammad Shahjan al-Nadawi articulated the notion of *siyyāḥa*, which means "wandering" or, in today's language, "tourism," to describe the practice of isolation and confinement in different religious practices.[12] Followers of Judaism, Christianity, Islam, Buddhism, and Hinduism practiced *siyyāḥa* by traveling through "deserts and wildness."[13] As these examples reveal, deserts have been associated with prophecy and trying hardship across religions, but the advent of spiritual Saharanism rerouted this spirituality toward imperialism and made it into a corruptive force.

Spiritual Saharanism is not *siyyāḥa*. As exemplified by Ernest Psichari's spiritual awakening in Mauritania before World War I,[14] this subarea of Saharanism deploys religious zeal and spiritual mobilization for the sake of domination in desert spaces, which stands in contrast to the concept of *zuhd*. Sa'd bin Salām al-Maghribi defines *zuhd* as "leaving this world and afterwards not caring who handles it."[15] Leah Kinberg argues that *zuhd*'s "spiritual basis" stands in contrast to the "materialistic approach toward life,"[16] concluding that the believer who engages in the practice of *zuhd* must relinquish worldly existence and concern.[17] These definitions are evocative of the early monastic isolation in desert solitude. Hence, it is crucial to make a distinction between *zuhd*-like practices, which are unworldly in their intentions, and spiritual Saharanism, which is the ideological use of spiritual undertakings to advance Saharanism's agenda of domination, extraction, and surveillance. The imbrication of spiritual Saharanism with military and institutionalized forms of power further distinguishes it from ordinary *zuhd/siyyāḥa*. Even though spiritual Saharanists may profess that they self-isolate or undertake their enterprises in the desert for a closer relationship to God or in search of a divine sublime, their endeavors are steeped in worldly power struggles. Unlike the *zuhd* practitioner's "living-dead" status,[18] the practitioner of spiritual Saharanism harnesses his unworldly knowledge to participate in a colonialist project that is antithetical to the interests of desert inhabitants, both human and nonhuman.

Spiritual Saharanism's attraction to desert spaces finds its explanation in a variety of factors. First, the existence of a strong, multireligious tradition of prophetic activity in deserts. Deserts in Judaism, Christianity, Islam, Buddhism, and Hinduism have been conceptualized as loci wherein individuals find religious illumination. Second, in the Bible the desert is associated with strong temptation and therefore is a space where it is possible to demonstrate will against sin.[19] Third, deserts are phenomenological places that evoke the sublime and its effects on the human psyche, further intensifying the spiritual experience. Edmund Burke defined the impact of the sublime in nature when he wrote:

> The *passion* caused by the great and sublime in nature, when those causes *operate* most powerfully, is *Astonishment*; astonishment is that state of the soul in which all its motions are suspended, with some degree of horror.... No passion so effectually robs the mind of all its powers of acting and reasoning as fear. For fear, being an apprehension of pain or death, operates in

> a manner that resembles actual pain. Whatever therefore is terrible, with regard to sight, is sublime too. . . . Indeed terror is in all cases whatsoever, either more openly or latently, the ruling principle of the sublime.[20]

Terror and astonishment are attractive to those who want to experience the thrill of spirituality, and spiritual Saharanism builds off the existence of these desires to further emphasize the desert as the ideal space for redemption.

However, spiritual Saharanism has shifted the image of the desert from that of an idyllic space for contemplation, solitude, and self-improvement to a springboard for racializing and even violent undertakings. It has supplanted the tradition of disinterested spiritual practice with a weaponized, imperialistic piety that, in its manifestation in the nineteenth- and twentieth-century Sahara, focused on the expansion of the French Empire and the reach of the church within it. French ecclesiastical authorities, who envisioned a return to a supposed Christian era that existed when the Romans colonized Tamazgha (the Amazigh homeland of the broader North Africa) more than a thousand years earlier, overrode the animist, Jewish, and Islamic spiritual practices that preexisted French colonization. The institutions that supported spiritual Saharanism reproduced the clichés of their time, a process that required a critical engagement with their preexisting legacy and impact on desert spirituality before French imperialism.[21] Even the desert itself was not spared the consequences of Saharanism's reductive ideas. If, for the believer, the harshness of the desert is a manifestation of God's will, for practitioners of spiritual Saharanism it is rather an enemy that must be dominated and reshaped.[22] Hence, it is only by writing the multiple manifestations of spiritual Saharanism into the broader history of Saharanism and colonialism that it will become possible to fully understand and account for the lasting impact this practice has had on deserts around the world.

Spiritual Saharanism's multilayered impact extends beyond the Sahara's physical boundaries thanks to a cast of individuals who have populated its ideational ecosystem since the nineteenth century. The list extends from Cardinal Lavigerie, who founded an ecclesiastic empire in Africa, to Foucauld, who inherited his precepts and transformed them to function on an individual level so as to prepare the terrain for the future evangelization of Muslims in Tamazgha.[23] It also includes individuals like Ernest Psichari and Henry de Castries,[24] who found their path to Christianity through their encounter with Islam, as well as misfits like Isabelle Eberhardt,[25] a Franco-Russian anarchist and writer who converted to Islam and lived in Algeria at the turn of the twentieth century, and even those like the Catholic priest Carlo Carretto, who acted upon a divine order and relocated to the desert in 1954.[26] The desert seems to accommodate those whom Paul Claudel explained had to disavow their religious feelings due to the generalized disregard for religion in French society.[27] As varied as their backgrounds were, these practitioners of spiritual Saharanism shared a centrifugal, if not obsessive, gravitation toward the desert, which became constitutive of what Berny Sèbe has called "popular imperialism" in France.[28] This obsession has outlived them, bequeathing to us an immense corpus of primary sources that continues to radiate (*faire rayonner*) their Saharanism into the world.

Spiritual Saharanism has proven its antagonistic, if not extermination-oriented, relationship with the Indigenous religions of desert inhabitants. As Daniel T. Reff has shown, Jesuit missionaries led to the impoverishment and decline of Indigenous languages, and the illnesses brought by the Europeans to the desert contributed to the discrediting of the "native priests and shamans"[29] who failed to "adequately explain, prevent, and cope with the unprecedented suffering caused by smallpox and other maladies."[30] Many factors motivated the colonialist desire to replace Indigenous people's beliefs with "civilized" European ones. Scholars have shown that Indigenous religious practices survived accusations of paganism and heresy in the American Southwest;[31] if Indigenous religions and the social institutions were the target of spiritual Saharanism in the Americas,[32] in the Sahara itself there was a phenomenal fascination with Islam, which then gave rise to disdain and antagonism. Whether Islam served as a path for individuals to return to Christianity (as in the cases of Psichari, Castries, Foucauld, and Claudel) or to embrace a new religion (as with Eberhardt), this polarizing religion fashioned much of what the French intelligentsia thought about the Sahara in the nineteenth century.[33] France was going through its own shift to secularism, and the intra-French politics of religion played out significantly in Algeria and its Sahara.[34] Though spiritual Saharanism unfolded in the Sahara, its ramifications lay at the heart of the politics of European modernity and the increasing separation between church and state.

The synergy of the military, church, and spiritual Saharanism is clear in the late nineteenth and the early twentieth centuries, the era of "celebrity colonialism."[35] Larger-than-life stars of the colonial system, such as Lavigerie, Marshal Hubert Lyautey (1854–1934), and Colonel François-Henry

Laperrine (1860–1920), wielded tremendous clout as they undertook actions and made statements that revealed their investment in spiritual Saharanism.[36] Lyautey wrote that Eberhardt was "everything that attracted me the most to the world: a refractory."[37] For Lyautey, Eberhardt symbolized not only obstinacy and resistance, but also "someone who is their real self, someone who is outside any prejudice, clichés, and who goes through life free of everything."[38] The truth, however, was that Eberhardt, or Si Mahmoud Saadi, as she was known, could not forsake her outright racist and dehumanizing attitudes vis-à-vis the Indigenous people of the Sahara.[39] While acting on the behalf of the army to colonize places that were still outside French control, including Morocco and large portions of the Sahara, Lyautey and Laperrine used the closed-off military status of the territory to selectively grant access to the land to people who were willing to serve their colonialist vision.[40] Hence, Lyautey sent Eberhardt on a reconnaissance mission to a Sufi order on the Moroccan-Algerian border. In turn, Laperrine facilitated, rather encouraged, Foucauld's establishment in the Sahara and mobilized his institutional connections to disseminate his brand of spiritual Saharanism, enmeshing it with spaces of significance that combined religious and military authority.[41]

The Catholic Church's active involvement in conceptualizing and actualizing its place in the colonization of the Sahara conferred ecclesiastical legitimacy on spiritual Saharanism. Lavigerie made full use of his influence to start settlements in the Sahara and harnessed the resources of his charity network to evangelize its population. This church-military complementarity continued well into the twentieth century in the relationship between Laperrine and Foucauld, who would be later credited with offering the Sahara to France, sealing the marriage between the clergy and the military in this land.[42] Since the early 1900s, Foucauld and Laperrine worked as partners, even though their visions may have clashed at times.[43] Their lives and even deaths have been intertwined in monuments, journal articles, and hagiographic writing (Figs. 2 and 3). Their memory is evoked even today by French stakeholders whenever they need to justify France's presence in the Sahara. Nevertheless, the convergence of state and church colonialist interests did not prevent antagonisms, as was displayed by the public disagreement between Lavigerie and the military and administrative authorities in Algeria, which had the fascinating consequence of placing the church on the side of those advocating "civic freedoms and economic liberalization."[44]

FIGURE 2. Stele of Charles de Foucauld and François-Henry Laperrine at Coëtquidan, originally in Ouargla. Bas relief in bronze by F. Bouffez (1931). Father Charles and General Laperrine were united by a strong friendship during their lifetime. Both of them died in the Sahara. Photo courtesy of Jean-Charles Gaillard.

MISSIONARY SETTLER COLONIALISM IN THE SAHARA

Cardinal Lavigerie played an instrumental role in the development and propagation of the most aggressive forms of spiritual Saharanism. An important figure of the Catholic Church in Africa and the Middle East, Lavigerie graduated with a doctorate from the Sorbonne before he moved to Syria-Lebanon, where he led the Œuvre des écoles d'Orient, an association "created to promote culture on the shores of the Mediterranean."[45] He would acquire even greater prestige when he was appointed archbishop of Algiers in 1866, and then three years later became the apostolic delegate to the Sahara and the Sudan after his request to Pope Pius IX, who held the papacy from 1846 to 1878.[46] As historian Bertrand Taithe writes, Lavigerie amassed both titles and power, becoming "bishop of Tunisia from 1881, and cardinal primate of Africa in 1882," positions which benefited his "instrumentalization of the [crusaders'] past and articulated most explicitly [his] missionary militarism."[47] During the posthumous establishment of his statue in the southern town of Biskra, a certain Mr. Roujon, director of the Beaux-Arts

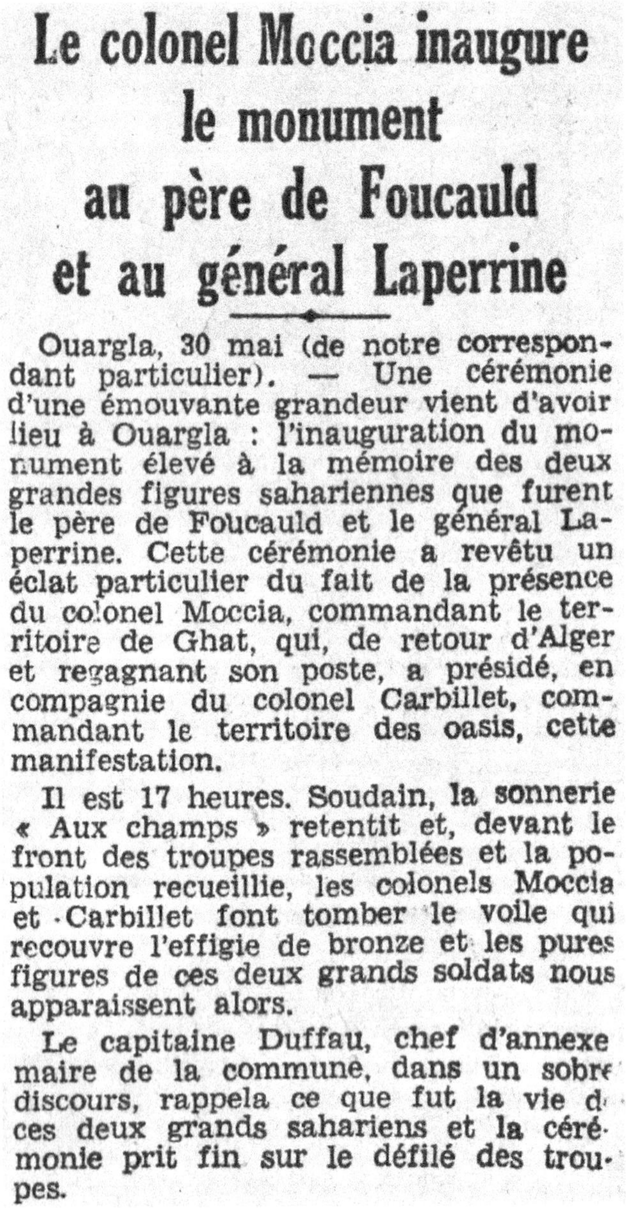

Le colonel Moccia inaugure le monument au père de Foucauld et au général Laperrine

Ouargla, 30 mai (de notre correspondant particulier). — Une cérémonie d'une émouvante grandeur vient d'avoir lieu à Ouargla : l'inauguration du monument élevé à la mémoire des deux grandes figures sahariennes que furent le père de Foucauld et le général Laperrine. Cette cérémonie a revêtu un éclat particulier du fait de la présence du colonel Moccia, commandant le territoire de Ghat, qui, de retour d'Alger et regagnant son poste, a présidé, en compagnie du colonel Carbillet, commandant le territoire des oasis, cette manifestation.

Il est 17 heures. Soudain, la sonnerie « Aux champs » retentit et, devant le front des troupes rassemblées et la population recueillie, les colonels Moccia et Carbillet font tomber le voile qui recouvre l'effigie de bronze et les pures figures de ces deux grands soldats nous apparaissent alors.

Le capitaine Duffau, chef d'annexe maire de la commune, dans un sobre discours, rappela ce que fut la vie de ces deux grands sahariens et la cérémonie prit fin sur le défilé des troupes.

FIGURE 3. The inauguration of the Foucauld-Laperrine monument in Ouargla. Photo courtesy of the Bibliothèque nationale de France.

and a delegate of the government, described Lavigerie as an "intrepid pioneer of civilization" and as a man who "thoroughly explored the lands of which he was considering the conquest."[48] An entrepreneurial priest, Lavigerie seized the opportunity to become the archbishop of Algiers to implement an ambitious religious-politico-militaristic program that encompassed the Sahara and the rest of Africa, extending as far east as Jerusalem.[49]

French authorities were wary of Lavigerie's ambitious personality and warned against his appointment as archbishop of Algiers. His record in Syria-Lebanon included stirring up an interconfessional discord, which pushed the Ministry of Cults of the Third Republic to express its reservations about his nomination to the archbishopric office.[50] Even the emperor warned Patrice MacMahon (1808–1893), then governor-general of Algeria, that he would not get along with Lavigerie, because the latter "lacked prudence and moderation."[51] French officials with different levels of authority depicted Lavigerie as a zealot and excessive individual, but MacMahon needed someone to fill the position created for Louis-Antoine-Augustin Pavy, who had passed away before serving in his new role.[52] Wielding consequential power through the years, Lavigerie lived up to these apprehensions throughout his tenure in the North African colony. Despite the security concerns that military and civil administrators brought to his attention, Lavigerie was intent on building a charity network that would serve as a launchpad for proselytizing Muslims, and by the time of his death in 1892 there were 600 priests and 282 churches and chapels between Algeria and Tunisia, as well as 230 schools in Algeria.[53] However, here I am specifically concerned with his propagation of an image of the Sahara as infested by Islam and barbarians, both of which Lavigerie set out to eradicate. His discourse and actions set the stage for modern Islamophobia and paved the way for clichés that continue to portray the Sahara as an inherently unsafe space.

Stoking Christian-Muslim enmity was crucial for Lavigerie's spiritual Saharanism. The entirety of his project rested on opposing Christianity to Islam and converting Muslims to Christianity in Algeria and the Sahara. Historian Joseph Peterson best captures the disruption Lavigerie's Islamophobic undertakings caused in Algeria: "Lavigerie's arrival in Algeria in 1866 ushered in a stark transformation of the Catholic Church's approach to colonialism and missions in Algeria. More than the colony's previous two bishops, Lavigerie was ready to provoke acrimonious debates with the colonial administration about the allegedly anti-missionary policies of the military administrators. He also engaged in public and dangerously offensive denigrations of Islam."[54] For Lavigerie, Islam was to blame for both uprooting Christianity from its former homeland and fueling resistance to French occupation. He firmly believed that his grandiose endeavor to evangelize Muslims was fully consistent with the existence of Christians who became Muslim after the advent of Islam,[55] going as far as to declare the Sahara as a site of a holy war.[56]

In a famous speech to a military audience in 1875, Lavigerie defined what could be called "the Muslim problem" in the Mediterranean. Entitled "The Army and the Mission of France in Africa," this long talk rereads the colonization of Algeria as a divine enterprise.[57] Lavigerie argued that among all the available armies, God chose "the army of France" to carry out this divine mission.[58] Accordingly, the French conquest of Algeria was God's punishment of Muslim pirates, hordes of criminals, and African barbarians who, together, posed a threat to civilization.[59] France's occupation of Algeria, which he describes as "the bloody lair of piracy,"[60] was also a manifestation of God's revenge on pirates who pillaged, killed, and enslaved Christians.[61] Even though MacMahon made it clear during one of their earliest meetings that "God and France did not speak the same language,"[62] Lavigerie used this speech to eloquently draw the parameters of the union of army and church through their joint colonization of Algeria. Notwithstanding the acrimonious fight with MacMahon,[63] Lavigerie maintained the ties between church and state in the colonial domain.

This speech was the culmination of a bolder Sahara-focused project that unfolded in 1869. That year, Lavigerie returned from a visit to the pope in Rome, in his own words, "Saharanized and negrified."[64] This was his way of quipping about the pope's agreement to add, upon his request, the Sahara and the Sudan to the purview of his spiritual leadership. The fact that one could be both "Saharanized" and "negrified" was a clear display of racism vis-à-vis different populations in the Sahara. The famine that struck the country in 1870 allowed Lavigerie to use charity to advance his evangelical agenda in Algeria despite the authorities' pushback,[65] but this racism-laden negrification and Saharanization enabled him to look further to "another spiritual province, encompassing all the oases of the immense desert until Timbuktu."[66] The Sahara thus became central to his endeavor to recover a supposed formerly Christian land and export Christianity beyond the borders of the colonized part of Algeria. Until his death in 1892, the Sahara was the focus of his obsessions, first as a place where he proposed to deport Muslims at the height of his fight with MacMahon,[67] then as a place to bring Christ to the one hundred million Africans who lived beyond this arid territory and who were "deprived of the Gospels."[68] As his project took root, so did his writings about the Sahara and the rest of Africa, which he reduced to a continent where there existed "the most awful barbarity, ignorance, bloodshed, anthropophagy, and universal slavery."[69] The desert emerges as a wall separating "millions of [African] souls" and "countless tribes [that] have plunged, without being able to extricate themselves, in the abyss of pains" from the benefits of Christianity and French civilization.[70]

The reduction of the Sahara, in Lavigerie's spiritual Saharanism, to a space of inhumane suffering with an immense potential for re-Christianization served multiple purposes. Acting as apostolic delegate of the Sahara and the Sudan, Lavigerie issued letters about slavery in the desert to different organizations. This helped him to constantly denigrate Islam and simultaneously federate the church's support for his evangelization project, which he had pitched to ecclesiastical authorities as a response to Protestant abolitionist successes in Africa.[71] Although the Franco-Prussian war of 1870 and the terrible famines that hit Algeria during the same period delayed his plans to expand toward the Sahara, he resumed his project in 1872 when he sent Father Charmetant to scout the south of Algeria for locations where the church could establish a foothold. Charmetant's successful mission emboldened Lavigerie to send three priests in 1875 with the intention of crossing the desert to reach Timbuktu and the Sudan.[72] The mission's goal was the establishment of a "station to buy slaves," for which Timbuktu, according to missionary literature, was an important center.[73] However, Fathers Paulmier, Memoret, and Bouchaud were murdered by the Tuaregs, further infuriating Lavigerie and unleashing his Islamophobic zeal.

Lavigerie chose to see nothing in the long history of the Sahara except for the Roman Christian past, which was to be restored through the reevangelization of Africans. According to his understanding, his endeavor was a return to the status quo after African Christian populations had sought refuge in the Sahara while escaping Muslim persecution. Although no non-Muslim who had crossed the Sahara provided any firm knowledge about these communities at the time, Lavigerie relied on flimsy and speculative evidence by Élisée Reclus to insinuate that they were white residues of an earlier Christianity.[74] He wrote that "the color of their faces and their language seem to indicate their European origin."[75] This reimagination of the desert as a formerly white, Christian land was a de facto delegitimization of Islam.

Lavigerie's role as apostolate of the Sahara and the Sudan led him to establish the Missionnaires d'Alger. The Pères blancs (White Fathers), as they were known, geared their actions toward the consolidation of control over the Sahara. These desert missionaries had to serve by example and teach people about religion gently through charity. Nonetheless, the push to use soft power to recover the Christian Sahara was not an alternative to military force, which, Lavigerie wrote in his letter to Emile Keller, the president of an antislavery committee in France, was also crucial to controlling the territory.[76] His recurrent descriptions of the desert dwellers as "savages of the Sahara" continued to strengthen the link between barbarity and the presumed instability in the desert, which by now must have been firmly impressed upon his congregants' imaginations.[77] Since the church did not have its own force to deploy in order to impose order and free slaves, it was incumbent on the French government to use its own military, hence "force should come from France and its army, and it is a must because security is a must and without it, we cannot have . . . any personal safety here."[78] Lavigerie thus invented a security problem, equating the Sahara's securitization with the ability to move forward with the church's imperialistic project.

The discursive vitriol against Islam was not enough to contain Lavigerie's colonial aspirations. The White Fathers spearheaded a multipronged strategy to achieve more effective colonization, including the establishment of Bit Allah (The abode of God) to foster universal brotherhood.[79] Foucauld would later recycle this idea during his first years in the Sahara. These abodes of God were to serve a primordial role in preparing the ground for Christian and military conquest by offering a foothold to these brothers of humanity who used soft power to infiltrate the enemies' hearts. Thus, a specific group was established under the name of the Khouan or the Frères du Sahara (Brothers of the Sahara), which Lavigerie considered to be "the auxiliaries of those who would later undertake the conquest by force."[80] The Khouans, which is most likely a derivative of the Wahabi Ikhwan that Lavigerie may have heard of during his time in Syria, were *défricheurs* (trailblazers) for those undertaking the "moral conquest," changing the thoughts and positions of the people of the Sahara vis-à-vis the Christians and Europeans.[81] These abodes of God would be spaces where they would carry out their "peaceful and civilizing" mission among a population that engaged in slavery and anti-Christian war as a result of being corrupted by Islam and fanatical groups like the Senusiyya order,[82] whose members mercilessly massacred Christian missionaries who tried to cross their territories.[83] The intention was not for the Brothers of the Sahara to replace the French state's role but rather to complement it.

The high stakes Lavigerie built into the Sahara made a church-led, armed solution necessary. In 1890, he formed an ecclesiastic militia that assumed the name of the Frères armés ou pionniers du Sahara, also known as the White Army. Taithe has described this enterprise as "missionary militarism," which consisted of the church's work to "raise, equip, and arm a paramilitary unit to serve in territory that the French North African army regarded as their playground."[84] The White Army was marketed in humanitarian terms as a means to eradicate slavery in the Sahara.[85] For Lavigerie, the scale of the desert's lawlessness and barbarity was such that he called it the "space of the biggest and most cruel brigandage" not only in Africa but also in the entire universe.[86] The Sahara thus emerged as a treacherous territory that required militarization even for the sake of abolitionist ideals that were but a small portion of the church's more substantial project of subduing the desert and opening the path to bring the rest of Africa under the mantle of Christianity.[87]

The White Army's founding documents further defined the nature of the church's militant spiritual Saharanism. Like explorers and pioneers of settler colonialism, each armed group was to be made up of fifty "brothers" who were to be subdivided into five smaller groups of various sizes that would carry out specific tasks. A group of nurses was to be in charge of hygiene and treating patients. There had to be a group of artisans skilled in construction, surveillance, and the maintenance of housing. Another group—farmers—had the task of producing the food. A group of subalterns was in charge of cooking and baking, and finally a group of hunters would bring in meat from wild game to supplement that produced by locals.[88] These groups were supposed to form a community of believers who, by "going native," would successfully provide their charitable services to the Indigenous peoples in order to demonstrate the superiority of Christianity over Islam. Since the conversion of Muslims through proselytizing was a quasi-impossible project, spiritual Saharanism emphasized the notion of "disinterested charity" (of which historian Joseph Peterson has debunked the disinterestedness).[89]

These undertakings required funding, which the church received from European donors. Hence, Lavigerie's "barbarization" and "fanaticization" of the Sahara participated in his endeavor to excite Catholic crowds and charity networks to donate. After all, the archbishop was tasked with the mission of bringing the Gospel to the interior of Africa.[90] However, the archbishop also wore the hat of a "*quêteur*—the alms-collecting priest—traveling across France to preach about his orphanages and take up offerings."[91] Therefore, casting the Sahara as a last bastion of Islamic fanaticism opposed to European civilization spoke to both the minds and the pockets of Catholic donors. The White Fathers' literature richly documents this mindset in its focus on their endeavors to create connections between the members of the "big human family" by pushing the boundaries of separation and barbarity represented by the Sahara.[92]

The prolific writings Lavigerie left behind reveal the centrality of storytelling to the brand of spiritual Saharanism that his actions and speeches embodied. During an era when cameras were not yet available to record and convey important events, church leaders' narrative prowess was the channel through which congregants received their ideas about the Sahara. Nobody was better than Lavigerie (not only a religious and academic authority but also a prodigious storyteller) at recounting tales that comforted the faithful and elicited their generous contributions. His 1875 letter to the families of the missionaries who were murdered by the Tuareg that year exemplifies storytelling's dual function as a conveyer of empathy and as a tool for justifying the missionaries' sacrifice in the pursuit of the Sahara's evangelization. Drawing on the Bible, history, and martyrology, Lavigerie conveyed his sentiments to the families and conferred martyrdom on their children, who had died on the path toward achieving the higher goal of Christian civilization in the Sahara. He wrote that Africa was "the last haven for nameless barbarities, of incurable mindlessness, of anthropophagy, [and] of the most repugnant slavery."[93] Accordingly, the missionaries' spilled blood became the water that would make the Sahara bloom again, and this imagery blurred the line between historical facts and religious scripture, on the one hand, and fiction and poetry, on the other. He wrote that the murdered missionaries were "sacred flowers where the whiteness of the lily allies itself with the crimson of the martyr and which first came to make these deserts flourish and fill up with fragrance."[94] The missionaries' blood was not lost since the dead desert itself needed this Christian blood to be revived and vivified. This metaphorical language trickled down to the White Fathers' literature, which repackaged and recycled it for the attention of its general public.[95]

Lavigerie's multipronged spiritual Saharanism was not merely focused on the discursive practice of militarized charity. In fact, this project also had a greening goal that gave it an experimental dimension through the church's farming orphanages. *Les missions catholiques*, a weekly bulletin of the Œuvre de la propagation de la foi, published an article in which the author highlighted Lavigerie's greening project *avant l'heure* in the fifteen acres of land he bought in Biskra to house the missionaries. The 1889 article cast these acres as having been "absolutely bare and uncultivated land" in order to contrast their original uselessness with the magic of the Catholic hands that were able to bring forth life from the fallow soil of the desert.[96] Hundreds of palm trees, fruit trees, and vegetables were planted to meet the needs of the missionary community.[97] This was part of Lavigerie's vision:

> The third condition necessary for the foundation of the pacific reservation that I am talking about is the habit of work specific to the desert and principally works of agriculture; not only the farming of palm trees, which are the basis of Saharan life, but also that of plants that are possible to bring into it from the coast, such as fig, apricot, and pomegranate trees as well as the vegetables of our gardens. What is marvelous, in fact, is that some of these vegetables that are useful for food, like potatoes, cabbages, lettuce, garbanzo beans, fava beans, and artichoke, among others, prosper and grow even faster than in our gardens in Europe if they are treated with adequately sufficient water.[98]

Lavigerie clearly omitted the millennial, oasis-focused agricultural traditions in the Sahara, which one of his contemporaries recorded as containing thousands of palm trees and also a variety of fruits and vegetables in addition to clover for the animals.[99] Despite Lavigerie's willful oversight, the bylaws of the Brothers of the Sahara required their staples to be "exclusively composed of the food items that are possible to procure in the Sahara."[100] Erasure does not mean lack of awareness of Saharan people's production of food, since the bylaws also required that the meat be "provided . . . conforming to the customs of the desert either from herds of camel, sheep or goats."[101] Even worse, however, the desire to heighten the contrast between Christians and Muslims led to racist commentary that desert people's abiding by Qur'anic injunctions made them fatalistic, which prevented them, in part, from making the desert green.[102]

These multiple initiatives and overlapping projects placed the Sahara at the center of attention in the Catholic Church's tentacular network and its underlying ideational ecosystem. The church's deep influence in Tamazgha, Europe, and the Middle East made the Sahara a household topic among congregants throughout the world. This was particularly thanks to charity and fundraising work that was, in turn, undergirded by an impressive publication infrastructure that allowed the ideas forming the core of spiritual Saharanism to reach a wide audience. These publication outlets conveyed all of spiritual Saharanism's prejudices about the desert as a land inhabited by savages whose only preoccupation was to enslave weaker people, wage war against each other, and murder missionaries who sought to bring them civilization. Misconceptions have the power to replace factual knowledge, but misconceptions relayed through spaces of faith in the name of religious authority have an even more powerful and enduring impact. Those who encountered the Sahara through Lavigerie's spiritual Saharanism in church literature consumed the "new virulence and [the] new racialization" that he and his followers had infused into their monumental Islamophobic and anti-Saharan intellectual output.[103]

A product of nineteenth-century European conflicts, Lavigerie's zeal to serve both his nation and God appeared amid France's imperialistic expansion.[104] As such, he endeavored not only to revive the past but also to "organize the present and prepare the future" of Catholicism in Africa at a time when supposedly mysterious, scary, and unknown places, including the Sahara, attracted both explorers and conquerors.[105] As a colonialist, Lavigerie never questioned whether the murders of explorers and missionaries who had encroached on the Tuareg's territories were anything other than barbarity. In his endeavors, the Sahara stood accused of being not only a natural barrier between the two lusher parts of Africa but also a barrier between the worlds of Christian civilization and Islamic savagery, slavery,[106] and the desire to shed Christian blood.[107] Analyzed retrospectively, Lavigerie's ideas were precursors to current European states' xenophobic and Islamophobic policies, which have militarized the Sahel, the Sahara, and the Mediterranean to limit all mobility under the pretext of fighting human trafficking.[108] In his own words, the "penetration of the Sahara imposes itself on France: it is its most pressing interest, the most direct for its Algerian possessions, for the security of its colonies, for its increasing riches."[109] France's failure to subdue the desert and its populations would result in the French being "thrown into the sea" by the savage inhabitants of the Sudan.[110] Lavigerie and his disciples are long dead, but the seeds they planted through their spiritual imaginaries of the Sahara have outlived them and continue to shape how Europe and, more recently, the US view the Sahara and its people, albeit in novel and constantly refigured ways.

FOUCAULD'S IDEATIONAL ECOSYSTEM: RACIALIZATION AND VIOLENCE IN THE SAHARA

Foucauld and His Ideational Ecosystem

Lavigerie's spiritual enterprise in the Sahara came to an end with his death in Algiers in 1892 and subsequent burial in the Cathedral of Carthage, where his remains stayed until his repatriation in 1964 when the church became property of the Tunisian state. Eight years after his death, in 1900, the French army extended its authority over the Saharan territory, subduing the recalcitrant Tuareg tribes and fulfilling Lavigerie's dream. His vision of a dominated Sahara materialized, but his missionary militia and the church superstructure that he had built over four decades was a thing of the past. His greatest failure, however, was not finding the white Christian communities he thought lived in the desert. Nonetheless, Lavigerie blazed the path for both desert-phobia and desert missionary action. Foucauld's relocation to the Sahara, first to Béni Abbès in 1901 and later to the Hoggar in 1905, would place the desert on the spiritual map of the Christian world in ways that surpassed anyone before him. This is partially due to Foucauld's ideational ecosystem, which intersected with a wide range of influential individuals who all shared a colonialist background. This ideational network of military officers and civilian intellectuals provided Foucauld's spiritual Saharanism with a legitimacy that has thus far allowed it to survive, if not entirely elude, criticism in the postcolonial period.

Foucauld's spiritual Saharanism would not have been appealing without his extraordinary life story. A graduate of the prestigious Saint-Cyr Academy and a former member of the Chasseurs d'Afrique in Algeria, Foucauld attained great acclaim after his exploration of Morocco in 1883–84. Morocco was the other Timbuktu in that it was impenetrable to non-Muslims except for diplomats and Jews.[111] Mentored by Oscar MacCarthy, the president of the local Société de géographie in Algiers, Foucauld applied himself to learning Arabic and passing as a Jew under the supervision of Mordechai Abi Serour, a Moroccan rabbi who agreed to serve as his guide into the country.[112] Disguised as Joseph Aleman, a Moravian Jew from Jerusalem, Foucauld entered Morocco, which was established in the European imaginary as being in a state of "medieval torpor, [and] ha[ving] no real contact with Europe and the rest of the world."[113] His book *Reconnaissance au Maroc, 1883–1884*, which crowned his adventurous enterprise there, sealed his reputation as an intrepid explorer and earned him the award of the Société de géographie de Paris in 1885, even before the book was published in 1888.[114] Henri Duveyrier, the highly esteemed explorer of the Sahara and author of the equally acclaimed *Les Touareg du nord*, wrote in his report for the Société de géographie de Paris that, at the cost of multiple sacrifices, Foucauld acquired "very precise information that has literally renewed almost all geographical and political knowledge of Morocco."[115] Félix Gauthier, another esteemed fixture of colonial geography, emphasized *Reconnaissance au Maroc*'s significance as the main reference work on Morocco's "Bled Siba," or the territory outside the direct control of the sultan of Morocco, even three decades after its publication.[116] The accolades the book received set Foucauld up for financial and academic success, but his choice to become a monk rechanneled this praise into his mythologization as a symbol of Christian sainthood in the desert.[117]

North Africa, more specifically Morocco, was Foucauld's source of worldly success and the place where he rekindled his Christian faith.[118] Witnessing the practice of Islam in Morocco was too powerful for him to ignore.[119] His declaration to Bishop Henri Huvelin ("I have no faith, and I am here to request that you teach me") during his confession in the Church of Saint-Augustin in 1886 was the culmination of his spiritual quest since his return from Morocco.[120] These words would become proverbial in terms of just how distanced he had been from religion prior to that fateful meeting.[121] Huvelin's spiritual directorship helped Foucauld make critical decisions, including later moving to Syria, Palestine, and the Sahara. His trajectory as a man who, despite tumultuous teenage years and a hedonistic adulthood, relinquished ordinary life and all the proceeds that he could have accumulated from his dangerous exploration in Morocco enhanced his reputation as an ascetic among his contemporaries. The profuse and ongoing hagiographic literature about him and his feats have sustained his brand of spiritual Saharanism beyond what could have been imagined in the nineteenth century.

Foucauld's reversion to Catholicism has been a crucial pillar of his spiritual Saharanism. His life story gave (and still provides) hope to those who need spiritual guidance—namely, a type grounded in experiential stories of isolation in a desert, evoking prophecy and spirituality. Similar to the lessons that Antoine de Saint-Exupéry's *Petit prince* learns from the desert, Foucauld's spiritual Saharanism drew on a life that was reconstituted in the desert and offered to God. Those who needed an example to follow in their struggle found it in the company of Foucauld. His status as a hero who overcame obstacles and proved his mettle was a source of inspiration for his contemporaries and those who came after him. Like the hero of Roger Frison-Roche's *La piste oubliée*, Foucauld became a prophetic figure who was drawn to the desert by a power that was mightier than his human ability to resist. Paul Lesourd even writes that the patience he gained during his travels in Morocco and Algeria allowed Foucauld to develop his latent, underdeveloped will, emphasizing that "nothing discouraged him, no obstacle daunted him or diminished his courage."[122] Because he wanted to live in isolation, he joined the Trappists in the Akbés monastery in Syria, but, as Louis Massignon writes, ten years of Trappist penitence were not sufficient for him to feel "detached enough" from the world.[123] During this time, Foucauld developed his ideas for the Petits frères de Jésus, an association whose members were to live in total poverty among the poorest people.[124] Hence, Foucauld's life trajectory and spiritual choices evoke the early Christian monks—the *ḥunafāʾ*—who forsook the world and focused instead on the hereafter. His spiritual

Saharanism rehabilitated this age-old practice that involved subjecting body and mind to extreme poverty in the harsh conditions of the desert.

The appeal of Foucauld's personal story in no way means that his spiritual Saharanism was divorced from Lavigerie's. In fact, Foucauld's spiritual endeavors were in many ways in keeping with Lavigerie's intentions, but without the latter's pompously explicit zealotry. Administratively, Foucauld was under the authority of the Apostolate of the Sahara. Although much reduced in size from Lavigerie's era, the Apostolate still had religious authority over the territory. The strongest point of consistency, however, was in Foucauld's recycling of prejudices against Islam in his epistolary writings throughout his life in the desert. He wrote to Henry de Castries that Islam "produced a profound upheaval in me; the sight of this faith, of these souls living in the continuous presence of God has allowed me to glimpse something bigger and truer than mundane occupations."[125] The admiration for the religion that brought him back to Catholicism was only matched by his adamant conviction that it was not a good religion. In another letter to de Castries, Islam becomes a seductive "islamisme" and threatens to stand between him and the "true religion."[126] Not only was Catholicism an easily provable truth, but this provability also served as evidence that "any other [religion] is wrong."[127] For him, the contrast between Jesus and Muhammad was a matter of chastity and poverty, on the one hand, and wealth and carnal pleasures, on the other.[128] It was between 1901 and 1902 that he sent these letters from Béni Abbès, and they can be interpreted as an indication that he had already dismissed the religion of the people among whom he chose to live.

A salient line of continuity of Lavigerie's spiritual Saharanism through Foucauld was his furtherance of Lavigerie's "nativization" of the White Fathers' dress code and behaviors. The success of the European missionaries was contingent on their success at being "as close as possible to the natives' way of life."[129] This insistence on frugality also had an economic dimension because of the limited resources in the colony.[130] Both efficiency and economy required the missionaries to wear the North African gandoura made of white wool, a haik, a red chechia, underwear made of linen or cloth, and a rosary around the neck.[131] Their type of shoes was to be dictated by the nature of the terrain.[132] Their dress code and food habits had to allow them to blend in with the natives. The abolitionist work these missionaries were called upon to accomplish was crucial for the evangelization campaign, so much so that they were required to learn the languages the enslaved spoke.[133] These requirements were in no way dictated by their concern for native traditions; rather, they were the result of a conviction that to better colonize the Saharan populations, the missionaries had to master their cultural frameworks. Maximizing proselytization and infiltrating every aspect of local people's lives pushed the church to nativize itself. These precepts suited Foucauld's excessive and obsessive personality, which desired a harsher ascetic experience than even the Trappists could provide.[134] The way Foucauld acted in the Sahara embodied every aspect of the Lavigerian ecclesiastic participatory approach. He lived frugally, dressed in local garb, and learned Tuareg Tamasheq, spending much of his time working on this language's grammar and literature. Foucauld went fully native, even in claiming his maraboutic status.

The discontinuity that Foucauld effected in the history of spiritual Saharanism resulted from his influential ideational ecosystem. Established around his own person over the decades, this extended network of prominent figures made Foucauld an integral, powerful voice within the military and civilian colonial systems alike. Regarding the military, he kept company with the heroes and celebrities of colonial expansion such as Lyautey, Louis Lacroix, Laperrine, de Castries, and Gustave Adolphe de Calassanti Motylinski.[135] Foucauld was first and foremost an officer who became a priest; thus, he embodied two pillars of the colonial situation. Nonetheless, he was aware that his continued existence in the Sahara was contingent on the approval of the military and ecclesiastic authorities.[136] Between 1901 and 1916, the cartography of Saharan existence was shaped by his collaboration with French officers, many of whom he had known before his renaissance of faith. In his letters to de Castries, he even took pride in the fact that the army and the Arab Bureau were building his chapel in Béni Abbès, commenting on the sympathy he received from the French soldiers.[137] Georges Gorrée, the director of *Cahiers Charles de Foucauld*, described him as the "right arm of the high military commandant of the Saharan oases and the constant and well-heeded adviser of the officers of the Algerian south."[138] Even Father Henri de Staoueli recommended him to the military authorities as someone who would "do what the great cardinal [Lavigerie] did in Tunisia for French influence."[139] Laperrine even went as far as to call Foucauld "the priest of the Tuareg."[140] Most importantly, the army needed Foucauld to stave off the nefarious effects of the widespread rumor among colonized populations that the French had no religion. As Hugues Didier put it, "Charles de Foucauld allowed soldiers established in the Sahara to be believers by proxy."[141]

The civilian side of Foucauld's spiritual Saharanism was equally important. Towering figures of French literature and thought like Claudel and Massignon, as well as René Bazin, are indissociable from its development and dissemination. Foucauld's exchanges with these figures gave him a prestigious platform of prolific, highly connected individuals to carry his message to audiences from all walks of life. At the time of his murder in 1916, Foucauld was only well known among the members of his close ideational ecosystem. However, Massignon wrote in his memoirs that people "love Charles de Foucauld because I made them love him," referring to his choice of Bazin to write his well-known biography, *Charles de Foucauld, explorateur du Maroc, ermite au Sahara.*[142] Bazin's 1921 book initiated a hagiographic fascination with Foucauld and generated a cult of personality, pushing illustrious members of his network to express their tacit disagreement with the biography, which fell on the side of bondieuserie or excessive devotion.[143] The result, as Dominique Casajus has written, was that "Foucauld's glory had become universal in a France that extended then from Dunkerque to Tamanrasset."[144]

The Sahara in Bazin's biography of Foucauld is nothing but a playground where the brave, enthusiastically devoted priest pursued his Christian ideas of charity and closeness to God. Foucauld's ardent colonialism, Islamophobia, and intentional delegitimization of Islam barely received any critical attention in the book. Some of these prejudices went unnoticed because they were left unnamed, and the cult of personality that emanated from the saintly image projected onto Foucauld made the critique of his œuvre impossible. In his respectful yet critical book *Charles de Foucauld: Moine et savant*, Casajus makes the forceful conclusion that, when reflecting on the literary genre used to depict Foucauld's life, one can see that "behind the figures deployed in it, the mythologies that animate it, and the feelings and bitterness that are expressed in it, there will appear, beneath the surface, another history: that of colonialism."[145] Foucauld's life in the Sahara and its phenomenal success were not a natural occurrence but rather the result of an active construction through a system of ideas, all of which collaborated to render him the Sahara's saintly figure in the popular Christian imagination.

Foucauld's ideational ecosystem demonstrates an overlap between Orientalism and Saharanism. Algerian scholar Ḥasan Dawwās has drawn on Orientalism to develop a variant of Saharanism;[146] although Dawwās rightly notes that the "Orient is not the Sahara,"[147] his definition of Saharanism as the "study of the Sahara" limits the theoretical and critical stakes of the novel approach and terminology he proposes.[148] This said, I agree with Dawwās's suggestion that Orientalism is no longer the appropriate way to approach the study of Tamazgha, the Sahara included, because it imposes a framework on a region that has its own cultural specificity. Unless Orientalism is overstretched to encompass anything and everything critical of colonialism and its legacies, as is the case with the current uses of "environmental Orientalism,"[149] physical deserts have both specific and broader significances that cannot be captured by Orientalism. For the specific context of North Africa, French Orientalism's misguided association of the area with the Orient has had a deep impact on the later marginalization of Amazigh languages and cultures.[150] The geographical Orient had indeed fascinated Lavigerie, Massignon, Foucauld, and Claudel, who all spent time in what is today called the Middle East, and they were part of the people influenced by imaginaries of the "biblical desert," which in Michel Roux's analysis were crucial for the Christian renaissance exemplified by Foucauld.[151]

Reconciling Spirituality and Racializing Violence: The Limits of Foucauld's Brotherhood

Time and again, Foucauld referred to himself as the *petit frère universel* (universal little brother).[152] Seen for the first time in writing, this phrase evokes ideals of equality and mutual respect without any distinction among those who are bonded through the notion of brotherhood. However, a close reading of Foucauld's discourse and a meticulous examination of his actions in the Sahara indicate that this universal brotherhood is counterintuitive, insofar as it was driven by his spiritual Saharanist vision of the world. Brotherhood entails the recognition of one's brother's absolute humanity, but Foucauld's vision of it normalized inequality and routinized racialization. There was a clear disconnect between Foucauld's actions and professed kindness and the metalanguage he used to talk about Saharans and their space. His conception of security alone reveals how his spiritual Saharanism stood between him and the materialization of the brotherly ideals that informed his writings from the desert.

One of the limits of this brotherhood is easily observable in Foucauld's obsession with portraying the poor people of the Sahara through the framework of his chosen dejection. Poverty, for Foucauld, had to take the material form of a chapel in Béni Abbès and a hermitage in Assekrem in the Hoggar. Both chapel and hermitage became consubstantial with the stories that Foucauld and others recounted in order to sustain the idea that the Sahara was a locus for personal transformation. Furthermore, these built environments were proof that French colonization was there to stay.[153] Foucauld took pride in his chapel being made of "dried bricks and logs of palm trees," adding that the chapel was "three cells and one guest room."[154] A few years later, he would write to de Castries from the Hoggar, describing his accommodations as "a small gourbi and a small garden."[155] Even Lyautey highlighted how his "chapel [in Béni Abbès] was a poor hovel with walls made of mud bricks and a dirt floor."[156] Similarly, Foucauld writes that his hermitage in Assekrem was "on the summit that overlooks almost all of the Hoggar, between savage mountains beyond which the horizon, which seems unlimited, evokes God."[157] It was the Belle Époque of all manner of excess,[158] but Foucauld, unlike his contemporaries, insisted on his harsh, frugal life aimed at intensifying the spiritual value of quietude and total satisfaction they procured for him.[159] It should not be forgotten, however, that this excessive frugality may also have been his way to prove his maraboutism to the Saharans by outwardly showing his piety, attempting both to impress them and earn their respect. Since Foucauld was always obsessed with the long-term impact of his actions, there is no doubt that his extreme display of religious zeal sought to outmatch his Muslim competitors.

Foucauld's correspondence with his European interlocutors reveals that his universal brotherhood applied transversally only to Europeans whom Foucauld treated as equals. As far as the people of the Sahara were concerned, this brotherhood was vertical and steeped in Saharans' infantilization. His participation in what came to be known as Laperrine's *campagne d'apprivoisement* (domestication/taming campaign) among the Tuaregs in 1905 is illustrative of this lopsided kinship, which uses the notion of brotherhood to disseminate a positive image about Foucauld's actions in the desert without necessarily questioning the methods employed in the colonial context. *Apprivoisement* refers to the process of making animals feel safe among or friendly toward humans. The notion of domestication presupposes that the tamer is human, whereas the creature being tamed is either nonhuman or shows faculties that can be considered less than human. The imaginary behind the language of taming the Tuaregs holds clear references to the association of the desert with wildness and lawlessness. The Tuaregs' murder of Captain Flatters and numerous other explorers and missionaries who adventured into their territory had garnered them the reputation of being "terrible children" or "terrible Tuaregs."[160]

At the turn of the century, it was common among practitioners of spiritual Saharanism to dehumanize and racialize Saharans, as is evidenced by this example from Eberhardt during her trip to the Kenadsa zawiya. She wrote: "I find blacks to be disconcerting and repulsive, mainly because of the extreme mobility of their faces: their ferret's eyes, and features plagued by tics and grimaces. They bring out in me a stubborn sense of their non-humanity, a lack of kinship which I succumb to childishly, every time, in the face of these blacks, my brothers."[161] This explicitly racist language, in tandem with the reference to brotherhood, is reminiscent of Foucauld's work. Later, Eberhardt reduces Black people of the desert to a state of animality and instinct, again serving as a reminder of Laperrine's *campagne d'apprivoisement*. Speaking about the sexuality of enslaved women, Eberhardt compares male and female desires, attributing the ability "to contain somewhat the urgings of their blood" to enslaved men while affirming that "black women are as frivolous as their loves."[162] This both bigoted and racist description of Black people was only matched by Eberhardt's antisemitic comments about Jewish men, whom she describes as distinguished by "vulgarity" and lack of "noble sentiment[s]."[163] Similarly, Psichari's encounter with Saharans in Mauritania was characterized by both fascination and a great deal of racism. Even though his spiritual awakening happened as a result of his encounter with the people of the desert, Psichari resorted to racist notions to explain Saharan spirituality. For him, the combination of environmental harshness, poverty, Amazigh primitivism, and a lack of civilization explains the preservation among the Moors of a "mystical character."[164] Since Saharans were "incapable of any artistic manifestation,"[165] they, like the arid land they lived in, could not be but an incarnation of a prehistoric or, at best, useless humanity.

Primitivism called for controlling and policing the Sahara and its inhabitants. Foucauld used his maraboutic status to play a security role for France, which calls attention to his double role as a spiritual man who addressed individuals sharing his spiritual quest and the security-minded Foucauld, who mostly dialogued with his former military colleagues. Although it is difficult to prove that Foucauld was enlisted as an official intelligence officer in the Hoggar, ample evidence in his correspondence reveals he was deeply invested in collecting information and sharing it with army officers. In July 1916, Foucauld wrote to Laperrine, "the Hoggar remains perfectly calm."[166] He again wrote to Laperrine, who was deployed to Europe during World War I, "No news from Ajjer since that of June 25, which I told you about in the preceding letter. The news from Adrar is very good: Moussa's people have killed Firhoun."[167] Firhoun was a Tuareg leader who fought against the French, and the way Foucauld broke the news to Laperrine indicates his joy that Firhoun was murdered by his Tuareg brothers on behalf of France. These letters contain infinitesimal details about the security situation across all four corners of the Sahara, including locations that were hundreds of miles away from Foucauld's headquarters. Whether Foucauld volunteered to furnish intelligence about the Saharans he lived with or if he was really a spy in the guise of a priest is beside the point. Rather, the focus here is on the meaning of brotherhood, spirituality, and solitude in the desert when they were instrumentalized to advance a colonial agenda. This is mostly apparent in his descriptions of ordinary intertribal raids, which he relayed to Laperrine as being "close to acts of revolt."[168] Not only did he attribute this situation to *incurie* (carelessness),[169] but he also suggested heavy-handed punishment, in his language, of revolt.[170] Speaking about the region of Adrar, where the raids of recalcitrant Moroccan tribes were particularly challenging to the French army, Foucauld exhorted Laperrine: "It is a must that all the raiders who appear be hunted and exterminated, down to the last one, so that the raiding tribes do not have any guides. . . . It is only by killing all the brigands, like we hang pirates in the yard, that we will have peace . . . later the Mauritanians will subdue the raiders of Seguiet El Hamra; our comrades in Morocco will subdue Draa and Tafilelt, etc, and definitive peace will exist."[171] While the letters that Massignon and Bishop Huvelin received from him preached brotherhood and spiritual care, these sentiments entirely disappeared in his officer-to-officer exchange with Laperrine.

Foucauld's reconciliation of violence and spirituality was fully fleshed out in his 1912 proposal to remap and reorganize the Sahara. Unsurprisingly, the control of space and people's movements within it was an essential aspect of his entire project. His plan for the pacification and disciplining of the Sahara provides the greatest road map into the types of questions that preoccupied him in his hermitic isolation. Entitled the "Plan d'organisation du Sahara,"[172] Foucauld's ambitious strategy was designed, in Gorrée's words, "to help implant French civilization in these oasis territories, which, in the past, were doomed to anarchy, pillage, [and] to raids of slaves and death."[173] For Foucauld, the Sahara was too vast and too dangerous to be policed by the four hundred native soldiers and the dozen French officers who were stationed in the vast annex of Tidikelt. He wrote: "It seems superfluous to demonstrate that it is impossible for a small number of officers of one annex to ensure: 1. contact with the natives, which is indispensable for their progress, gaining their confidence, and knowing them; 2. the constant presence of officers in the centers of the main regions necessary for the administration to have centers and so that we know where to find a representative of the authorities; 3. the constant presence of officers among the mobile military troops necessary for maintaining order."[174] The three elements that motivated Foucauld to submit his plan were all linked to his vision that tight authority had to be kept over the Sahara and its inhabitants. This reorganization of the territory's military management actively sought to curtail the Saharans' freedom of movement and disable their agency by consistently exposing them to the existence of a military power in their midst. Foucauld wanted the people of the Sahara to internalize surveillance and discipline according to the rules of colonialism.

Foucauld's plan entailed the division of the Sahara into three military zones: Tidikelt, Ahaggar, and Ajjer.[175] Each of these annexes had authority over an immense territory. Specifically for the annexes of the Hoggar and Ajjer, Foucauld suggested the construction of forts in Ahaggar and Adrar because of the nomadic lifestyle endemic to these regions. In his own words, "a fixed and permanent center of authority was indispensable for their discipline and administration," because "some tribes lived permanently in this portion of the territory in Adrar."[176] Similarly, the construction of a fort in the annex of Ajjer was crucial for "the surveillance of this important region that is coterminous with Tripolitania."[177] Bringing centers of power to a population he describes as being "lazy, wasteful, feisty, violent, intelligent, and bold"[178] was integral to the "civilizing" project of colonization, which Foucauld supported. The officers who were to be appointed to manage the "primitive and half-civilized" Tuareg population had a double-edged function of both "administering and civilizing" the inhabitants. This required the officers to enjoy respect that would give them the ability to "influence minds."[179]

The civilizational terms Foucauld used are reminiscent of Lavigerie's antagonistic binary that opposed Islam to Christianity in the Sahara. Foucauld started from the premise that the population of the Sahara was backward and primitive, living outside the scope of civilization, and the task of colonial officers—and the church, by extension—was to civilize them. He wrote in his plan: "The progress of the natives toward civilization is especially contingent on the esteem and confidence that they have for the French with whom they are in contact. It also depends on the wisdom of the measures taken by those who govern and on the happy impulsion they know how to give. Therefore, the officers chosen to administer [the Sahara] have to be well known; known for a personality that is worthy of esteem and confidence; that we know their acts are motivated by the public good and not their personal interest."[180] His emphasis on justice and equity was not for the good of the natives but rather for the good of the colonial project, the sustainability of which was contingent on the enforcement of these elements.[181] This awareness is reflected in his assertion that if France failed, it would be pushed out of the Sahara.[182]

As a universal brother, Foucauld never stopped to ponder the consequences of such proposals for the mobility of desert dwellers. His tendency to overgeneralize and exaggerate the threat represented by intertribal strife created a dark image of the Sahara, justifying its reorganization in a way that would keep it pacified—or subdued. However, his plans to control and surveil the Saharan territory aimed to impose a vision of security that was foreign to the desert populations' nomadic way of life. His designs did not stray far from Lavigerie's view, insofar as his view of the desert was dominated by a worldview that filled the Sahara with belligerent, savage, and bloodthirsty tribes. The reality, however, is that many of these accusations were amplified and blown out of proportion to "barbarize" the people and the territory for the sake of more security-focused interventions. Instead of asking himself why the people of the Sahara resisted French colonization of their territory, Foucauld avoided looking into the root causes of this rejection of colonialism and focused instead on increasing the natives' docility and fostering his vision for civilization.

The monastics and *zahids* founded cloisters in the desert to disengage from the concerns of the material world and dedicate their existence entirely to seeking God.[183] As I have demonstrated throughout these sections, spiritual Saharanism, by contrast, had a hard time divorcing from the world and focusing on the divine alone, because colonialism, domination, and inequality in the desert were at its core. Although Foucauld preached spiritual solitude in his letters and other writings, the desert was never a tomb for him. It was rather a bizarre and dangerous milieu that increased his Christian capital among his widening ideational ecosystem. His *rayonnement* onto the world was as much about carving out borders and spaces of influences to control, if not entirely Christianize, non-European populations as it was about monasticism. Encompassing work on Tuareg literature, a translation of the Bible into Tamasheq, and even the emancipation of some enslaved individuals whom he bought, particularly in Béni Abbès, Foucauld had a versatile profile that spoke to individuals and groups from all walks of life. His relationship with Laperrine sealed his fate as a priest-soldier who was worthy of philatelic commemoration alongside Laperrine in 1935 by the famous artist Mohammed Racim (1896–1975) (Fig. 4). The dissemination of his image by French postal services wedded his name to the Sahara, foregrounded his fort in Tamanrasset, and allowed him to be a central figure in many Christians' understanding of desert spirituality (Fig. 5). While only specialists nowadays know of Lavigerie's Islamophobic undertakings in Algeria, many faithful Christians across languages and cultures had savored curated versions of Foucauld's spiritual Saharanism even before his canonization in 2022.

FIGURE 4. Commemorative stamp designed by Mohammed Racim, a famous artist in French Algeria.

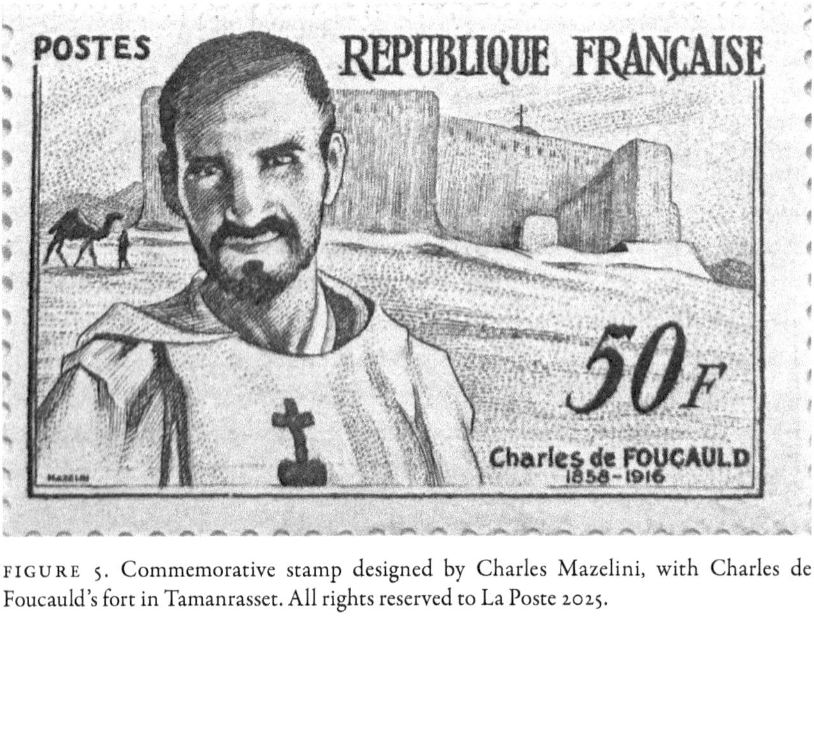

FIGURE 5. Commemorative stamp designed by Charles Mazelini, with Charles de Foucauld's fort in Tamanrasset.

EGOCENTRISM IN THE SAHARA: AFTERLIVES OF SPIRITUAL SAHARANISM AND EXTRACTIVE SPIRITUALITY

Between 1999 and 2004, I worked as a teacher in the High Atlas Mountains, and this marked the first time I encountered Foucauld's legacy. Groups of men and women were dressed in gray djellabas and wearing khaki pants and sturdy boots, resembling the uniforms of the Moroccan "auxiliary forces," themselves a version of the native force established by the French called a goum.[184] These trekkers, who walked along the Ounila Valley from Telouet on the way to the city of Ouarzazate, sought no engagement with the local population. One evening at sunset, they set up a makeshift camp outside the village where I was teaching. Curious about these people whom I encountered several times over those years, I tried to ask them questions about the meaning of their trek, but only once did someone drop the name Les petits frères de Jésus. It turned out that they were a group of believers who commemorate Foucauld's exploration of Morocco through this march that takes them through the main areas he had visited in 1883–84. More than twenty years later, I cannot but think of this surviving practice of celebrating Foucauld's legacy as an important feature of spiritual Saharanism. Once again, Foucauld has withstood the test of time and outlived every other colonial figure who resided in the Sahara, specifically thanks to the afterlife given to his brand of spiritual Saharanism through the myriad writings and commemorative acts of those who considered themselves to be his spiritual heirs. However, the clearest space where one sees this afterlife is in the literature that constantly reinvents his spiritual journey, repackages it, and endows it with new meanings that speak to contemporary audiences.

The self-focused, egocentric avenue that Foucauld opened in spiritual Saharanism paved the path for the disengagement of contemporary individuals from the concerns of the real world. In *Letters from the Desert*, Carlo Carretto (1910–1988) presents one such afterlife. In 1954, corresponding to the beginning of the Algerian War of Independence, Carretto, a forty-two-year-old Italian priest, arrived in Algeria to fulfill a divine order to renounce his worldly life and move to the Sahara. A voice ordered Carretto: "Leave everything and come with me into the desert. It is not your acts and deeds that I want: I want your prayer, your love."[185] Indeed, Carretto relocates to the Saharan town of El Abiodh Sidi Cheikh and the local annex of the Petits frères de Jésus established by Massignon, Louis Gardet, and others in

Foucauld's memory in 1933. Carretto describes his experience in the desert and the discovery that pursuing Foucauld's path was "the way for him."[186] This life in the desert required Carretto to make a break between his past life and the life he was about to live for the next ten years.[187] Family, friendships, connections, and memories that he had built until that point all became burdensome, and Carretto needed to free himself from them. He even burned his address book as a symbol of this rupture with the world,[188] which only, and paradoxically, increased his love and prayers for his friends. Carretto would crisscross the Sahara under colonial authority for the next decade, and his continuation of Foucauld's spiritual Saharanism reveals the Sahara's function as a playground for spiritual improvement and an experience of purgatory.[189]

The Sahara, for Carretto, was a purely physical experience. For him, the description of the territory as a purgatory necessarily implied that the people of the desert were sinners or, at the very least, deserved the harsh conditions in which they lived. Instead of hearing the wails and cries of those who were going through the Algerian War (1954–62), he chose to hear "silence in the desert, silence in the cave, silence in the Eucharist."[190] Since he was aware that the potential readers of *Letters from the Desert* were urban, egocentric beings, he chose to satisfy their need for silence and spirituality in their busy lives. His focus on the desert as a sonic, corporeal experience is only matched by a dangerous desire to fix it as a bodily experience that leads to spiritual fulfillment without any intellectual stakes. He writes that one "must simplify, deintellectualize,"[191] despite the Sahara's multisecular tradition of learning and intellectual production in all manner of science. A close reading of the book, however, indicates that the desert is only a foil for Carretto to teach his followers about Christianity by adopting the path of Foucauld's spiritual Saharanism. The desert is de-spatialized—as in the call to find one's own internal desert—and removed from its own rich context so as to serve a Catholic renewal in crisis.

Carretto was neither Foucauld nor Lavigerie. He lived in a different time, and his discourse reflects the spirit of the era of ongoing decolonization in Africa. He was very careful not to reproduce the same colonialist violence that Lavigerie and Foucauld bequeathed in their writings. He even clearly stated the dangers posed by colonialism and underscored his understanding of the colonized people's struggle for liberation, going so far as to critique the imbrication of colonization and the church in writing, "A missionary wasn't always synonymous with a man of God, nor an official with generosity and justice."[192] In this regard, Carretto demonstrated a strong understanding of the significance of decolonization and the need of colonized people across the globe to shake free of its legacies. Nonetheless, awareness of independence and decolonization did not translate for Carretto into a departure from Foucauld's own colonialist endeavors. He instead emphasized them by furnishing a reading that particularized his experience as being different from that of the colonial missionary. Carretto selectively read Foucauld's history in the Sahara, writing that he "arrived alone, defenseless, poor."[193] Not only were these assertions counterfactual, given that Foucauld had arrived with the blessings and support of the military, but Carretto also attributes to Foucauld intentions he did not have, particularly in emphasizing that he acted as if decolonization had already started.[194] Casajus has already demystified much about these hagiographic assertions, affirming along the way that the Tuaregs were aware that Foucauld was "protected by the army of a foreign nation."[195] Yet these counterfactual assertions remain tenets of spiritual Saharanism's instrumentalization of the Sahara.

Prejudice against Islam and Muslims—or in today's terms, Islamophobia—is where Carretto continues Lavigerie's and Foucauld's vision. The times may have changed for colonialism, but the image of Saharan Islam as a haven of violence against the Other had not, and even Carretto subtly insinuates that violence and fanaticism were entrenched among the Muslims he encountered in the colonial desert. An impoverished Black child whom Carretto had built a friendship with had expressed distress that Carretto would go to hell if he did not convert to Islam. Whether this truly happened or whether it was only a story Carretto invented to galvanize his readers, the outcome is the same: Muslims do not distinguish between adults and children, and everyone learns fanaticism at an early age. Carretto deftly conveys this in his reply: "Oh, what a thought, Abdaraman [*sic*]! Who told you that I would go to hell if I didn't become a Muslim?"[196] Abderrahman's real or invented concern for his Christian friend's well-being in the hereafter serves not as a moment of care and religious *convivencia* but rather as fodder for denigration of Islam by recycling the memory of a supposed Islamic fanaticism in the Sahara. Carretto serves a poisoned chalice in velvety rhetorical gloves: "Poor little Abdaraman [*sic*]! You, too, are a victim of fanaticism, the stormy zeal of religious people, the so-called 'men of God,' who would send half the human race to hell, just because they are not 'one of us.' How can the thread of love which links me to a brother be broken by an alleged purity of faith, or that religion, instead of being a bridge of union, should become a trench of death, or at least of unconfessed hate? We're best off without it, this religion which divided us."[197]

Carretto's nicely crafted generalities would seem entirely disinterested and leveled at all religions save for the fact that they are directed at the behavior of a Muslim child who supposedly drank the milk of hatred. The takeaway for the reader is that Abderrahman was being indoctrinated by the religion whose adepts murdered Foucauld in 1916. This was all too clear in the previous paragraph, in which he stated that Foucauld came to the Sahara as a Little Brother (*petit frère*), but he was "murdered, through ignorance and fanaticism, by sons of the same tribe as Aleck and Abdarahman."[198] Aleck is Abderrahman's father, whom he depicts as a fatalistic person who lacks any agency. Although Carretto announces the birth of a new world with decolonization, it seems that that new world has left Muslims out of it. Muslims in the Sahara, as has been established since the nineteenth century at least, still bask in the barbarian and savage image that was painted of them and that sustains Islamophobia and fear of their terrorism even today.

CONCLUSION

This chapter has developed the concept of spiritual Saharanism, which I have defined as a spiritual ideology that encompasses all forms of institutionalized and individual deployments of deserts in religious discursive and actionable practices. Drawing a distinction between spiritual Saharanism and the long tradition of desert spirituality, I have shown that, unlike traditional monastic and ascetic practices, spiritual Saharanism feeds off religious antagonism and aspirations for colonial hegemony. Disinterested piety is, of course, not subsumed under the scope of spiritual Saharanism as long as its practice in the desert and treatment of desert inhabitants does not fall in line with the rhetoric of emptiness, incivility, and violence that has characterized spiritual Saharanism. While the ascetic who self-isolates in the desert is in search of internal illumination or immunity from perceived corruption in the world, the practitioner of spiritual Saharanism brings the corruption of the material world into the desert in order to achieve domination. Foucauld represents an embodiment of the contradictions of spiritual Saharanism. He espoused universal brotherhood while inciting the French army to murder recalcitrant Saharans. He also advised French authorities to corrupt the Tuareg leader Moussa Ag Amastan (1867–1920) by giving him a salary and paying off his debt. Here, spiritual Saharanism acted as an agent of corruption to advance the goals of colonization.

The chapter also furnishes the concept of an ideational ecosystem to explain why spiritual Saharanism has been able to survive and prosper, reaching its apogee with Foucauld's canonization. The existence of networks of individuals and institutions focused on the Sahara established interconnected spaces where like-minded people anchored an ideational space that has undergirded spiritual Saharanism since the nineteenth century. Individuals like Claudel and Massignon were attracted to ideals of universal brotherhood and spiritual exploration. Others, like Laperrine and Lyautey, were hardcore executers of colonial military policy. Still others, like Lavigerie, were at the service of the church. The ideational ecosystems in which they evolved made the Sahara a terrain for myriad undertakings that included, but were not limited to, conquest, proselytizing, and policing.

Spiritual Saharanism continues to feed off the Islamophobia and racism that were built into it in the nineteenth century, and it uses these frameworks to inform European policy vis-à-vis immigration from the Sahara, especially now that the Sahara is increasingly associated with narcotraffickers, migrant smugglers, and even gun traffickers (particularly after the demise of Muammar Qaddafi's regime at the end of 2011). In its 2020 report, Frontex, the European Border and Coast Guard Agency, assessed the sources of migration and ranked sub-Saharan Africa and Southeast Asia as future sources of undocumented migrants.[199] Regarding curbing immigration from Africa, the report suggests that "a permanent military presence by the EU (incl. civilian EU missions) and other international partners in key areas in the Sahel-Sahara will hamper the expansion of smuggling, kidnapping, and racketeering activities in the region."[200] If this is not a novel iteration of Lavigerie's spiritual Saharanism–infused endeavor to secure the threatening Sahara in the nineteenth century, then what is?

TWO

Extractive Saharanism

EVERYTHING IN DESERTS IS EXTRACTABLE!

A VARIETY OF FACTORS made the period between 1920 and 1960 suitable for the rise of a new and aggressive kind of economic Saharanism, which I propose to call extractive Saharanism. Although French policy regarding the Sahara during this period has been the subject of abundant scholarship, none to date has explained or conceptualized the phenomenon behind the rush to excise the Sahara from the rest of Africa and create a fully French Saharan territory, one that some people involved in this project called "the French Sahara." Spearheaded by the top brass of French civilian administrators, extractive Saharanism conceived of the desert as an entirely available space with wind, sun, oil, and mineral resources that could all be exploited to support the French economy, further ensuring France's strategic importance among other post–World War II nations. A combination of nationalism and prescient awareness of the changes taking place in the postwar world inspired French officials and their supporters in the intellectual and civilian society to advocate for the creation of new entities, the reorganization of the Saharan space, and the remapping of its administrative contours, all in order to expedite extraction of its resources and ensure that the territory remained French after African decolonization. In tandem with the development of these policies, propagandists of extractive Saharanism engaged in public lectures, wrote books, churned out articles, and even traveled abroad to convince banks and multinational companies to participate in the Sahara's *mise en valeur*.[1]

Algeria's independence in 1962 cut these efforts short and diverted attention from their legacy, which allowed them to remain untheorized until now. While enveloped in ideals of humanism and universal brotherhood, extractive Saharanism, at its core, was a colonialist project that maneuvered until its last breath to carve out a French Saharan dominion that was simultaneously located in and separated from Africa. Bernard Simiot, a novelist and journalist, best described this project in writing that the annexation of the Sahara to France would "represent the European head placed on a giant African body for which the Maghreb and Africa would be the limbs."[2] Extractive Saharanism is the most advanced form of discursive and material extraction that the Sahara has ever witnessed.

French Saharanism went through two important phases. The first was an army-led phase that conceived of the Sahara as a security problem between the murder of Captain Flatters in 1881 and the end of World War II in 1945.[3] The second phrase was civilian led, and it marked the entry of civil engineers and administrators as well as economic institutions into the desert to implement exploitative projects.[4] Although the army continued to play a crucial role in the Sahara, which remained a military zone, its presence in the public arena receded into the background as civilians dominated the production and implementation of Saharanism. Both military and civilian Saharanisms are extractive, but the articulation of Saharanism as an inherently extractive practice took shape in the hands of the civilians or officers-turned-bureaucrats who had a say in the desert's exploitation. As historian Perrin Selcer has demonstrated, the postwar period witnessed the bureaucratization as well as the scholarization of work around deserts through UNESCO's Arid Zone Program.[5] Despite its failure to regreen deserts, this program "succeeded in cultivating an epistemic community of experts that transcended disciplinary and political boundaries. This international knowledge infra-structure made a global view [of deserts] from above possible."[6] French desert experts, who at some point in their careers transited through the Sahara, played a major role in building and disseminating this expertise, part of which incentivized extraction.

The discovery of immense oil reserves in the Gulf, along with the need to reconstruct Europe after the war's destruction, led to the emergence of this new class of expert Saharanists. Unlike the Saint-Cyrians of the past, Saharanists were now engineers, graduates of the National School of Administration, technicians, and government officials, and they entered the desert to implement grandiose visions of extraction. Starting in 1947, Erik Labonne (also written as Eirik Labonne; 1888–1971), a former French ambassador to the Soviet Union (and a former general resident in Tunisia [1938–40] and Morocco [1946–47]), would become France's Sahara superman. He understood that moving French military assets to the Sahara in the postwar period could be harnessed to strengthen military-civilian industrialization.[7] The importance of Labonne's work as a master civilian Saharanist was recognized by Max Lejeune, the minister of the Sahara in 1957, who referred to him in a speech as "the first to have believed in the Sahara and [the one] who, starting in 1947, attracted the attention of the government to its mineral and industrial potential."[8] In the USSR, Labonne witnessed the industrial *combinats* (Russian, *kombinat*) put in place in Siberia and represented France at the Kirkuk agreements.[9] The respect Labonne enjoyed among French elites gave credence to his ideas about the Sahara's industrial potential,[10] setting in motion Saharanism's methodical exploitative ideology that would dominate French thinking through the end of the colonization of Algeria in 1962. Both the projects proposed for Saharan development and the stature of the men involved in these endeavors gave Saharanism a grand extractive identity.

Certainly, Saharanism did not just become extractive in the 1940s. In fact, the Sahara had been viewed as a space for extractive enterprises at least since the first cargo loads of enslaved people were dislocated from their homes and shipped out of Africa.[11] Historians have already shown how the tragedy of slavery displaced hundreds of thousands, if not millions, of people from where they lived in the Sahara or its bordering lands.[12] In a moment of truth, engineer Émile Bélime, the governor of the colonies famous for his nickname the "Master of Water" in Niger, found parallels between slavery and the extraction of resources from the Sahara.[13] He wrote that the morals of every given historical period determined what was extractable: "Sword and cross in hand, the Portuguese and the Spanish rushed to the New World. Following their example, we, like them, grabbed sugar- and spice-rich islands, and, in order to develop them, we imported slaves who were duly evangelized. Everything has been said about the slave trade's calamities and cruelties, but [we have] always omitted the fact that the times lent themselves to it. During this period, serfdom was a common practice in Europe, and slavery was far from being abolished everywhere."[14] For Bélime, France's exploitative undertakings in the Sahara and other colonies in the 1950s were no different from what the Portuguese and Spanish had done in the Americas and other colonies. When people were all the Sahara had to offer, the dominant powers of the time—meaning North African traders and their European partners—extracted the people to ship to the New World. In the twentieth century, however, the focus shifted to the oil and minerals sedimented in the desert. In Bélime's uncensored understanding, slavery was phased out because it was no longer morally acceptable, and also because mechanization had replaced manpower. Accordingly, the extraction of resources replaced the extraction of people.

In the 1950s, when most of the conversations and ideas I cover in this chapter were unfolding, extraction had taken various discursive, legal, economic, and even social forms, including, but not limited to, the exploitation of oil reserves, minerals, wind, solar energy, arable land, and labor. Starting in the 1930s, Albert Sarraut, French minister of the colonies, officialized the dissemination the concept of *la mise en valeur coloniale* (colonial investment/enhancement for extractive purposes), which sought to optimize the use of colony resources for their benefit and that of the "motherland."[15] Later French officials and technocrats who oversaw desert-focused schemes drew religiously on Sarraut's *mise en valeur* to maximize the utilization of anything exploitable in the Sahara.[16] Already in 1890, French inventor Charles Tellier had published a book entitled *La conquête pacifique de l'Afrique occidentale par le soleil,* in which he made a case for solar energy.[17] Many decades later, Pierre Cornet, a member of parliament, published *Sahara: Terre de demain*, which catalogued, among others, Saharan mineral and energy resources.[18] Physician Edmond Sergent authored *Le peuplement humain du Sahara*, which furnished a rationalization for the kind of labor that could participate in the desert's exploitation.[19] The 1950s, in particular, witnessed a profusion of writings whose authors' laid out their visions for the colonial development of the desert territory and its resources. This literature participated in creating the key concepts that spurred and sustained extractive Saharanism.

Extractive Saharanism urged the French state to make structural legal and administrative changes that would accelerate exploitation of the desert's resources. These included passing Sahara-specific business laws, creating new administrative entities, and remapping the Sahara's cartography as virgin lands whose prospection and exploitation required the recognition of this new status.[20] Saharanists, particularly those with political and economic positions within the French polity, engaged in massive propaganda campaigns in the US and the UK to attract well-resourced companies to invest in the extraction of desert resources in exchange for favorable business arrangements.[21] Imbricating American and British petroleum oil interests with France's future domination of the Sahara was part of a strategy to stave off these governments' support for Algeria's independence. French technocrats also developed plans for a desert industrial complex, which would, they argued, integrate the Sahara into Europe's economy and military strategy within the nebulous Eurafrique.

A VIOLENT ENCOUNTER: THE SAHARA AS A SECURITY THREAT FOR THE FRENCH ARMY

As detailed in Chapter 1, French Saharanism dates back to the nineteenth century, when French explorers joined their German and British predecessors to penetrate the fabled desert.[22] The French feelings of inferiority vis-à-vis their German and British counterparts came to an end when Frenchman René Caillié arrived in Timbuktu in 1828 and shattered the city's mythical image; he was preceded by Henri Duveyrier.[23] Their feats sustained the "Saharan myth" and made the Sahara itself a "legend, forgotten at times, but always resurgent."[24] In tandem with the arrival of these explorers, the French army slowly adopted a pincer movement that would culminate in the colonization of Timbuktu in 1898 and of In Salah in 1900. While these military achievements were celebrated, subduing the Tuaregs would become the next obsession,[25] particularly after the murder of Colonel Paul Flatters in 1881, which etched the Sahara into the French imagination as a security threat.[26] Historian Benjamin Brower has eloquently summarized the complexity of this history in writing that "A rich body of aspirations, myths, and fantasies accompanied economic and geostrategic concerns and formed a part of the complex matrix that drove the Saharan conquest and shaped its violence."[27]

Before the French, the Romans had also perceived the desert as a threat and built *limites* to separate it from their domains.[28] In the nineteenth century, the French, who considered themselves the heirs of the Roman Empire in North Africa, absorbed and deployed the Roman perspective, borne out by the bloody cost of the conquest. Early in the colonial enterprise in Algeria, certain capitalist interests (which were involved in the creation of a trans-African railway and several other projects) sent out scouts to determine the best ways to build a rail line that would link the French dominions in North and sub-Saharan Africa.[29] One such mission was led by Flatters, whose murder slowed down the colonization of the Sahara and had an even deeper impact on the memory of the French army, which constructed the vast territory between Touat, the Hoggar, and Adrar as a lawless terrain.[30] This landmark event would fashion discourses that created an administrative reality in which the Sahara became a military zone.

The Sahara would be policed and controlled by a combination of classical army and Indigenous desert police. By 1920, it was entirely pacified, which, in colonial vocabulary, meant that the populations' resistance was weakened. In the words of General Boisboissel, the "Sahara was saved" thanks to

General Laperrine, who brought it under French authority.[31] The image of the desert as a security threat survived, but it became counterproductive to the development efforts of proponents of extractive Saharanism by the end of the 1940s. The discourse of this new brand of men shifted attention from security to optimizing the exploitation of natural resources. Suddenly, everything that France had accomplished in the Sahara for at least fifty years had to be rethought in light of new development requirements that demanded experimentation with extraction-friendly institutional, legal, military, and commercial setups. The dangerous Sahara of the pioneers was slowly replaced by the advent of a developmental imaginary that foregrounded a fully exploitable territory. In fact, extractive Saharanism saw no boundaries to what could be done with the wealth and the space of the Sahara, fueling a cultural and economic community, both energetic and dynamic, whose ideology set the tone for desert-centered discussions throughout the 1950s.[32]

THE SAHARA AND THE BIRTH OF *MISE EN VALEUR* AS AN EXTRACTIVE IDEOLOGY

French extractive Saharanism emerged in conversation with Sarraut's 1923 concept of *mise en valeur*.[33] The notion of *mise en valeur*, which means colonial investment and enhancement as well as "development" or "making profitable" for colonial and extractive purposes, emerged within the French colonial system in tandem with the concept of *aménagement* (developing/development). Although the notion of *mise en valeur* certainly predated Sarraut's book, his publication brought this idea to a larger audience.[34] *Mise en valeur* became a key concept for understanding the extractive interdependence between colonized and colonizer in the colonial world.

A lawyer and multiterm member of parliament, Sarraut was minister of the colonies when his book was published. As a colonialist, Sarraut saw the colonies as an extension of the *mère patrie* (motherland), which meant that France was one whole unit regardless of where its territories were situated. In the preface to his book, his friend André Touzet, a governor of colonies,[35] wrote, "Under the nostalgic eyes of this France of Asia, where your effort supported mine, we conceived, for the glory and wealth of France, of the robust development of its colonial fortune."[36] Dispensing with any diplomatic language, Touzet explicitly declared that the colonies were a source of wealth for France, arguing that the *mise en valeur* he and Sarraut set in motion contributed to the enhancement of their country's glory.[37] Sarraut himself started his preface by evoking the ongoing Colonial Exposition in Marseille, highlighting how French people from all walks of life "returned [from the exhibition] amazed by the unexpected revelations of this New French World, acquired by the perseverance of the motherland, pacified by its justice, fertilized by its science, and entirely attentive, throughout an immense territory, to the labor of fecundity, which in the meantime augments its human richness as well as its material wealth."[38] According to Sarraut's analysis, the exhibition was only the tip of a large colonial domain that would enrich France and contribute to its economic and political strength.

Sarraut's plan for colonial exploitation was costly, and his book was partially a plea for funding. Sarraut, who was governor of Indochina for five years, drew on facts to prove that the *mise en valeur* undertaking was worth its enormous cost. First, when World War I broke out, France's colonies had provided eight hundred thousand soldiers and workers to the metropole.[39] Hence, the motherland's future security depended on the colonies. Second, like all colonialists, Sarraut was a staunch nationalist and believed that France's financial independence could be reached by maximizing the exploitation of resources available in the colonial domain.[40] He wrote, "Our colonies produce or can furnish cottons, wools, silks, rubbers, wood, fats, [and] materials that the French market requests from foreign warehouses for billions of francs."[41]

Even before Sarraut and his contemporaries, the Belgians had a long history of applying the concept of *mise en valeur* in the Congo. In her book *The Colonial Disease: A Social History of Sleeping Sickness in Northern Zaire, 1900–1940*, historian Maryinez Lyons defines *mise en valeur* as "economic exploitation," detailing the various ways in which the Belgian colonial establishment exploited the Congolese people, including women and children, to make the colony profitable.[42] Unlike other definitions that focus on the notions of "improvement," "rehabilitation," and "investment" that are embedded in the concept, Lyons strongly articulates the exploitative nature of the combination of labor and resource extraction and details its impact on the health of those who were exploited. She writes that the difficulty of finding African labor "was an enormous problem as the *mise en valeur*, or economic exploitation, of the Congo in the early decades of its existence depended almost entirely upon obtaining sufficient numbers of African labourers."[43] Sarraut could not have been unaware of the Belgian violence in the neighboring Congo, where the grand idea of development led to a drop in food production, causing malnutrition as a result of the enlistment of adults who could farm the arable land to work in mines instead.[44] The Belgians needed to build the extractive infrastructure that would facilitate the exportation of this vast country's treasures, and their *mise en valeur* played out in a particularly brutal way. Geographer Maurice Zimmerman wrote for the *Annales de géographie* that the Belgians' results in the Congo were the outcome of "an administrative and economic system that appears to be doomed because it seeks to force nature and leads to the oppression of the natives."[45] While Zimmerman's comment on Belgian oppression could be inscribed within the context of Franco-Belgian competition in Africa, the fact remains that Zimmerman recorded the inhumane manner in which the Belgian *mise en valeur* decimated Congolese populations and exposed them to the health issues that Lyons discusses in her book.[46]

Despite its cruel history, *mise en valeur* was marketed as a humanitarian approach to economic exploitation. Sarraut argued that the colonies had already given tremendously to France, and that it was time for France to give back to them while also ensuring its economic independence.[47] Since the financial resources required for colonial development were enormous, Sarraut attempted to convince lawmakers by insisting that France's generosity "should profit the colonies for which it ensures economic growth and human development. Hence, the French colonial operation, which is designed to serve the two parties, is no longer the spoliation of one race by another, but rather an association."[48] For France's colonial *mise en valeur* the time had come, though long overdue, for "resolute, powerful, and relentless action," and "energies, capitals, wills, arms and minds; all these active forces should bravely take the direction of Overseas France to complete its development following a methodical and precise plan."[49] These synergies, Sarraut proposed, should be harnessed for the great projects, which included "major public works, economic infrastructure, and social actions."[50] These exploitative infrastructures would make up for the time France had lost in making its colonies profitable.

As the notion applied to the Sahara specifically, the publication of Sarraut's book triggered the Académie des sciences coloniales to launch a competition between 1925 and 1927 on the theme of the Sahara's development. The Académie invited participants to submit unpublished manuscripts in which they reflected on the "search for a general and long-term policy for the development of the Sahara."[51] The competition specifically required participants to submit manuscripts that contained "scientific data," "technical procedures," "stages of execution," "financial methods," and "future perspectives."[52] Anyone who aspired to the award of twelve thousand francs was asked to conceive of a holistic program that would support their idea for the Sahara's development. In addition to the prize money, the winner's manuscript would be published by the Académie. The committee received eight monographs from men who all "possess[ed] historical, geographical, scientific, and administrative knowledge that gave their work a solid basis and piqued attention."[53] However, it was geographer Fèlix Gautier's *Le Sahara vaincu peut-il être dompté? L'aménagement du Sahara* that won the competition.[54]

Established in 1922, the Académie was a hub for colonialist intellectuals. Its first president was none other than Albert Lebrun, who conceived of the methodical exploitation of the colonies and who would go on to become president of France from 1932 to 1940. During the Académie's official inauguration at the Sorbonne on May 18, 1923, Paul Bourdarie, the Académie's permanent secretary and long-term member, articulated its colonialist agenda, which included defending the "French colonial idea," demonstrating the role French scholarship and human morality played in France's colonial project, and, finally, serving as an intellectual and scholarly ambassador of the French government's colonial policy to other nations.[55] For the occasion, Sarraut, the Académie's honorary president, improvised a speech in which he reiterated his concept of *mise en valeur,* whereby the benefits of colonialism were to be shared between colonized and colonizer.[56] Thus, the convergence of the Académie's colonialist goals with Sarraut's notion of *mise en valeur* played out in how the organization conceived of the development of the Sahara. The Académie's award revealed that Saharanism was becoming an institutionalized project with a perception of the desert informed by colonial conceptions about the space and its economic potential.

The Académie thus paved the way for the application of the *mise en valeur* and *aménagement* to the Sahara. These two concepts would be the key terms that civilian administrators and Saharanists deployed obsessively in their conversations about this desert throughout the 1950s. The notion of development and civilization embedded in them was also attractive to Anglophone companies, which the French government endeavored to attract in the 1950s in order to benefit from their immense capital and advanced technical know-how in its implementation of its plans for the Sahara. *Mise en valeur* allowed proponents of extractive Saharanism to use every means available to expedite the exploitation of desert riches. *Mise en valeur* was the keystone of the French technocrats' extractive Saharanism and their plans to keep the Sahara French forever.

GOODBYE TO THE SAHARA OF CAMELS AND CARAVANS

Nationalizing the Sahara

Writing the obituary for Ambassador Labonne, lawyer and judge Pierre Escoube indicated that the diplomat's major legacy had been the replacement of the Sahara of caravans with one of oil derricks, and the emphasis on the collective synergies that its exploitation entailed.[57] In Escoube's words, by "replacing the Sahara of caravans with the Sahara of oil derricks and oil wells, he [Erik Labonne] proved the fecundity of the principle of 'joint forces,' public and private, civilian and military, [and] national and international."[58] Escoube's argument that one man changed the clichéd perception of the Sahara from a place traversed by caravans and inhabited by nomads following the ways of their ancestors to a place supporting modern technology is certainly edifying. The power of Escoube's description of his friend's achievement lies precisely in his recognition of the imagination's ability to produce lasting ideas about space, and about deserts, specifically.

Labonne's extractive ideology was geared toward making the Sahara look and sound exactly like what France needed it to be, regardless of what its history and its people had already actually made it. He represented state visionary Saharanism with its giant capitalistic projects and politico-administrative capacity to facilitate the relocation of companies, investments, and specialized labor to the Sahara. His vision was representative of the shifting notion of state sovereignty at a time when the rise of technical knowledge and corporations forced the state to join forces with other entities. This reality is best captured by philosopher Jacques Ellul in writing that the state is "compelled to modify and rationalize its administrative, judicial, and financial systems on the model of the great commercial and industrial enterprises."[59] The Sahara of business, oil deals, and derricks required a new regime of governance, a new *code pétrolier* (oil code), and other reforms designed to accommodate the efficient establishment of an extractive superstructure.[60] Hence, it was not only camels and their caravans that became irrelevant in this new desert,[61] but also the old, arbitrary division of the territory into administrative siloes under different regimes of governance.[62] The clash of Franco-French sovereignties within this older structure became not only "obsolete" but also a hindrance for business and an obstacle to the extractive enterprise French bureaucrats worked to achieve in the Sahara.[63]

The obsolescence of the Sahara's political and administrative structures triggered a passionate debate about its nationalization. Bélime, the president of the association of Les Amis du Sahara and the aforementioned colonial administrator in Niger, was the first to call for the incorporation of the Sahara into France. In 1951, he expressed his disagreement with the establishment of the Union française, stipulated in the constitutional reform of 1946. Bélime took issue with the consequences of the colonies' autonomy, which in his analysis would deprive the colonial system of the labor it needed to build and maintain the colonial infrastructure.[64] However, the main issue Bélime took up in this essay was the position of a weakened France in the postwar context, specifically voicing his concern about France's "criminal" acceptance of the disbandment of its colonial domain.[65] Bélime lamented the fact that France had long overlooked the Sahara as a result of having "considered [these desolate areas] as wastelands, sterile shreds of the earth's crust, wrapping valuable fragments of our possessions in their troublesome gangue."[66] Bélime could not but compare France's negligence of the Sahara to the investments of the US and USSR in their "depopulated spaces."[67] Accordingly, Bélime asserted, France was fifty years behind the Americans and the Russians, who both were able to exploit the resources concealed under their respective Alaskan and the Siberian desertic territories.[68]

The discovery of the Sahara's resources lent urgency to its nationalization so as to ensure its wealth would remain French. An unapologetic colonialist, Bélime had no qualms about publicizing his belief that everything that the desert offered was harvestable. Mixing a strong understanding of global technical developments with a shameless conviction that natural resources should be used for human progress, Bélime drew on different examples from deserts and forests across the world to make his case for the exploitation of the Sahara. Notably, he remarked that that the Sahara was already being exploited in nonextractive ways, including by trains and passenger planes.[69] Yet material extraction was his main goal, in reference to Labonne's ideas about the Sahara's industrialization,[70] and focused in particular on the exploitation of the coal and minerals so central to the desert's industrial future.[71] In Bélime's final analysis, the "Sahara [was] bursting with resources,"[72] which was both good and bad news. He predicted that as discovery of resources brought greater visibility to the land, this would in turn lead to economic competition or even to the questioning of France's ownership of the territory. As such, Bélime proposed that annexing the territory to France would bar the road for any future claims of ownership by the Sahara-neighboring nations.[73] Along the way, Bélime recycled Saharanist ideas of emptiness, martyrdom, and French blood spilled in conquest as evidence of France's eternal ownership of the land.[74]

Bélime's article became a classic propaganda piece that blazed the path for a yearslong debate. Motivated by strategic and economic stakes projected upon the Sahara at the time of decolonization, the responses published in *Hommes et mondes* defended the Sahara's nationalization as the solution to any attempts to share its newly discovered resources. Bernard Simiot, a famous writer, journalist, and editor of *Hommes et mondes*, repeated Bélime's call for the Sahara's annexation to the metropole. Based on a fully Saharanist approach that harkened back to ideas of emptiness and uninhabited-ness, Simiot denied the existence of any Indigenous desert populations, urging Europe to take advantage of the space's welcoming climate for the "white race" to populate it.[75] However, what interested Simiot was the Sahara's subsurface, still largely unknown and which, in his words, indicated the existence of a "great variety and evident mineral wealth."[76] Simiot inserted the word "petrol" in his discussion of resources, but also emphasized that not much had been done to make sure that oil deposits actually existed in the Sahara.[77] The map accompanying Simiot's article represented a tentacular system whereby the blood of the desert was sucked up by pipelines to feed the French economy and enhance the motherland's strategic position (Fig. 6).[78] In a telling question, Simiot wondered whether the Sahara was "an enormous heap of stones and sterile sand? Or a powerful reserve of energetic and mineral resources?"[79]

Hommes et mondes broadened the debate by inviting contributions from "geologists, engineers, economists, military officers, jurists, physicists, medical doctors, diplomats, and high-ranking colonial administrators."[80] Their responses revealed how the Sahara was reduced in their ideology's eyes to a resource-gorged, exploitable space. The highly engaging, albeit considerably varied, papers reflected their authors' entrenched Saharanism, which clearly conceptualized the territory as a malleable terrain whose geography, physical borders, human population, and millennial history mattered less than the resources purportedly located underground.[81]

Remembrement, which means "regrouping lands together,"[82] entered the lexicon at this stage of the discussion. Simiot's vision involved getting rid of

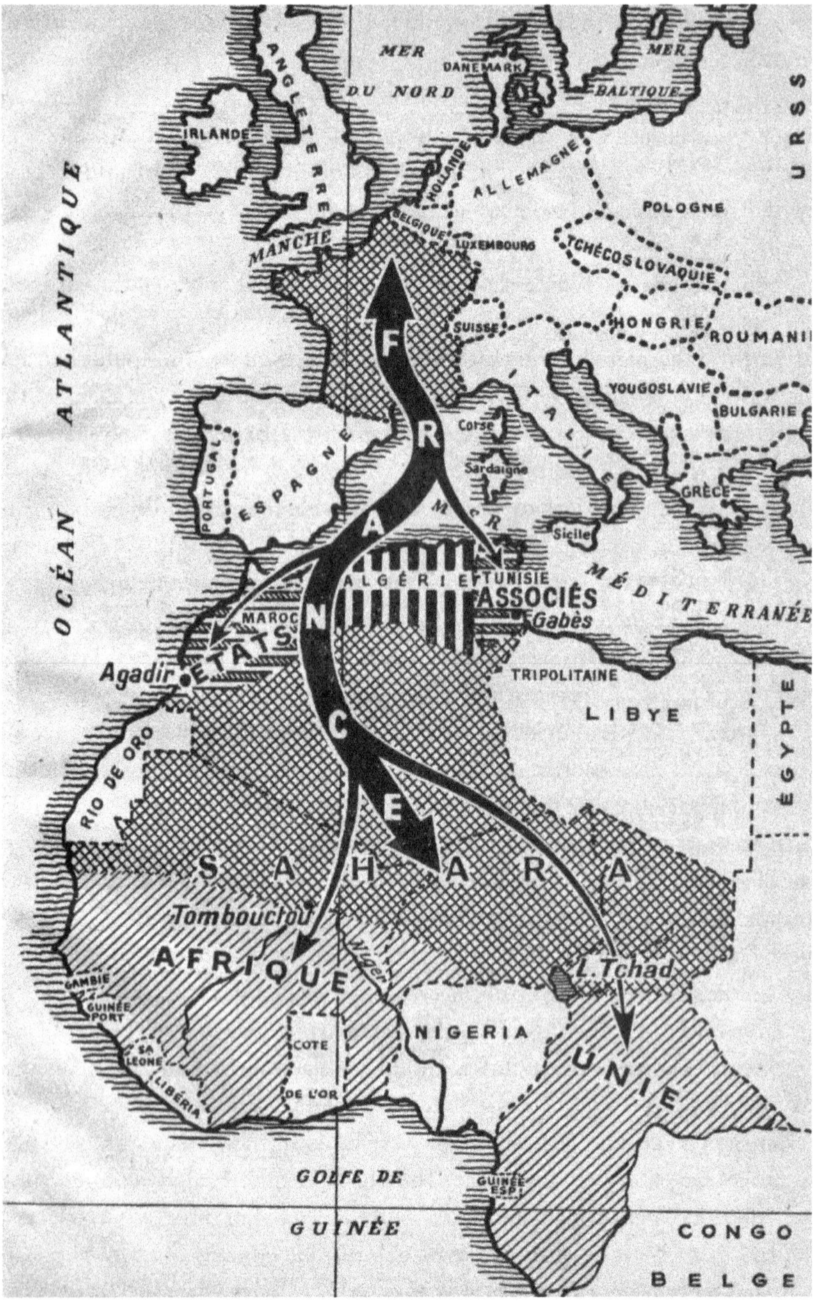

FIGURE 6. Representation of Eurafrique, from *Hommes et mondes* (1961), portrayed as cementing the ties between Africa and Europe. Photo courtesy of *Revue des deux mondes*.

the divisions based on the different administrative regimes of Algeria, Morocco, Tunisia, Niger, the Sudan, Chad, and Mauritania.[83] The consolidation of the desert territories into one unit was supposed to fend off neighboring states' territorial claims and, in the meantime, facilitate the use of the riches that had suddenly become the focus of the world's attention.[84] For Georges Catroux (1877–1969), a general who played a major role in the occupation of southeast Morocco,[85] if France was to exercise its sovereignty in the sparsely inhabited space of the Sahara "without sharing or contestation," it would need to be regrouped into one territory.[86] This was all the more necessary because the desert had shifted from being viewed as "unproductive" to being a promising land that opened up some "new perspectives."[87] These new and promising positions were none other than Labonne's initiatives, thanks to which "the desert, which has heretofore been barren, has liberated its hidden energies."[88] Whether we interpret energies in a literal or metaphorical sense, the Sahara was first and foremost a deposit of resources that had to be staunchly defended.

In his contribution, lawyer Gustave Mercier, who was a close collaborator of Louis Armand, the director of the SNCF, further complicated Saharanism's extractive logic. Mercier found a curious, but very illuminating, parallel between the US's nationalization of Alaska and Bélime's idea of nationalizing the Sahara. Ignoring the fact that the US had bought Alaska from Czarist Russia, Mercier built on this example to project how a nationalized Sahara would "allow our engineers, our prospectors, our hydraulicians, [and] our agronomists to apply their knowledge and develop their entrepreneurial spirit in this immense, empty territory, which certainly conceals unknown riches. This would open up a seductive quarry for our national vitality."[89] The *mise en valeur* of the Sahara was a pathway toward the extraction of its industrial and mineral potential.[90] However, a fascinating proposition, which Simiot felt the need to refuse immediately, came from Ambassador Gabriel Puaux, who suggested the creation of "an organ that resembles the one the Americans have conceived for the development of the Tennessee Valley; a sort of technical headquarters that would ignore the administrative borders" of the different parts of the desert.[91] This "Saharan Corporation" would "receive special powers regarding the exploitation of minerals as well as land and air lines that would allow it to act rapidly and efficiently beyond the parliamentarian and bureaucratic slowness."[92] As they unfolded, these intellectual debates became a political agenda, and by 1956, even Guy Mollet, the French prime minister, adopted this idea of a Saharan corporation in inviting "all of Europe to develop Africa."[93] Extractive Saharanism was the backbone of the efforts that culminated with the 1957 decision to move forward with restructuring the Sahara.[94]

What is striking about this brand of Saharanism is its awareness of extractive enterprises in other deserts across the globe. The contributors to the dossiers published by *Hommes et mondes* paid particular attention to American endeavors to exploit Alaska and Soviet efforts to develop Siberia. These references to Russia and the US were mainly meant to foreground their successes in their cold deserts while France was still several decades behind in its exploitation of Saharan resources. In 1955, Armand, the SNCF director and the president of the BIA, which was established in 1952 to maintain Eurafrique,[95] highlighted Russia's construction of railways in East Siberia, which permitted it to develop an area that was larger than France itself.[96] Highlighting other states' achievements did not downplay French Saharanism's role but rather emphasized how France had previously focused on policing the desert instead of exploiting it. France had to catch up to its peers, but the US and Soviet achievements were proof that extraction was both possible and the right course of action.

As these discussions reveal, Saharanism consolidated a community made up of a coterie of influential and like-minded people. Its influence was such that, from the outside, it would be difficult to distinguish their ideas from one another. Their analyses were marked by several commonalities that included, first, the Sahara's emptiness as proof of its unpopulated-ness, which translated to it being unowned. Phrases like "absolute desolation,"[97] "solitudes stériles" (sterile solitudes),[98] "grand vide saharien" (great Saharan emptiness),[99] and "solitudines" (solitudes) were constantly recurrent in the writings of different generations of stakeholders. Desolation gave rise to extrapolations that then opened up space for musings about danger, as is the case in Roger Frison-Roche's trumpeting of the achievements of the 1898 Foureau-Lamy Mission from Ouargla to Timbuktu through the Sahara to assert how, once they passed the land of the Ajjer Tuaregs, travelers found themselves confronted by the "dangerous unknown of the Hoggar and the Aïr, [and] the mysteries of Black Africa."[100] Second, this emptiness naturally bred anarchy in the Sahara, which only France's occupation eliminated. Since France had paid a very high price for the pacification of the Sahara, it had earned perpetual ownership of the desert.

The construction of the Sahara as a source of endless wealth occurred in lockstep with the rise of global capitalism. Petrol trusts and strong American and British banks set the economic agenda for other regions, including the Sahara. Their interests required accommodations that were reflected in the French state's invitation of foreign companies to invest in prospection in the territory.[101] Their agreement on France's ownership of the Sahara did not prevent extractive Saharanists' disagreements over foreign investment and its encroachment on their nation's sovereignty. Bélime objected to any notion of *mise en valeur* that would relinquish even the smallest degree of French sovereignty over the Sahara to global finance.[102] Aware of this reality, Armand, who believed that the means needed to exploit the Sahara were bigger than what France could afford alone,[103] wrote that some French individuals "were against the entrance of foreign capital into French Africa," whereby he mostly meant the Sahara.[104] Like former soldiers who had served in the Compagnies méharistes sahariennes and had a nostalgic loyalty to a certain vision of a rustic desert, Bélime was an old-timer, and his vision for the Sahara was antithetical to the one being promoted by influential technocratic Saharanists. Their disagreements were never about whether or not to colonize but rather on the most efficient way to maintain the Sahara under French control and optimize the commodification of its resources even as Algerian nationalists were claiming the Sahara's independence.

Remapping the Saharan El Dorado: Competing Levels of Governance

The moment the petrol flew from the Sahara in commercial quantities in 1956 marked a new phase in extractive Saharanism. French historian Charles-Robert Ageron called it "the year of petrol," which promised "a new El Dorado" in the desert.[105] Extractive Saharanism was triumphant. The French government created the Organisation commune des régions sahariennes (OCRS) and a Ministry of the Sahara in 1957. These two supraregional institutions to administer the integrative exploitation of the desert were preceded by the establishment of the Zone d'organisation industrielle africaine (ZOIA) and the BIA in 1950 and 1952, respectively.[106] The aim of these institutional arrangements was the "creat[ion] of an important common market for the entirety of the Saharan territories, which would allow for the organization of investments, the creation of the conditions for exploitation, and the conception of the Sahara's entire future under the control and political responsibility of the French state."[107] The inauguration of these institutions was the clearest indication of the special governance that was being developed to manage the Sahara and exploit its resources at a time when independence was in vogue globally.

This institutional landscape reflected the clashing visions between those who supported the Sahara's annexation to France and those, mostly in Algeria, who defended maintaining the status quo. The hardliners grouped under Les Amis du Sahara, who believed that the territory should be annexed to France, imposed their agenda on French society, gaining the support of other Saharanists in the government. Georges Guide captured their proliferating propositions, writing that the "promoters of the 1952 movement of ideas, like the authors of the different legislative proposals, unanimously signaled that the Sahara's administrative dispersion between different state structures would certainly not facilitate the powerful action necessary for valuing its riches."[108] While Morocco and Tunisia were protectorates, or technically independent states under French rule, the Algerian Sahara reported to the governor of Algeria. The deserts of the Sudan, Mauritania, and Niger were answerable to French West Africa in Dakar, whereas the Chadian desert reported to French Equatorial Africa in Brazzaville.[109] These five different territorial and administrative distributions meant that there were different currencies and customs regimes,[110] which both complicated and hampered the Saharanists' vision for a fluid, unified, undividable, and forever French Sahara.[111] The prescience of the discussions about the Sahara's nationalization in 1951 indicated the strategic thinking at the heart of the initiatives so dear to extractive Saharanism's proponents. The establishment of the ZOIA, the BIA, and the OCRS (Map 2) were the clearest indication that extractive Saharanism had made the Sahara into a societal and political issue for the entirety of France.

Labonne became the godfather of all desert-centered extractive projects, particularly after the establishment of the ZOIA. It was a structure of "conception and coordination" that brought together members of the army, public figures, and individuals interested in developing the Sahara.[112] In less cryptic terms, it was the conceptual powerhouse of French extractive Saharanism. This institution was in charge of "defining orientations and the outlines of [desert development] programs."[113] Labonne's own definition of his priorities stressed the importance of starting from the concrete reality of the Sahara in order to come up with integrative economic and industrial projects for the totality of the Union française,[114] which was constitutionalized in the reform of 1946 to conform to the geopolitical reality of decolonization. Most importantly, however, Labonne insisted on the transborder

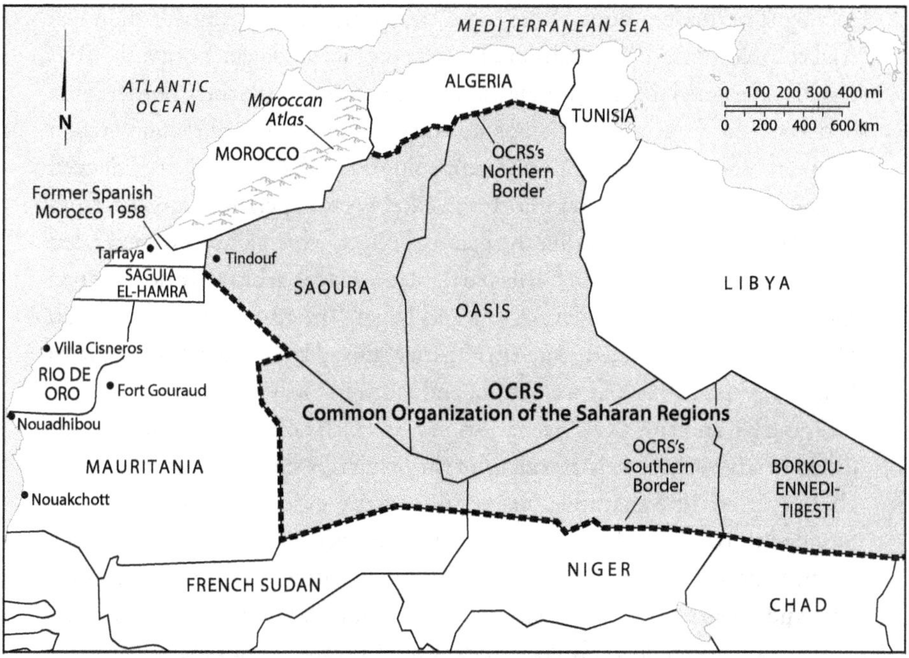

MAP 2. The proposed borders of the Common Organization of the Saharan Regions (OCRS). Cartography by Bill Nelson.

mandate of his organization, which was empowered to conceptualize its projects independently of the administrative lines that separated the different parts of the Union française.[115] Labonne's supracolonial entity placed the Sahara within a larger colonial dominion, which included development projects in Gabon and Madagascar.[116] Specifically, given the Sahara's mineral resources and proximity to France, it was central to the ZOIA's five industrial complexes, two of which were to be located in the Saharan border territory: on the Moroccan-Algerian and Tunisian-Algerian borders.[117] These plans for inter-Saharan economic integration aimed to create a de facto different administrative reality for the French-controlled desert.

Two years after the establishment of the ZOIA, Pierre July, a minister in Edgar Faure's government and a proponent of the administrative unification of the Sahara, formed the BIA,[118] adding yet another layer to the administrative governance and extractionist superstructures. Conceived of as the executive branch of the ZOIA,[119] the BIA was placed under the leadership of Armand, described by André Deutsch as "a brilliant engineer and man of great foresight."[120] Armand defined the BIA's main mission as establishing a catalogue of "underground riches" and "the technical 'planning' for an industrial complex."[121] Although limited in terms of its actual authority, the BIA was also designed to navigate the compartmentalized, arbitrary borders that had resulted from the reality of military conquest and the competition between officers belonging to different colonial military zones, as evidenced by the almost-deadly encounter in 1904 between Laperrine's mission from Algeria and another one from the colonial Niger, which almost degenerated into an internecine battle.[122] This particular incident arbitrarily determined the current borders between Algeria and Niger. The administrative division of the Sahara that ensued from this history proved to be a major obstacle to France's desire to extract, transform, and monetize its resources.

The BIA and the ZOIA were not, however, the only institutions established to advance the *mise en valeur* of the Sahara. A slew of other structures, all immersed in Saharanist discourse and its extractive ideology, were founded to facilitate the exploitation of desert riches. The Inter-Ministerial Commission for the Saharan Trains was directly attached to the prime minister and oversaw the development of industrial transportation.[123] In 1946, the Bureau de recherches du pétrole was put in place. Its mission was primarily focused on the Sahara; however, France's search for oil dated back to the 1920s, when the Compagnie française des pétroles was created.[124] British and American companies' discovery of oil in Iran, Iraq, Saudi Arabia, Kuwait, and the United Arab Emirates made France realize that by having its own source of energy, it could harness the power of the future.[125] Geographer Ivan du Jonchay articulated France's focus in this search by emphasizing the economic and security benefits of energy sovereignty.[126] In addition to state-level extractive entities, other more local institutions, like the Office for the Search for Petrol and the Company for Mineral and Industrial Equipment, were established to optimize resource-discovery endeavors in the Sahara.[127] In the meantime, France created the Commissariat à l'énergie atomique (CEA),[128] which aimed to acquire nuclear expertise, build a uranium stockpile, and harness the necessary human and material resources for France to enter the nuclear club. The Sahara was integral to nuclear and fossil-fuel energy projects, as was clearly indicated in placing atomic energy under the purview of the minister of the Sahara.[129]

Meanwhile, Saharanism spilled over into French society at large. This societal aspect took the form of a strong Saharanist civil society, which advocated for the creation of extractive institutional setups. The Comité du Sahara français, which Bélime founded in 1951, along with the Association

Charles de Foucauld, the Amis du Sahara, and the Association Eurafrique, among others, advanced their Saharanist ideas through publications, political advocacy, and lobbying, and they had a strong presence in the public sphere. Their publications and staunch involvement in public debates about the Sahara and its development kept the territory fresh and intimately present in the French public's mind. The abundance of these institutions and the fact that they had both state and civic dimensions clearly manifested "the unity of action" that Louis Chevalier advocated for the Sahara's industrialization.[130] The number of individuals involved in these Sahara-centered debates with a background in the military or colonial administration also underscores the continuities between the different stakeholders, which made any distinction between state and civilian society very difficult. The maze of Saharanist overlaps indicates how important the Sahara became for France's own conception of itself.

As a result of its ubiquity in the news, political discourses, and cultural production, the Sahara acquired a crucial significance not only for French officials but also for the lay people who were constantly consuming the discourse of Saharanism. Everything that was said focused on the wealth the Sahara provided, particularly after the introduction of oil stocks in the Paris Stock Exchange. The discussions from this period show that Saharanism has the ability to reinvent geographies, recreate maps, insinuate unrealistic imaginaries of wealth, and endow itself with self-sustaining power though ideals of resource extraction.

MAKING SAHARANIST EXTRACTION A REALITY

Extraction of Material Resources and Human Labor

When translated into action, extraction is multidimensional in its targeting of material, labor, and intangible resources. Thus, every exploitable good offered by the desert's soil was considered fair game for French companies and global capitalists drawn to invest in the Sahara. French Prime Minister Guy Mollet put this exploitative ideology into words in 1956: "France is a great power. It will mobilize its forces to realize the Saharan miracle. The southern territories' immense riches in coal, iron, petrol, and natural gas will be developed. The Metropole will bring its technology and investment. Algeria will bring its executives (*cadres*) and its increasingly qualified labor. The economic exploitation of the desert is the great task of our generation."[131]

Mollet's road map underlines the imbrication of material and immaterial extraction in France's designs for the Sahara. Mollet also stated as a fact the division of labor between the Sahara, which would furnish both labor and natural resources, and the metropole, which would contribute the capital and technical knowledge. Mollet's goal was achieving the "Saharan miracle," which he made into an entire generation's mission. Unlike the ongoing, and equally problematic, discussions about creating reblooming deserts, the French extractive endeavor was very clear.

Mollet's words were expressive of a general mood in France. René Pottier concluded his 1947 book *Histoire du Sahara* by writing that France had nothing to expect from the Sahara but treated it as though it "had been the richest of the colonies."[132] French interest in the desert, in Pottier's argument, was attributable to France's benevolence and proof that it was "capable of noble gestures."[133] As evidenced by Mollet's vision, this type of humanist discourse about benevolence would disappear entirely from Saharanist literature as it was replaced by a focus on the Sahara's economic benefits. The reader of Saharanist literature from the late 1940s until the independence of Algeria in 1962 cannot help but notice the hyperfocus on resources, which were listed meticulously in every book, article, and booklet produced about the Sahara.[134] Suddenly, the Sahara had become the linchpin of an entire developmental modernity that almost completely contradicted previous literature, which had depicted the desert as an empty territory and in which France was invested for civilizing and humanitarian purposes. Almost all Saharanists turned their attention to the *sous-sol* (underground), which shifted the nature of expertise needed to furnish a detailed register of proven or potential underground resources and the best ways to create the infrastructure required for their extraction, transportation, and transformation.

The institutionalization of this extractionist ideology manifested in public-facing writing and conferences about the Sahara. Jean Imberti, a businessman and founder of the Confédération générale des entreprises du Maroc (CGEM), wrote in 1951 that the "mineralization of the Sahara is a fact."[135] The magazine *Entreprise* published an unsigned article in 1957 entitled "Ne trahissons pas le Sahara," in which the unknown author emphasized the undoubtable existence of wealth in the Sahara, specifying how "tens of billions have been invested in order to prospect this underground rich in petrol, iron, copper, manganese, and, without a doubt, uranium and thorium."[136] Jacques Soustelle, the deputy minister in charge of the Sahara and atomic energy, made several appearances at conferences and gave interviews in which he promoted the Saharan underground as the most interesting territory in the moribund French Empire.[137] Soustelle proudly announced that it was not until the 1950s that systematic prospecting of underground wealth had taken place, yielding a plethora of minerals, including manganese, iron, copper, and uranium, in the region including Colomb-Béchar, Mauritania, and the Hoggar.[138] Soustelle provided his audiences with estimates of the Sahara's proven underground and aboveground riches.[139] However, the discovery of coal, oil, and gas had an even greater significance.[140] Discovered in Edjeleh, on the Libyan-Algerian border, and also in Hassi Messaoud and Laghouat, among other places, oil fields with a minimum capacity of fifty million barrels (called "Class A" in the professional jargon of the oil industry) seemed abundant and easily exploitable.[141] The need to assert that this wealth was in French hands was a tenet of the optimistic portrayal of the Saharan treasures. Soustelle, for instance, stressed the public and private French capital's ownership of the Compagnie de recherches et d'exploitation de pétrole au Sahara (CREPS), the Compagnie française des pétroles (of Algeria), the Société nationale des pétroles d'Aquitaine (SNPA), and the Société nationale de recherches de pétrole en Algérie (SNRPA), which were all involved in the first oil discoveries.[142]

Soustelle foresaw no end to the extractive Saharanism he represented. For him, the great results achieved in Algeria were only part of the ongoing prospection that would not be completed for years.[143] In an interview with the American magazine *Time* in 1959 (Fig. 7), he likened the Sahara to California, arguing, "This desert should come to mean to France what the Far West meant at a certain period to American states on the Atlantic coast."[144] A specialist of Mayan civilization, Soustelle was familiar with North American history and aware of the implications of drawing similarities between the significance of Sahara for France and the West for the US.[145] Although the journalist scoffed at his comparison of the Sahara to California's Death Valley, Soustelle was not wrong in equating the importance of oil and gas in the Sahara to what gold represented for Americans in California.[146] Others used "new Texas, France and Europe's new Ural [Mountains],"[147] which insinuated, once again, how ideas that undergird extractive Saharanism are nourished by the same Saharanist imaginary that has traveled across different deserts independently of their locations.

Along with driving heady discussions about the material resources of the desert, extractive Saharanists emphasized the necessity of human beings for this development. Although they worked toward the same goal, there was a

FIGURE 7. Cover of *Time* featuring Jacques Soustelle, the French Minister of the Sahara (August 17, 1959). From TIME. © 2025 TIME USA LLC. All rights reserved. Used under license.

difference between Armand, who underscored the importance of new technologies in executing the Sahara's *mise en valeur*,[148] and Soustelle, who saw the use of human labor as part of a political operation to improve natives' living conditions.[149] Industrializing the Sahara would require manpower to build the "tremendous quantity of highways, airports, railways, tele-communications,

[and] domestic housing" that were essential for the oil industry.[150] Building this infrastructure necessitated the proletarianization of the "unskilled" Saharans who would, in exchange, benefit from the fruits of capitalism's investment in this infrastructure.[151] The expected exploitation of Saharan labor generated a wide array of reflections that all pointed out how their participation would both ameliorate their living conditions and accelerate social transformation of nomadic and sedentary communities.[152] However, there was no disagreement over the need to enlist labor from the Sahara itself.

The focus on extracting labor from inhabitants of the Sahara was not new. In fact, it dates back to the nineteenth century. As early as 1887, the French army had planned to conscript oasis inhabitants. The difference, however, is that the extraction of labor as articulated in the 1950s was capitalistic, aiming to harness all the manpower and energy available in the Sahara for France's economic exploitation of the territory. The question among the stakeholders then centered around determining who could bear the harsh conditions of life and work the desert. In *Le peuplement humain du Sahara*, Edmond Sergent, the director of the Pasteur Institute of Algeria, drew on his medical authority to hierarchize the people most likely to comfortably tolerate the Sahara's inclement weather based on their skin color. Sergent's racializing system was mostly based on ideas he had culled from Saharanist literature about relationships among the different ethnic groups in the Sahara.[153] His entire book does not contain much hard medical data to support his claims. Thus, material extraction went hand in hand with the reproduction of reflections on race and hierarchization of humans.

Immaterial Extraction: Imperialistic Harvest of the Sun

In addition to its focus on minerals and gas, extractive Saharanism manifested in a variety of other endeavors to procure immaterial resources. In this section, I will specifically discuss the extraction of solar energy, the early debut of which envisioned the Sahara as an ideal place for its expansion. Extractive Saharanism tapped into every possible option available to dislocate, use, and monetize underground and aboveground resources, but discussions about solar energy were more full-fledged from an early date. This should not be surprising, because solar energy was deeply intertwined with colonialism since the nineteenth century.

French inventor Charles Tellier was a pioneer of solar energy who tapped into Saharanism *avant l'heure*. Known for his contributions to the invention of commercial refrigeration,[154] Tellier was inspired by the Sahara's 70°C conditions to write that desert heat was the most significant that humans experienced on Earth.[155] He proposed what he called a "bold" idea to use solar energy "to cross the Sahara without any difficulty and to fertilize it along the way."[156] In Tellier's analysis, the Sahara, which he considered a land of "solitude, aridity, and the absolute domain of the sun,"[157] offered enough energy that if harnessed could power a trans-Saharan train. Tellier's technical discussions foregrounded the major role the sun could play in consolidating the economic ties between North and sub-Saharan Africa. Evoking the idea of the Trans-African Railway, which was also unfolding during his time, he wrote that his method could make it "possible to remove the locomotives from the rails to be constructed and replace them with machines that use the stored power of the sun."[158] Tellier expanded on how the sun could be exploited in myriad ways to support the railway, accommodate workers in the desert, and even make the territory more arable.

Tellier's project marked the beginning of a trend to generate solar energy in the desert. A few years after Algeria's independence, Marcel Perrot, the former director of the Institut de l'énergie solaire de l'université d'Alger (IESUA), wrote that most of the initiatives to harvest and utilize solar energy never went beyond the "stage of ideas and preliminary projects, which were most often grandiose."[159] According to Perrot's historical research, solar energy research only took off in Algeria after 1945, and it was mainly linked to global need for energy and the relaunching of the Méditerranée-Niger Railway.[160] Established in 1959, by 1962 the IESUA had "a hundred researchers, technicians, engineers, and other staff members," in addition to about two dozen professors who were conducting research in scientific fields related to energy.[161] The construction of a "Saharan sun house," as well as the building of a "Saharan solar city," were all experimental projects that exploited the Saharan sun, further advancing Saharanism's tradition of using deserts for testing purposes.[162] The fascinating aspect about this history is that all the expertise acquired in the desert was repatriated to Marseille, where the technicians and scholars who started in Algeria developed pioneering solar energy research for France.

American inventor Frank Shuman was inspired by Tellier's work to take his inventions one step further. According to the Emirati newspaper *The National News*, in 1908, Shuman founded the Sun Power Company with the aim of building power plants with large capacities for energy production. Shuman's dream had always been to build "a massive solar array in the Sahara with an installed capacity of nearly 200 megawatts."[163] This was a dream that "could have met global power demand, at least around midday," should the inventor have succeeded in his endeavors.[164] This retrospective reevaluation of Shuman's gargantuan ambitions erases both the colonial origins and the venture capitalist nature of Shuman's project. When Shuman failed to raise the $40,000 he needed to fund the project, he accepted an offer of sponsorship by his London friends.[165] Colonized Egypt, of all places, was his testing ground for the new technology. As writer Jeremy Shere notes, Shuman's invention offered Lord Horatio Herbert Kitchener, the British consul general and minister plenipotentiary in Egypt, the tools he needed to implement his own vision of *mise en valeur* for Egypt's desertic lands flanking the Nile River.[166] Solar energy then became a factor in British colonialism's designs to increase the profitability of the colony by decreasing the cost of energy needed to pump water from the Nile into arable desert land.

Shuman further articulated his extractive ideas in several publications that appeared in *Scientific American* between 1911 and 1914. In 1911, he published an article entitled "Power from Sunshine: A Pioneer Solar Power Plant," in which he explained that the sun was nature's main underused source of heat. Tracing Shuman's scientific lineage, the article cites the names of engineers who advanced research and developed inventions in the field of solar energy, including (rather unsurprisingly) Tellier's.[167] Desert spaces figure prominently in Shuman's scholarship. For him, a modernized irrigation system powered by the sun could save thousands of acres of arable land as well as thousands of cattle.[168] In his 1912 letter to the editor entitled "The Solar Engine in Egypt," Shuman took issue with an article that had mentioned his return from Egypt with his experimental project still incomplete. He attributed the interruption of the experiment to the abundance of the sun, explaining that his 100 horsepower solar plant "gave even better results than we expected," only to add that his zinc boilers, which worked in the mild sun in Philadelphia, could not withstand the heat in Egypt.[169] For Shuman, this was a reason for celebration, because, in his words, the "inventor of a new fuel which burns out his boilers" should be happy with results that exceeded his expectations.[170] Although he only talks about Egypt in the article, the logic underlying his enterprise was that the desert sun was to be harvested to optimize British exploitation of its colony. This silence on the Sahara was, however, preceded by his description of the Australian desert in "Power from Sunshine" as a "valueless" place that could be revived through the use of sun power.[171] When all was said and done, the sun for Shuman was the source of energy for the future.

Like the rest of the Saharanists of his generation, Shuman never missed an opportunity to respond to an article. In his retort to a 1915 article that he believed underrepresented the state of solar power, Shuman argued that his experiments had "brought sun power from the ideal stage into the real,"[172] and he specified the Sahara as a place where his scheme could succeed. He wrote to the editor, "It would only be necessary to cover 20,259 square miles of ground in the Sahara Desert with our sun heat absorber units, spaced as wide apart as they now are [in Cairo], to give *perpetually* the two hundred and seventy million horse-power per year required to equal all the fuel mined in 1909."[173] Similar to Shuman, Armand argued in 1954, "It would be sufficient to pave in silicon a chunk of the Sahara of an area equal to that of a medium-sized *département*" to generate all the energy France acquired from coal, petrol, and hydroelectric power combined.[174] Global warming was not an issue then, and Shuman's argument merely focused on the free energy that would be produced in perpetuity once the $98 billion his project would have cost was invested. The "human race," as a result, would "survive all the coal and oil fields by many thousands of years."[175] It is reasonable to assume that Shuman was probably thinking of white Europeans and Americans as the beneficiaries of his enterprise, since he lived at a time when people were racially hierarchized according to their race, language, and geographical location. White colonizers were, indeed, the principal group that extracted energy from the sun in Africa at this time.[176] Part of this privilege was also conspicuous in the fact that Shuman never had to contend with issues of property or sovereignty over the desert spaces where he proposed to build his multibillion-dollar plant.

Although solar energy has become a crucial element in the fight against global warming, it is important to note that its history is steeped in Saharanism and its assumptions about deserts. Tracing solar energy's genealogies through Tellier and Shuman alone would be sufficient to show that this clean energy was originally a solution for technical questions that arose with conquest and the need to maximize economic exploitation of colonies. Retracing the history of solar energy and its embeddedness in extractive Saharanism is not meant to argue against this source of clean, sustainable energy. Rather, the goal is to draw parallels between solar energy as an imperial tool and the ongoing uses of deserts to carry out all manner of extractive enterprises in the name of human good. Colonial states were deeply invested in optimizing the exploitation of the colonies, and when classical methods reached their limits, they relied on new ideas that could enhance their profits.

The aforementioned Simiot asserted in 1951, "It would not be entirely fanciful to consider, in the near future, the domestication of the torrents of light and heat that are lost daily amidst these *solitudes*."[177] Simiot was not entirely wrong. The rise of green neoliberalism relegated this colonialist history to oblivion, which turned into an amnesia that facilitates the invitation of more solar extraction in deserts across the globe.

In Africa, Morocco has been at the forefront of synergies to harvest sunlight. Since the 2010s, a sprawling project called Noor-Ouarzazate has covered eight thousand acres just outside the city of Ouarzazate. Managed by the Moroccan Agency for Sustainable Energy (Masen), Noor-Ouarzazate (Fig. 8) is presented in terms that are reminiscent of Soustelle's musings about the oil welfare in the Sahara in the 1950s. Hence, Masen's strategy "contributes to territorial equity and the sustainable development of the places that host the project." With savvy marketing strategies that address global audiences, Masen officials double down on their project's contribution "to environmental protection and to the reduction of greenhouse gas emissions."[178] Similarly, US President Biden's administration placed solar energy at the heart of its efforts to curb greenhouse emissions and "Develop a Clean Energy Economy." In 2022, it approved two large solar projects in the Mojave Desert that would cover the electricity needs of more than 250,000 California residents.[179] Centered on 10.8 million acres of desert areas of several counties in California,[180] the Desert Renewable Energy Conservation Plan (DRECP) is first and foremost defined by its existence within deserts. Both the Noor-Ouarzazate facility and DRECP evoke spoliation of desert lands and expropriation of land from Indigenous inhabitants. Noor-Ouarzazate's excessive consumption of water is now threatening the only man-made lake on the Draa River, while the production of solar energy in the American Southwest is now endangering lands that, in the words of Brendan Cummings, conservation director of the Center for Biological Diversity (CBD) in Tucson, Arizona, serve as "habitat for imperiled species, [and which] are themselves functioning ecosystems that conserve carbon naturally."[181] Despite similarities in the way Saharanism operates in these deserts, journalists in the US have access to information that can help uncover green energy's environmental costs. Unlike the prevalent silence in Morocco, journalist Barclay Ballard wrote an article in which he revealed that the Ivanpah Solar Electric Generating System has cost the lives of six thousand birds annually since its operation in 2014.[182]

It is true that solar energy offers a perfect, freely harvestable source of immaterial energy. However, harvesting solar rays has caused significant

FIGURE 8. Aerial view of Noor-Ouarzazate. Image created by Benjamin Grant / Overview, source imagery © Maxar.

environmental and humanitarian harm that the focus on clean energy and global warming has overshadowed. The displacement of Indigenous populations from their ancestral land is just one of many ways in which Saharanism has turned deserts upside down in recent years. Although solar energy projects are now conducted by national governments rather than independent prospectors, the visions projected onto deserts are conceived through technologies and notions of environmental consciousness produced elsewhere. The colonial continues in different ways, and Saharanism is there to give it a more palatable attire.

THE SAHARAN INDUSTRIAL COMPLEX

Soustelle told *Time* magazine that a large portion of French industry would be concretized in the Sahara,[183] although oilmen "pooh-pooh[ed] Soustelle's industrialized Sahara as visionary."[184] In fact, Soustelle was not the only one within the French state to have believed that the industrialization of the Sahara was not only possible but that France could federate the means to make it true. The idea of the Saharan Industrial Complex (SIC) was widespread among almost all the stakeholders in the Sahara. The discursive hype around the creation of the SICs was stoked by nationalist grandeur and die-hard colonialist positions at a time when the Sahara figured on the radar of capitalist movers and shakers in the US and the UK. Saharanist tropes for developing the desert and transforming it into something new underlaid these discussions.

The SICs were Labonne's brainchild. However, it was Armand who propagated the possibility of their creation throughout the 1950s. A technocrat, Armand commanded respect and admiration among the members of his generation. He was the one who said, "The Sahara filled up lecture halls in Paris!"[185] Armand wrote a slew of articles and gave a series of talks in which he explained his ideas for the SICs. For five years, Armand argued that setting up integrated factories in the desert was not only possible but in fact necessary to prove France's ownership of its Sahara.[186] Rather than considering the ideas that he promoted as being his alone, it is important to perceive them as part of a larger institutional thinking that placed extraction and transformation of desert resources at the very core of French economic prosperity. It is also important to remember that Armand was an institution with an army of assistants, advisers, and strategists who drafted his lectures and articles, which, again, says a lot about Saharanism's profound existence as a mindset.

Armand believed in the power of technology to transform deserts. In a talk he gave to the Société française de géographie économique in 1953, he praised how new technologies had "made deserts recede" in the US, India, Australia, and South Africa, which were using modern technology to develop their arid territories.[187] Per Armand, technological development, easier access, improved infrastructure, and the existence of mineral and energy resources would facilitate the establishment of the SIC in the Sahara. Buttressing his argument by advocating for complementary economic activities, Armand made the case for an available resource–based integrated chain of production.[188] In this conception, establishing SICs in deserts was anything but a choice: "It is necessary to closely link the industrial equipment to energy projects and especially to public works—notably means of transport—some of which are and can only be within the domain of the state. There needs to be a direction, a plan—not one fixed according to preestablished data (since we are in a field that is still very poorly understood) but a plan that is likely to concretize 'integrated development' in the zone."[189] Following in Labonne's footsteps,[190] Armand in his vision for the SICs imagined them as an integrated whole, including work with coal, iron, metallurgy, and acids. The Moroccan-Algerian border city of Colomb-Béchar was presented as the perfect site to pioneer the SICs. In addition to its proximity to mineral-rich areas, the city's strategic location linked it to Algiers via the

Méditerranée-Niger Railway and to the Atlantic Ocean via Agadir.[191] Thanks to its less harsh climate and the abundance of water resources, the city was presented as inhabitable to Europeans.[192]

The focus on Colomb-Béchar was also linked to the desire to implant heavy military industries to protect French assets from future wars. In fact, even before France established the Centre saharien d'expérimentations militaires (CSEM) in the Reggane Plateau and the Centre d'expérimentations militaires des oasis (CEMO) in the Hoggar in 1958, it had started the nucleus of a military industry in Colomb-Béchar with the Centre interarmées d'essais d'engins spéciaux (CIEES) in 1947.[193] Similar to the later nuclear-testing facilities that France built in the desert, this sprawling military complex included a firing range, an administrative section, communication facilities, storage and workshop facilities, and barracks.[194] The existence of this center must not be overlooked as one of the reasons that development at Colomb-Béchar was mainly focused on heavy industries.[195] France even attempted to secure NATO funding for some of these projects, but it is not clear whether it succeeded or not.[196] As such, the SICs could be said to have functioned as the civilian dimension of the experimental Saharanism, the larger ramifications of which I discuss in Chapter 3.

Beyond the practical benefits that the proponents of extractive Saharanism encoded into the SICs, the desert space itself was turned into an opportunity for transformation. Armand's depiction of the Sahara as an untapped space for novel developmental initiatives meant that administrative and financial structures could be as flexible and innovative as the investment schemes.[197] Once conceived, the French Union was called upon to legally formalize the existence of such "virgin lands" in order to accommodate their exploitation.[198] The invention of this new category aimed to "facilitate prospection and efficiently help companies that will take the risks of setting up in the desert."[199] Armand stressed, "The moment has come to liberate ourselves from ancient ways of seeing, ancient traditional formulas that were able to ensure the success of France's economy in the nineteenth century, but which are now outdated, particularly in untouched land."[200] Hence, the land was not just a space for imagining new industrial complexes but also for diverse forms of capitalist ventures that would accelerate both the extraction and transformation of Saharan resources. The *pays neuf* was conceived as a territory for innovative partnerships between the public and the private sectors that are inconceivable in other areas. These partnerships were not only necessary but fundamental to the very existence of the extractive enterprise in the desert.[201]

Sustaining France's grandeur was a significant factor in the way extractive Saharanists conceptualized their plans for the desert. After all, France was "responsible, in the world's eyes, for the exploitation of the Sahara,"[202] and this responsibility had a cost, insofar as France had no choice but to prove that its technical know-how, financial strength, and national stamina were capable of living up to the challenge. The creation of SICs would entrench France's presence in Africa, and its commitment to the Sahara's *mise en valeur* would demonstrate its "African vocation" within the *longue durée.*[203] Internally, the establishment of SICs would not only mobilize French techniques but would also "resuscitate a new spirit" among the French youth who were being invited to partake in the "grand task of the century."[204] Faithful to this nationalist discourse, Soustelle declaimed, "Young men, go South!" adding that it was in that direction, specifically toward the Sahara, that "French dynamism of this end of the twentieth century should be oriented and developed."[205]

The utopic imaginings of a SIC-ed Sahara and the injunction to French youth to go south were oblivious to the Algerian War of Independence, which raged from 1954 to 1962. There was even a correlation between the violence of the war and Saharanism's heightened stakes in the Sahara, which was slowly conceived as a linchpin of Euro-American capitalistic and strategic interests. However, Algeria's independence put an end to these schemes. As though by magic, the "Sahara disappeared from the [French] collective imaginary" with the cessation of the particularly abundant literary, scientific, and social scientific publications of the postcolonial period.[206] French extractive Saharanism and its multi-decade legacy receded to archives, where it escaped critical and conceptual articulation until now. It has become Saharanism.

CONCLUSION

This chapter has conceptualized how Saharanism functions as an extractive practice. Tracing the shift from military governance to the rise of civilian control of its development, the chapter has examined multiple institutions that were created to implement various notions of the Sahara's *mise en valeur.* While the army's construction of the desert as a dangerous and threatening space had been prevalent ever since French encounters with the Sahara in the nineteenth century, the 1950s witnessed the rise of discourses around development and exploitation, the bulk of which focused on the underground resources. This "underground turn" was the clearest and the most truthful depiction of Saharanism's inherently extractive nature. For almost a decade, French society was bombarded with continuous propaganda about the wealth of the Sahara, which contributed to the dissemination of many assumptions about the place and its people. The chapter has shown how the Sahara was reorganized and its morphology reshaped by French attempts to accommodate global oil capitalism and its corollary extractive enterprises.

THREE

Experimental Saharanism

DESERTS AS A TESTING GROUND

IN APRIL 1927, BOTANIST WALTER T. SWINGLE, who worked for the US Department of Agriculture, was invited by French authorities to participate in an investigation into *Fusarium oxysporum*'s infestation of palm groves in the Moroccan desert.[1] Swingle, who happened to be affiliated with the University of Lyon, was asked by his French contacts to accompany them to Figuig and Boudnib, which had a reputation for the high quality of their dates,[2] but whose groves suffered from this illness that made palms wilt and die.[3] This proved to be a once-in-a-lifetime opportunity for Swingle to set foot on what he called "the greatest single date planting in all Africa."[4] In addition to learning about Bayoud disease,[5] Swingle observed how local people tended to the groves, pollinated the trees, and cleaned them in preparation for the harvest season. During his time in Boudnib, he met a tribal leader who sold him eleven Medjool palm offshoots that he sent to Washington, DC. Once there, the offshoots were quarantined on a Native American reservation in the Nevada desert for a period of two years.[6] A hundred years later, Swingle can be said to not only have imported a new plant but also to have placed the Sahara at the heart of the multibillion-dollar Medjool (pronounced *Mejhoul/ljihl* in Morocco) date economy in the US. Swingle's story is only one manifestation of a practice that I propose to call "experimental Saharanism," which subsumes all endeavors to test new ideas and undertakings in desert spaces.

Swingle's stint in Morocco speaks to a long tradition of the extraction of desert animals and rare plants for experimental purposes. His importation of palm offshoots from southern Morocco followed from an intense effort to develop a commercial-scale date industry in the US since the nineteenth century.[7] A few decades prior, the US had imported camels and their trainers from Egypt for its warfare against Mormons and Native Americans in Utah.[8] However, these inter-desert experimental enterprises were not unidirectional.[9] They were, in fact, part of a larger network of exchanges that included, among others, Swingle's first visit to North Africa, David Fairchild's and S.C. Mason's efforts to identify and import Saidy offshoots from Egypt,[10] and French botanist August Chevalier's attempt to import botanical techniques from Arizona into Reggane in 1930.[11] This trans-desert experimental endeavor would become transnational policy through UNESCO's Arid Zone Program, which "considered the results of arid zone research in areas including hydrology, plant and animal ecology, climatology, and wind and solar power, among others, to be universal to all arid lands and broadly applicable."[12] However, experimental Saharanism is not limited to plants; it is an all-encompassing phenomenon that draws on notions of a desert's availability not only for the extraction of everything it contains and application of theories for a universal applicability of knowledge, but also for its being a space that is inherently sacrificeable for the testing of lethal and nonlethal products.

Experimental Saharanism has underpinned the production and deployment of deserts as spaces where new ideas, inventions, and undertakings can be made into a reality. Because of Saharanism's racism toward desert inhabitants and its disdain for arid environments, experimental Saharanists' endeavors are usually oblivious to the desert's nature as home for both human and nonhuman subjects. Focusing on a variety of projects that unfolded in deserts, this chapter conceptualizes experimental Saharanism and demonstrates its construction and weaponization of deserts' desolation to justify their uses for testing purposes. Most importantly, this chapter articulates how experimental Saharanism reached its height with the militarization of the atom, which made deserts into secretive sites for cutting-edge and oftentimes deadly technologies.

DEFINING THE CONTOURS OF EXPERIMENTAL SAHARANISM

Experimental Saharanism transformed deserts into testing grounds for all types of environmentally unfriendly technologies and products. From "high-performance gliders to race-ready flying cars,"[13] trains, and planes, deserts across the globe immediately come to mind as ideal spaces for proving new technologies. Arid areas are constructed as places of choice to test a variety of known and unknown products, a practice that, oftentimes, went hand in hand with colonialism, which left native communities no say on how their territories were used. When France occupied the Sahara, its army and industrial sectors, particularly Citroën and Berliet, used the territory to test myriad innovations. Similarly, General Motors, Toyota, Honda, Nissan, and Kia have owned more than 28,000 acres of desert land in the American West for testing their vehicles since 1953.[14] This association of deserts with testing is neither new nor accidental, but rather the result of their discursive production as empty and, most importantly, remote and secure areas, where the secrets can stay safe.

Deeply seated in anthropocentric approaches, experimental Saharanism has prioritized humans over nature. Hence, the efforts to tame or subdue these expanses of land for the benefit of humans has involved enterprises to modify, engineer, or even transform them. The construction of the Suez Canal, which required the mobilization of the most sophisticated technologies of the nineteenth century, was one of experimental Saharanism's greatest achievements. The completion of the canal represented a triumph of European architecture and technology, which instigated other equally ambitious projects. Both France and Britain undertook trans-African desert train projects, which involved synergies and tight collaborations among civilian, military, and business stakeholders, representing a wider technological trend at the time.[15]

Although ubiquitous, experimental Saharanism has not previously been articulated in conceptual terms. As exemplified by the aforementioned botanical and equine exchanges between the Sahara and the Sonoran deserts, experimental Saharanism links different deserts as ideal spaces for trying out new ideas. It has perpetuated what historian Philipp Lehmann has called a "technological imagination," which is constitutive of the efforts to engineer and transform natural spaces, particularly deserts.[16] Undergirded by discursive practices that hark back to an entrenched history of ideas about deserts, this subtype of Saharanism involves powerful corporations that wield both the wherewithal and the authority to turn ideas into measurable actions. Although enterprises undertaken by individuals may be subsumed under the appellation of experimental Saharanism, their long-term impacts cannot come close to equaling the consequences of state- and business-sponsored initiatives. Nevertheless, individual undertakings have contributed to experimental Saharanism's discursive existence and continue to nourish imaginations that sustain it. Hence, experimental Saharanism, in its deeper and broader ramifications, has the power to both theoretically inform and physically shape the way a desert is experienced, lived, used, and considered.

Proponents of experimental Saharanism have deliberately shaped discourse to represent deserts as empty, desolate spaces. This is clearly apparent in the rationale for choosing arid areas as testing sites for weapons and lethal technologies. Historians Terrence R. Fehner and F. G. Gosling of the US Department of Energy explain how the Nevada Test Site (NTS) was established in 1951. "Uninhabitedness," meteorology, and economic impact were, according to Captain Howard B. Hutchinson of the Armed Forces Special Weapons Project, factors that determined the choice of the location to avoid "harm to population, economy or industry."[17] Despite the even better meteorological conditions on the East Coast, which would take the fallout into the sea, its demographic density and the highly prized fisheries in the Atlantic Ocean meant that the best option in terms of its decreased risks was not a viable option for other reasons. Hutchinson's report emphasized the desert's emptiness and the availability of the land in the Southwest, although the winds would carry fallout to remote populated areas.[18] The main takeaway from Hutchinson's report is that the safety of human beings, the economy, and the industry prevailed over that of the environment.

This anthropocentrism has not only been limited to lethal testing; it also extends to desires to remake deserts and engineer their climate. Although created by accident in 1905 in California,[19] the Salton Sea disaster was caused by technological and architectural initiatives that inform experimental Saharanism. Similarly, experimental Saharanism is at the heart of Muhammed Bin Salman's construction of Neom City in the western desert in Saudi Arabia.[20] Nonetheless, climate engineering in deserts is not a new phenomenon. Captain François Élie Roudaire (1836–1885) endeavored to create an internal sea in the chotts between Algeria and Tunisia.[21] Inspired by the successful feat of his mentor Ferdinand de Lesseps with the Suez Canal, this military geographer thought that creating a *mer intérieure* by connecting the Sahara to the Mediterranean would create milder weather in the Sahara,[22] an idea that geographer Henry Chotard celebrated: "It was like wildfire, and enthusiasm broke out; we saw under the beneficial influence of these waters borrowed from the Mediterranean the appearance of the country change as if by magic: the sands became fertile lands that were covered with woods, meadows, crops; the few villages were replaced by numerous, well-populated towns where industry and commerce developed, and before which our ships arrived at full sail or at full steam."[23] For Chotard, bringing the Mediterranean into the Sahara was a newsworthy event that marked man's triumph over nature.[24] Similarly to Roudaire, British geologist Ernest Hubert Lewis Schwarz proposed a plan to redeem the Kalahari Desert in South Africa, conjecturing, "On the Kalahari project, everyone in South Africa, whether he wants it or not, will receive the additional rain, will see his land rendered more fertile, and all his difficulties from drought, famine and pestilence disappear."[25] George P. Marsh also highlighted and commended the positive effects of Captain Allen's plan to dig a canal that would connect the Mediterranean to the Red Sea via the Dead Sea. Despite several caveats about the risks of the project, Marsh still insisted the "climate of Syria would be tempered, its precipitation and its fertility increased, the course of its winds and the electrical condition of its atmosphere modified."[26]

France's control of the largest desert in the world until 1962 may give the impression that it has dominated experimental Saharanism. While it is true that French engineers, geologists, botanists, hydrologists, and husbandry experts attended to all aspects of the desert between the nineteenth century and the independence of Algeria, the advent of the atomic bomb in 1945 placed American scientists at the helm of cutting-edge experimentation. First developed in French and German laboratories, nuclear research reached its apogee in the US, where the scientists involved in the Manhattan Project perfected the fission of the atom achieved by Otto Hahn and Fritz Strassmann in Nazi Germany in 1938 to produce plutonium and weaponize radiation.[27] The US put an end to World War II and changed the course of history when its army dropped nuclear bombs on Hiroshima and Nagasaki on August 6 and 9, 1945, respectively. Plutonium, a lab-produced radioactive metallic element that is crucial for the development of nuclear weapons, has "a half-life of 24,100 years."[28] This long life is not good news for deserts, which have since the 1940s received significant amounts of radioactive residue that continue and will continue to impact their entire biomes for hundreds, if not thousands, of years.

The US's construction and use of the atomic bomb set in motion a race for nuclear armament and for deserts in which to test them. This rush for deserts went hand in hand with spy agencies' recourse to unorthodox means to access the secrets of the bomb,[29] which the US refused to share even with its closest allies.[30] Nevertheless, when other states unlocked the secret of the atomic bomb, deserts both hot and cold, from Nevada to the Sahara, and from the Maralinga area in Southern Australia to Semipalatinsk in Kazakhstan, became embroiled in atomic politics. After the US, the USSR tested its first bomb in 1949 on the steppe of the Semipalatinsk Test Site in Kazakhstan, while Great Britain borrowed a 3,300-acre desert in the area they renamed Maralinga in the Great Victoria Desert to conduct its tests in 1954. France, in turn, used the Sahara to carry out its first seventeen nuclear experiments between 1960 and 1966. In comparison with all previous uses of deserts for experimentation, nuclear tests involved the construction of atomic cities, the deployment of thousands of expert and nonexpert workers, and the mobilization of cutting-edge scientific expertise that marked a new leap in experimental Saharanism's ability to cause destruction.

Preparation for war also turned deserts into proving grounds for humans' capacity to bear the stresses of war and fighting in the harshest conditions possible. Faced with the Nazi occupation of North Africa in 1942, General Lesley James McNair (1883—1944) issued an order for the creation of the Desert Training Center (DTC) that "would prepare American soldiers for desert warfare."[31] In order to train on terrain that presented similar challenges to the ones soldiers would encounter in the Sahara, General George S. Patton (1885–1945), who was designated to lead this effort, reproduced the Sahara at the Arizona-California DTC. In the words of historian Sarah Seekatz, "over a million troops trained in its desert heat, in an area roughly 18,000 square miles," which is bigger than the joint area of both Maryland and Delaware.[32] This hardening of bodies and their acclimation to desert conditions required soldiers to run a mile in full military gear in under ten minutes.[33] The end of the war led to the repurposing of the DTC, but even today, television programs show the desert's image as a place to prepare bodies for harsh battlegrounds or difficult experiences.

This mimicry of the Saharan space in the California desert cannot be dissociated from its origins in Saharanism, which has a monolithizing tendency in which deserts are presented as mutually interchangeable. Literary scholar Brian T. Edwards has argued that this swapping of desert terrains in American films from the 1940s, like *Casablanca* (1942) and *Sahara* (1943), "detached [them] from the specificity of the North African landscape."[34] Edwards further clarifies the implications of reproducing North African landscapes in California, writing that these films were made "with little attention to the geography and architecture of Casablanca or Libya, [but] both remap North Africa as they plot their vision of Americanness onto the cleared space."[35] This transposition of two different deserts without regard for their topographic and ecological specificities—qualities that give each its own unique identity—extend beyond film to encompass a variety of enterprises that reflect how Saharanism operates. Since, as writer William Atkins has sarcastically pointed out, literature depicts "the deserts of the world as one,"[36] Saharanism subjects them to the same treatment, independent of their location. Most importantly, however, this absence of specificity turns the desert landscape into an open space for testing that knows no boundaries.

The persistence of experimental Saharanism is not impacted by the changes in warfare technologies or those used to fight natural crises. New technologies, particularly drones, found their proving grounds in desert spaces. As recently as 2017, National Public Radio (NPR) reported that the US Army was "testing [in the Mojave] how much of this know-how can be put in the hands of troops on the ground who may have to fight someone with intense cyber capabilities like the Russians or Chinese."[37] In April 2022, several news outlets, such as Utah Public Radio, announced that the Utah desert was going to be the terrain for the US Army's testing of a drone swarm, indicating that the small drones would be launched from a variety of platforms to then converge and attack the same target. Most recently, the Food and Agriculture Organization (FAO), a UN initiative, provided Mauritania with the resources to use drones for its battle against locusts. In 2020, the country witnessed a preliminary trial, which, according to the British Broadcasting Corporation, was "expected to confirm the durability and adaptability of drones in different desert conditions."[38] Although the fight against locusts, which devastate crops throughout the Saharan region, may be worthwhile, the desert is presented as an open land where AI-manned drones can be perfected safely. Because of drones' dual uses, several scholars have drawn attention to the threats embedded in their deployment, as they can also monitor migrants.[39] Since migrants from sub-Saharan Africa have to take routes through areas monitored for locusts, there is no guarantee that, once developed, drone technologies will not be used to surveil people or that the findings from this research would not be militarized.

These examples reveal that experimental Saharanism has made it almost an expectation to outsource experimentation to deserts. French artist and writer Odette de Pingandeau described this state of mind on the eve of France's testing of its first nuclear bomb: "What place could be better suited for testing the monstrous weapon than these uninhabited regions of sand so familiar to movie-goers and popular travel magazine readers! To many it even seemed fortunate that France had available such an ideal testing ground at its very back door."[40] Pingandeau cuts straight to the heart of the issue of experimental

Saharanism: It requires people to be grateful that lethal experimentation is taking place in desolate areas far from their homes. Instead of merely describing this phenomenon, Pingandeau attributes its origins to the familiarity of the sands to moviegoers and magazine readers. In subsuming this phenomenon under experimental Saharanism, it is possible to account for the cultural and ideational processes that prepare humans mentally and psychologically to accept the misuse of deserts and the mistreatment of their biomes. Saharanism deactivates its consumers' critical- thinking abilities by normalizing and making ordinary the death of the desert.

The interest in nuclear experiences and their consequences has addressed every facet of their advent from their environment impacts to Cold War politics.[41] Nevertheless, the deserts where these experiments unfolded were simply glossed over. As Rebecca Solnit reveals in *Savage Dreams: A Journey into the Hidden Wars of the American West*, even antinuclear activists overlooked the physical test site.[42] Although Solnit is referring to the NTS, her observation applies to desert experimentation sites globally. Solnit observes, "Nuclear war, whether you are for it or against it, is supposed to be a terrible thing that might happen someday, not something that has been going on all along."[43] This future-oriented fear of the annihilation that could be caused by nuclear power has thus prevented many, including staunch antinuclear activists, from perceiving the actual scale of the ongoing atomic war in desert environments. This fact can only have one explanation, that is, the internalization of the desert's emptiness and lifelessness.

It is within this gap between what has been, what is, and what might be done in the future that experimental Saharanism has survived. Between the fear of a future nuclear war and the actual decimation of desert biomes throughout the world, Saharanism has legitimated deserts as the "proper" places where death can happen for the sake of anthropocentrism. As the authors of a recent article write, the "desert holds its secrets—which is why it's been an ideal place to test out what's next."[44] This "what's next" offers experimental Saharanism the latitude as well as the impetus it needs to always be on the lookout for something new, whereby the consequences of experiments can be buried in desert land first. As I will explain later in this chapter, the idea of modernity as representative of a difference in the way time is lived and experienced is essentially ingrained in the depiction of deserts as being out of step with modern time.

In the imagination of experimental Saharanism's proponents, the desert appears more like a stage or playground than a natural space that is a habitat for myriad forms of life. Christopher Nolan's 2023 film *Oppenheimer* is an excellent example in this regard.[45] Although several parts of the film unfold in the desert laboratories of Los Alamos, the desert itself is the biggest absence in the movie. It is only mentioned once, when the rain suspensefully delays the first trial of the bomb. However, *Oppenheimer* does not mispresent the reality of how the desert figures as a presence-absence in the experimental endeavors that take place within it. Interestingly, experimental Saharanists care more about their gadgets, measurement charts, and performance reviews than they do about the desert spaces they occupy. This may be a result of their presumptions that the desert is already empty and dead. After all, only human presence counts as life, which disregards the desert's own internal biodiversity.

The treatment of deserts as dead should be situated in time in order to avoid facile overgeneralizations. The authors of *Origins of the Nevada Test Site* rectify experimental Saharanism's views by nuancing the notion of life in the NTS area: "Although no locale can be said to be ideal or optimal for nuclear weapons testing, the Nevada Test Site was perhaps the best continental site available for avoiding collateral damage and radiation exposure to plants, animals, and, most importantly, human beings off site."[46] Unlike the self-assured blanket statements that have been promulgated since the inception of the nuclear weapon, relating mainly to radiation's minimal effects on desert ecologies and biomes, the new language contains words such as "no locale" and "perhaps," which clearly indicate the desire to plant doubt in and nuance past affirmations about nuclear weapons. With this very important quotation, the authors imply that, of all the inhabited places that the nuclear bomb could have been tested, the NTS was the one that would lead to the least damage. This is, of course, predicated on the idea that the remoteness of desert areas is equivalent to less presence of life, be it plant, human, or animal.

This backtracking was not even conceivable sixty years ago, despite demands from Third World governments representing populations that would be impacted by radiations' then poorly known effects. In the face of protests made by Morocco and other African nations in the years leading up to the 1960s French experiments, Jules Moch, France's ambassador to the UN, defended his country's decision to use the Sahara as an experimental ground, claiming, "The populations of all the states bordering on the Sahara—Morocco, Tunisia, Libya, the Sudan, Ethiopia, Ghana, Liberia, Guinea and the states of the [French] Community—will be in less danger than the inhabitants of Siberia and of California, who were in no danger at all, when a greater number of experiments were being conducted."[47] The logic underlying Moch's argument was that the Sahara was not only more remote from large urban centers than the sites where the US and the USSR had conducted their experiments, but it was also emptier than the steppes in Kazakhstan and the American Southwest. In a manner reminiscent of Pingandeau's insightful critique, France, therefore, deserved to be applauded for its concern for African lives by choosing their unpopulated, lifeless desert for its nuclear tests.

As this discussion reveals, experimental Saharanism cannot be divorced from Saharanism's production of the idea of deserts as remote and desolate. The coalescence of discursive emptying of deserts with the undertaking of actions that require the removal of populations and livestock effectively created a self-fulfilling imaginary of emptiness.

FRENCH EXPERIMENTAL SAHARANISM: THE SAHARA AS A PROVING GROUND

Between Desert within the Desert and the Land of Thirst

Once France came to the decision to make its atomic bomb, the question of the site where it would be exploded arose. Already in 1956, Jacques Britsch wrote that France would have no alternative to the Sahara as a test site for atomic weapons, should it decide to make them.[48] A year later, General Charles Ailleret, who had been the commander of the Armes spéciales (Special Weapons, SW)—an equivalent of the American Special Weapons Project—since 1956,[49] set out to scout the Sahara for an appropriate place in which to test the bomb.[50] Upon his death in a plane crash in 1968, *The New York Times* depicted this trusted advisor of General Charles de Gaulle and his chair of chiefs of staff as a nuclear hawk who advocated for "an all-out [nuclear] war in the event of a major Soviet attack."[51] Indeed, Ailleret became very interested in atomic weapons in the 1940s, which earned him the position of commander of SW. However, in reference to his call for a NATO-led nuclear war on the USSR, *The New York Times* cautioned, "it is often difficult to separate General Ailleret's ideas from those of his imposing chief [de Gaulle]," to indicate the extent of the overlap between their ideas.

The Commissariat à l'énergie atomique (CEA)'s white paper *France's First Atomic Explosion* and Ailleret's 1968 memoir *L'aventure atomique française* are two crucial texts that explain the complex system France put in place to acquire what came to be known as its proverbial *force de frappe* (striking force),[52] also known as the *force nucléaire stratégique* (nuclear strategic force).[53] The Press and Information Service of the French Embassy in the US translated the CEA's report into English. A propagandist text, *France's First Atomic Explosion* was prepared to control the damage ensuing from the experiments in the Sahara and justify the French bomb to the world. However, beyond its public relations' role, *France's First Atomic Explosion* as well as *L'aventure atomique* contain important information about the division of labor between the CEA and SW. Accordingly, the CEA, which included civilian and military components as well as the Direction des applications militaires (DAM), was "responsible for conducting preliminary studies for the experimental atomic explosions and for the preparation of the scientific parts of the tests."[54] Hence, the task of the CEA was to study and construct the bomb for the Ministère des armées, which had funded the entire project.[55] Ailleret's SW, on the other hand, was tasked with the "choice, organization, operation, and logistical support and security of the shooting range."[56] These complementary roles were not entirely seamless, as Ailleret and scientist Pierre Billaud clearly indicate in their memoirs. Despite their close collaboration, Ailleret almost never discussed CEA scientists except to complain about the preferential treatment they received compared to their military colleagues.[57]

Ailleret's rationalization of choosing the Sahara as testing site is a testament to experimental Saharanism's construction of emptiness. Because the Sahara met the criteria to optimize the results of the experiment, the SW emptied it for Moch even before the 1959 UN debate in which he had to defend its choice. Among several other factors, the French army needed a location close enough to mobilize the large-scale logistical and human know-how necessary for the preparation, construction, and security of the field. Also, since the experiment was going to be an aboveground atmospheric one, the testing ground had to take into account radioactive fallout, which required the SW "to have at its disposition a considerable space."[58] This space could be "maritime or desertic," but the most important requirement was for it to be effectively devoid of any human activity that the fallout could impact. Options included the Kerguelen Islands, Clipperton Island, the Tuamotu Archipelago, and the Sahara, but the remoteness of the first two locations from metropolitan France, the impossibility of building airports on them, and their windspeeds led to their elimination in favor of the Sahara.[59]

Hence, the Sahara was chosen from a map in Paris even before Ailleret and his team made their first scouting trip to the area in 1957. Ailleret wrote,

"We a priori eliminated the site of Touamotou for the sake of the Sahara and in all likelihood for the sake of the part of it named Tanezrouft."[60] Ailleret was already convinced that the Sahara was the appropriate place to conduct the explosion, and his scouting mission was only intended to confirm the choice and define a specific place for the construction of the test site. To further convince his readers that the choice was perfect, Ailleret gives them a glimpse into his ideational universe, recycling Saharanist clichés that Tanezrouft was "the land of thirst and fear,"[61] a land "known for the absence of any life in the immense spaces separating Reggane from Tessalit."[62]

In casting the Sahara in these terms, Ailleret was not inventing anything new. There was already a long lineage of Saharanism that he drew on for his own musings about the dangerous, empty desert. Historians Benjamin Brower and Philipp Lehmann have revealed in their respective works the imbrication of violent conquest and geoengineering in the Sahara. Brower specifically has demonstrated how violence in the Sahara was romanticized by French officers and soldiers, reifying their readings of the Romantics in the form of excess violence committed in this sublime space.[63] Lehmann went in the opposite direction by demonstrating how a coterie of writers gave literary life to Roudaire's aforementioned project of an "internal sea."[64] Between the romanticization of violence and the literary dissemination of an earlier manifestation of experimental Saharanism, the history of ideas that underlie experimental Saharanism connect its various components across different times and generations. When Ailleret and his team went to the desert to find the ideal location to build their atomic facilities, their feet stood on the firm ground produced by generations of Saharanists who had already thought about, initiated, or undertaken experimental enterprises in deserts.

Located in southwestern Algeria toward the Mali border, Tanezrouft had come to prominence during the French conquest in the twentieth century. The area witnessed some gory battles, including the Battle of Tanezrouft in 1917, during which three hundred Tuaregs attacked a military convoy, killing one French officer and wounding another, in addition to killing eight native *sahariens* enlisted in the Compagnies méharistes sahariennes established by Captain François-Henry Laperrine in 1897.[65] In 1923, General Georges Estienne (1889–1973) evoked Tanezrouft's infamous reputation as a deadly place among the few Saharan explorers who had tried to cross it.[66] Surprisingly, however, it was geographer Félix Gautier who popularized Tanezrouft's emptiness. A respected connoisseur of the Sahara, Gautier, who was a professor at the University of Algiers, produced influential scholarship that shaped the thinking of multiple generations of the French establishment. In 1923, Gautier wrote that Tanezrouft "designates the part of the Algerian Sahara that is entirely dead."[67] Six years later, Gautier doubled down on these assertions by reporting that in Tamasheq (the Tuareg variety of Tamazight), *Tanezroufts* meant the "land of thirst and death."[68] Accordingly, Gautier asserted that "Tanezrouft—in our Sahara—is the maximum desert, unapproachable, haunted by terror."[69] He qualifies this part of the Sahara as the "unexplored zone, the blank on the map."[70] Gautier does not stop here, however, going on to argue that Tanezrouft acted as a barrier for communication between North and sub-Saharan Africa.[71] In 1935, Captain Léon Lehuraux, who would later become an expert as well as a member of the Algerian Assembly,[72] depicted Tanezrouft as the land of choice for the "Saharan motorist," mentioning in passing its "absolute aridity."[73] According to Lehuraux, six-wheelers and vehicles on caterpillar tracks "waged an ardent, passionate, and moving" struggle in this space that had "neither fences nor spectators."[74] Nonetheless, Chevalier, the aforementioned French botanist, even attempted to start an experimental botanical garden in the area in 1931.[75] Gautier's powerful writings cemented the image of Tanezrouft, and the Sahara by extension, as a land of emptiness and death, a cliché that would particularly thrive in the 1950s when French bureaucrats, politicians, technicians, and army officers deployed it to justify the Sahara's economic *mise en valeur* and its corollary experimental enterprises.[76] Jacques Soustelle refers to Tanezrouft as "an entirely desertic expanse" that was forbidden to nomads.[77] Edmond Sergent, the director of the Pasteur Institute of Algeria, cites botanist and explorer Auguste Chevalier to emphasize that in Tanezrouft one only finds "some lizards and insects."[78]

This intellectual arsenal about Tanezrouft's desolation was already there for French military to exploit in defense of the French nuclear tests. During Ailleret's two stints in the desert in 1957, he found confirmation in a certain Commander Catignol's statement that the area south of Reggane was both "rigorously deserted" and easily accessible.[79] The legacy of Saharanism and its extended reach provided the atomic scouts with the rationale to justify a choice they had already made. Ailleret wrote that for those coming to Tanezrouft for the first time, the "most striking thing was the total, I say total, absence of animal or vegetal life."[80] In order to preemptively counter any arguments to the contrary, Ailleret made a comparison between Tanezrouft and Colomb-Béchar, where France had established the ultra-secret 3,728-mile test center for chemical and other weapons under the name B2-Namous.[81] B2-Namous, which remained under French control until 1978, was a desert, but one that had lizards, vipers, and some plants. Yet in Tanezrouft what "stunned us [Ailleret and his team] was that there was no trace of any form of life."[82] This absence of life, as defined by Ailleret, in this "desert within the desert" led him to conclude that his mission found "the ideal place to conduct nuclear explosions without posing any danger to the neighbors, since there were none."[83]

As Ailleret dealt with the Sahara, the reader cannot fail to notice how he embraced a desert mystique. He was himself a prophetic figure, abreast of the most cutting-edge military inventions, and his meetings with some of his fellow countrymen serving in the Sahara underlined the distinction between his modern temporality and their rustic life among the inhabitants of oases and desert hamlets. He sarcastically described the welcome he and his team received from the *saharien* officer in charge of the Bordj Etienne as "absolutely charming."[84] Ailleret had no qualms about the fact that his experimental Saharanism marked a new dawn for the desert. In this long passage, he explains how the nuclear enterprise radically differed from that of the soldiers and army officers who had policed the desert since the nineteenth century:

> During our reconnaissance mission, we encountered several officers who served as chiefs of posts of Saharan Affairs. In general, they were excellent officers with a great conscience and very devoted to their tasks of civil administration before all else. However, they appeared to us as very specialized in a way that is more than narrow in their Saharan problems and also, although they strove to promote a modern Sahara, they were attached to old methods, which were also outdated for the most part. The automobile and radiotelegraphy, and even the plane, which brought mail and provisions once or twice a week, were introduced into the desert, but these new processes were only used to facilitate the execution of old methods and not in order to promote new ones.[85]

Here, the proponent of the French nuclear age announced that experimental Saharanism required new skills from people who were not too immersed in the traditional desert way of life. As much as the Saharanist officers were representatives of the colonizing power, many of them remained loyal to the relationships they had built with Indigenous Saharans and their environment over the years. Whether out of romanticism or aversion, some *sahariens* espoused a notion of desert conservation, or rather musealization, which was antithetical to Ailleret's nuclear modernity. Because *sahariens*' "respectable traditions . . . have become old-fashioned,"[86] Ailleret decided that they were not fit for the experimental enterprise and hypermodern age it symbolizes. The atomic era reduced the desert into an irradiatable ground, but the nostalgic officers who had lived too long in the desert were not prepared for this sea change.

Once Ailleret had established the emptiness of the Sahara, French diplomacy championed the premises of experimental Saharanism, starting in 1959. Ailleret's short reconnaissance missions generated a truth that spread like wildfire in French and international venues in the years leading up to the explosion of Gerboise bleue in 1960. Moch, a former socialist minister, played the devil's advocate at the UN, defending not only France's right to own a bomb but also the legitimacy of its testing in the Sahara. Faced with arguments from Asian and African countries, Moch insisted, "[The] Sahara lends itself better to this experimentation because the site chosen for it is . . . deserted."[87] The first characteristic of experimental Saharanism this statement reveals is the disregard Moch had for the thousands of inhabitants in a string of oases who would be all affected by the nuclear fallout in the Sahara, admitting as much in his speech. Moch's impassioned defense of an explosion that he was aware would be detrimental to the entire biome contained a self-contradiction of experimental Saharanism and its own science. The second trait that can be discerned in Moch's speeches at the UN is the use of science to downplay the long-term effects of radiation.[88] Experimental Saharanism's logic was reflected in historian Dominique Mongin's reassertion of the qualifications of remoteness, expansiveness of territory, and ease of equipping the area.[89] In 1959, those engaged in French diplomacy used Saharanist tropes to mentally and emotionally prepare the world for their country's entry into the atomic club.

Although French nuclear experiments were probably the most mediatized atomic tests because of their imbrication in the emerging decolonial context in Africa and the ongoing war in Algeria, France only followed in the footsteps of its atomically endowed predecessors. During its operation between 1951 and 1992, the NTS's 1,375 square miles witnessed more than a thousand tests, which were conducted to gauge "the impact of nuclear weapons on man-made objects and structures, plants and animals, and the physical environment, and experimental testing in the search for possible peaceful uses."[90] Similarly, the Australian parliament's investigation of the effects of the British experiments in the country's southwestern desert starting in 1954 revealed the rationale behind the choice to have the test sites in Australia. When the British government failed to secure approval from the US to use the NTS, it approached Australia to find "a site which would be located either on a remote island or in a desert similar to the Nevada test range in the United States."[91] Interestingly, the Australian officer who drafted the report about the Montebello Islands used the same imagery typically evoked to describe deserts by insisting on the lack of potable water, the inhospitality of the space, and the absence of any infrastructure.[92] Jacob G. Warren states that Australia's and Britain's "nuclear authorities" displaced the Indigenous populations of Ooldea Mission to Yalata, emptying the desert "physically and conceptually."[93] Although the inquiry commission that Australia put in place in 1985 raised many questions about the dangers to which the Aboriginals were exposed,[94] its narrative accepted the premises of experimental Saharanism, which led to its focus on minimizing risks rather than on fully elucidating the impact on the actual desert spaces.

French proponents of experimental Saharanism were not, however, the sole stakeholders invested in the Sahara. Morocco, a country that considered much of the Oriental Desert annexed by France in the nineteenth century to be its territory, brought the issue of the French experiments to the UN General Assembly in 1959. Ahmed Taib Benhima, Morocco's representative at the UN, refuted the scientific and ethnographic validity of the French arguments, contesting how a "section of the press, about two years ago, described the Sahara as a gloomy and uninhabited desert."[95] Benhima went on to explain that the media campaign sought to "prepare minds in Africa and elsewhere to accept without difficulty and in due course first of the existence of guided missile bases and then of the testing in the Tanezrouft of the first French nuclear bomb."[96] While Tanezrouft was the linchpin of the French strategy to vacate the desert, Benhima focused on Reggane, which was, in his words, the "center of a great arc of valleys between southeast Morocco and Mzab, one of the most fertile oasis regions in the Sahara."[97] Reflecting this argument, the British newspaper *The Observer* reported that the "Atom City" France built in Hammoudia was "not in the center of a bleak desert" but rather in the middle of a department that had a population of two hundred thousand people.[98] These counterarguments made no difference in the minds of the French proponents of experimental Saharanism, for whom this bomb symbolized the success of "a purely national effort."[99] They were intent on using the discursively deadened land of the Sahara to prove the lethal power of their national creation.

Experimental Saharanism's Dark Geography

According to American geographer Trevor Paglen, the geography of testing in deserts is part of a larger and deeper "black world."[100] Paglen asserts that this black world is not solely about the secret communications, air traffic, and clandestine careers that connected the different sites, which all happened to be mainly in deserts, but also results from "the power to create these geographies, to create places where anything can happen, and to do it with impunity."[101] Experimental Saharanism thrives in the secret geography of isolated and inaccessible desert spaces. Ensured of their impunity, proponents of experimental Saharanism have no limits to what they may do in deserts. Much like other atomic states, France made a dark geography of the Sahara for its nuclear, ballistic, and chemical testing between 1957 and 1978.[102]

After the 1957 reconnaissance mission, the Commandement interarmées, which Ailleret chaired, set in motion a three-year process that culminated in the construction of the atomic city, where much of the known and still-unknown proceedings unfolded. France's largesse allowed the experimental Saharanists to turn discourse into reality, and, at the request of Prime Minister Guy Mollet, the French resident general in Algiers designated an area of 108,000 km^2 (41,699 square miles, which is equivalent to the state of Virginia or one-fifth the area of France) as a military zone.[103] Called Zone 42, this space was to host the Centre saharien d'expérimentations militaires (CSEM), which had been established for the purposes of all operations related to testing the French bomb. The construction of the atomic city required large-scale synergies between the army and civilian industry, including companies working in the fields of engineering and architecture and which lent their expertise to the military. Thus, experimental Saharanism cannot be seen as one field alone but rather as an interconnected series of industries that all built expertise from their work in the desert.

Describing what the French built in the Sahara as an "atomic city" is not an exaggeration. Between the summer of 1957 and January 1960, the city sprang up from the desert, defying both nature and history (Fig. 9). Comprising three sections that stretched over sixty kilometers, the atomic city had a living area called Reggane-Plateau, a military zone situated in Hammoudia, forty-five kilometers away, and a Ground Zero location in Tanezrouft, fifteen kilometers from Hammoudia and sixty kilometers from the Reggane-Plateau. All personnel with clearances had access to the living area, but only a limited number of scientists and technicians were allowed

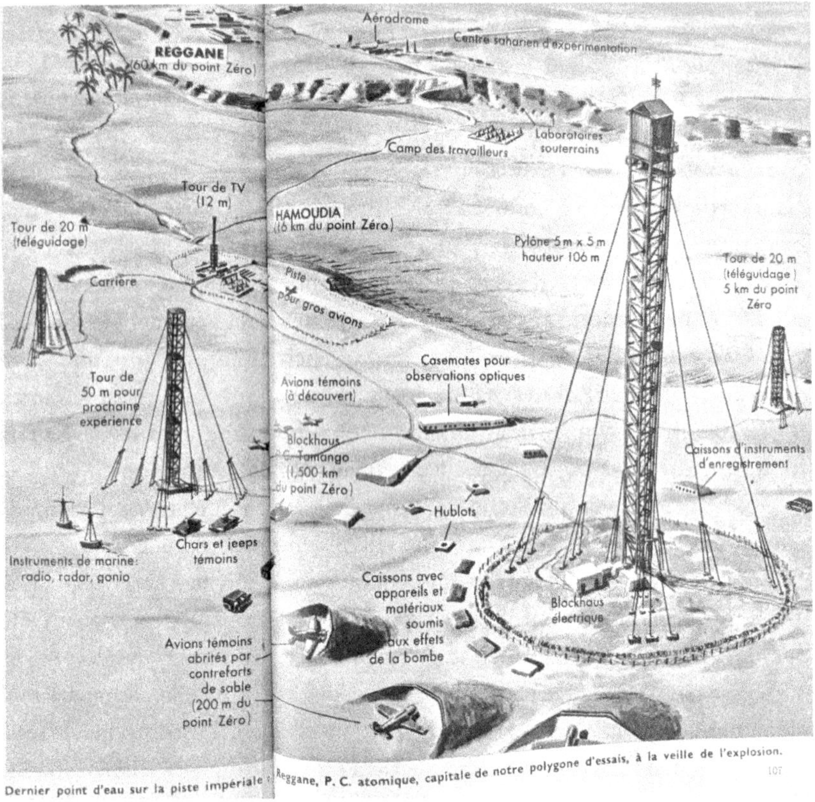

FIGURE 9. Sketch of the Atomic City in Reggane, from *Science et vie*, April 1960. Courtesy of *Science et vie*.

into Hammoudia and Ground Zero. The layout of these facilities and the strict security took into account the need to minimize personnel's exposure to radiation as well as the need to gather as much data about the experiment as possible.

The free land and abundant cash flow from the state expedited the construction of the atomic city. The Reggane base was made up of 175 buildings, including offices, dormitories, dining halls, a bakery, a modern hospital, and a swimming pool. Not only that, almost all the buildings were air-conditioned. The Reggane base was also the location of the airport as well as underground tunnels that served as laboratories and storage areas for scientific equipment. In Hammoudia, which was an advanced military post until 1957, the army built an airfield for planes and helicopters as well as a radar station. Ailleret and the important personnel tasked with observing the experiments had their headquarters in Hammoudia. Finally, Ground Zero consisted of a tower one hundred meters high where the bomb was placed and several underground bunkers of different sizes, which contained all the testing equipment to register the impact of the explosion. Two smaller towers contained cameras set to record the explosion. Ground Zero was also littered with a variety of military and household material, as well as animals that would be exposed to the atomic blast in order to test the effects of radiation.

Scientific exchanges with American colleagues influenced the French atomic city. Although the US government was prohibited by Congress, as a result of 1946 Atomic Energy Act, from sharing nuclear knowledge with other countries, the US had allowed French atomic experts to visit the NTS. They had also been invited on a mission called *Aurore* to visit the testing sites in Nevada and meet nuclear authorities in the US in 1958.[104] French scientists received help from their American colleagues to pursue their research, and American companies supplied them with radiation-detection monitors.[105] These military-scientific collaborations aside, the layout of the test site itself was influenced by the American NTS. Like their US counterparts, the French built a tower to detonate the bomb in order to reduce the atomic fallout. A. Constandina Titus wrote that the NTS saw the construction of "Doom Towns," which were "full-scale homes [that] were built and furnished with everything from brand-name foods in the refrigerator to current magazines on the coffee table" to test the impact of radiation on ordinary life.[106] Although there is no evidence that the French built any such towns in the Sahara, they did learn from their visits to the NTS how to position materials and instruments in ways that would allow them to achieve the results they needed. Instead of an artificial doom town *à l'américaine*, however, the entire Reggane area, which Ailleret kept referring to as "the desert of deserts,"[107] was the colonial doom town.

Although much of the discussion about the French experiments in the Sahara has centered on the four atmospheric experiments in Reggane and the thirteen underground ones in the Hoggar, what has been missing from scholarly treatment of these experiments is analysis of the logic and ideational apparatus that enabled these tests to take place the way they did. Delineating the transnational aspects of experimental Saharanism is crucial for understanding the transformation of deserts into incubators for discovery and testing of new technologies writ large. The construction and detonation of the atomic bomb in the Sahara was the culmination of a complex operation that brought together experts in areas far afield, such as engineering, architecture, armament, hydrology, and climatology, but who put national defense and technological prowess over the desert environment. Appraising his achievement after the explosion of the 70 kt Gerboise bleue, Ailleret admiringly wrote that this desert, "so scary in its natural form," had been made "inhabitable in its artificial form created by the hands and minds of mankind."[108] Long before the horrifying prospects of artificial intelligence and the possible realities it will enable, Ailleret demonstrated that experimental Saharanism could, if it so chose, obliterate humanity.

EXPERIMENTAL SAHARANISM INVISIBILIZES DESERTS

A common feature of scholarship on nuclear experiments is the omission of discussions about desert environments. Diverting attention from the space directly impacted by radiation has been the main way the atomic brand of experimental Saharanism has eluded attention since its violent iterations in the 1950s. The present section reveals how experimental Saharanism has invisibilized the environment throughout the course of debates about French experiments in the Sahara. Even as the discussions about banning nuclear experiments raged, deserts as receivers of the nuclear residue remained overshadowed partly due to a lack of conceptual frameworks that define the ideology that has undergirded the use of deserts for experimentation in the first place.

Rather than engaging with experimental Saharanism from within its own framework, a radical approach requires focusing on the former's effects on deserts per se. Atomic states have, indeed, the power to withhold archives from the public view, but they are not able to silence deserts, which act as un-archives that disclose the scars of the myriad experimental enterprises that were forced upon them.[109] Although archives may contain a large portion of truth about the actions of states in deserts, one has to also contend with the fact they collected this information to serve their own internal purposes. Therefore, the desert biome, including human inhabitants, should remain the main archive for how experimental endeavors have impacted desert ecosystems. Even if the French archives of the nuclear experiments were to be fully and unrestrictedly accessible, they can no longer account for sixty years of the tests' legacy on the Sahara and its populations. Thus, it is important to return to deserts themselves in order to recover experiences of survivors and environmental evidence to understand the scale of experimental Saharanism. This said, experimenting entities' archives are crucial for the reconstruction of experimental Saharanism's genealogies and the extensions of the system of ideas at work in its continuity.

The discussions that unfolded throughout 1959 reflect the invisibilization of desert environments. The Sahara was most often not the focus of the UN and other international organizations because the member-state ambassadors used an anthropocentric approach to emphasize how the French nuclear tests were going to hurt all humanity. V. K. Krishna Menon of India gave a steadfast, well-argued speech against the experiments, but the impact on the desert was omitted from his compelling statements. Other than a few reminders about the populated and oasis areas of the Sahara, Menon declared, "Any explosion of this kind, anything that leads to more ionizing radiation, is harmful to the people around, to those who are handling it, and to the world as a whole."[110] Similarly, the experiments elicited a great deal of anger from individual nations as well as regional and transnational bodies. Tawia Adamafio, the secretary general of the People's Party of Ghana, gave an incendiary speech in September 1960 to an audience in Accra against the ongoing French experiments. Like his predecessors at the UN, Adamafio condemned France's "nuclear imperialism" and how it was "desecrating the African soil with nuclear explosions," but the Sahara, where the experiments were happening, was reduced to the "soil of mother Africa," and the impact of the tests was conceptualized as "endangering the health, life, security and prosperity of the African peoples and of mankind."[111] The desert as the main environment in which atomic warfare was unfolding was buried in discussions about geostrategy, ethics, and even the legality of atomic weapons. The desert was simply a launchpad for doctrinal opposition to nuclear weapons for the sake of humanity.

This anthropocentric response to the anthropogenic threat of nuclear annihilation suited experimental Saharanism. As long as the rehabilitation of deserts was not the main issue, its proponents could always argue that experimentation could happen in safer conditions in even more remote and more deserted areas. A radical departure from this commonplace scenario requires a desert-centric approach that adduces desert biomes as the main reason to oppose testing in deserts. Then and only then would deserts no longer be treated as containers in which life happens to exist but rather as living organisms that are nurturing in their own terms. Experimental

Saharanism has been able to circumvent this factor because human safety has always been put forward as the primary driver behind the choice of deserts for experimentation. However, this is not an either-or issue. At its core, this is a fundamental question about how the planet Earth has been overly exploited, mistreated, and polluted to accommodate this unsustainable anthropocentric conception of life.

The scientists who participate in experimental Saharanism treat deserts as though they were nonexistent entities. Scientists seem to actively avoid desert spaces in their accounts, as though any attention they may pay to the physical terrain would bring out their liveliness and complicate the scientists' tasks. Hence, experimental science focuses on results, graphs, sensory tools, and data, all of which remove the scientists from the reality of the desert. For instance, the words *desert* and *deserted,* as well as *environment,* were mentioned only twice each in very technical terms in *One World or None,* the 1946 book written by several scientists who contributed to the Manhattan Project in order to draw attention to the dangers of atomic weapons.[112] Yves Rocard, one of the few civilian scientists to collaborate with the CEA, recounts his observations in Reggane before and after the explosion of Gerboise bleue in *Mémoires sans concessions.* Rocard provides many details about measurements, seismic movements, and earth tremors registered miles away from Ground Zero, but had very little to say about the desert itself.[113] He could have been anywhere, and the same observation applies to the period he spent working in atolls of the Pacific Ocean. Likewise, *Oppenheimer* offers a journey into the genesis and execution of the American nuclear bomb but fails to depict the desert in any meaningful way.

There is a crucial difference between the handling of the island-based nuclear experiments and the ones that were carried out in deserts. Both the US and Britain used the Bikini Islands in the South Pacific and the Montebello Islands in Australia, respectively, to test their bombs. However, Australia, which was joined later by New Zealand and Fiji, brought a case at the International Court of Justice (ICJ) against France's experiments in the Pacific in 1973. In its written argument to the ICJ, the Australian government emphasized the injurious impact that the fallout would have on Australia, stating that the "interference with ships and aircraft on the high seas and in the superjacent airspace, and the pollution of the high seas by radio-active fall-out, constitute infringements of the freedom of the high seas."[114] Interestingly, the environment and sea life, as well as cargo ships and fishermen, became quite central to this case, and the main question was whether France's tests were harmful to Australians and New Zealanders.[115] Even before Australia used this rationale, the Asian-African Legal Consultative Committee had heard a similar argument from the representative of the United Arab Republic (UAR) in 1961, within the context of rallying against French experiments in the Sahara. The UAR's representative argued for the illegality of thermonuclear experiments primarily because of the indiscriminate "destruction of life and property."[116] The UAR representative also drew on international maritime law, which prohibits nuclear tests on the high seas for reasons linked to interference with the flow of air and sea navigation.[117] Although the Sahara was the direct reason the Asian-African Legal Consultative Committee was asked to stipulate the illegality of nuclear tests, the UAR's argument focused on the sea instead of the desert.

The concentration on the sea relied on a jurisprudence regarding maritime navigation and seafaring. Deserts' economic importance in fact declined as a result of the development of seafaring and its technologies. The Sahara, for example, lost its primary role as a commercial connector between North and sub-Saharan Africa when European powers succeeded in reorienting trade routes from the Sahara to the Atlantic Ocean. The result was more trade activity on the ocean and less and less use of the desert routes in commerce. This widespread use of oceanic shipping meant the Sahara was not involved in legal cases that would have had the same jurisprudential impact as maritime ones. For instance, the story of the three British seamen who murdered and ate their cabin boy in 1884 aboard their vessel, the *Mignonette*, on their way to Australia left its imprint on legal doctrine.[118] Two of the men were found guilty of murder, and their case outlawed the practice of "the custom of the sea," which allowed seafarers to draw lots and decide who should be eaten by the others to survive.[119] Although there has been much speculation about the case, one important aspect was the justice system's desire "to resist the harsher implications of Social Darwinism."[120] Since deserts had lost their importance for trade, they could only be useful if they filled that gap and accommodated extraction and experimentation.

Just a few decades before the decision that outlawed killing at sea for whatever reason, General Aimable Pélissier led his famous *enfumades* (fumigations) in Dahra in 1845, and seven years later the siege of Laghouat happened in 1852.[121] The bloody scenes which Eugène Fromentin documents in *Un été dans le Sahara* are sufficient to support the idea that deserts elicited unbounded violence,[122] a notion that Benjamin Brower points out in stating,

"French military leaders and politicians considered such attacks against defenseless populations as a necessary step to achieve victory and peace. Such individuals claimed that the cruelty of these encounters was a normal feature of armed conflict in Algeria. This led to horrifying events like the 'enfumades' at Dahra (1845) and helped mitigate the controversy afterwards, shielding its perpetrators from political repercussions and allowing them to continue their grisly work."[123] The British legal system, on the one hand, protected the sea, while the French colonial system in Algeria, on the other hand, legitimized violence in the desert. As a result, there is no transnational desert jurisprudence that matches the maritime one. Local jurisprudence exists in the desert laws and customs, which operate internally, but they have not garnered any international enforceability.

Racism is another way experimental enterprises have camouflaged their impact on the biomes targeted. Oscar Temaru, a pro-independence politician from Polynesia, made a powerful statement about the French nuclear tests on the islands in 2017. Temaru noted that France had continued its nuclear experiments in Polynesia, instead of metropolitan France and Corsica, because of what he called "a form of nuclear racism."[124] Much is, of course, known about the coalescence of science, colonialism, and racism that led to myriad forms of experimentation on people of color without their consent.[125] This racialization extended to territories, some of which were more likely than others to be chosen for experimental projects. Inner cities, poor neighborhoods, Indigenous lands, deserts, and islands belong to the territories impacted by scientific racism. However, "nuclear racism" is even clearer among Indigenous communities whose territories have been constantly used for proving deadly products. Hence, the US used Native American territories to conduct its tests, while Great Britain and Australia agreed to use Aboriginal peoples' land to test the British bomb. France chose the Sahara, south of Algeria, which did not enjoy its own sovereignty, to conduct its tests. In adding nuclear racism to the already abundant terminology about nuclear testing, Temaru reorients attention to the form of racism that targets both environments and the humans living in them that are constructed as disposable.

It is not far-fetched to say that the detonation of Gerboise bleue and subsequent atomic bombs in the Sahara was also the result of colonial racism. French colonies, including Algeria, were racially hierarchized structures, where Europeans were at the top of the pyramidal system. While the Décret Crémieux of 1870 granted French citizenship to native Jews, spurring their gradual Westernization and incorporation into French society, the majority of Imazighen and Arabs (meaning Muslims, specifically) were kept under the notorious Code de l'indigénat.[126] The Sahara has been home to the Tuaregs, Blacks, and mixed populations that French geographers, ethnographers, and military officers have written about amply. The Tuareg, particularly, occupied a central location in this discourse. Hailed as chivalrous and honorable people, particularly thanks to the work of Henri Duveyrier,[127] the Tuareg were demonized and vilified as ruthless barbarians after they decimated Lieutenant Paul Flatters' mission in 1881. Their resistance to occupation changed their status from that of a free and trustworthy people to criminals given to banditry and high criminality, as was exemplified by the mythified Medaganat.[128] Thus, the conflictual relationship between the Tuareg and France cannot be overlooked as a possible explanation for the military's choice of their homeland for its experimentation.

French military officials' racism vis-à-vis the Indigenous people of the Sahara was not even subtle as they celebrated their groundbreaking achievement. The hyper-scientific atomic age was contrasted with the folkloric outlook of the natives, cast in primitivistic terms. Ailleret, for instance, writes that racialized Populations laborieuses du Bas-Touat (PLBT) "introduced to the American-style work site, which was endowed with powerful and well-managed resources, a stunning note of romanticism and folklore."[129] This observation establishes a light-years–wide temporal gap between Ailleret's teams and the PLBT who were still leading a life that was thousands of years behind. Differences in temporality are intrinsic to racism's weaponization of difference. Antoine Schwere, a CEA executive, insinuated that Saharan populations were malnourished, mentally retarded, and physically weak.[130] This racializing is manifested in Schwere's definition of a PLBT as someone "of Arab origins, but [who] also had black blood and some drops of Berber blood."[131] André Bendjebbar, a military historian, later reproduced this racism in his *Histoire secrète de la bombe atomique française*, in which he makes the stunning statement that the French experimenters found "prehistoric" people in the Sahara.[132] However, understood within what historian Muriam Haleh Davis subsumes under the prevalent "racial capitalism" under which "human difference determined which kinds of bodies would be subjected to extraction, violence, and legal exception,"[133] these dehumanizing views of PLBT and the Populations laborieuses des oasis (PLO) belong to a larger grammar that relies on a system of ideas that continues to discard human equality. Hence, French scientists and military personnel could declare their enterprise safe, regardless of the fact that Saharans called 1960 *ʿām al-suʿāl* (the year of tuberculosis), *ʿām al-maraḍ* (the year of illness), and even *ʿām al-wafayāt* (the year of deaths).[134]

EXPERIMENTAL SAHARANISM AND THE POLITICS OF DEFLECTION

As if racialization were not enough, the proponents of experimental Saharanism have demonstrated their adeptness at the politics of deflection, by which I mean the skill to direct attention to another, less controversial topic. The clearest examples in this regard are carmaker Berliet's two missions, which were dubbed Mission Berliet Ténéré and Mission Berliet Tchad and carried out in 1959 and 1960, respectively. The two missions were cross-country automotive treks undertaken to test the hardiness and navigational capacity of the French auto manufacturer's vehicles. Authorized by the governor of Algeria, these two missions evoked the nineteenth-century attempts to scout a route for the trans-Saharan railway. The difference, however, was that the French authorities needed the information culled by the nineteenth-century missions to dominate the Sahara, which had remained beyond France's control in 1900, whereas the coincidence of Berliet's operations in 1959 and 1960 with the controversies around atomic testing raises questions about their purpose. There is room to think that they were part of a public relations effort to refocus public attention on the Sahara outside the Reggane area.

In *L'Afrique de Berliet*, historian Mériem Khellas unearths the history of the carmaker in Algeria and the place the Sahara occupied in its business strategy. Khellas has captured the imbrication of military conquest and commercial colonization with the construction of roads in Algeria.[135] Indeed, the establishment of Berliet's first subsidiary in Algeria in 1908 took place within a larger context of cooperation between the army and the colony's business community.[136] The army was one of Berliet's main customers, and the former's requests incentivized the construction of "faster and better-performing vehicles."[137] However, Berliet was not solely a provider of military material, since it also played a major role in the search for and exploitation of oil and gas in the Algerian south. In serving the military and the oil industry, Berliet designed new types of trucks that would carry heavy loads across desert terrains.[138] As Khellas rightly observes, the Sahara was a testing ground for the "development of novel innovative products adaptable to the significant geographic constraints."[139] Berliet thus directed its research capabilities to construct vehicles that would optimize their clients' endeavors in the Sahara.

The Sahara also served to promote new products and startups, as was the case with André Citroën's company, which was established in 1919. Using government funds earmarked for the conquest of the Sahara, Citroën enlisted the services of engineer Adolphe Kégresse, who, as chauffeur for Czar Nicholas II, had developed a solution for cars in snow.[140] In 1921, the Citroën *auto-chenilles*, or half-track, was revealed, providing potential solutions for vehicles to be used on agricultural lands and in inaccessible areas. When Kégresse's car crossed from In Salah in Algeria to Timbuktu in the Sudan on Christmas Eve in 1922, it marked the first successful motorized crossing of the Sahara without any casualties. Citroën, empowered by this success, organized two missions named *Croisière noire* (the black expedition) for Africa and *Croisière jaune* (the yellow expedition) for Asia in 1924. These missions paraded the carmaker's products and connected businesspeople in France to the colonies, creating "traditions of patronage" from which Berliet benefited in its own missions.[141] In addition to the automobile industry, Citroën had a vision for Saharan tourism manifested in his hotel "Le Territoire," which he had built in 1929 to host the king of Belgium.[142] French politician Louis Castex commented that he was "an energetic and audacious man who had guessed the desert's resources; a mover and shaker whom the French industry misses so much today."[143]

By the time Berliet launched its first mission, it already had a blueprint to ensure its success. However, the mission took place at a time when France was at the vortex of global antinuclear campaigns because of its upcoming atomic tests and the raging Algerian War of Independence. Mission Ténéré Tchad started from Ouargla in November 1959 and crossed Djanet into Fort Lamy (the current N'Djamena) before returning to Ouargla in January 1960.[144] The second mission departed from Ouargla with the stated aim of finding a better way to reach Chad and lasted from October 29 to December 9, 1960. Both missions were organized in tight collaboration with military and civilian authorities in France and Algeria. General Édouard Laurent (1896–1972), a member of the armed forces, led the first mission. Participating institutions included the Bardo Museum, the National Scientific Research Center, the French Institute of Black Africa in Dakar, the Institute of Saharan Studies, and the OCRS. Even Soustelle was present when the mission started on

FIGURE 10. Berliet truck, Mission Ténéré Tchad. Courtesy of Archives Fondation Berliet–Lyon / France, www.fondationberliet.org.

November 8, 1959. In the words of Roger Frison-Roche, this was "sufficient to immerse the participants in the grandeur and difficulty of the tasks that fell to them."[145] The mission is evoked in proud terms, and Henri Lhote, one of the scientists, is described as an "intrepid Saharanist," while Maurice Berliet himself is referred to as "a seasoned Saharanist."[146] Frison-Roche even evoked the 1898 Foureau-Lamy Mission, which left Ouargla with 1,000 camels to reach Chad, thereby implying that there were historical continuities between these trans-Saharan missions.[147]

Two voluminous books and several articles and films were made about the Berliet missions.[148] Despite the rich information they contain about Saharan geography, geology, routes, populations, and history, the books are an exemplar of the collaboration between private companies and officials to enhance scientific knowledge of the desert and find a direct commercial route that would link North and sub-Saharan Africa.[149] At this juncture, a truck could replace a ship for trade between the different countries of the reshuffled France-Afrique. Berliet also proved the mettle of its Gazelle trucks in the Sahara (Fig. 10). Equipped with six wheels, a Magic engine, and five different speeds, Gazelles could "pass through practically anywhere."[150] In addition to celebrating them as a solution for problems of provisions for long-distance travel in the desert, the literature from this period highlights the entirety of this enterprise as a sign of French development even as the twilight of the French colonial empire was drawing near.

Everything that surrounded the Berliet mission reveals that the publicity was a camouflaging strategy. Retrospectively, the announced goals and rhetoric clearly indicate that its objective was far more complex than simply opening a faster route across the desert between the two parts of Africa. The other goal was to open a breach in the wall of public opinion opposed to the proliferation of nuclear weapons by foregrounding France's humanitarianism even as it was preparing for the atomic tests. Curiously, the books published about these missions were resoundingly silent on the nuclear experiments.

EXPERIMENTAL SAHARANISM AND HYPOTHECATING DESERT FUTURES

Algerian scholarship has grappled with the legacy of French experimental Saharanism for several decades now. In 2000, Al-Markaz al-waṭanī li-al-dirāsāt wa-al-baḥth fī al-ḥaraka al-waṭaniyya wa thawrat awwal nuvambr 1954 (The National Center for Research on the National Movement and the Revolution of November 1, 1954) published an important book entitled *al-Tajārib al-nawawiyya al-faransiyya fī al-jazā'ir: Dirāsāt wa buḥūth wa shahādāt* (*The French Nuclear Experiments in Algeria: Examinations, Studies, and Testimonies*).[151] The result of seminars and testimonials organized by the center, the book clearly states that reckoning with French experiments in the Sahara requires "discussing the entirety of health and environmental consequences that resulted from them, in addition to issues of radioactive pollution and nuclear waste."[152] The book underlines the fact that the legacy of nuclear and radioactive residues defies closure, which in turn requires approaches that combine scientific, legal, and humanistic expertise.

The impossibility of closure does not mean that efforts to document experimental Saharanism's impacts are futile. In fact, Algerian scholars have routinely probed the effects of France's atomic experiments despite a report by the International Atomic Energy Agency (IAEA) that concluded there were no dangerous residues in most of the area that witnessed experiments and made any protective intervention in the "Gerboise Bleue, Gerboise Blanche and E2 tunnel sites" contingent on its use for development and human activity.[153] A contribution to the edited volume entitled "The French Nuclear Experiments and Their Lasting Impact" traces the history of France's nuclear obsession and attends to its impact on humans against the background of French assurances of the safety and cleanliness of the tests.[154] Enumerating the various ways in which the people of Sahara were impacted, the chapter lists blindness, miscarriages in both humans and animals, internal hemorrhaging, and death. The aforementioned Antoine Schwere recorded how the mouflon was exterminated in Tan Afella because of the atomic explosion.[155] The long-term effects were the appearance of medical issues that the populations had not seen before, including stillbirths, deformities from genetic mutations, and sterility.[156] Research has also shown that the "inhalation and ingestion of contaminated particles (dust), for both underground and atmospheric nuclear tests" were the main pathways of contamination.[157] Scholars Ghitaoui Abdelkader and Bahmaoui El Cherif have situated the deaths resulting from radioactivity between 30,000 and 42,000, without counting the ongoing contamination in the region.[158] Libyan scholar Muḥammad Saʿīd al-Qashshāṭ, who was a witness to the aftermath of the French experiments in the 1960s, has written that during a visit to the Algerian Sahara between 1972 and 1973, he "learned that the bomb killed many Arab Sahrawi citizens and that that Sahrawis call that year the year of *al-kuḥḥa* or the year of coughing because radiation impacted children and the elderly and killed many of them."[159] Although incomplete or based on hearsay or flawed estimations, this engagement with the legacy of experimental Saharanism demonstrates that local people have indeed kept alive the everlasting impact the experiments have had on the life of the desert biome.

Time has also proven that the media content produced by French experimental Saharanists was full of deception. French officials used media outlets and their political might to entrench the ideas that the part of the Sahara chosen for the experiments was lifeless. However, sixty years later, Algerian scholars have revealed that the experiments had a deep impact on the arable land and palm trees.[160] The desert was not deserted, but the French experiments desertified it by exterminating the crops that ordinarily grew in the area where experiments took place.[161] French philosopher Jacques Ellul refers to a study that captures the impact of the use of chemical waste in the Sahara on palm trees, which in turn accelerated the impoverishment of the Saharan populations.[162] This devastating impact was not only attributed to the atmospheric tests but also to the irradiation of water. Crops, humans, and animals alike imbibed the radioactive water.[163]

All this continues to happen while France's deadly legacy of atomic waste is entombed in the Sahara. Thousands, if not millions, of tons of contaminated material has turned the Sahara into a source of emergent radiation, continuing to spew death among inhabitants and their sources of livelihood. Danielle Endres defines "nuclear colonialism" as "a form of environmental injustice that works at the intersection of settler colonialism and nuclearism and has disastrous effects for Indigenous Lands, peoples, and nations."[164] Anecdotally, Ailleret expressed his desire to leave Reggane immediately after the explosion of the Gerboise bleue, although he was instructed to supervise a second experiment before he was finally allowed to take up his new position in northern Algeria. While the French soldiers and technicians were able to leave the Sahara and return home, bringing with them their own share of contamination,[165] the Saharans who called the desert home have since suffered from the legacy of nuclear colonialism.

CONCLUSION

Building on Saharanism's earlier construction of deserts as empty, dead, and uninhabited spaces, this chapter has defined the myriad aspects of experimental Saharanism. The chapter showed that deserts have been placed outside the realm of life through notions of emptiness and uninhabited-ness. Because of their constructed desolation, they were forced open for experimental Saharanism's enterprises. Thus, deserts became dark spaces for violent technological imaginations. Although the chapter has focused specifically on the testing of technologies that have lethal effects on desert environments and their inhabitants, experimental Saharanism is a far more substantial subcategory of Saharanism that has affected and will continue to affect the integrity of the desert ecosystems for centuries to come.

The projects this chapter has subsumed under the category of experimental Saharanism cover a wide range, including farming projects that exhaust aquifers, solar energy installations that take up thousands of acres of land, and test sites for unsafe technologies or harmful products. However, not all of these projects have the same consequences for desert biomes. Some are more dangerous than others, but none of them could surpass the dangers that emerged from the rush toward nuclear experimentation after the US built and used the first atomic bomb. Since 1945, the testing of bombs, rockets, and space exploration technologies have dominated desert news. The radical novelty and destructiveness of atomic weapons was a sign of both mastery of technology and scientific advancement. Hence, for some states, including France, attaining national grandeur and proving scientific progress meant participating in an unbridled race for the nuclear bomb. The race played out on deserts, drawing on Saharanism's long, trans-desert legacies, which continue to be adduced to justify the unjustifiable that has unfolded in deserts.

FOUR

Sexual Saharanism

TRANSGRESSION AND IMPUNITY IN THE DESERT

ANDRÉ GIDE (1869–1951) made his second trip to Algeria in 1895. While checking out of the Grand Hôtel d'Orient in Blida before catching the train to Biskra, he glimpsed the names of Oscar Wilde and his lover, Lord Alfred Douglas, on the blackboard listing the hotel's guests. Wilde's notorious reputation and legal troubles in England had preceded his Algerian trip, and Gide's initial impulse was to leave the hotel furtively in order to distance himself from Wilde, whom he had met for the first time in Paris in 1891.[1] Gide surreptitiously erased his name from the slate and made his way to the train station, but, feeling guilty, decided to return to the hotel for fear that Wilde might have already seen his name on the public guest log. Reflecting on the reason for his behavior, Gide wrote, "spending time with Wilde meant putting yourself in a compromising position."[2] However, shame brought him back to meet Wilde and Douglas. That fateful reversal of his trajectory has since become a key moment in the way his story has been told and retold for more than a hundred years.

Once all three of them returned to Algiers, Douglas left Wilde and Gide in the city and took off to Biskra, "seduced" by Gide's descriptions of his experience in the oasis.[3] Douglas stopped in Blida to find Ali, an adolescent *caouadji* (coffee server) he had met there, in order to elope with him to Biskra. Douglas's escape to the Sahara left Gide under Wilde's supreme influence, which was to forever impact how he was read, discussed, and remembered. Although this was not the first time Gide had engaged in pedophilia or homosexual activities, the sojourn with Wilde in Algiers confirmed his pedophilic and homoerotic penchants. As he relates in his autobiography *Si le grain ne meurt* (*If It Die . . .*), Gide had expressed his admiration for a boy named Ceci, whom he and Paul Laurens took as a guide during their stay in

Sousse in Tunisia in 1893. However, while Gide did not act on his desire for Ceci, he did later with another boy, named Ali.[4] Gide consigned his sexual adventure in the Sahara to the novel *L'immoraliste*, which fictionalized his experiences during his visits to North Africa.

More than a hundred years later, in 2006, famed Australian writer and literary critic Robert Dessaix was in Algeria following in Gide's footsteps. During an interview with the Algerian newspaper *Liberté* about a Gide-inspired autobiography he was writing, Dessaix was asked directly about the French novelist's pedophilic activities. Not only did Dessaix dismiss the ethical ramifications of the question, but he also made the bold and insensitive declaration that pedophilia was not frowned upon during the time that Gide was in Algeria. Dessaix went even further, absolving Gide and his ilk of their sexual crimes by stating that Gide "behaved [with children] like a gentleman."[5] Clearly scandalized by this provocative statement, Samir Benmalek, the Algerian journalist who conducted the interview, reminded Dessaix that what the latter was really invested in was not Gide's sexual life in the colony but rather his newfound liberty.[6] For Dessaix, Gide was the epitome of counterculture, self-discovery, and transgression, which blinded him to the fact that Gide's self-liberation and fulfillment took a toll on Algerian children. Gide's actions in the desert and Dessaix's continued defense of his demigod, even a century after the fact, is a testament to the continued persistence of what I propose to call, beyond any moralistic judgment of nonheteronormativity, "sexual Saharanism."

Gide's and Wilde's pedophilic practices in Tamazgha are only a small fraction of a colossal, underground sexual phenomenon. In 2021, French American essayist and well-regarded intellectual Guy Sorman made some devastating revelations about Michel Foucault's sexual life in the Tunisian city of Sidi Bou Said, where he was offered his first academic job in the 1960s. Sorman told television channel *France 5* that he "witnessed what Foucault did with young children in Tunisia . . . ignoble things. The possibility of consent could not be sought. These were things of extreme moral ugliness."[7] Haytham Guesmi, the Tunisian academic who wrote about this story for *Al Jazeera*, pointed out the power dynamics involved in these revelations, which, he predicted, "will likely be swept under the carpet without much debate."[8] Indeed, the story did not receive much attention, and academics and journalists have since continued their ordinary discussion, citation, and teaching of Foucault's work without much care for the ethical ramifications of Sorman's bombshell. This amnesic attitude is the continuation of the historical disregard for and racialization of colonized people. During a talk I gave at an Ivy League institution in the Boston area about Gide's sexual Saharanism in *L'immoraliste*, two white scholars pushed back against my conclusions, one arguing that the novel was "about gardens and flowers," while the other quipped dismissively that my reading of Gide was "a nice twist." Both responses seemed to reject any ethical take on Gide's much-celebrated route to self-liberation, even though Gide himself did not shy away from admitting that he had sexual relationships with underage children in the Tamazghan French colonies.[9] The attitudes of Gide's defenders mean that spaces that are considered peripheral to the center of power, of which deserts constitute an important part, continue to be conceived of and acted upon as lawless margins of civilization.

TOWARD A DEFINITION OF SEXUAL SAHARANISM

Sexual Saharanism, as I define it, requires a distinction between it as a practice that emanates from and goes hand in hand with an ideological position of power and privilege, and romantic or frivolous incursions into the "heterotopic" space of the desert by couples who want to experience their sexuality in a different landscape.[10] Sexual Saharanism captures both the ideational processes and the practices that have established deserts as havens for sexual experimentation and sex-related violence. Sexual Saharanism cannot be dissociated from "the colonizer's dormant desires and his repressed racism," which has constructed desert people as primitives, dominated by "instincts and frivolities."[11] Arab literary critic Joseph Massad has emphasized, in his critical reading of Hanan al-Shaykh's novel *Misk al-ghazāl* (*The Deer's Musk*), that "civilization in the novel seems to be a time and place when and where natural desires prosper while primitivism [in the desert] is a time and place when and where unnatural desires prosper."[12] Hence, sexual Saharanism refers to the different ways in which deserts have been imagined and acted upon as spaces outside the realm of ethics and legality that are foundational to organized society. Through a mixture of discursive strategies that center self-discovery and anti-conformism, sexual Saharanism has evolved into an imaginary in which deserts are constructed as ideal places for exploring desires—including, but not limited to, fetishes—in a way that is limitless, both in the material and ethical sense, and with a quasi-guaranteed impunity. Sexual Saharanism symbolizes the desertion of ethics, law, and morality when it comes to engaging in criminalizing actions in deserts. Building on deserts' so-called emptiness and timelessness, sexual Saharanism upholds both the imagination that sustains this sexualized perception of deserts and the actions that treat them as ideal places for countercultural transgressions. Due to various constraints, much of the activity of sexual Saharanism's practitioners will elude scholarly examination, but it is high time that the scholarly *desertion of* the ethical questions that have arisen from these actions is critiqued, because it has allowed this imaginary to persist and infiltrate much scholarship about sexual liberation.

There is no doubt that sex and sexuality have always been central to transgression.[13] The body particularly is the locus of the struggles between conformists and nonconformists, who each want to see their antithetical values reflected in both physical and social bodies. The pedophilia that played out in the Sahara during the colonial era was one of the ways in which those involved in sexual Saharanism enacted their vision of bodily liberation as a form of countercultural rebellion against the social norms of their time.[14] However, Saharanism's success at establishing the desert as a territory to which normative ethics and morality do not apply has overshadowed the troubling ethical dimensions of this counterculture's treatment of deserts as places for guaranteed impunity. A double standard was at work whereby the criminalization of pedophilia in Europe, which placed such abuses outside any countercultural or nonconformist ethos, met with no reprehension from the same European artists, intellectuals, and writers who flocked to the Sahara to engage in that same taboo sexual practice. This said, the ideas and the actions that I subsume under the notion of sexual Saharanism are broader than pedophilia alone, and they include all forms of prostitution as well as pornographic reportage—whether in popular magazines, newspapers, or literary and artistic works—that commends, raves about, and conveys hyperbolic ideas about sex and sexuality in deserts.

Sexual Saharanism has taken different shapes and forms, but its main constant feature is the centrality of the desert as a haven for the fulfillment of carnal desires. The enthusiasm about sex in the desert is conveyed by British travel writer Geoff Nicholson in his sardonic statement that he "liked the idea of making love to a woman in the desert."[15] Albeit radically different from each other, variants of sexual Saharanism were or have been at work in the major European figures' rush into the desert in the early twentieth century; in the orgiastic image of Las Vegas; and in the self-branded countercultural Burning Man festival in Black Rock City, Nevada. That deserts are theaters for imaginaries and acts of moral or social transgression is inscribed in politics of representation, as historian Julia Clancy-Smith has noted about Algeria,[16] and in a politics of social rebellion that seeks to undermine the status quo. Be that as it may, sexual Saharanism is undergirded by and disseminated through countless articles, novels,[17] photographs, magazine stories, and new media. The colonial obsession with the women of the Awlād Nāyl (also written Ouled Naïl or Ouled-Naïl, depending on the source), whom Egyptian explorer Mohammed Thabet called "desert Geishas,"[18] was also imbricated in an us-versus-them colonial agenda in which the degenerate status of the Arab woman proved their inability to be assimilated.[19] The intense focus on the Nāyliyyāt (Ouled Naïl women) is the clearest evidence of sexual Saharanism's ability to instrumentalize difference to both abet and justify what now appears to be a legacy of sexual violence in the desert.

The Burning Man festival is the modern global manifestation of sexual Saharanism and the continuity of its underlying ideas into the twenty-first century. An annual gathering that started on the beach of San Francisco in 1986, this festival has since 1991 found a home in Black Rock City in the Sonoran Desert, accommodating ever-increasing numbers of revelers—as of late, it has drawn crowds of nearly one hundred thousand. The festival's literature as well as the countless online materials produced by its participants reveal how the desert space serves as a haven for myriad unbridled types of body-centered experimentation. Highlighted as a gathering where everyone is "pushing their boundaries and feeling their bliss,"[20] Burning Man has built its image as a countercultural hub, the aficionados of which resist what they call the "Default World," governed by the rules of capitalism, which subdues humanity to governmental and corporate power.[21] Like the decadence movement in the nineteenth and twentieth centuries, the body is central to Burning Man's rejection of norms, which celebrates participants' desires "with almost no regulations or limitations."[22] This supposed absence of rules is only a rhetorical illusion, since Burning Man is patrolled and anyone who violates the laws regulating drug use, sex in public, or any other criminalized acts under US law risks being charged.[23] Nevertheless, the festival has to sustain the myth of lawlessness to fully live up to the desert imagination underlying the enterprise.

This insinuation of absolute freedom in Nevada is another manifestation of the Saharanism-infused misconception that one acts with utter autonomy in deserts. Hence, this illusory promise of absolute liberty emanates not from the absence of laws and regulations, but rather is a metaphorical freedom that is afforded them by the fact of being in the desertic space. The well-known phrase "what happens in Vegas stays in Vegas" encapsulates this construction of the festival's desert location as a consequence-free container for almost any transgressive desire. Although some scholars have already emphasized how the festival is a combination of contrasts between the beauty of humanity and its "immorality and some [of its] darkest aspects,"[24] this chapter does not set out to judge what revelers do but rather to comprehend how the venue itself is viewed as a moral *terra nullius* that escapes the restrictive order experienced in ordinary life in urban areas. Exploring the meanings that the festival has taken on in the revelers' imaginations after it moved to Nevada will shed light on the ideational continuities that exist between Burning Man and sexual Saharanism. Relocating the festival's annual meeting point to Black Rock City was meant to accommodate its thousands of revelers, but the move can also be interpreted as enactment of the notion that the desert has the capacity, in both the literal and metaphorical senses, to absorb that which is not to be known and to absolve revelers of any moral guilt that might result from their transgressions.

Theoretical articulations of deserts as an ideal space for unbridled exploration and self-assertion have undergirded sexual Saharanism. For instance, in his discussion of identity between modernism and postmodernism, Zygmunt Bauman has argued that the desert was "a land not yet sliced into places, and for that reason it was the land for self-creation," conceptualizing it, in the meantime, as "the archetype and the greenhouse of the raw, bare, primal and bottom-line freedom."[25] Bauman comments on Edmond Jabès's notion that one enters the desert "to lose identity and become anonymous."[26] In Bauman's reading of Jabès's words, the desert is a space for freedom, power, and anonymity. Desert-goers, or pilgrims, as Bauman calls them, have the capacity, once they penetrate the desert, to both be and act like God, "unbound by habit and convention, by the needs of their own bodies and other people's souls, by their past deeds and present actions."[27] Here, the desert is not just a space for absolute rebirth and an unrelenting, perpetual self-invention, but also a locus where people can be whoever they want to be without consideration for what was before and what comes next. The difference lies in the pilgrims' intellectual resourcefulness and their ability to transcend their own internalized boundaries. Seen through the prism of sexual Saharanism, these ideas depict deserts as malleable places that invite constant self-refashioning.

Bauman's problematic use of the desert—albeit for theoretical purposes—affirms that his pilgrims' quasi-divine nature stems from the fact that "whatever they did they did *ab nihilo.*"[28] Working in nothing and from nothing, these pilgrims invented a new world, established its laws, and created its values. Even though Bauman advanced these ideas within the context of the study of identity, his propositions participate in a larger tendency among theorists of nomadism to present deserts as a terrain for limitless freedom. The trend of deploying the metaphorical desert for thinking about modernity, poststructuralism, and postmodernity has been around for almost four decades now, but these theoretical works rarely engage with the desert as a concrete, lived reality. The focus is more on the meaning of the desert in contradistinction to Euro-American struggles against trends within their own societies.[29] Caren Kaplan is a notable exception, in that she gestures to the appropriation of the desert by what she calls "theoretical 'tourism'" in her critique of poststructuralism's "desire to become like or merge with the periphery or margin that one's own power has established."[30] Accordingly, nomadism's abstracted desert bears no resemblance to the existential conditions experienced by real nomads, whose life is romanticized and idealized to the extent that its harshness is made invisible. In what can be read as a critique of Baumann's pilgrim, Kaplan notes, "[The] desert symbolizes the site of critical and individual emancipation in Euro-American modernity; the nomad represents a subject position that offers an idealized model of movement based on perpetual dis-placement."[31] Whether manifested in the search for wilderness or touristic pleasures in the desert, this subject position enacts a desire to convey disillusionment with modernity.

In their canonical book *A Thousand Plateaus: Capitalism and Schizophrenia*, Gilles Deleuze and Félix Guattari engage in a discussion about the creation and challenges of the rhizome, which emphasizes connection and entanglement instead of a one-root tree model. According to the authors, the creation of the rhizome requires the maker to "enter a becoming, people your desert. So experiment."[32] As the primary founders of nomadology, Deleuze and Guattari imagine their desert as a depopulated nothingness, where everything is possible.[33] Kaplan's "theoretical 'tourism'" can be seen here: It is a hegemonic practice that theorists from the Global North use in the attempt to erase the boundary between their position of power and that of the periphery, which in itself was a creation of their powerful colonial homelands.[34] The romanticization of nomadism has become foundational for the Saharanism associated with the desert as a disculpating space that can free the theorist from the guilt of not having real relationships with the people who inhabit the periphery. One result of this situation is that the theory's metaphorical nomad is given free rein over the real nomad, whose life depends on different visions of deserts, her home.

COLONIAL SEXUAL SAHARANISM: STRIPPING THE DESERT OF ETHICS AND MORALITY

The intertwinement of deserts and sexuality is nothing new. Deserts were, in fact, sexual refuges for Church Fathers of the Roman era. Joyce Salisbury has written, "Among the most influential theorists of sexuality during this time of paradigm shift between Roman and Christian were men and women who renounced sex to seek God in the solitude of the desert."[35] These Desert Fathers misconceived sexuality as a social phenomenon, thinking that "simply moving to the desert would avoid sexuality."[36] However, isolation in the desert did not immunize them against their innate desires. As Salisbury demonstrates, the Fathers learned that the human body itself is the locus of sexuality.[37] Sexual Saharanism marks a shift from this spiritual attitude, which associated isolation in deserts with protection against sexual desires, and instead perceives the desert as a land where all carnal possibilities are not only imaginable but also entirely possible. Hence, desert solitude does not provide shelter from a misconstrued moral corruption but rather offers a haven for extreme experimentations with the body that defy the prescriptions of social order.

Geishas of the Desert or the Moral Alibis of Sexual Saharanism

When France colonized Algeria in 1830, what ensued was a settler-colonial system, which faced staunch resistance from the existing religious and tribal establishments. One such resistant was Abd al-Qadir al-Hassani al-Jaza'iri (Emir Abdelkader), who garnered support among tribes throughout the country and whose name became synonymous with the experience of an early anti-colonial war. The Arab Ouled Naïl was one of the tribes that rallied behind Abdelkader. Boasting an eastern and a western branch, the Ouled Naïl extended across different Algerian regions, including Chlef, Ghardaia, M'Sila, Laghouat, Biskra, Ouarghla, El Khroub, and Oum El Bouaghi.[38] As Abdelkader was engaged in his seventeen-year resistance against the French, one of the Ouled Naïl's leaders, Mūsā ibn al-Ḥasan al-Darqāwī, crisscrossed the desert on "marathonic visits" with "'ulama, nobles, and sheikhs, who rejected the French occupation and who enjoined the inhabitants to participate in jihad in many parts of the Tell."[39] The Ouled Naïl's jihad against French occupation continued even after al-Darqāwī's martyrdom in Biskra in 1849.[40] Guy de Maupassant, the French novelist and essayist, wrote that the village of Boukhrari (he probably meant Boghari), which is five hours away from Biskra, had "a singular political importance, because it makes it a kind of a link between the Arabs of the coast and those of the Sahara. So, it has always been the pulse of insurrections. That's where march-order comes from and that is where it goes back to. The most distant tribes send their people to find out what's happening in Boukhrari. Eyes are watching this place from all the regions of Algeria."[41] This is Maupassant's way of highlighting Ouled Naïl's strategic location in the Sahara. Historian Benjamin Brower has shown that the dismantling of the tribe included targeting its food sources and levying high taxes.[42] These measures extended beyond the military and economic restrictions to encompass the imposition of leadership that did not emerge from the ranks of the tribe itself.[43]

This history of the French authorities' willful fragmentation of a tribe resisting their authority was rather overshadowed by a constructed story of dancers and prostitutes. Instead of a rebellious Biskra, where al-Darqāwī was killed by the French army, Biskra stood for another Ouled Naïl, for those who, in the Western imagination, merely evoked tourism, pedophilia, and prostitution in the desert until Algeria's independence in 1962. The profusion of scholarly, literary, and journalistic articles that depicted the Ouled Naïl as morally corrupt tribes whose daughters were sent to towns to become professional dancers (aka prostitutes) at a very early age is a testament to Saharanism's hegemonic power. The cultural industrialization of Ouled Naïl as a source of eroticism in the Sahara served the interests of the budding tourism industry, for which the lascivious image of the Ouled Naïl women was profitable. Euro-American authors who visited the Sahara doubled down on the imaginaries of debauchery, salaciousness, and sexual fantasies of all kinds. Powerful and pervasive, this depiction pushed Mohammed Thabet, an Egyptian national, to refer to the Ouled Naïl women as "geishas of the desert."[44] Heavily influenced by the French literature of the time, Thabet wrote, "Among the tribes of the desert near the oasis of Biskra, the Ouled Naïl come to the cities to earn money by specializing in dance and prostitution, then they return to their homes to continue a veiled way of life and wait to get married."[45] Thabet did nothing more than translate the colonial misconceptions of his French contemporaries into Arabic and disseminate them among his readers in the 1940s.

Starting in the nineteenth century, the Nāyliyyāt were established in the colonial imaginary as vessels of Europeans' sexual desert fantasy. Eugène Fromentin depicted the village of Boghari in the 1850s as "populated by beautiful women, the majority of whom come from the Saharan tribes of the Ouled-Nayl [*sic*], A'r'azlia, etc., where manners are easy and where girls have the habit of going to make a fortune in the surrounding tribes. The Orientals have charming names to disguise the true nature of the profession of this type of women, whom I will, in the absence of a better name, call dancers."[46] It is clear from this description that Fromentin was convinced that the dancers were prostitutes. When he attended a dance, he utterly objectified and dehumanized the Nāyliyya (singular of Nāyliyyāt) who, he opined, "was not pretty, had this type of beauty that was suitable to dance."[47] Always with the same objectification, he writes, "When she extended her naked arms, which were adorned with bracelets up to the elbows, and moved her long, skinny hands with an air of voluptuous fear—she was definitely stunning."[48] The surgical description of her beauty, her quantities of jewelry, and her voluptuousness clearly sexualize this unnamed woman who, in Fromentin's mind, had become a prostitute even though she did nothing but dance.

This was only the beginning of a century-long obsession with the Nāyliyyāt. Almost all the important intellectual, artistic, and military figures who visited the Sahara during this period found a way to mention these women, whether to express fascination or contempt. The insertion of names of Algerian towns such as Bou Saâda, Laghouat, and Biskra, where Ouled Naïls were located, into their publications not only increased sales but also enhanced their image as sites of brothels. Maupassant, one of France's most illustrious literary figures, called them "prostitutes," and the editor of his *Les carnets de voyage* in 2006 inserted a note stating the "Ouled-Naïl are the erotic curiosity for the traveler."[49] Artist Théophile Gautier reproduced and disseminated the aforementioned dance scene from Fromentin's book in his own memoir, *Voyage en Algérie*.[50] French scholar Patrick Aurousseau has argued that interest in the Ouled Naïl's precolonial customs participated in the "creation of an Ouled-Naïl label" that became integral to an economy of "prostitution and mass tourism."[51] Hence, sexual Saharanism did not just convey what its practitioners saw and did, but it also contributed to a vision of the desert as a place where there was no distinction between Indigenous morality and immorality. Prostitution was accepted and elevated into a social value, which benefited Europeans but also put their societies and their culture on a higher moral ground.

This self-serving discourse has since been debunked by Algerian scholars. Malek Alloula revealed how postcards of Algerian women—one of the most important tools of (mis)representation under colonialism—produced the unrealistic image of the bedecked and bejeweled Algerian model whose portrait stripped Algerian society of its opacity in an endeavor to mark its subjugation to the colonial order.[52] Sociologist Marnia Lazreg has also argued that colonial producers of the myth of the Nāyliyyāt overlooked the fact that these women participated in Muslim society and contributed to its culture.[53] Contrary to Lazreg's assertion, ignorance of the importance of modesty in Islamic culture cannot be the only explanation for the propagation of the image of the Nāyliyyāt as a symbol of sexuality and licentiousness. Exaggeratedly lewd depictions of the Nāyliyyāt on colonial postcards and in all manner of literature had the immediate effect of incentivizing tourism; it also had the long-term goal of revealing what its propagators thought were Islam's internal contradictions, as a religion that pretended to defend virtue while its practitioners encouraged their women to become prostitutes.

This imbrication of racism and Islamophobia is best found in the work of Émile Masqueray (1843–1894). Described as a pioneer of knowledge production in French Algeria, Masqueray, who was also the author of a French-Tuareg dictionary and the director of the Algiers School of Letters,[54] drew on his knowledge of ancient mythology to establish continuities between Nāyliyyāt performers' Arab origins and the ancient Babylonian practice of offering virgin women to appease the dreadful half-human, half-animal creatures of their time.[55] His bias against the Nāyliyyāt's Arab ancestry pushed Masqueray to equate their Arab descent with vice and the destruction of civilization.[56] Consequently, these women are distorted as Cupids (goddesses of desire, after Greek mythology), pseudo-Muslims who performed an original sin in the colonial Sahara. Nowhere is Masqueray's racism more evident than in his description, where he states that the Nāyliyyāt "offer themselves, no longer to the Babylonians who were artistically coiffed and perfumed with myrrh, but to all the nomads and to all the sedentaries of the Barbarian Africa."[57] None of this, however, stops Masqueray from sticking three pieces of gold on one of the dancers and asking her if she would take him; an offer that the dander declined because, for her, the occasion of the dance was a religious ceremony that commanded respect.[58]

Lazreg provides a different history that counters Nāyliyyāt's over-romanticization. Confirming the existence among the Ouled Naïl of a tradition of dance that predated the advent of French colonialism, Lazreg argues that a

"Nailia [*sic*] is not a prostitute in the sense that we know it today."[59] However, the colonial imagination perverted a limited practice that had its own cultural, social, and economic codes coherent with its society's values and transformed it into a source of fascination for colonizers. Lazreg reveals that the colonial construction of dance as "a rite of passage before marrying" was not even coherent with the cultural context in which these women practiced this profession.[60] Barbara Wright has also rightly cast doubts on the false depiction of the Nāyliyyāt as prostitutes.[61] The persistence of this sexual Saharanist stance will come as no surprise to anyone who is aware of the deep intertwinement that existed among the growing Saharan tourism industry, the exploitation of these women, and their transformation into prostitutes. The Nāyliyyāt became an essential marketing tool for French desert tourism.[62] The Syndicat d'initiative, representing the interests of the tourism business community, included Ouled Naïl Street, where most of the prostitution activity was headquartered, in their tour guide.[63] Under these circumstances, the traditional dance that the Nāyliyyāt performed in accordance with their own social values was not enough for the tourism industry, which knew that catering to the sexual needs of tourists and French servicemen in the desert was where the big money was to be found. Hence, tourism companies "determined the contents of the Nayliyyat's performances, insisting that they appear naked before their visitors."[64] As a result, the French and their European counterparts could "enjoy the spoils of colonial domination of women in the south,"[65] making up for their inability to live out such dreams in northern Algeria, where women were veiled.

Owing to sexual Saharanism's powerful cultural machine, the Nāyliyyāt became the beacons of a sexual geography that dotted the landscape of the desert (Fig. 11). Algerian towns in the Tell—namely Biskra, Blida, and Bou Saâda, among others—became must-visit locations for pleasure-seekers throughout the colonial period. Robert Hérisson, a military doctor, wrote about his passage in Biskra in 1909 that there were "English, Austrian, German, and Russian men" at Hôtel de l'Oasis, where he stayed, adding, "Nordics were attracted to this African land by the romantic reputation of the young Arab women of Ouled-Naïls."[66] Despite the abundant literature about it, this sexual geography remained outside the purview of critical analysis and stayed confined to memoirs and literary texts that reek of exploitative sex practices within the colonial economy. Swedish historian Sven Lindqvist has rightly explained the vicious circle in which the Nāyliyyāt were trapped as a result of colonization's termination of their social order

FIGURE 11. Biskra, Rue des Ouled Naïls. Photo courtesy of the Library of Congress.

when he emphasized how "war and occupation had led to social anarchy. With the misery also came prostitution, first around the garrisons, then around the tourist hotels."[67] As this passage demonstrates, it was not the ways of the tribe that were loose, as French writers famously depicted them, but rather colonial policy had created the geography of Saharan sex markets. But colonialism had to preserve its discursive higher moral ground, and the fiction of Saharan women's wantonness and moral corruption had to predate French colonization, which provided colonial customers of prostitution with "a moral alibi."[68] By placing the Nāyliyyāt outside the purview of ethics and moral normalcy, sexual Saharanism cleared the way for European pleasure-seekers to live out their desires and fantasies in its unethical desert.

Clancy-Smith has written that the translation of the novel *Musk, Hashish, and Blood* into English "suggests that French colonial representations of the Arab Muslim woman as hooker and harlot had begun to feed into the underground pornographic press of the English-speaking world."[69] Indeed, sexual Saharanism mobilized a powerful imaginary that perpetuated the colonial fascination with colonized Muslim women's sexuality. In 1931, British writer Edgar Fletcher Allen highlighted how the Saharan town of Biskra was "the capital of tourism" and the unparalleled "natural centre of the holidaymaking, sun-seeking people who make any stay in the country."[70] Writing admiringly of the establishment of a casino in the town, he interpreted the decision as a reflection of Biskra's willingness to "give its visitors what they want."[71] And what the visitors wanted was amorphous, voluptuous, and deeply steeped in sexual Saharanist imaginations. Fletcher Allen does not spare the Nāyliyyāt the stigma of the profession that they were coerced into by the burgeoning tourism industry, despite his admission that they were "generally the chief attraction" of the desert.[72] Notwithstanding his voyeurism and the pleasure he certainly took in attending nightly dances with girls as young as thirteen,[73] Fletcher Allen audaciously observed, "However attractive these *danseuses prostituées* may be to their own folk, their charm is entirely lost on the desert air of Occidental people."[74] This is one of the many contradictions of the practitioners of sexual Saharanism, who enjoyed being voyeurs while also pretending to criticize the morals of the same women on whom they preyed. These men flocked to the desert to attend naked dances performed by underage girls, but they always portrayed themselves as virtuous bystanders rather than participants. They still insisted on their higher moral ground, revealing how sexual Saharanism, like its experimental counterpart, has a formidable intrinsic ability to reconcile the irreconcilable.

Sexual Saharanism crossed the Atlantic, fascinating American journalists and travelers, starting in the nineteenth century. French colonial propaganda played a crucial role in disseminating the story of the Ouled Naïl through its touristic literature in English. This Orientalizing "pornographic press" drew on state propaganda outlets like *French Colonial Digest*, which was published by the French Bureau of Information in the US. *French Colonial Digest*'s implication in this trade is evidenced by its serialization of an article by Floyd Gibbons.[75] However, American writers also produced their own desert pornography. Alexander Powell published an article entitled "Sirens of the Sands," which, in addition to recycling the platitudes Powell had most likely culled from the French propagandistic literature, emphasized the "sensuous and barbaric" Nāyliyyāt lifestyle.[76] Most important for Powell was the need to cast the Ouled Naïl as an immoral, uncivilized, and lawless people whose way of life was diametrically opposed to that of the West.[77] Writing in 1925, William Dickson Boyce glorified the Nāyliyyāt, going so far as to say that they were "the happiest of their sex,"[78] even comparing them to American Roma.[79] Adventurer and photojournalist Jack Mortimer Sheppard evinced the same fascination with desert prostitutes in the Saharan town of Tindouf in 1956. Going against the grain of American puritanism, Sheppard expressed his admiration of the "somewhat dignified manner" in which prostitution was practiced under the French colonial establishment.[80] Quoting an officer who told him about the equilibrium and discipline two women prostitutes brought to the troops' life in the Sahara,[81] Sheppard justified the French army's exploitation of the so-called Nāyliyyāt to keep their soldiers happy. This American desert pornography reached new heights with Paul Bowles, whose sexual adventures with George Turner—an American citizen he met in Algeria—among the Ouled Naïl were recorded by his biographer, Christopher Sawyer-Laucanno. In Bou-Saâda, the two companions paid for a sixteen-year-old girl to dance for them.[82] For seventy-five francs, Bowles and his companion were entitled to a five-minute naked dance as well as intercourse with the underage girl.[83] Thus, travel literature and journalism circulated Ouled Naïls' stories in the English-speaking world, inspiring Americans to fully partake in sexual Saharanism.

The Nāyliyyāt's dancing primarily in order to raise a dowry fascinated those who wrote about them. Pierre Bonardi, a French officer turned writer, argued that Ouled Naïl girls were groomed from childhood "to earn [their] dowry through prostitution."[84] Maupassant adduced the idea that dowries were the main motivation for these performances, but he also underlined that the practice was not solely limited to Ouled Naïl.[85] Dessaix talks about Gide's and Lauren's sexual exploitation of the adolescent girl Meriem during their Biskra visit in terms that evoke the dowry story as well. In Dessaix's words, the "two young men were simply losing their virginity in the time-honored way while she was earning her dowry in the same spirit. Mutual exploitation of a very North African kind."[86] Having made a fortune, or so the myth went, the women would go back home to buy a husband and settle down.[87]

To these writers, the women's abundant jewelry indicated that Saharan prostitution made them wealthy (Fig. 12). In 1884, Maupassant painted the image of women whose "chest[s are] drowned under necklaces, medals, [and] heavy jewelry."[88] Maupassant insists on quantifying the gold and silver that the Nāyliyyāt wore, calling it a fortune.[89] Likewise, writer Melville William Hilton-Simpson depicts the Nāyliyyāt of Bou-Saâda as being more "covered with bright colours and jewelry" than their counterparts in Biskra.[90] Fletcher Allen provides a vivid description of a thirteen-year-old girl he had met in a brothel in that town: "Around her neck were four gold and silver necklaces. She had two slabs of gold dangling like breastplates, held by a chain round her shoulder, and she carried a golden girdle."[91] Sheppard reports that the two women who serviced the French soldiers in Fort Trinquet (Bir Moghrein in Arabic) near Tindouf "were well on the way to becoming independently wealthy by Arab standards."[92] By focusing on the dowry story and adducing culturalist factors to explain the exploitation of both adult and underaged Nāyliyyāt, sexual Saharanists revealed their hypocrisy, accepting and even defending the prostitution of colonized women at a time when all forms of sex trafficking were being increasingly outlawed in Europe and the US.

Sexual Saharanism is not just a relic of the past—it is very much present in current desert-centered tourism. Exotic local bodies captivate the imaginations of this ideology's heirs. While the image of the harem has become almost a cliché, what sexual Saharanism does is quite different.[93] Anthropologist Jessica Jacobs has discussed the premodern as well as the postmodern implications of ethnosexual relationships between Egyptian Bedouins and Euro-American women in the Sinai.[94] For Jacobs, these relationships show that the desert has been constructed as a space to stop time and find a lost freedom in an arena untouched by modernity and where time is experienced differently than in Europe or the US. This codification of the desert as being associated with nostalgic ideas about time brings these Euro-American women to the desert wilderness, where they can live outside

FIGURE 12. "Types Algériens, Femme des Ouled Naïls." Photo courtesy of Library of Congress.

modernity in the form of ethnosexual relationships.[95] Both the rhythm of life and the dwellers' lifestyles make the Sinai premodern,[96] allowing the Euro-American tourist to live outside modern and urban temporalities.[97]

The lingering legacy of sexual Saharanism in cultural production continues to inform novel sexual relationships in deserts. Jacobs points out that the impetus for sexual relationships in the desert is "filtered through literary and cinematic imaginaries," which bring tourists to the desert with expectations that locals need to meet in order for the multilayered socioeconomic dynamics that are built into this desert imaginary to be satisfied.[98] Similarly, Corinne Cauvin Verner has shown how tour guides in the southeastern Sahara in Morocco have strategically embraced the image of the Tuareg created by literature in order to entice European women.[99] The desert space operates as a metaphor, whereby the "landscape in the Sahara is eroticized: the sand dunes are frequently compared to the curves of a woman's body; the sensorial perceptions are amplified with quivering, caressing, biting or dizziness."[100] Sexual Saharanism is thus relived as a local phenomenon that exploits Western fantasies for economic benefits in a totally reconfigured Saharan space in which the power dynamics have shifted between the male descendants of the formerly dominated and the female descendants of the race that formerly dominated their ancestors.

Transgressive Desert Sexuality as a Healing Force

Sexual relationships between the colonized and colonizers were a manifestation of the imbalanced power dynamic between the Indigenous people and their invaders. Lindqvist has brilliantly captured the ethics of this colonial situation, writing that in "the colonies, while one represented the highpoint of civilization, it was possible to escape much of civilization's unpleasantness: the banality of the bourgeoisie, the *tristesse* of marriage, the inhibiting control of impulse—and become party to murder, child abuse, sexual orgies and expressions of urges which at home largely found their outlets in dreams."[101] As dreamscapes of desires that are criminalized elsewhere, the sense of impunity in deserts intensifies the willingness to make fantasies a reality.

Homosexuality was one of the sexual tendencies that played out in the Sahara. In his discussion of Ouled Naïl in *Au soleil*, Maupassant uses homosexuality to contrast Arabs' barbarity and Europeans' civilization. Speaking for his own people, Maupassant claims, "Our ideas, our customs, our instincts are so absolutely different from those that we encounter in these countries that at home we barely dare talk about a vice so frequent there that Europeans are no longer surprised nor scandalized by it."[102] The "vice" was the Arabs' supposed acceptance of "counternatural love between beings of the same sex."[103] While Maupassant overnormalizes homosexuality in the Sahara, he abnormalizes it in Europe. As historian Todd Shepard indicates, this discourse would outlive colonization in French constructions of Arab men's sexuality.[104] This supposed tolerance of homosexuality was a "deviation of instinct" for Maupassant,[105] who simply exploited the contact with Arabs to express his homophobic positions. When Maupassant explains why homoeroticism exists in the Sahara, he misguidedly removes homosexuality from the realm of human society, where it is a reality, and places it in the realm of desert immorality: "Where does this deviation of instinct come from? It is probably due to several causes. The most apparent is the rarity of women, sequestered by the rich who have four legitimate wives and as many concubines as they can feed. Perhaps also the intensity of the climate, which excites sensual desires, has blunted in these men of violent temperament the delicacy, finesse, and intellectual rectitude that preserve us from disgusting habits and contacts."[106] Maupassant's comparison of the Sahara to the Romans and ancient Greeks conveyed the idea that the Sahara belonged to a "vicious," premodern time.[107] Joseph Massad, meanwhile, offers a brilliant discussion of this binary opposition. Taking *Misk al-ghazāl* (*The Deer's Musk*),[108] a novel by Lebanese novelist Hanan al-Shaykh, as his point of departure, Massad critiques its author for reproducing the European division between civilization and primitivism vis-à-vis homosexuality, writing, "The desert kingdom is to be described and judged as a primitive place where uninhibited sexual desires of all varieties reign supreme, free from civilized regulation, thus approximating Western social Darwinist and Freudian descriptions of primitive and infantile sexuality."[109]

Gide was the most important literary figure to have explicitly and unabashedly documented his brand of sexual Saharanism. His was a "dive into [the] dark well," to use Lindqvist's words, but not one that performs the historical and ethical work that has yet to be completed in order to "clean out" the well of pedophilia in the Sahara.[110] Both *L'immoraliste* and his autobiography *Si le grain ne meurt* bring his reader into the underworld of the prostitution of underage girls and boys in the colonial Sahara.

Published in 1902, *L'immoraliste* is a fictionalized rendering of his experiences during his trips to Tunisia and Algeria, starting in 1893. The novel's protagonists, Michel and Marceline, are a recently married couple who embark on a long honeymoon that takes them from France to Algeria via Tunisia. Twenty-four-year-old Michel is a famous, wealthy scholar who decided to marry the twenty-year-old Marceline as a way to comfort his dying father, who feared he would be leaving him alone when he passed away. Once in Tunisia, Michel falls sick with tuberculosis and Marceline nurses him throughout their journey, including on their trip to the desert town of Biskra. While in Biskra, Michel slowly emerges from his lethargic state by walking in the fields of the oasis and spending time in the gardens in the town. During these outings, a feeble Michel meets several children who offer to carry his shawl and other belongings, which he is too fatigued to carry on his own. The sunny weather and the sudden presence of children around him infuse Michel with new life.

Michel's transformation over the course of the novel is not just related to his regaining of health but also ushers in a shift in his ideas about sexuality. In fact, his pedophilic acts with the children in Biskra are part of a deep ideological process that occurs within Michel and pushes him to rebel against his bourgeois socialization. Michel willingly strips himself of his mannerisms and slowly slips into decadence under the influence of his friend Mélanque, a character inspired by Gide's friend Oscar Wilde. This sensual awakening results in a reconfiguration of Michel's own understanding of the existence he has led up until that point. He declares, "My senses, awakened now, were recovering a whole history, were reconfiguring their own past."[111] Michel can finally give up exalting the mind to instead glorify the senses.[112] Acting like a vampire, Michel is able to literally and figuratively suck the health and life from the children of Biskra in order to pump their blood and energy into his own tuberculosis-ridden body. The result is an extraordinary declaration of his metamorphosis,[113] a transformative change resulting from his predation on the children.

Michel's renunciation of his European rationalism to immerse himself in pedophilic vampirism equates the Sahara with the hedonism and primitivism that supposedly flourish in uncivilized places. His renewed sense of himself as an individual and his embracing of his homosexuality require him to escape civilization for a world of carnal and instinctual pleasures. The desert is depicted as the ideal site where Michel can live out his dreams, fantasies, and desires without restraint. Marceline summarizes his new ideology, referring to it as a doctrine that "eliminates the weak."[114] Michel becomes a disciple of Darwinism, whereby those who do not fit his selfish conception of beauty, health, or attractiveness are described as ugly, unclean, and disposable. When arriving in Biskra on his second visit with Marceline, Michel finds that the children he associated with during his first visit have grown up:

> I didn't recognize the children, but the children recognized me. Informed of my arrival, they all came to meet me. Could these be the right ones? The disappointment! What had happened? They had grown up—hideously.... In just over two years—could it be possible?... What exhaustion, what vices, what sloth had already imprinted such ugliness on these faces in which so much youth once had bloomed? What servile labors had warped these lovely bodies so quickly? It was a kind of bankruptcy.... Would I find among these boys just what I most hated at home?[115]

The deep internal change that Michel experiences leads him to "disdain culture, propriety, rules."[116] His brutal new doctrine rejects honesty and any morality, because they are nothing but a set of inhibitions and restrictions. Moktir—the child who stole Marceline's scissors during their first trip to Biskra—is the only one Michel still finds worthy of his attention. The reason Moktir remains unchanged, even surpassing Michel's own memory of him, is attributable to his deviousness—he is a petty criminal who left prison just before Michel's second arrival in Biskra.[117] Broadly speaking, Michel's new doctrine runs roughshod over moral considerations. It requires an active desertion of a principled way of existence within any normative ethics that distinguishes between right and wrong. For him, morality cannot serve as an obstacle to self-discovery, no matter what the cost for others might be.

Mélanque, Michel's iconoclastic friend, is the philosopher of the sexual Saharanism Michel enacts. He praises unbounded immorality, making living life to its fullest more important than any celebration of its abstractions. In Mélanque's eyes, European civilization has become trivial and meaningless because it is "cut off from life."[118] Thus, instead of simply engaging in art for art's sake, which is precisely what Michel had done before his trip to Biskra, Mélanque advocates an experiential doctrine that places lived experiences above the production of ideas. The dichotomy between Michel and Mélanque shows that Michel represents the "man of principles" whom Mélanque, himself freed from the moral pressure of social norms, abhors.[119] This polarization between the principled and the unprincipled drives the novel, which describes Michel's struggle to become a version of Mélanque by constantly endeavoring to act in ways that undermine the bourgeois Puritan education instilled in him through years of education and social conditioning. The Sahara as well as the forest that is part of Michel's estate in France serve as shelters where he can live out his pederastic desires. Michel's second trip to Biskra reveals his Mélanquian self in which there is no room for social norms and their resulting inhibitions. Instead of taking care of Marceline in her sickbed, Michel chooses to spend the night with Moktir's Nāyliyya in Touggourt, leaving Marceline to die alone in the desert.

The parallels between *L'immoraliste* and Gide's own life story are very clear. Gide visited Algeria and Tunisia almost six times in a span of a few years after 1893.[120] His travels took him to Algerian towns popularized by colonial tourism, specifically to Biskra and Bou-Saâda, where he was to have several pedophilic encounters. However, he suddenly stopped visiting Tamazgha in 1906 and would not return until 1926.[121]

The similarities between his experiences during his long stays in Tamazgha and his fictionalized rendering of it are so close that some critiques have mixed the two in their readings. During Gide's first visit to Tunisia and Algeria in 1893, he was not accompanied by a woman but rather by his friend, the artist Paul Laurens, who had received a fellowship to spend a year abroad.[122] During their time in Tolon, Gide fell sick, but his tuberculosis was not diagnosed until he saw a doctor in Kairouan, Tunisia. After this diagnosis, Laurens took care of Gide, and they changed course, abandoning their plans to cross the desert from Sousse to Biskra to opt for a less adventurous route by train.

Gide's autobiography leaves no room for doubt about the experiential nature of the pedophilic actions depicted suggestively in *L'immoraliste.* He first acted upon his pedophilic desires in the desert of Sousse in Tunisia, where he had intercourse with a boy named Ali. For Gide, this was "a small episode that had a significant impact on [him]. It would be more false to silence it than it would be indecent to recount it."[123] The way Gide describes Ali's invitation to him on the sand dune reverses roles and attributes the act of solicitation to little Ali, instead of Gide contending with his own decision to pursue a desire that purportedly caused him to hesitate at first. In his retelling, Gide insinuates that he had intercourse with Ali to please the latter, since his indecision made the boy's "laughter fade slowly, his lips close on his white teeth; an expression of disappointment and sadness darkened his charming face."[124] Readers will never know what really happened at the moment when Gide walked with Ali to the sand dune. Gide had the last word about the encounter because he was the holder of the pen, and his enthusiasts, like Dessaix, have taken on the role of embellishing his sexual Saharanism. Thanks to sexual Saharanism, not only does the perpetrator outlive his victim, but he also continues to shape how the story of his pedophilia has been *deserted* by scholars, literary critics, and historians.

Gide's premeditated construction of the desert as his terrain for moral transgression is clear from his decision to not bring his Bible on his trip with Laurens to North Africa. This act of deserting a book that may inhibit his personal urge toward an unprincipled existence was an indication of his readiness to exploit the Saharan space to cross the Rubicon of pedophilic sexual Saharanism. Leaving the Bible back home was the culmination of Gide's enactment on his understanding of "classicism," which in his words, was "opposed to [his] Christian ideal."[125] Gide's abdication of the Bible, a book to which he had always returned for moral nourishment, marked a rupture with his Protestant upbringing and "its fear of the particular, the bizarre, the morbid, and the abnormal."[126] By leaving the Bible back home, he left law and moral inhibitions outside the desert. The colonial Sahara thus became a place where religious and moral constraints were removed.

Gide's desert both invites and accommodates what he has called "vice."[127] His choice of that word explicitly conveys his internalization of a social awareness that his pederasty was reprehensible. Nevertheless, awareness did not lead to the suspension of his sexual conquests among Saharan boys. In fact, the arid landscape abetted his pedophilia. Once he finished with Ali, he blessed the desert's splendor, declaiming, "How beautiful the sand was! My joy was donned in the lovely splendor of the evening, in such rays!"[128] As John Weightman noticed, the identities of Gide's boys in the Sahara were unimportant due to their interchangeability,[129] and Ali is no different, disappearing from the picture afterward. As readers already know from *L'immoraliste*, Michel—Gide's alter ego—could not care less about what happens to the children he vampirized.

Sexual Saharanism is clearly manifest in the scholarly *desertion* of the ethical dimension of Gide's pedophilic history in favor of a more sympathetic reading of his homosexuality. As such, Martin Halliwell's reading of Thomas Mann's *Death in Venice* and Gide's *L'immoraliste* emphasizes that in these works the "protagonists fall for adolescent boys despite themselves."[130] Although this happens in the realm of fiction, the fact that Halliwell focuses on Michel "falling for" a boy instead of foregrounding his agentive choice to pursue pedophilic relationships absolves Michel—and Gide by extension—of any responsibility for his actions in the desert. Similarly, Frederick Grubb highlights how Gide's art is about "new possibilities in man" and constitutes a departure from already established ways of being in search of "what can be achieved."[131] This sympathetic reading prevents Grubb from fully addressing Gide's pedophilia, even though he warns that this search for the new and its potential is "a valid impulse put in action wrongly" in *L'immoraliste.*[132]

Arab writers have not fared any better in confronting this dimension. Egyptian scholar Samih Murkus both confounds homosexuality with pedophilia and recycles Orientalist clichés, writing: "Tolerance of homosexuality continued in the Orient until the beginning of the twentieth century, contrary to Europe, where it was criminalized; encouraging several European writers and artists, such as André Gide and Oscar Wilde, to travel to Algeria, Morocco, Egypt, and other Arab countries to practice what Europe had prohibited."[133] Murkus's failure to distinguish homosexuality from pedophilia led him to praise how the southern bank of the Mediterranean became a sexual haven for pedophiles. That said, there are notable exceptions, like Anthony Copley, who, in his book *Sexual Moralities in France*, calls out Gide's perversion.[134]

Positive attitudes toward figures of sexual Saharanism are neither surprising nor unexplainable. The discussion of Gide and Wilde, who represent the avant-garde of public homoerotic transgression, verges on infatuation. Jonathan Dollimore has conceptualized this relationship, dating from the time of their encounter in Paris in 1891, as marked by a tension between Wilde's "anti-essentialism" and Gide's "essentialism," which he claims "epitomizes one of the most important differences within the modern history of transgression."[135] Wilde's disregard for the social conventions put Gide in Wilde's thrall and led him down the path of transgression.[136] The two men's beliefs about transgression and liberation produced different, albeit effectively similar, conclusions. For Wilde, it was the "essential self" that was let go in the act of transgression, whereas for Gide, the "liberated desires" led necessarily to self-renewal and reinvention.[137] The now (in)famous scene in Algeria when Wilde asked Gide if he desired the underage flute player named Mohammed shows Gide as a man who was entranced, firmly under Wilde's liberating (or corruptive) influence. This scene from Gide's autobiography has been widely commented on,[138] and the focus on Wilde's influence on Gide has excluded Mohammed, who has been *deserted* by scholarship and the historicization of sexual Saharanism in the colonized Sahara (Algiers is, of course, not in the Sahara, but the logic of sexual Saharanism applies to this scene). Dollimore's forceful conclusion that "Gide's experience in Africa is one of the most significant modern narratives of homosexual liberation" sums up this ethical desertion.[139] The focus in the retrospective reconstructions and readings of the story are never about the forcibly sexualized child but rather about celebrated white men who achieved their sexual liberation. Hence, naming and identifying sexual Saharanism is only a pathway toward the tremendous work required to rehabilitate the stories of its victims.

This tendency to trivialize sexual Saharanism's impact on its victims is further enhanced in Dessaix's reading of Gide and Wilde's sexual adventure with two boys in Algiers in January 1895. Dessaix rhetorically asks: "Why dwell for even a moment on a callow young Frenchman and an Irishman with bad teeth picking up boys together in Algiers one night in 1895? Strictly speaking, it wasn't even André's first time—not quite, although, admittedly, the other two times, in Tunisia and on Lake Como, hadn't unlocked anything in him."[140] Guided by his own sexual Saharanism, Dessaix never really seeks to understand what Gide's self-discovery meant for Saharan children. Dessaix, like other readers, as though guided by some sort of fatalism, attempts to reflect on the inevitability of these actions for Gide, whom he envelops in a desert mystique. Dessaix even finds himself defending Gide when Yacoub, an Algerian contact Dessaix met during his visit to Algiers, reminds him of Gide's sexual acts in Algeria.[141] Dessaix pays no attention to the ramifications for others of his demigod's self-liberation as he follows in his footsteps and refreshes the story of sexual Saharanism in the minds of his readers who, in their turn, will find their way to North Africa in due course.

The ethical double standards become all too clear when desert pedophilia is compared to the reception of Wilde's homosexuality in Britain. Lord Queensbury was scandalized by his son Alfred Douglas's relationship with Wilde, to such a degree that he called the latter a "posing Sodomite."[142] However, even as Lord Queensbury denounced Wilde, his son eloped to Biskra with the underage Ali—his Aladdin—whom he had brought from Blida. Racism, fame, power, and colonialism were all imbricated in this episode. Accused of indecency in England, Wilde avoided arrest because of the staging of his plays in London.[143] Indecency, however, did not apply to Douglas's, Gide's, and Wilde's sexual acts with boys in the Sahara, despite the fact that Biskra was not very far from London. The abdication of criticism combined with the desertion of the law allowed sexual Saharanism to foreground a romanticized transgression whose underage victims remain unaccounted for. In Britain and France, pedophilia and homosexuality were crimes, but not in a Sahara enveloped in ethical, legal, and moral desertism.

The story of pedophilia in the desert embodies Saharanism's racialization and dehumanization of the people who call the desert home. Although Gide's work has inspired countless studies, the desert remains elusive in this scholarship. It continues to act as an empty, primitive space that fails to register as a real place whose inhabitants actually have real emotions. The worse part of sexual Saharanism is its overpowering ubiquity, which makes local scholars reproduce European silences. For instance, Algerian historian al-Ṭayyib Būderbala writes that Gide was "organically and intimately wedded to Algeria, and the new land provided him with the meaning of life and its significance, which is the discovery of himself, the world, and others. Thanks to his Algerian experience, Gide was able to liberate himself from French bourgeois values and their philosophy."[144] Whether this positive depiction of Gide is due to their author's failure to actually read Gide's works or is attributable to the impactful Euro-American readings of Gide's experience, it is clear that Būderbala, like the aforementioned Murkus, participates in the dehumanizing of Indigenous Saharans that is at the core of sexual Saharanism. The complete opposite of this lax attitude, Farid Laroussi, a Canada-based Algerian literary scholar, has deftly deconstructed Gide's strategic instrumentalization of his siding with the natives, highlighting how his desert craze was motivated in part by his pedophilic penchants.[145]

The desert fatalism that appears in the way that these men's paths converged in Algeria cannot justify their desertism. These European men could have asserted their *homosexual* identity without creating victims among Saharan children. Eerily, critical studies about this period have—consciously or unconsciously—abandoned their ethical compass in favor of these powerful men's tales of liberation, ignoring the toll their personal freedom took on Saharan children whose side of the story will never be told. Sexual Saharanism has survived for so long because its crimes have been overshadowed by the amalgamation of pedophilia with homosexuality. However, the examination of pedophilia in the colonial Sahara should not be a way to criminalize homosexuality or question gender nonconformity. Rather, it should be construed as a project that uncovers the complicit silences that have enabled sexual Saharanism to avoid detection, articulation, and ethical examination of its dangerous depictions of deserts as havens for sexual freedom of all sorts, regardless of those whom it has put in harm's way. Outside of Africa, sexual Saharanism has rid itself of this pedophilic history and taken more contemporary forms that continue to sustain deserts as loci for myriad countercultural undertakings.

WESTWORLD AND BURNING MAN: COUNTERCULTURE IN THE AMERICAN WEST

Westworld: *A Desertic World of Possibilities*

The American television series *Westworld* is an excellent embodiment of sexual Saharanism. Unfolding in a man-made desert that resembles the landscapes of Arizona and Utah, *Westworld* is a recreational hub where an endless number of Hosts, or humanoid robots, are programmed to satisfy the most fantastical sexual and gory needs of their Guests. Unlike the Hosts, Guests are human and pay to enter the theme park of *Westworld*, where they can pursue their "basest instincts" without any consequences.[146] In addition to making the androids into "the playthings of wealthy visitors, who could sexually assault, beat and even kill the lifelike beings,"[147] the programmers deprive them of the capacity to retaliate by erasing their memory and disabling their ability to remember the abuses they experience.[148] Deprived of memory, the Hosts can be ceaselessly exploited and violently mishandled by their Guests without any hope for manumission from this new form of slavery.

The Host-Guest relationship in *Westworld* is rigged against the Hosts. Almost all their behavior is mechanized and coded to serve the humans who pay for the service. While the guns used by Guests cut through the Hosts' flesh and dismember their bodies, which get repaired countless times in the ultra-modern lab facilities, the Hosts' own guns only cause a pinch if they are fired. The logic underlying the show is that humans, as represented by Guests, have dark desires that they are willing to pay to fulfill. However, desires have consequences when they turn into punishable acts. Thus, when the Guests enter this desert-like fantasy world, inhibitions for violence, whether physical or sexual, fall and disappear. Guests pay to enter a consequenceless realm in which they reemerge physically and legally intact after engaging in violent rampages. *Westworld* allows the Guests to commit all the murders they want and participate in all the sexual orgies they desire, but everything remains confined to the phantasmagorical desert. The landscape serves as an open world of possibilities for unregulated shooting, prostitution, racism, and mass murder.

In his book *Sex Robots: The Future of Desire*, Jason Lee argues that sex robots have always existed in the human imagination. Tracing the evolution of robotic creations as technologies changed and developed, Lee focuses particularly on the sexual fantasies that have been projected onto these creations. For Lee, the existence of the "sex robot is the manifestation of our deepest desire, and therefore is our dream manifestation."[149] The editors of *Reading Westworld*, Alex Goody and Antonia Mackay, offer a distinction between robots and droids and problematize how the series depicts sex robots. Unlike the impression that automata give of autonomous functioning and self-empowerment,[150] the robots in *Westworld*, Goody and Mackay argue, are distinguished by their resemblance to humans and their capacity to transcend the preprogrammed actions.[151] The human appearance of *Westworld*'s robots places them within the "android" rather than the robot family.[152] Beyond these technical distinctions, Goody and Mackay reveal that the gender dynamics embedded in *Westworld*'s approach to sexuality cannot be divorced from notions of accumulation and commodification.[153] Seen through this prism, *Westworld* is a fantastical realm where men can live the wildest fantasies capitalism affords them. In the absence of real women, the androids are there to be on the receiving end of the desires to control and accumulate. Rebecca Solnit has clearly articulated the fact that feminism is the antithesis to capitalism, writing, "under the one women are people and under the other they are property."[154] It is not difficult to extend Solnit's conclusion to *Westworld* as a realm in which capitalism turns the desert and everyone in it into a commodity for the rich males who can afford it. As Goody and Mackay observe, "If *Westworld* is a game, it is one where gendered identity appears biased towards male fantasies for Guests and female subordination for Hosts."[155]

Pursuant to this capitalistic logic, there is nothing that Hosts cannot do to satisfy the desires of their guests in *Westworld*. After all, Guests pay to enjoy the services Hosts are programmed to offer. This entire high-tech structure is designed and controlled to maximize Guests' enjoyment. The desert emerges as the ideal place to go in order to indulge in aggressiveness and hedonism without fear of judgment. Given *Westworld*'s focus on the fulfillment of extreme sexual and murderous desires, the show perpetuates the obsession with deserts as places where unbridled sexuality is not only encountered but remains free of any ethical or moral judgments. *Westworld* thus harnesses the power of technology and the promises of artificial intelligence to create a simulacrum world so that men can engage in actions that elsewhere would be subject to moralistic scrutiny. Interpreted differently, underlying *Westworld* is the notion that the desert has the capacity to absorb sin and cleanse crimes. However, it is important to reflect on why the desert specifically is capable of containing such atrocities. Constructing the desert this way is not just an artistic choice but rather the result of Saharanism's preconceived ideas about the space and its uses. The desert is the realm of primitivism and as such is able to accommodate actions that cannot be conceived of transpiring in civilized areas governed by rationality.

In *Westworld*, the greatest manifestation of sexual Saharanism is to be found in the depiction of the Pariah area. In an interview with *The Hollywood Reporter*, Richard Lewis, *Westworld*'s co-executive producer and supervising director, explained the rationale behind the introduction of Pariah in the third season. Lewis said, "We wanted it to feel like it was not only fairly tough to get to and remote, but also that you had an aggressive desire to want to go there and to get there."[156] This is not only reminiscent of Saharanism's construction of the desert as a remote, vacant land that requires arduous efforts to reach, but also the fact that the ardent desire to be there is fueled by an unvanquishable mystique. Thus, Pariah, as its name suggests, is the far edge of the desert, and it best represents the imaginary of Saharanism: "Pariah, a city filled with outcasts, delinquents, thieves, murderers and a whole bevy of horny hosts. As a reward for their work in apprehending a stash of explosives for the local mercenaries, William and Logan are invited to attend a sexy party—and as it turns out, nobody throws an orgy quite like the people of Pariah."[157] While the entire imaginative framework underlying this passage has already been explained throughout this book, the point about Pariah residents' mastery of orgies is an excellent example of Saharanism's association of the desert with sexual excess. And yet, much of the scholarship surrounding *Westworld* has focused on the technological aspects of the distinction between humans, robots, and androids, leaving the significance of the desert unaddressed.

Westworld chatbot Aeden, which was created in partnership between Google and HBO and to which viewers could ask questions in 2017, defined Pariah as "the gateway to ultimate danger and sin in Westworld. The delicious orgy of decadence that awaits you is beyond any indulgence you've ever experienced."[158] A creation of what is currently called artificial intelligence, Aeden had already internalized the idea of the desert as a limit to ethics—a place where all decadent behaviors are not only accepted but also invited. *Westworld*'s Pariah is probably the clearest example that sexual Saharanism's effects are deeper and more influential than previously articulated. After all, Aeden declares, "there is no law in Pariah," before asking the inquirer, "what law are you interested in breaking?"[159]

Burning Man: Sex and Drugs as Foundational Pillars of Counterculture

Since 1986, Burning Man has been an important annual event in the US. Started as a friendly initiative between like-minded people on Baker Beach in the San Francisco area, Burning Man has grown to become one of the most famous self-branded countercultural events on Earth. Characterized by its participants' bizarre art, weird costumes, and complete freedom to break the laws and customs of their ordinary world, the festival is indeed an experiment in countercultural activism. In a manner reminiscent of Wilde's and Gide's contentions that contravention of social mores is crucial for freedom, Burning Man represents an experimental world made for pushing limits. Unlike nineteenth- and early twentieth-century transgression, however, Burning Man's version of counterculture is very much in sync with the values of its time, which leave no room for criminal sexual conduct, pedophilic or otherwise, although sexuality is a foundational element of the experience.

In her book *Future Sex*, American journalist and essayist Emily Witt has reflected on the entanglements among sex, class, and privilege at the festival. From the get-go, Witt admits that her participation in Burning Man in 2013 was motivated by her interest in "sexual experimentation, psychedelic drugs, and futurism."[160] Through her own experiences of sex and drugs, combined with observations of other revelers' behavior in the different encampments, Witt reflects on the drug-sex culture that undergirds Burning Man's countercultural movement. She asserts that people who are "interested in sexual experimentation,"[161] like her, are sure to find inspiration at Burning Man. The wide array of "lectures on orgasmic meditation, 'shamanic auto-asphyxiation,' 'ecosexuality,' 'femtheogens,' 'tantra of our menses,' 'sex drugs and electronic music' and the opportunity to visit the orgy dome" promises the participant a comprehensive countercultural experience of sexuality.[162]

The overemphasis on sex and drugs is not surprising. Established by Larry Harvey, the co-founder of the festival, Burning Man's guidelines highlight three sets of values that supposedly tie its community together.[163] The first can be described as values of collectivization, which emphasize inclusivity, a barter economy, the exchange of gifts, and "decommodification."[164] These values reflect an intentional rejection of all forms of the monetization of the experience, despite the fact that the participation fees and the rental of the material required for the experience are fairly high. The second set of values foregrounds experimentation and participation, thus giving the festival an experiential dimension that centers on the capacity for creative expression.[165] Finally, the third set of guiding principles emphasizes civic and communal engagement through the diverse forms of responsibility that are expected from the participants vis-à-vis both the community and the environment. Hence, the revelers are not only encouraged but actually required to fully take advantage of the opportunities Burning Man offers them.[166]

The desert is foundational to the experience of Burning Man. Saturated with Saharanism's sexy images of romanticized deserts, revelers seek experiences that they would not otherwise encounter in their ordinary world. Burning Man acts as a *zone franche*, where social and legal risks are minimized because living out one's desires and excesses are part of the package. Steven T. Jones, a journalist from the Bay Area, argues, in a manner that is reminiscent of Bauman, that Burning Man is a ritual that helps people turn their old selves into something different through the variety of experiences involving sex and drugs that they have throughout the duration of the festival.[167] Adding to the desert's malleability, British scholar Barry Taylor has counterintuitively argued that there is also spirituality amid Burning Man's "unbridled sexuality, widespread drug use, and other wild and hedonistic goings-on."[168] In this reading, a quest for the spiritual, which is experienced at the intersection of the sacred and the profane, underlies Burning Man.[169]

Beyond the hedonistic image conjured by the festival's focus on "Sex Positive Communities,"[170] Burning Man also aspires to refashion society based on a different ethics. Again, the desert here serves as a ground for experimentation of possible future societies. However, the aspiration to transform social relationships elicits challenging questions regarding issues of class, access, and inequality. Witt calls for a reflection on the difference between radical change within society and Burning Man's aspirations of change relocated to a remote desert location:

> To protest against these things in everyday life carried a huge social cost—one that only people like Jean were grimly willing to bear—and maybe that's what the old burners disliked about the new ones: the new ones upheld the idea of autonomous zones. The $400 ticket price was as much about the right to leave what happened at the festival behind as it was to enter in the first place.
>
> Still, I'd been able to do things here that I'd wanted to do for a long time, that I never could have done at home. And if this place felt right, if it had expanded so much over the years because to so many people it felt like "home," it had something to do with the inadequacy of the old ways that

> governed our lives in our real homes, where we felt lonely, isolated and unable to form the connections we wanted.[171]

Reading Witt, one cannot help but think about Burning Man being its own *Westworld*, in that it provides a protective environment for its revelers to be themselves. The desert serves as a place for revelers to absolve themselves of the guilt of not being participants in transformative actions in their everyday society. Instead of all-liberating change, festivalgoers opt for a temporary one that is designed for like-minded people for a defined duration.

This reality leads Witt to examine the limits of Burning Man's radicalism. The absolute freedom turns out to be ephemeral, and the urban world imposes its order on the revelers' lives. The desert, experienced through Burning Man, acts as a digression or a liminal space in one's life from which one can temporarily escape—both in the physical and legal terms. She writes: "The hypocrisy of the 'creative autonomous zone' weighed on me. Many of these people would go back to their lives and back to work on the great farces of our age. They wouldn't argue for the decriminalization of the drugs they had used; they wouldn't want anyone to know about their time in the orgy dome. That they had cheered at the funeral pyre of a Facebook 'like' wouldn't play well on Tuesday in the cafeteria at Facebook."[172] What is striking about Witt's words is the sense of disengagement that this desert liminality allows festivalgoers to have. Many of Burning Man revelers are wealthy and hold much economic and social clout, but, since the desert already meets their needs, they seem to refrain from using their power for social transformation elsewhere. Desertism, as a result, leads to the desertion of costly and transformative action in society, allowing its practitioners to live out their aspirations in the desert.

CONCLUSION

This chapter has drawn on a variety of materials across the Sahara and the American Southwest to conceptualize sexual Saharanism, which captures a plethora of sexual fantasies that are projected onto deserts and acted upon in them. Sexual Saharanism refers to systematized acts that are undergirded by the ideology of Saharanism, which has associated deserts with imaginaries of primitivism, emptiness, lawlessness, and impunity. As spaces inhabited by humans, deserts hold their own people's notions of sexuality and morality, but, as this chapter has demonstrated, sexual Saharanism tends to construct them as liminal spaces in which ethical and moral principles do not apply.

Colonialism and Saharanism's powerful legacy turned deserts into ideal spaces for sexual exploitation, predation, and experimentation. The Algerian Sahara in the nineteenth and twentieth centuries was constructed as a brothel for European tourists and French servicemen. The imbrication of the tourism industry in conjunction with the prolific output of military and civilian cultural producers created an image of the Sahara as devoid of ethics, law, and morality to invite sexual exploitation of Nāyliyyāt and Saharan children. Since colonial practices fascinated people encountering them for the first time, American and British travelers and journalists brought the French version of sexual Saharanism to their readers. Thanks to a network of literary, journalistic, cinematic, and other mediatic outlets, sexual Saharanism thrived and grew to reach audiences well beyond the colonizers themselves.

Although the chapter only focused on manifestations of sexual Saharanism in the colonial Sahara, *Westworld*, and the Burning Man festival, its arguments are relevant to similar experiences that unfold in other deserts across the world. In its broader implications, this chapter has revealed that deserts have served as canvases for the realization of sexual fantasies regardless of their outlandishness, excessiveness, and, in the case of pedophilia, illegality and immorality. Between abusive and criminalized sexualities that found refuge in the colonial Sahara and the experimentation with sex and drugs in the high-tech–dominated countercultural Burning Man festival, historicizing how sexual Saharanism pervades the way deserts are constructed as realms in which societally censured desires find their truest expression is crucial for understanding why these actions have happened in deserts and continue to be associated with them in the first place.

FIVE

"Unity of Creatures"

SAHARANISM MEETS DESERT ECOCARE

SAHARANISM'S DISCURSIVE DENIGRATION and actual mistreatment of deserts has normalized lack of empathy toward them as living ecosystems. From the Sonora to the Kalahari and from the Sahara to the Gobi deserts, arid spaces have suffered from Saharanism, which has deemed them desolate wastelands. Saharanism has been at the core of capitalistic and scientific enterprises that have unfolded in deserts and which have been misleadingly presented as beneficial for humanity's common good.[1] For instance, arguments for "panopticonizing" borders and building separation walls in deserts may be justified politically as enhancing border security but, as Vanda Felbab-Brown, Luis Alberto Urrea, and Jason De León have shown, these measures' humanitarian, socioeconomic, and environmental impacts are dramatic and long-lasting.[2] This represents a bleak reality that American figural painter Willie Binnie has captured in his painting *Border* (Fig. 13), which depicts an unbridgeable separation between the United States and Mexico in dark colors. Likewise, nuclear experiments may seem necessary when marketed as a deterrent against an outright nuclear war with real or imagined enemies.[3] However, a deeper examination of these policy justifications reveals that they are steeped in Saharanism's view of deserts as empty and dangerous, which warrants their necro-ecological outcomes—that is, the deadly toll these projects have taken on both human and nonhuman subjects in desert environments in the past, present, and in the future.

This chapter examines how Saharanism's threat to desert life in Africa and the Middle East has elicited an array of creative ecological responses. Saharanism's widespread dissemination in all manner of culture production has erased deserts' character as homes to people, plants, animals, and other invisible lives.[4] By historicizing works in which writers from the Sahara and

FIGURE 13. Willie Binnie, *Border*, 2020. Acrylic wash on raw canvas. 60 × 90 inches (1.52 × 2.43 m). Image courtesy of the artist.

the Arabian Deserts have conveyed their ecologically conscious worldviews of their homelands' encounter with various aspects of Saharanism, this chapter articulates Indigenous cultural producers' philosophical and critical engagements with Saharanism and its necro-ecological impacts. Saharanism, particularly in its industrial, extractive, and experimental forms, has instrumentalized the construct of desert "emptiness" to be an excuse for its horrifying pursuits in arid places. In 1962, the Australian historian Ivan Southall wrote that the desert in Woomera was "one of the greatest stretches of uninhabited wastelands on earth, created by God specifically for rockets, a magnitude of emptiness."[5] Unlike Southall's conception of the desert, the arid places this chapter examines are inhabited by people and other nonhuman subjects. If the desert of Saharanism is a void, the desert this chapter recovers is rich in ideas, mythologies, political struggles, and theoretical significance. It is a place where ritual and literature, combined with local environmental consciousness, coalesce to lay the foundations for an environmental humanities suited to the desert biome. As evidenced by the legacy of French atomic explosions in the Sahara, colonizers' insistence on the desert's uninhabited-ness and lifelessness did not spare its Indigenous populations the tragic consequences of the deadly experiments.[6] Indigenous engagements with the tragedies of Saharanism demonstrate that there is more to deserts than their supposed emptiness, dilapidation, and nonlife.

Indigenous thinkers, activists, and writers from Tamazgha and the Middle East have presented an image of their homelands that is antithetical to Saharanism. Saudi writer and oil economist Abdelrahman Munif and Tuareg novelist and philosopher Ibrahim al-Koni have carved out an entire subfield of Arabic literature dedicated to deserts.[7] Munif's *Mudun al-milḥ* (*Cities of Salt*) and al-Koni's *Nazīf al-ḥajar* (*The Bleeding of the Stone*), along with their nonfiction interventions, have historicized the myriad brutal consequences of anthropogenic activities in their respective homelands. Even before the editors of *Environmental Humanities: Voices from the Anthropocene* invited readers to reconsider life based on "the fundamental inseparability of the human and the nonhuman in their shared earthly rootedness,"[8] al-Koni coined the concept of *waḥdat al-kāʾināt* (unity of creatures), which captures the indispensable complementary of all lives in his desert home.[9] Al-Koni's concept not only undermines Saharanism's clichés about lifeless aridity but also predicates the sustainability of any anthropocentric life on the preservation of *all* lives. A few years before al-Koni emerged as a world-class writer, Munif revolutionized the desert by presenting it as a political terrain for reevaluating the relationship among space, resources, and the need for Gulf States and societies to think sustainably beyond what he called "cruel and inimical cities" of salt.[10] To say that Munif's work is transformative would greatly understate the role he played in putting the Arabian Desert on the map of both literature and critical sustainability studies worldwide. Deeply realistic, both Munif and al-Koni have argued for an ecological care (ecocare) approach that requires the rational management of the finite natural resources that are crucial for sustaining life in the desert.

Munif's and al-Koni's expansive body of works has not prevented the emergence of a younger generation of cultural stakeholders in the desert.[11] Malian Tuareg author Omar Al Ansari, who wrote *Ṭabīb tinbuktū* (*The Physician of Timbuktu*), writes in Arabic, while Algerian microbiologist Hocine Hacene writes in French.[12] *Ṭabīb tinbuktū* was probably the first novel in Arabic to depict the impact of French nuclear experiments on the Sahara, including the fact that a joint Nigerian-British scientific commission detected high levels of radiation just one day after the first experiment on February 13, 1960.[13] Likewise, Hacene's *Le Sahara dans l'enfer* is a scientifically grounded book that historicizes the French nuclear program and its impact on Saharans. From Reggane in the Touat area and Tan Afella in the Hoggar, *Le Sahara dans l'enfer* tells the story of four workers in the racialized category of *populations laborieuses du Bas-Touat* (the working population of the Lower Touat, PLBT)[14] hired as unskilled labor to support the construction of the facilities needed for the testing of French nuclear bombs.[15]

These works participate in a desert Indigenous ecocare philosophy that has engaged with Saharanism and its consequences both directly and indirectly. Except for al-Koni, who, as I will show in the following pages, has recently talked about "ideology" vis-à-vis deserts, the rest of the Indigenous authors whose works I analyze through this lens are aware of Saharanism's manifestations without necessarily fleshing it out in clear ideological terms. Their works do, however, deconstruct the interrelated system of ideas that, over the course of the centuries, has made deserts into wastelands in which anything can happen. Even as they leave it unnamed, these local thinkers' depictions of Saharanism's dire humanitarian and environmental consequences help us define the contours of an intellectual trend and actionable practice that has thus far eluded articulation.

Rooted in desert ecologies and global trends of environmentalist thought, these local conceptions of ecocare present worldviews that refute Saharanism's assumptions about the barrenness and uselessness of deserts that go undeveloped or unexploited. Based on their intimate knowledge of the land and its traditions, the local cultural producers whom this chapter examines have grappled with the various deaths, traumas, displacements, and ecocides that Saharanism has brought to their desert homelands. Their records of the wounds Saharanism inflicted on their desert ecosystems are the core of their ecocare, which, as this chapter demonstrates, is not merely a manifesto of environmentalist thought in deserts but also—and most significantly—a reparative approach to justice for a biome that is threatened because of its very nature.

Ecocare-imbued visions of deserts are antithetical to Saharanism. In Indigenous imaginings, deserts are neither empty nor monolithic. They are geographically diverse, with mountains, ravines, valleys, and varied flora and fauna. In terms of their human makeup, the social organization of deserts, as demonstrated by sociologists and historians since the time of Ibn Khaldun, is embedded with significant hierarchies, political awareness, rebellions, claims to sovereignty, forms of knowledge, and methods of trade that are crucial to the study of their politics, religions, lineages, and commerce.[16] Deserts are thus no different from other, ordinary places, in that they are sites for all social and communal struggles.[17] Thus, they are far from being apolitical, since all plans to dominate them have led to resistance from their inhabitants, like the Tuaregs, who defended their territorial autonomy in the face of explorations, invasions, and capitalist schemes.[18] Instead of Saharanism's *terra nullius* and *terra incognita*, deserts are, for their inhabitants, both known and subject to ownership rights. If they actually were empty, as Saharanism stipulates, deserts would not be the loci of "wars, conflicts, and competition between rulers" or sites for "attempts at annexation and efforts to impose a form of unity [on their people]."[19] For these Indigenous insiders, deserts are not just what meets the eye. However, Indigenous knowledge, which does not align with Saharanism's understanding of methods of knowing, ends up being dismissed.[20] Knowledge formation beyond this Euro-American–centric world encompasses diverse habits that are grounded in a deep awareness of interactions between people and their environment. Ecocare is, therefore, all the more crucial for sustaining Indigenous ecological practices and keeping the threatened desert ecosystem alive.

HEALING THE WORLD: AL-KONI'S *WAḤDAT AL-KĀʾINĀT* IN THE DESERT

Ibrahim al-Koni has argued that the tourist's camera view reduces the desert to scarcity.[21] Al-Koni allows us to draw a distinction between the "superficial view" founded on impressions made from behind the camera and a "thick view" (to paraphrase Clifford Geertz's famous concept of "thick description") that is the result of a long-term interaction with desert biomes.[22] The superficial view is that of the "overlander," which Geoff Nicholson describes, based on Quentin Crewe's definition of the phenomenon, as "passing over the land without in any way touching the culture."[23] The thick view is grounded not only in experiencing life in the desert but also in understanding its symbolic significance and observing its codes of conduct. Saharanism most often reflects its propagators' shortsighted, touristic view, which fails to capture the deeper meaning of the environment. Even when they enter a desert with the best of intentions and a clear awareness of what not to do, practitioners of Saharanism oftentimes are prevented from embracing deserts' radical difference and attempting to grasp its significance for its full-time inhabitants.

Al-Koni's multipronged approach has successfully put the Sahara at the center of a critical literary and nonliterary oeuvre. He has, for instance, paid attention to the way the desert (*al-ṣaḥrāʾ* is definite in Arabic) is talked about and depicted as a space of nonlife because of its aridity. He has grappled with the literary disregard for deserts, writing, "Since the beginning of humanity, the desert has remained marginalized, neglected, forgotten, and alienated from the world."[24] He has tackled what he called "tanmīṭ ṣaḥrāʾ" (the stereotyping of the desert), which, combined with ideology, leads to *tazwīr* or "fabrication[s]."[25] Although he does not call it Saharanism, al-Koni's discussion of ideology corresponds to my definition of this concept. He writes:

> Self-evident truth is always a product of ideology. When the desert becomes a wasteland [in ideology], there is no guarantee that the banal mentality that markets the desert as a void won't prevail; since it is a ruin and because ruins are desolation, because they are remnants, we can shed tears over reality but we cannot recognize it as a dwelling, since in the myths of the nations of the ancient world, ruins are always inhabited by evil souls, and we have no choice but to leave them. Is this where we get the deadly conviction that the desert is a void, that it is a wasteland, and that there is no guardian, custodian, or heir in its space because it is communized? What does communized mean? It means that every action is permissible! This certainty is the reason why the firman which legitimizes the most vicious sins against it as it is exploited as a site for conducting nuclear tests or dumping chemical waste, and its representation as a sacrificial offering for terrorism and the merchants of prohibited goods, finds a safe haven.[26]

Al-Koni can be said to have depicted both Saharanism and its antidote in this article, and the most striking observation is that the ideology of emptiness has a universal impact on *all* deserts. This confirms that Saharanism's mistreatment of deserts is not about specific arid lands but about the category "desert," which indicates that this is an issue grounded in a long history of deserts symbolizing nonlife.

These distinctions allow al-Koni to offer an Indigenous philosophy of desert ecocare. Aided by a decentered mode of knowledge and cosmogony that accept both science and mythology as valid ways of explaining the world, al-Koni's ecocare shifts away from an anthropocentric view to one that sees humans as just one species among others whose existence is contingent upon the ecological balance that will sustain all creatures. Al-Koni has theorized this ecocare in his notion of *waḥdat al-kāʾināt*,[27] which should not be confused with the Sufi notion of *waḥdat al-wujūd* (unity of being/existence).[28] The latter refers to the relationship between humans and God, while the former refers to the complementarity between all creatures in the desert. *Waḥdat al-kāʾināt*, a recurrent theme in al-Koni's interviews, is the idea that human life in arid lands is only sustainable so long as other creatures' lives are also nurtured and sustained. Accordingly, anthropocentrism in the desert simply and predictably leads to anthroponihilism.

Waḥdat al-kāʾināt is particularly compelling in light of climate change's disruption of the Earth's ecological balance. Hence, the apocalyptic end that awaits us should global warming not be curbed gives an even greater significance to al-Koni's prescient formulation of this unity of creatures. A 2022 report of the UN Intergovernmental Panel on Climate Change (IPCC) warned with high confidence that human-induced warming would lead to a variety of risk-laden climate dangers that threaten both humans and ecosystems.[29] This report paints a dire picture of the mayhem that anthropogenic climate change will spur and which includes irremediable losses in both terrestrial and aquatic ecosystems.[30] The IPCC report, drawing on global warming's impact on deserts throughout the world, sounded the alarm for the impact of environmental disruption on water sources and desert plants as well as the degradation of desert communities.[31]

The difference, however, is that al-Koni grappled with ecological sustainability in the Sahara decades before an understanding of global warming became widespread. His novella *The Bleeding of the Stone* articulated a first version of this notion of interspecies harmony.[32] In his own words, it was

> an early warning against what would befall the world if it continued in its blindness and its disregard for this unity of creatures. It was a siren, like the novel entitled *Gold Dust*, that predated the current environmental catastrophe. The lesson is that the disruption of the unity of creatures is a disruption of the global balance and an extermination of all animal and plant species, which paves the way for genocide against human species, because the law that rules this world is similar to the one that governs the human body: any microbe that affects any member of the body is a tumor capable of destroying the entire body.[33]

At its core, *waḥdat al-kāʾināt* is a philosophy of human and nonhuman interdependence in the shared desert environment. The notion grants equal significance to all the lives that coexist in this reputedly harsh space. This complementarity of existences is now, in the age of the Anthropocene, almost a given in both environment and animal studies.[34] Anna Tsing has argued that interspecies collaboration is a must for an inhabitable world, for trans-species death will be the result of an absence of cooperation.[35] The key distinction here, however, is that al-Koni developed *waḥdat al-kāʾināt* from the interdependence of all lives for survival in the desert, specifically. To live in the desert environment means nurturing other lives, which, in turn, means taking seriously this interspecies unity.

Asouf, the main character in *The Bleeding of the Stone*, leads an isolated—but not lonely—life in the Massak Mallat in southern Libya: tending to his animals; watching over the old Amazigh petroglyphs; and guarding the *waddan*, a desert animal important in Tuareg mythology. A mystical loner, Asouf has learned the importance of keeping one's word to the *waddan* and of not hunting it. Embodying the interdependence between the human and nonhuman subjects of the desert, Asouf abides by the cherished codes of conduct that command respect of all existences to avoid tragic disasters. Asouf's duty to be an agent of sustainability and unity, and not of necro-ecological catastrophe, limits his latitude to hunt by adhering to values passed down to him by his father who impresses on him that "to hunt a pregnant animal is a great sin."[36] These teachings are deepened by his father's own death as result of his recanting his vow to not hunt the *waddan* again. These teachings allow Asouf to understand and internalize the desert as a site for interspecies respect and the preservation of both human and nonhuman subjects.

Asouf's embodiment of this unity does not mean that everyone shares the same values. Qābīl and Masʿūd, two agents of extractive Saharanism, appear unannounced in Asouf's remote desert home and turn his ecologically balanced life upside down. The parallels between Qābīl and Asouf's encounter and the Quranic story of Qābīl's killing of his brother Hābīl (Abel) are all too clear.[37] Driven by jealousy and anger that God accepted his brother's offering and not his, Qābīl committed what is believed to be the first murder in history. This Quranic killing, however, was a very specific fratricide, whereas Qābīl's eventual murder of Asouf is a necro-ecologically disruptive act. While Asouf thinks of the *waddan* as an extension of human life, Qābīl, whose anthropocentric Saharanism entails the relentless consumption of meat, shows no concern for desert animals' sustainability. Unable to understand Asouf's vegetarianism and his unconditional love for animals, Qābīl kills Asouf because he is blind to the latter's environmentalist wisdom and jealous of his ability to embrace the habitat he shares with other creatures in such a loving way.

Qābīl's obsessions with meat and hunting bring about the downfall of the desert ecosystem in the oases. His access to deadly American weapons, including a helicopter, emboldens his ecocidal nature, which feeds off his merciless desire to kill. In a short period of time, Qābīl's murderous guns reap herds of gazelles, which fall "like clusters of dates torn apart in a storm"[38] and spill "rivers of blood" to the point that "the herds virtually [die] out."[39] All of this is exacerbated by Qābīl's "little thought for the rules of nature."[40] His relentless need to consume meat and sell the excess to John Parker, an American officer stationed in the desert who furnishes him with the lethal ammunition, pushes him to run roughshod over the biome and eventually turn to cannibalism by exterminating animals and killing Asouf.[41] Qābīl's cannibalistic act is, to borrow Lisa Kröger's words about a different time period, evidence that "the nature of humanity is to corrupt."[42] Just like the American tractors and bulldozers that, in search of oil, wipe out Wādi al-ʿUyūn in Munif's *Cities of Salt*, the "introduction of rapid firing guns to the desert" precludes the self-renewal of desert life.[43]

Accounts of the French occupation of the Sahara reveal that thousands of mouflon, gazelles, tigers, and rabbits perished as a result of colonial enterprises. Both the last Atlas lion and the last Saharan crocodile were exterminated under colonial rule. Although geographer Émile-Felix Gautier documented the *méharistes*' extermination of the addax and antelope in the Algerian portion of the Sahara,[44] the steep toll that colonialism took on desert wildlife has yet to be fully investigated. Hunting aside,[45] various French desert-crossing missions cost countless camels their lives. The Foureau-Lamy Mission started its three-year crossing of the Sahara in 1898 with a thousand camels, most of which had died by the time it reached its destination in Chad.[46] French authorities' reliance on camels for military and exploratory missions spelled economic and ecological disaster for native Saharans who depended on these animals for their livelihoods and mobility in the desert. As both colonial and postcolonial scholars have demonstrated, the camel is essential to the desert way of life, and any change to its existence directly impacts people's ability to exist in their desert homelands.[47] Controlling camel herds and their numbers could also change mobility patterns. The extermination of Saharan wildlife would only intensify after the French experiments in Reggane and Tan Afella between 1960 and 1966, which caused an unspecified number of deaths and miscarriages among livestock.

In its broader environmentalist message, *The Bleeding of the Stone* speaks to the dire environmental consequences of any infringement on the unwritten desert *nāmūs* (laws). In fact, there is a link between Qābīl's mistreatment of the environment and his merciless slaughter of Asouf. His careless breaching of unity of creatures prepares him to cross the forbidden line of homicide.

He equates Asouf's life with a *waddan*'s, and he harnesses his expertise as "one who'd slaughtered all the herds of gazelles in the Red Hamada" to murder Asouf.[48] Qābīl's trivialization of the death of the desert animals throughout his hunting career has cheapened the value of all life in his eyes. Greed and a zero-sum approach to satisfying his desire for meat blind Qābīl to his ecocidal violence. However, his blatant transgression of the laws of nature and his destabilization of its order release an ecocare imaginary in which nature is (re) endowed with agency: murdering Asouf unleashes the ecosystem's capacity for self-repair and self-renewal as it removes the deregulating factor (Qābīl) in a deluge. When Qābīl's actions exceed what nature could tolerate, the natural order intervenes to bring back the lost order into life.

Al-Koni's theory of desert environmentalism does not, however, focus exclusively on the extermination of wildlife. The superficial touristic view he critiques conceals the desert's civilization while drawing unwanted attention to its millennial Amazigh petroglyphs. The corrupting power of the tourist's camera reveals what is supposed to remain protected in the remote recesses of Wadi Methkhandoush. While accompanying a delegation of paleontologists, an employee of the Archaeological Department warns Asouf: "A lot of people will come, from all races and religions, to look at these ancient things. See that they don't spoil the rocks. These rocks are a great treasure, and these paintings are our country's pride. Keep your eyes open. People are greedy, ready to grab anything. If they can, they'll steal our rocks to sell them in their own country, for thousands, or millions even."[49] The urbanite official offers Asouf money for this service, but he falls short of understanding that Asouf embodies *waḥdat al-kā'ināt*, which makes his own survival in this isolated area contingent on that of everything around him. By defending other existences with which he shares his environment, Asouf, in fact, preserves his own life.

Al-Koni, like Munif, to whom I will turn shortly, considers the discovery of gas and oil a turning point in the treatment of deserts. In Libya, the oil wealth of the 1960s brought both economic opportunity and an opportunistic view of the desert environment. Through their encounter with global gas and oil capitalism, local people internalized Saharanism's extractive approach to deserts. As al-Koni has put it: "They disdain the lives of the creatures of this land, which yesterday were an integral part of the human community; these creatures are undomesticated animals and desert plants, and the traces of the ancestors inscribed on the walls of caves for thousands of years. This also includes the exhaustion of the underground water, which was not water before today but rather a life and a condition of existence for future generations."[50] A *ghanīma* (spoil of war) mentality replaced the more ecologically responsible ancestral treatment of the desert.[51] The shift from an approach characterized by creaturely unity to one that is entirely anthropocentric could not be starker.

Waḥdat al-kā'inat has wider ramifications. It encapsulates an ethics of living in the desert not as a parasitic agent whose own survival outweighs all other life but as one who can only be when and if all creatures are equally afforded the same right to be. This creaturely unity also strikes a balance between need and greed, which scarcity of resources teaches desert dwellers to take seriously. However, this desert ethics is not available to just anyone, since it is the result of the thick view of lived experience and ancestral traditions that make lives in deserts interdependent, more so than in other places. Hence, *waḥdat al-kā'inat* holds a radical promise for the perception of the complementarity between all lives not only in deserts but also anywhere human action has triggered environmental damage.

Al-Koni's ecocare is embedded in the Amazigh notion of *tagat* (ⵜⴰⴳⴰⵜ). Sometimes also pronounced *tagatut* (ⵜⴰⴳⴰⵜⵓⵜ), *tagat* is a malediction that befalls or catches up with someone who hurts any form of life. Since the Sahara is also occupied by spirits, Amazigh people are aware that other subjects, including *wida ur ḥlinīn* (ⵡⵉⴷⴰ ⵓⵔ ⵃⵍⵉⵏⵉⵏ; evil spirits), are there to punish wrongdoers. Amazigh children are raised with the firm belief that hurting an animal, uprooting a plant, or muddying clear water are unforgivable sins that will come back to haunt them. *Tagat* is nature's power to take its revenge on those who break its rules and injudiciously exert their dominion over other, powerless beings. Therefore, *tagat* encompasses everything, and woe to those who transgress its *nāmūs*.[52] Al-Koni captures this eco-conscious system in writing that the desert taught him that "the tree, the smallest tree or plant, is my equal. Also, in the desert I learned the prohibition against dislocating any green branch. In the desert, I learned not to break open a bird's egg."[53] The belief in retribution through *tagat* plays a crucial regulating role in the relationship between desert people and their environment. Hamid Ait Slimane's short story "Tanezrouft" conveys how *tagat* befalls a people whose greed and covetousness lead to their ruination. An Amazigh sage transformed Tanezrouft, the harsh desert that French geographers and military officers wrote so much about, into an Eden, but nature takes away its water when its people engaged in excessive behaviors that deviated from the early path traced by their forefather.[54] Saharans understand that abiding by the *nāmūs* is the only way to survive, and that an ecumenical disposition toward other creatures spares one *tagat* and its disastrous visitations.

Rooted in desert ecocare, al-Koni's literary and theoretical work thus refutes Saharanism's claims that deserts are inherently barren, as well as their later construction as spaces where anything can be undertaken. By portraying the dangers that threaten desert ecosystems and the elaborate ethical and cultural systems that Indigenous Saharans have put in place to regulate their lives under the harsh conditions of the desert, al-Koni's practice of ecocare complicates the arid lands' story. Instead of an in-spite-of-the-desert position, al-Koni presents a thanks-to-the-desert framework to illuminate its occulted way of life. Through his multilayered conversations with the Sahara, al-Koni's ecocare foregrounds a thick view that is grounded in an experiential, culturally sensitive approach to desert life. This thick view has underlaid his prescient conceptualization of creaturely unity, which has made humankind's own sustainability reliant on the well-being of all creatures.

THE MURDERED DESERT: REGISTERING HUMAN AND ENVIRONMENTAL TRAUMAS

Petrocapitalism and Its Threat to Sustainability

If al-Koni has constructed a philosophy of ecocare based on a balanced relationship between all creatures in the desert, Saudi novelist and essayist Abdelrahman Munif's ecocare placed the desert at the center of the twentieth-century political, social, cultural, and capitalistic upheavals of the Middle East. More than any other desert-centered fiction or critical scholarship published in Arabic, Munif's work paved the way for the study of the sociocultural and politico-economic struggles that have ensued from desert societies' discovery of oil. His practice of Indigenous ecocare was rooted in an intimate knowledge of Bedouin culture and a critical understanding of petroleum economics, in which he held a doctoral degree.[55] Focused intensively on the sustainability of life in the Gulf after oil wealth's transformation of the Bedouin way of life, Munif's fiction and nonfiction do not simply deconstruct the models of governance adopted in oil-rich Gulf countries; they also chart alternative paths toward a more sustainable future in the post–fossil-fuel era.

Until the publication of *Cities of Salt,* Arabic writers did not address the issues related to oil and deserts.[56] As Munif declared in a televised interview in 1993, these questions had been unexamined, remaining "mawāḍī bikr" (virgin topics).[57] As Stacey Balkan and Swaralipi Nandi have argued, oil's elusion of examination is imbricated in "spatial amnesia" and a refusal to admit its ecocidal and necrological impacts.[58] Oil specifically was not an issue that could be ignored because of its role in shaping the "political and geographic contours" of the twentieth-century Arab world.[59] As a result of his tapping into this uncharted territory, the Saudi state pressured other Gulf States to ban his books, adding another layer to the revocation of his citizenship in 1963.[60] This aggressive response to Munif's fictional and scholarly work reveals that deserts are not as inconsequential as Saharanism has portrayed them. In fact, Munif's desert is a vivid site of struggle among antagonistic visions of authority, identity, and livelihood,[61] which threatens the political system that was shored up by petrodollars after American and British prospectors struck oil. Hence, the oil industry brought wealth and planted the seeds of authoritarianism, which Munif brilliantly depicted in his portrayal of the inhumane prison systems.[62]

Drawing on Munif's work, Robert Nixon has argued that in most cases, reliance on fossil fuels has generated states that are "undemocratic, militaristic, corruption-riddled, and governed without transparency."[63] These phenomena cannot be divorced from the process that Graeme Macdonald has described about the internationalization of oil sites that invites foreign technologies, expertise, and labor,[64] which invite, as corollary, local despotism. Despite these insights, most scholarship has overlooked the desert itself as a locus of Indigenous people's theorizations, political struggles, and mobilization against hegemony. While many studies have examined *Cities of Salt*, the ecological road map that Munif proposed for sustainability of life in the desert of the Arabian Peninsula requires a more substantial engagement with his multipronged ecocare project, which identifies and reflects on the disruption of desert societies and the impawning of their futures to a finite resource.

Munif's depiction of the life ushered in by oil capitalism unveils how desert communities in the Gulf were thrust into what can be called petro-Saharanism's hypermodernity. In *Bādiyat al-ẓulumāt*, the last volume of the quintet *Cities of Salt*, the narrator captures the significance of the emir's death as a persistent, powerful wind that "changed a lot of the landmarks and forms" as well as "the ideas, the convictions, and relationships of many, who became humans of another type."[65] Munif gives us one of the most damning assessments of the impact of petro-Saharanism, by which I mean all visions for deserts motivated by oil and its revenue. Petro-Saharanism and its schemes undermined desert societies and their age-old way of life: their tribal customs "are overridden sometimes as a result of competition and struggle. . . especially in the context of a transition of power."[66] The dramatic, heartbreaking toll that this hypermodernity took on the Wādi al-ʿUyūn oasis and community speaks volumes about the overnight transformation it brought upon the desert as a whole. A landmark of desert life in the books, Wādi al-ʿUyūn is disrupted by the arrival of American oil prospectors who, unbeknownst to the local populations, unleash the irreversible chain of events that will benefit petro-Saharanism at the expense of the community.[67] Petro-hypermodernity dispossesses the Wādi's Indigenous tribes and throws them into the vortex of proletarianization at the service of the oil industry.

In addition to the subjugation of nomads to the capitalist system, *Cities of Salt* recounts how the discovery of oil also caused ecological mayhem. This ecocide, which transformed familiar places into entirely alien, deserted spaces, is poignantly rendered through descriptions of the Wādi before and after the Americans' arrival. At first, the Wādi is described as "an outpouring of green amid the harsh, obdurate desert, as if it had burst from within the earth or fallen from the sky."[68] However, American oilmen utterly disfigure it and end its role as a life-giver in the harsh desert despite the inhabitants' objections.[69] Fawaz, the son of the recalcitrant leader Miteb al-Hadhāl, returns one year later to get a job with his brother Shaalan, who stayed to work for the Americans, and finds that the Wādi has become "a place he had never seen before. There was no trace of the wadi he had left behind; none of the old things remained. Even the fresh breezes that used to blow at this time of year had become hot and searing in the daytime, and a bitter cold penetrated his bones late at night."[70] The decimation of the oasis deregulates the desert climate, which is now described as being excessively hot or cold depending on the time of the day.

The merciless attack on the natural space of the Wādi instantiates the correlation between unchecked technological advancement and petro-Saharanism's callous attitude toward desert nature. The community of Wādi al-ʿUyūn is so severely uprooted that Fawaz realizes that "what had happened was not just the loss of a place called Wādi al-ʿUyūn, not any loss that a man could describe or grow accustomed to."[71] The loss "was a breaking off, like death, that nothing and no one could ever heal."[72] Obviously, the American oil prospectors are not emotionally connected to the place, and their Saharanism blinds them to the Wādi's importance.[73] Their "tractors. . . attacked the orchards like ravenous wolves, tearing up the trees and throwing them to the earth one after another, and leveled all the orchards between the brook and the fields."[74] This violent scene is nothing short of a cold-blooded ecocide that, like in *The Bleeding of the Stone*, is enabled by Saharanism and American technology.

In Munif's ecocare, nature is anthropomorphized as it undergoes petro-Saharanism's ecocide. The novel gives a voice to plants; the trees "shook violently and groaned before falling, cried for help, wailed, panicked, called out in helpless pain and then fell entreatingly to the ground, as if trying to snuggle into the earth to grow and spring forth alive again."[75] Nevertheless, the willful American workers, armed with deep-seated, guiltless Saharanism, pay attention neither to the wailing of the trees nor to the trauma of the desert inhabitants. Once the Americans' genocidal attack on the oasis comes to an end, the outcome of their work is "a cruel, wicked sight that resembled death."[76] The powerless desert inhabitants feel all the guilt and remorse for being witnesses to these brutal scenes. Unlike the Americans who treat the desert as a worksite, its inhabitants treat it with reverence as a home. Desert ecocare resides in this gap between the two. Home, for the desert natives, has a sense of permanence, whereas worksites are temporary. However, this sense of permanence and homeliness is disrupted by the expulsion of the inhabitants to the emerging oil town of Ujra.

The discovery of oil ushered in what has been described as the "resource curse."[77] According to this theory, natural resources have, instead of being a source of prosperity, led to intractable problems for oil-rich societies. Producing a commodity that has strategic importance for world economies, oil companies were empowered to make decisions that were beneficial to the owners "regardless of the results or losses that might be inflicted on the host country."[78] The powerful oil cartels, also known as the "Seven Sisters," have dominated the oil industry since it was constructed on the remains of the Ottoman Empire in the 1920s.[79] These companies have not always used democratic or clean means to ensure the continuity of their extractive endeavors. They supported coups, funded militias, and nurtured corruption to achieve their goals at the expense of Indigenous populations. Indeed, the discovery and extraction of oil has had deep societal impacts,[80] but the focus has mainly centered on the connection between fossil fuels and global warming. The questions of human and environmental murder that has unfolded in deserts as a result of the extraction of oil have not been broached. More specifically, traumas inflicted on human beings whose connections to their ancestral world were severed and transformed forever do not figure as much in current scholarship. Miteb al-Hadhāl, the recalcitrant tribal leader in Munif's novel, points to this reality. Overpowered by this environmental butchery, Miteb, a Bedouin and a free man, "felt alone, like a meaningless grain of sand no one cared about" for the first time in his life.[81] His pride is hurt, and his existence subjected to untold violence. His traumatic experience pushes him to act as if he "had been struck by fear and then dumbness,"[82] leading him to self-exile in the desert.

Munif did not invent this tragic story. As he revealed in an interview, the novel is based on his own continued examination of "historical events and relationships of a certain mode" after his study of the "oil period."[83] This task required "archival work and historical readings as well as the examination of events and people," which allowed him to combine this "documentary material" with "material from the imagination."[84] This method enabled Munif to delve into aspects of the oil industry that may have been absent from the written record, such as his depiction of how some people were so attached to the desert that they simply surrendered to death. For instance, although Umm Kosh shows tremendous resilience to the long absence of her son, she loses her will to live after the Americans dismember the orchard. Her sudden death is a rejection of life under "petrocapitalism,"[85] which is another local response to combat homogenization, global capitalism, and neoliberalism.[86] By recovering real stories of little people like Umm Kosh, Munif eternalizes the experiences of those who have been omitted from the history of this dizzying hypermodernity, which made the desert into a complete sacrifice zone.

Munif's desert ecocare leaves out no aspect of the interconnected transformations the oil industry has imposed on the condition of desert populations. As if the trauma of displacement and the loss of their home were not enough, the Bedouins have also had to contend with their proletarianization. Once begun, their sacrificial operation remains open-ended to impact not only their present but also their future. The disconnect between their nomadic skills and the new ones required by the oil industry humiliated them. Mocked by the Americans, the throats of the Bedouins-turned-workers became "filled with a bitterness that gave everything the taste of colocynth."[87] Petro-Saharanism demoted the nomads to a lower-class status in what was only the beginning of their relentless descent into an even deeper and sinister proletarianization, which incorporated them into a well-oiled system of disempowerment.[88]

The oil industry also forced Bedouins to endure spatial segregation. In *Cities of Salt*, the gated, orderly American part (American Harran) and the open, disorderly Arab town (Arab Harran) are contiguous,[89] but the difference between them breeds resentment:

> [The Bedouins'] depression was never deeper than when the workers looked around to see, in the east, American Harran: lit up, shining and noisy, covered with budding vegetation; from afar they could hear the voices of Americans splashing in the swimming pools, rising in song or laughter. . . . To the west were the houses of Harran, from which smoke rose at sundown and the sounds of human and animal life came. Last of all they saw the barracks they lived in and this dry, harsh, remote life, at which point memories flooded back and their hearts ached with longing, and they found endless pretexts for quarrels, sorrow, and sometimes tears.[90]

The psychological effects of this Manichean division, which is reminiscent of Frantz Fanon's distinction between colonial and colonized cities,[91] translate into somatic troubles and behavioral issues that encapsulate the impact of Saharanism's destabilization of these desert dwellers' lifestyle. Their space sacrificed, their homes lost, and their freedom lost, the Bedouins plunged into the abyss of Saharanism-fueled petromodernity.

The nomads' disempowerment vis-à-vis petro-Saharanism feeds a ghostly imaginary that relies on equally powerless miracles to get rid of the Americans. In addition to the somatic trauma inflicted on the nomads, who are now forced to work in extreme weather conditions, trauma impairs the Bedouins' ability to speak and express their feelings. As Dori M. Laub has argued in other contexts,[92] linguistic trauma pushes characters to introversion. Wadha al-Hamad, Miteb al-Hadhāl's wife, presents a case of traumatic loss of language due to being displaced from Wādi al-ʿUyūn. However, the older women around her think that "fever had tied her tongue."[93] As the months pass and her condition does not improve, her continued trauma is blamed on "a black devil [that] had entered her body between her stomach and the upper chest through the water of Rawdhat al-Mashti."[94] Wadha's illness proves that the demons, devils, and spirits that the desert inhabitants invoke to explain their world are powerless in the face of new illnesses brought about by petromodernity. Hence, the oasis dwellers are not only expropriated and displaced, but their ability to speak is also impacted, making their experience all the more traumatic.[95] The oil industry took their words and replaced their worldview with one mired in destruction. However, it was only the beginning of a future-oriented sacrificial project that would perpetually transform who they were and what they would become. In fact, Saharanism thrust them into petro-postcoloniality.

In his works of nonfiction, Munif portrays the "shock" of oil and gas as molds that gave shape to contemporary Gulf societies. After its discovery and exploitation, oil initiated a new era in the Arabian Peninsula in which petroleum "determined" everything.[96] For Munif, "everything" meant all aspects of life. Omar AlShehabi, a Bahraini sociologist, has addressed this reality in arguing that oil dominates the most infinitesimal details of life in the Gulf, likening it to "the blood that runs in its veins and feeds all the other aspects of its life."[97] Sudden, sizeable wealth caught desert societies by surprise and paved the way for a phenomenon that uprooted entire peoples. However, Munif laments the treatment of the oil industry as a financial resource that never became part of an integrated economic and industrial vision in the Gulf. This financializing approach turned the oil industry into a bearer of "disfigurations and [irreparable] risks"[98] instead of being a catalyst for positive, multifaceted, sustainable development.

The risks and disfigurations that Munif highlights in various articles and book chapters were spurred in part by desert peoples' encounters with petro-Saharanism. Munif, like al-Koni, located the impact of Saharanism in the dissipation of traditional ecocare and the transformed attitude toward land.[99] In a book chapter entitled "Baʿḍ āthār ṣadmat al-nafṭ fī al-jazīra al-ʿarabiyya" (Some of the Effects of the Oil Shock in the Arabian Peninsula), Munif lists the commodification of land and accompanying vertiginous transformations that the oil industry set in motion. Land became coveted and, sometimes, powerful entrepreneurs dispossessed its rightful owners. Because the logic of extraction underlying these practices is antithetical to desert ecocare, it was difficult for the Bedouins to understand the shift from a desert-friendly existence to one that internalized profit-making.[100] Nonetheless, it is not just the rapport to the land that shifted; money also "has [acquired] the highest value" and is perceived as being "able to make anything happen."[101] The monetization of social relationships is another consequence of oil money, to which Munif attributes the "consumptive voracity that reigns over petrol societies."[102] Hence, the oil industry introduced modes of thinking and behaving that deepened the disconnect between the Arabian Desert and its people.

Munif's ecocare, unlike al-Koni's more philosophical trend, is particularly steeped in his studies in social sciences. That said, both men share a deep concern for the sustainability in their respective deserts. In *Waṭanī ṣaḥrāʾ kubrā*, al-Koni returned to the theme of the extraction of desert resources, particularly the use of pipelines to take aquifer water from the Libyan Desert to the coastal cities in order to meet the needs of the urbanization ensuing from the country's oil reserves.[103] However, concern for sustainability is even more salient in Munif's critical output, particularly in his attention to the transnational influences that led Gulf businesspeople to adopt unsustainable construction models borrowed from the US and Hong Kong.[104] For Munif, "This construction style may fit Western Cities because of the demographic density and the nature of the climate and the land available, and also the high prices [of rent] and because of the businesses and their independence and complementarity, but it does not suit areas that are sparsely populated or have disjointed demographics. Also, it does not suit the hot weather or rather, the intense heat, which in the summer most often surpasses 50°C in the shade."[105] Most importantly, however, Munif wondered whether these skyscrapers would be able to outlive the depletion of oil in the future. These are questions that contributions to the edited volume *al-Bīy'a fī al-khalīj* (*The Environment in the Gulf*) have further complicated through considerations of oil's domino effect on demographics, consumerism, urbanism, and the environment in the Gulf in the age of the Anthropocene.[106] We can see that Munif was prescient in placing sustainability as a sine qua non for the tenability of life in post-oil Arabia.

Munif died in 2004, but his four-decades-long engagement with petro-Saharanism's impact on Gulf societies paved the way for a multifaceted understanding of its continuing effects. AlShehabi has demonstrated that between 1932 and 2015, the Gulf countries had earned 9.60 trillion dollars from extracting and exporting their oil, and argued that much of this revenue was spent on welfare and large public constructions, with some of this wealth only recently being put into revenue-generating investments.[107] As these numbers indicate, Munif's fiction and scholarship can be read as a cry against petro-Saharanism and its reductive notions about the desert, but also against native societies' adoption of its worst elements. Munif was a visionary in both respects, and his warnings against the worst kinds of development in oil-producing countries in the Arabian Peninsula have proven accurate. Nevertheless, not everyone heard Munif's message cautioning against the construction of dissoluble "Cities of Salt," or what AlShehabi has called "mudun al-ḥadātha al-nifṭiyya" (cities of petromodernity), which have no ability to survive should the oil reserves reach depletion thresholds.[108]

The ongoing development of the 10,230-square-mile Neom City in western Saudi Arabia is the clearest manifestation of petro-Saharanism's continuity. Launched by Mohammed Bin Salman (MBS) in 2017, this "smart city," which has been under construction on the Red Sea between Egypt and

Jordan in Saudi Arabia's northwest since 2019, boasts plans for "regreening" and "rewilding" projects in a hypermodern megapolis. Major media outlets have covered plans for the Line—an area within Neom that extends more than 175 kilometers from the coast into the Arabian Desert, with 500-meter-high buildings that will house a self-selecting population of nine million people—extensively.[109] Supervised by Giles Pendleton, an Australian citizen, this 200 billion dollar project "will be the largest megastructure in the world—a futuristic, mirrored residential and business block that rises over an expanse of desert, emerald waters, rocky inlets and white beaches of the rugged Tabuk province."[110] Neom not only runs roughshod over forty years' worth of ecocare wisdom that warned against the importation of a prepackaged petromodernity, but it also promotes a Saharanism-infused Hollywood-esque city that attempts to forget its homeland's desert nature.

Neom is only another manifestation of the politico-economic and petrol-dominated world that Munif depicted. The city represents a vision in which everything harkens back to Saharanism's local and global ramifications, and MBS's plan is infused with imaginings borrowed from sci-fi movies. The prefabricated models of the city, which depict a lifeless desert that human intervention can transform into dreamy oases even as Saudi courts are busy issuing capital and imprisonment sentences for recalcitrant Indigenous inhabitants of the northwestern region,[111] recycle Saharanism's many clichés. The Howeitat's protests against the expropriation of their land belie the image of a quiet, seamless, depoliticized, and highly curated desert that is conveyed by the professionally produced graphics. This said, there is no greater testament to Saharanism's power than the fact that it has been adopted by a powerful local leader who ties his own political legitimacy to the grandiose "un-deserting" of his homeland.

Saharanist extraction in Neom has fantastical dimensions. A linchpin of MBS's *Ruʾya 2030* (Saudi Vision 2030), the construction treats this rich and inhabited part of the Tabuk desert as a blank space in which an aspiring leader can exercise his lust for power. As Ali Dogan, a research fellow at Leibniz-Zentrum Moderner Orient, has written, "Neom, as MBS' own megaproject, serves as a key tool for him to consolidate his power in Saudi Arabia and foster the regime's security."[112] The project's website describes it as "a transformative and ambitious blueprint to unlock the potential of its people and create a diversified, innovative, and world-leading nation,"[113] all in the very short period of fourteen years between its launch in 2016 and 2030. Underpinned by Saharanism, Neom will be a glass miracle in the desert.

Saharanism's all-permitting discourse, combined with the belief in humans' ability to perform miracles in the desert, depicts Neom as a breakthrough for the future of humanity.[114] This convergence shows once again that the desert is relegated to oblivion in order to foreground yet another brainchild of petro-Saharanism.

Unsurprisingly, sustainability figures prominently in MBS's Saudi Vision 2030. According to the official literature, not only will the country attempt to achieve "a Net Zero future by 2060," but it will also diversify its energy sources to include cleaner energies through novel solutions like the "Circular Carbon Economy (CCE)."[115] Accordingly, renewable sources will account for fifty percent of energy consumed in the kingdom. Sustainability concerns also include attention to biodiversity and conservation as well as agriculture. The website touts the project, which still has a long way to go before completion, as a "global model of the journey towards a sustainable future."[116] Since petrol money has, as Munif argued, created a media empire that has taken control of culture and journalism,[117] it is rare to encounter any criticism—even in the West—of this environmental mayhem. For instance, Robert Mogielnicki, a senior resident scholar with the Arab Gulf States Institute in Washington, DC, extolled all of Neom's achievements and future potential without ever pausing to reflect on its developers' transposition of an obviously European toponymy to expropriated Bedouin lands.[118] The Las Vegas–ization of the Arabian Desert, which is antithetical to sustainability, does not seem to be an issue for Neom's developers, as it clearly dovetails with MBS's declaration in 2018 that "the Middle East is the new Europe."[119]

In the late 1990s, Munif drew a connection between human rights violations and the arrogation of petrol resources by the ruling families. In his view, the prison system in the Gulf was one of the outcomes of petromodernity. This link between Saharanism, development, and imprisonment could not be any clearer after the revelation of the human rights violations that accompanied Neom's construction.[120] According to the *Alestiklal* website, MBS's project required the displacement of twenty thousand desert dwellers and the demolition of their homes to clear the space for Neom.[121] These expulsions and displacements are reminiscent of Munif's poignant descriptions of similar operations in the 1930s. Subject to the continued heavy-handedness that accompanied the discovery of oil, Abdulilah al-Howeiti and Abdullah Dukhail al-Howeiti, cousins who are native to the area, were sentenced to fifty-year jail terms along with travel bans for the same period for "supporting their family's refusal to be forcibly evicted from their homes in the Tabuk province of northwestern Saudi Arabia."[122]

Petro-Saharanism harnesses abundant resources to disregard human rights; this is even true of companies that operate in democratic and law-abiding countries. In 2020, an open letter to Boston Consulting Group, Oliver Wyman, and McKinsey & Co. by a collective of human rights organizations drew these major Western companies' attention to their participation in the violation of the Howeitat people's rights. The letter invited the companies "to reflect upon your responsibilities, and unless and until the adverse human rights impact can be addressed, urge your companies to reassess involvement in the NEOM project, and to cease engagement entirely."[123] However, as American urbanist Adam Greenfield has argued, architects adore despots such as MBS because, unlike in liberal democracies, an authoritarian leader encourages them to "dream big" and says their visions will be realized.[124] With Neom and its underlying politics, as well as its reliance on American and British corporations to implement a supposedly green vision for Saudi Arabia in the midst of the global warming crisis, we come full circle to where Munif started in 1984 with the publication of the first volume of *Cities of Salt*. Neom's future environmental disasters are concrete proof of Saharanism's threat to humanity at large. After MBS launched a nine-year war in Yemen and ordered the brutal assassination of journalist Jamal Khashoggi in his country's consulate in Istanbul, greenwashing and undeserting the desert were his ways of refashioning himself as a civilized leader. MBS did not reinvent the wheel; rather, he acted like an attentive disciple of Saharanism's textbook written over the last two hundred years.

Munif would certainly have been unhappy with the continuity of the disturbing construction trend he warned against in the 1980s. Nevertheless, he would have been vindicated to observe the link between MBS's power grab and the rush to transform the desert. In 2020, the British newspaper *The Guardian* revisited what happened in November 2017 in Saudi Arabia, writing, "nearly 400 of Saudi Arabia's most powerful people, among them princes, tycoons and ministers, were rounded up and detained in the Ritz-Carlton hotel, in what became the biggest and most contentious purge in the modern kingdom's history."[125] The torture and pressure exerted on these powerful individuals ended "with $106bn recovered" from the jailed businesspeople, according to *Al Jazeera*.[126] This same Ritz-Carlton was the venue where MBS launched his Saudi Vision 2030 in 2016.[127] Political scientist Mark Beeson has argued that "'environmental authoritarianism' may become an increasingly common response to the destructive impacts of climate change in an age of diminished expectations."[128] But Beeson's conclusions, which attribute somewhat altruistic intentions to dictatorships, do not seem to apply to Neom, which will cost the Saudis almost a trillion dollars. Whether Neom succeeds or fails, its materialization has unleashed Munif's prescient ecocare-inspired warnings into the world to haunt the living practitioners of Saharanism.

FRENCH NUCLEAR TESTS: A "NUCLEAR HOLOCAUST" IN THE SAHARA

In the nuclearized Sahara, ecocare has taken the form of a multifaceted fictional and nonfictional contention with the irreversible legacy of French nuclear experiments. Between February 13, 1960, and April 25, 1961, France carried out four *Gerboise* atmospheric (or ground-level) nuclear experiments in Reggane in the Tanezrouft area of southwest Algeria, where it had established the Centre saharien d'expérimentations militaires (CSEM) in 1957.[129] Though French government officials and military officers alleged that the location was uninhabited, Tanezrouft was an important connector between Algeria, Mali, Morocco, and Mauritania.[130] Algerian scholar Ahmed Boussaid has argued that even if Tanezrouft itself was barren, it nonetheless served as a geographical and civilizational extension of the famous populated corridor of Touat oases.[131] After joining the nuclear club, France used its Centre d'expérimentations militaires des oasis (CEMO) in the In Ekker area to run a series of thirteen supposedly "cleaner" underground tests in the Hoggar between 1961 and 1966. The bombs of this series were named after gemstones;[132] of the thirteen experiments in this second series, Béryl, Améthyste, Rubis, and Jade failed and exposed military and civilian personnel to radiation leakage,[133] which caused human and environmental casualties.[134]

Ultimately, these experiments introduced radioactive matter into the lives of thousands of people and contaminated thousands of acres of land, ushering in the age of "nuclear colonialism" in the Sahara.[135] Bruno Barrillot, the foremost expert on French nuclear history, wrote about the human and environmental impact of the different French tests in the Sahara, underlining that France's smaller and undeclared "cold tests in the Sahara were particularly devastating. Some of them have led to deadly accidents."[136] Beyond these deaths and identified cases of contamination, the entire territory was exposed to radiation. Nuclear colonialism intersects with experimental Saharanism in their opposition to desert ecocare in that both of them encompass all forms of past, present, and future ecocide resulting from the use of deserts for lethal experiments and the storage of radioactive waste. In Tan Afella in the Hoggar alone, thirty thousand inhabitants were endangered by exposure to higher levels of radiation.[137] In this specific context, desert ecocare means both refuting Saharanism's myths of the empty desert and historicizing the impact of nuclear colonialism from the perspective and in the language of its victims.

Ecocare as it pertains to nuclearism is the embodiment of local engagement with the history of nuclear colonialism and its underlying Saharanism. The ongoing academic discourses on French nuclear experiments have mostly failed to account for the knowledge produced by local scholars about the experience and their understanding of its continued impact. These experiments not only left radiation in the Saharans' bodies and ecologies, but also left a lasting imprint on their identities and sense of being and not being. Nigerian Tuareg poet Mahmoudan Hawad sums this reality up in saying, "We, the Tuareg, the inhabitants of central Sahara, do not exist for those who planned 'experiments' and 'tests,'"[138] showing how the planners' approach was consistent with the long-lived ideology, informed by Saharanism, vis-à-vis the desert. Unlike the prevalent complaints about France's silencing of the history of its nuclear experiment in the desert, local Algerian scholars from all disciplines have, in fact, examined the impacts of these tests' on the people, fauna, and flora of the Sahara. The local scholarship participating in this ecocare has presented detailed theories regarding France's responsibilities in terms of international and humanitarian law, broadening the ramifications of nuclear testing to include questions of reparations, the clearing of the waste created by the experiments, and assigning the responsibility for the damages that ensued from testing to France.[139]

Placing emphasis on the absence of French archives has led an important number of foreign scholars to shift attention away from the suffering of Saharans and their desert environment even though their story is amply documented in Arabic sources and in Amazigh social memory. The historiographical centering of France has come at the expense of the knowledge produced by those who survived these tests. Consequently, engagement with Indigenous notions of desert ecocare and the myriad ways in which formerly colonized Saharans and their fellow citizens have tackled the legacy of nuclear Saharanism has also been delayed, if not diminished.

Official archives, and specifically those contemporaneous with the tests themselves, are unquestionably significant. *Le Parisien*'s revelation of a declassified map that dates back to the first experiment in 1960 and which sheds light on the levels of nuclear fallout throughout the region and the world confirms these archives' importance.[140] Nevertheless, the inhabitants of the Sahara have produced their "other-archives"—other forms of documentation that do not necessarily fall under the definition of traditional archives and that relate their embodied experiences with the nuclear tests and their aftermaths.[141] While France, like all states, can afford to remain silent on this matter, Saharans have no such luxury because the trauma of nuclear colonialism occupies their bodies, shapes their genetics, and inhabits their ecosystems. Hence, shifting attention from official French archives to desert ecocare can also bring to light that which the Saharanism-informed, racialized vision of Tanezrouft and the Hoggar wanted erased, forgotten, and unspoken. Paying attention to Indigenous Saharan experiences articulated in Darija, Tamazight, and Modern Standard Arabic, even more than French, reveals the ramifications of what Hocine Hacene has described as a "nuclear holocaust."[142]

Scholarly and ethnographic investigations of French nuclear tests from a local perspective refute the widespread misconception that the desert is nonliving. Scholar Abdelfatah Belaroussi has rightly suggested that these experiments "targeted humans, the ecosystem, fauna and flora, and water," noting the countless problems, particularly cancers, that decimated people's health in Reggane.[143] Iraqi nuclear physicist Abdelkadhem Aboudi, who was based in Algeria until his death in 2021, explained the dangers of nuclear experiments in the Sahara and their impact on human, animal, and plant life.[144] Based on conversations with local people, Australian anthropologist Jeremy Keenan captured the birth defects and genetic mutations observed among the inhabitants as well as the disappearance of specific plants in the Hoggar.[145] Keenan himself asserted that a "crime had been committed against the people of this region, and it has been covered up."[146] But an event of this magnitude that affected about sixty thousand people cannot simply be covered up because French archives were either withheld or deliberately laconic, or even because diplomats and military officers claimed the land was empty.[147] Guided by their sense of ecocare, Algerian and Algeria-based scholars and writers have recorded the experiments' continuous impacts since years before this history became of interest for the international community.[148]

Ecocare employs both hard science and literature to tackle the consequences of France's nuclear tests in the Sahara. This hybridized method has enabled a process whereby the science of the horrific experiments is interpreted through a humanistic lens as part of an Indigenous history of nuclear colonialism. Al Ansari's *Ṭabīb tinbuktū*, which Moroccan literary critic Aḥmad al-Madīnī views as an anthropological testimony to the Tuaregs' life and history in the Sahara,[149] and microbiologist Hacene's *Le Sahara dans l'enfer*, which relays historical and scientific data in the form of a narrative, are the clearest expressions of this ecocare. Indeed, *Ṭabīb tinbuktū* and *Le Sahara dans l'enfer* present the Sahara as a united block in which mobility was the lifeblood of existence before French colonialism annexed parts of the desert to different nation-states; they also demonstrate that French nuclear Saharanism tore the Saharans' history asunder, into a pre- and post-1960.

Ṭabīb tinbuktū tells the story of Muhammad, a medical assistant who witnessed important historical events that unfolded in the expansive area between northern Mali and the Sahel in 1960. Set against the backdrop of the French transfer of power to President Modibo Keïta's (1915–1977) southern army, the novel establishes crucial connections between the disenfranchisement of Malian Tuaregs and France's imperialistic vision for the Sahara. The tension between a postcolonial state that was trying to assert its authority, on the one hand, and the recalcitrant Tuaregs who claimed the right to move freely within their homeland, on the other, turned into a "horrific massacre" at the hands of the Malian army in Kidal.[150] The Tuaregs' refusal to abdicate their right to free movement culminated in a confrontation in which the Sahara morphed into "a prison for those who live[d] in it."[151] In addition to the impacts of war, the novel depicts the complicated geography of France's necro-ecological enterprise in which exposure to deadly violence was a common denominator among humans, air, fauna, and flora.

Unlike *Ṭabīb tinbuktū*, which follows events located far from the sites of nuclear testing, *Le Sahara dans l'enfer* is set within the test sites and their immediate environs. The combination of historical research about the genesis of the French nuclear bomb with accounts of lived experiences of people who witnessed the tests closely has allowed Hacene to provide vibrant, plausible testimony about nuclear Saharanism and its disregard for the basic well-being and safety of Indigenous populations. Through the story of Boudjemaa, Hussa, Salem, and Mohamed, four native workers in the PLBT, Hacene penetrates the invisible underworld of the atomic city of the CSEM in Reggane, as well as of the CEMO. Both CSEM's PLBT and the CEMO's *populations laborieuses des oasis* (PLOs) had firsthand experience of what was happening inside the closed-off military bases where experiments were taking place. By presenting the infernal conditions that these tests inflicted on the Sahara and its populations, *Le Sahara dans l'enfer* paints an image of a traumatized and disoriented population whose biome is pulverized by nuclear bombs.[152]

Both *Ṭabīb tinbuktū* and *Le Sahara dans l'enfer* portray the colonial deception that surrounded the experiments in the Sahara. The two recount how France withheld information about its enterprises in the desert before and after the explosions. General Charles Ailleret and Ambassador Jules Moch famously dismissed the existence of any people or other forms of life in the area where their government planned to test the bombs. Nonetheless, even as they denied the presence of any life, the French army hired some thirty-five hundred local laborers to work in construction and other manual jobs.[153] These workers were kept in the dark regarding the true nature of the project and the risks they were running by being at sites that would later be exposed to radiation. *Ṭabīb tinbuktū* centers the ignorance of the causes of sudden illness and deaths that unfolded in Muhammad's homeland, which is hundreds, if not thousands, of kilometers away from Ground Zero in Reggane. Muhammad reflects on this, saying:

> People have confirmed to us that something serious happened in the Northern Sahara towards the Hoggar and Tassili. They said that the successive noises of a huge earthquake were heard in the outskirts.
>
> The witnesses said that they saw a mushroom cloud take off from the ground into the sky . . . and that a huge cloud of smoke ascended from it. Before that they had seen *Ikufar* [French] planes hovering in the sky. And some travelers who escaped from that region said that *Ikufar* have cordoned it off . . . and that they met people who looked as if they had been stricken with chickenpox, and the skin of some of them started peeling off.[154]

The earthquake, the mushroom cloud, and the chickenpox marks left by the aftermath of the explosions throughout the Sahara hint at the scientific reality unknown to the narrator. According to French sources, the Gerboise bleue explosion led to radioactive fallout that spread up to a radius of 150 kilometers during the first day and thousands of kilometers afterward.[155] Since the uncontainable nuclear residue became a mobile source of contagion (Map 3),[156] the geography of nuclearization and its "environmental catastrophe," as Algerian scholars Imān Sūrī and Bin Sahla Thānī Bin Ali referred to it, exacted a high price throughout the Sahara.[157]

These novelistic works confirm fiction's capacity to capture and historicize disorienting experiences. Historicization includes both registering the shock-

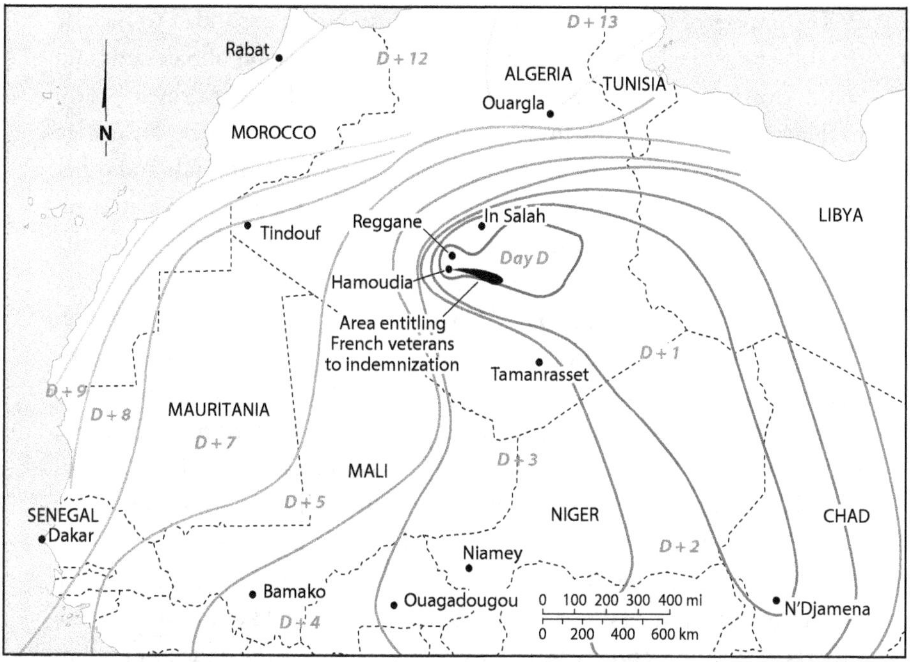

MAP 3. Nuclear fallout contamination area after Gerboise bleue. Cartography by Bill Nelson.

ing nature of the traumatic experience and recording the Saharans' responses to it. An important facet of ecocare in *Le Sahara dans l'enfer* is the attention it pays to France's atomic age as a deeply traumatizing experience for workers, villagers, children, and all other members of society. The absence of reliable information about sudden illnesses and deaths exacerbated this disorientation: "A few hours after the explosion, some had developed eye inflammations and symptoms of momentary or permanent deafness, others developed symptoms of acute irradiation syndrome. Some had decided to leave this cursed area outright to settle elsewhere or join relatives in Adrar. . . . Throughout the Touat region, we talked only of this explosion and its consequences. The whole population had felt it very strongly."[158] As an airborne source of contamination, the deadly nuclear fallout transcended the arbitrary borders French officers had drawn on the Saharan territories during the Niamey Convention after they defeated the Tuaregs.[159] The Saharans called 1960 *ʿām al-wafayāt* (the year of death).[160] The reenactment of this episode has become nature's annual ritual, as winds carry contaminated sands from the Sahara to remind Europeans of French nuclear Saharanism's legacy.[161]

The impact of the experiments in the desert can be expanded to include the disregard of ethical testing methods. The racialization of Saharans and other Algerians took an even more sinister—albeit still unconfirmed—form in the supposed use of humans as guinea pigs. Algerian prisoners of war were allegedly placed in areas close to Ground Zero alongside animals and other disposables to observe the impact of explosions and radioactive matter on these beings.[162] Bruno Barrillot and some Algerian scholars have skeptically mentioned the use of Algerian prisoners during the experiments, but these accounts remain unsubstantiated.[163] Hacene draws on the fact that Algerian workers were not given the same protective gear as their French counterparts, "neither glasses nor protective overalls or masks,"[164] to surmise that they were deliberately exposed to radiation in order to test its impact on humans. Hacene has called them "neutron fodder."[165] In the absence of factual data, *Le Sahara dans l'enfer* adopts a comparative approach to reveal the difference between the overly protected French scientists, military officers, and families and the absence of similar safety measures that could have mitigated the impact of the atomic fallout on Indigenous Saharans. Hacene writes, "The experts of the CEA and the military were well aware of the dangers of radioactivity, and instructions were given to decontaminate the staff and material rapidly, without any concern for the PLBT and even less for the region's inhabitants."[166] Not only were these hundreds of Algerian workers conscripted to participate in "the most difficult tasks,"[167] but, unknowingly, their bodies also served as test kits for measuring the bombs' efficiency.

If the immediate and most visible aspect of nuclear experiments was death, their indirect consequences have been even more insidious. Hacene refers to a "real genocide with witnesses in the short, medium, and long term" among the Indigenous workers.[168] Nuclear Saharanism is not limited in terms of its timescale, and its danger stems directly from its colonization of the future. This can be seen especially in the amount of radiation and contaminated equipment buried in the desert;[169] it continues to release lethal doses into the territory even decades after the test sites closed. This deferred, continual effect of nuclear Saharanism has made it very difficult to determine the exact number of victims it has claimed. Algerian legal scholar Hacene Hachemi documented the variety of material and immaterial damages these experiments inflicted on Algerians in the Sahara, speaking in the meantime of forty-two thousand direct and indirect victims.[170]Algerian scholars Abdelaziz Rajʿi and Nawī Bin Mabrūk have contended that France carried out a total of fifty-seven known and secret nuclear experiments in the

Algerian desert,[171] including the four well-known atmospheric tests in Reggane and the thirteen underground ones conducted in Taourirt Tan Afella, which is located 150 kilometers north of Tamanrasset.[172] The power released by the sum of these experiments was, according to these scholars, forty times the power of Fat Man, the nuclear bomb the US dropped on Hiroshima during World War II.[173] The unimaginable amount of radioactive matter left behind has inscribed the tests' nuclear necro-ecological impact within a longer history of continued ecological colonialism and its crimes in Algeria.[174]

These ecocare-based approaches to the legacy of French nuclear Saharanism also reveal a sensitivity to the impact of the tests on the desert as an environmental place. Hacene notes that immediately after the first experiment, the people in the Adrar region noticed a "decrease in the flow of foggaras, an event that was more important than the explosion itself because they are for the inhabitants of the Touat what the Nile and the Euphrates are for Egypt and Iraq—i.e., life or death."[175] This indicates that there is a geological dimension to nuclear Saharanism. In Elisabeth Leuvrey's documentary *At(h)ome*, the owner of a small plot of arable land in Tan Afella talks about the sickness of soil.[176] Instead of talking about the barrenness of the land, the farmer uses a term that is usually associated with humans to describe the suffering of *akal* (land) in Tamazight. Algerian specialists and farmers have pointed to a decrease in crops and overall agricultural production.[177] Scholar Faḍīla Rābiḥī has argued that the region went from being autarkic in terms of agricultural products to experiencing shortages in the production of staples such as tomatoes and wheat.[178] Citing Algerian nuclear physicist Ammar Masouri, Rābiḥī concludes that Reggane, once an agricultural powerhouse, has become "a barren land whose products no longer have the quality they did before."[179]

French nuclear experiments also catalyzed a demographic transformation in the Sahara. Desert populations driven by fear left in the immediate aftermath of the explosions. Moreover, the pollution of water sources and the depletion of the foggaras drove the Saharans and their livestock out of their homeland. These migrations have led to some surprising outcomes, as in the case of al-Koni, whose family left the Sahara as a result of the first experiments. When asked about why he writes in Arabic instead of Tamasheq, his Tuareg mother tongue, al-Koni counterintuitively attributed this shift to the French nuclear experiments. The tests forced his family to move, severing his relationship to the homeland:

> An oppressive colonial empire like France issued me a death sentence when it poisoned the land of the heavenly visions, the Great Desert, with its nuclear bombs, forcing people to be alienated from the paradise of reality, which it made even further from being within reach. It made it a lost paradise, and I consider my journey through the world to be nothing but a tragic, persistent attempt to recover this lost Eden. The issue of being alienated from one's mother tongue then seems a lot easier when it is compared to there being a place of origin that you can see but where you can't live.[180]

By extending the impact of nuclear Saharanism to language, al-Koni broadens the horizons of desert ecocare to include recording and interrogating the myriad tangible and intangible ways in which nuclear Saharanism has infinitely and indefinitely affected deserts and their inhabitants.

CONCLUSION

This chapter is the culmination of the book. It is also the chapter that highlights how the different strands of Saharanism direly affected Indigenous desert dwellers in the Sahara and the Arabian Deserts. The chapter has probed the myriad ways in which various ecocare cultural practices have challenged Saharanism by grappling with issues of extraction, development, and experimentation in the Arabian Desert and the Sahara. I deployed a multipronged analysis to conceptualize how ecocare, as a desert-focused practice of environmental consciousness, has been informed by the disasters that Saharanism has brought upon these two deserts. Balancing the critique of Saharanism with a theorization of ecocare based on fictional and nonfictional sources, this chapter is also an attempt to center local experiences and languages as the main source for ecocare's theorization.

The chapter has also revealed the multiplicity of ways ecocare has been a site of critical engagement with Saharanism. Al-Koni developed the umbrella concept of *waḥdat al-kāʾināt*, which combines both tangible knowledge with desert mythologies, while Munif focused mainly on the transformative role the discovery of oil played in Arabia and the challenges of establishing sustainable post-oil societies. Hacene and Al Ansari foreground the murdered desert as a result of French nuclear experiments. These different approaches and practices of ecocare intersect in their focus on the desert and in revealing the critical existential questions confronting desert natives.

In the abstract, deserts may seem smooth and beautifully nomadic. However, the works this chapter has examined focus solely on Saharanism's disruption of millennia-old endogenous ties within desert biomes. Ecocare-informed works are significantly concerned with the annihilation that development, capitalism, and experimentation brought upon deserts. The prevalence of an anthropocentric view that places humans above and beyond all other nonhuman subjects in deserts has had the perverse effect of incentivizing anthropogenic transformations that have forever threatened deserts' ways of life and, even worse, made nuclear colonialism an integral part of their futurity. The chapter demonstrates that the path these authors chart requires humans to act not like nuisances, as they currently do, but rather as agents of desert ecocare, which commands that we treat these arid living landscapes with attention, knowledge, and respect.

Epilogue

DESERT LEGALESE, ART, AND THE PATH FORWARD

DESERT IMAGINATIONS WILL HAVE ACHIEVED its goal if readers emerge with even more questions than answers about the fate of deserts worldwide. Spurring readers' curiosity about arid spaces and challenging their assumptions about them would also be a major achievement for this project, which I undertook out of the conviction that the rehabilitation of desert ecologies requires a different way of thinking about them. In its broadest conception, the book has drawn on a wide array of materials to explain what generally makes deserts the targets of so much rhetorical violence, not just in literature and film but also via actionable enterprises that have political, scientific, economic, sociocultural, and security-related consequences. Instead of merely discussing these actions and their outcomes, the book examines the reasoning behind the grand schemes that deserts are made to seem to invite across the globe. By understanding the manner in which Saharanism has shaped how deserts are viewed and (mis)treated over time, the book has uncovered the rationale behind the long-term invisibilization in widespread public discourses of both the biodiversity they nurture and the threats that they face. As such, parsing a handful of Saharanism's insidious manifestations across a variety of sources has allowed *Desert Imaginations* to link different deserts to one another and connect what unfolded or is still unfolding in them through the common factor of this ideology.

I should note that charting an alternative path for a more ecofriendly and ecologically aware treatment of deserts was not my primary concern in writing *Desert Imaginations*. That would require another book—but before it can be written, it was necessary to define the problem that deserts face today. Therefore, I leave sketching out a road map on how to save deserts from Saharanism's disastrous effects to community planners who know better than anyone else the concrete challenges confronting their specific desert environments. My aim, however, has always been to unearth and clearly articulate the system of ideas that continues to threaten deserts by ignoring their homeliness to diverse human and nonhuman populations and reducing them to soulless spaces amenable to various forms of pillage and sacrificial acts to conserve or preserve environments that are considered more important. This might be an obvious conclusion for those who grew up in an arid area, as I did, but this may not be the case for those whose mental constructions of deserts derive from Saharanism-infused cultural production. Therefore, *Desert Imaginations* is primarily concerned with the sinister world of Saharanism, which has surreptitiously colonized most imaginaries about deserts. It is equally important to establish Saharanism's parameters in order to redress the wrongs that the persistence of this ideology has condoned, continually allowing ecological mayhem to be committed against deserts and their futures. Spreading knowledge about Saharanism as the scourge that has maligned deserts will certainly lead to greater consciousness about the need to put an end to the ongoing ecocide that has decimated arid lands across the world.

Although the Sahara is its centerpiece, the conclusions of *Desert Imaginations* can be applied to various deserts, hot and cold, independently of their location. The mere evocation of a "desert" is enough to pull Saharanism, with its deep-seated penetration of culture, politics, and society, into action. Whether the issue is fossil fuels or solar energy, security threats or nuclear testing or waste storage, arid places are, despite being considered remote, at the center of political and economic maneuvers and discussions that often claim to defend citizens' best interests. As these chapters have demonstrated, lying behind that which is portrayed as beneficial to different national constituencies is the powerful ideology of Saharanism, according to which anything that can supposedly benefit "ordinary" human life in livable urban or nonurban areas can, without hesitation, be removed from deserts or deposited in them. Saharanism has thus rationalized deserts as sacrifice zones, acting as both sources and dumps. This oxymoronic, albeit prevalent, function of arid lands is reflective of contradictory constructions of deserts as both salutary and demonic spaces, depending on whether they enable the extraction of resources or the depositing of waste. Nonetheless, this false binary fails to account for the true nature of deserts and their significance for their human and nonhuman residents. The existence of Saharanism cannot be blamed on any lack of scientific knowledge of deserts but rather on the dissemination of the superficial, "touristic view" that al-Koni critiqued and which is the air that Saharanism breathes to sustain itself.

Methodological considerations have warranted the focus on what I consider the four main pillars of Saharanism, followed by a chapter on counter-Saharanism through Indigenous practices of ecocare. Although Saharanism is a tentacular ideology, with vast implications for deserts across the world, I have dedicated separate chapters to religion, extraction, experimentation, and sexuality rather than to individual deserts. These four themes, analyzed in an interdisciplinary manner, extend across a vast number of subjects that encompass but are not limited to colonialism, geopolitics, literature, economics, demography, sexology, and science and technology. The integration of these elements within Saharanism means that deserts are central to some of the most intimate aspects of human existence. The delineation of spiritual and sexual Saharanisms reveals how imaginations of deserts are enmeshed with human desires, pleasures, fantasies, quests, and transcendental motives. Spirituality is foundational for mental and emotional security, whereas sexuality is an innate biological need that has deep psychological ramifications. The fact that deserts have been viewed as loci for the intersection of sexual and spiritual quests since the time of the Desert Fathers made it possible for Saharanism to repackage these pursuits and deploy them to achieve present goals. Meanwhile, the existence of extractive and experimental Saharanisms is a reflection of the technical, scientific, and economic enterprises that coalesce in what their proponents construe as an open-sky lab where unfettered human innovation can test the boundaries of human genius. The history of French enterprises in the Sahara leaves no doubt that extraction and experimentation are two sides of the same coin. The exchange of expertise between oilmen and the nuclear authorities in the 1960s in the Sahara is a testament to this reality. These four subcategories of Saharanism furnish a generalizable model of the expansive ways in which Saharanism unfolded to various degrees in different deserts. By conceptualizing the religious, sexual, experimental, and exploitative dimensions of Saharanism, *Desert Imaginations* offers both a multipronged and historically grounded articulation that disentangles the main ideas humans have built around deserts and, most significantly, facilitates a critical understanding of how these ideas have become decisive in determining the way arid lands are approached.

The need to fill the conceptual void in desert studies, particularly in terms of how deserts are (mis)treated, does not, however, mean that the book presents a uniform, one-size-fits-all definition of Saharanism. Instead, *Desert*

Imaginations formulates Saharanism as a dynamic, ever-evolving system of ideas and behaviors as well as undertakings that play out in deserts. Saharanism's multiform nature is what has enabled it to operate differently across deserts and times. As revealed throughout this book, Saharanism's variable geometry in separate locations and temporalities endows it with resilience and local flavors, though its core attitude toward deserts is deeply ingrained in an exploitative, reductive, and racializing mindset. This variable geometry is governed by an internal logic that is the outcome of centuries of portrayals of deserts as inimical spaces with people who need to be dominated and dispossessed, climates that have to be regulated, and resources that are only good when they are extracted. These ideas, the legacy of centuries of myriad encounters with deserts in the contexts of colonial expansions and enterprises, solidified over time into attitudes that inspire and frame what happens in deserts. In attending to Saharanism's multiscalar aspects and manifestations, *Desert Imaginations* blazes the way for its readers to further examine Saharanism's malleability and manifestations in their own specific contexts.

As presented here, Saharanism is also topical and newsworthy, as evidenced by current events. In December 2023, just a few months into Israel's multidimensionally lethal war on Palestinians in Gaza in the aftermath of Hamas's attacks on Israeli settlements on October 7, 2023, Joel Roskin, an Israeli geologist and geographer at Bar-Ilan University, penned an opinion article entitled "Why Moving to the Sinai Peninsula Is the Solution for Gaza's Palestinians."[1] Roskin starts by assessing the irreparable damage Israel's unbridled bombing had done to the entire built environment in Gaza, affirming, "The metropolis has to be fully evacuated, redesigned, monitored, and only then rebuilt to provide habitable and economic[ally] conducive conditions."[2] What might at first glance seem to be a sympathetic and humanitarian position vis-à-vis the Palestinians' suffering soon reveals itself as clearly supporting the idea of ethnically cleansing Gaza by relocating Gazans to the Sinai Desert. Roskin follows the well-trodden path of Israeli Saharanism, for which, as countless scholars have already discussed, the notion of "a land without people for a people without land" has been crucial, and he summarily states that Sinai's 23,166 square miles make up "one of the emptiest places in the Mediterranean region."[3] Roskin further alleges that the state-of-the-art infrastructure Egypt built in northern Sinai renders the area the place of choice for the enforced resettlement of Gazans. Roskin's concern for Palestinians is such that he opines that this land "can easily host large-scale development projects that, if led by the Chinese and supported by local labor, for example, can easily mature in just one to two years."[4] This very short article is a concrete example of how notions of desert emptiness, development, and experimentation, which are discussed at length in this book, continue to operate even in the midst of a tragic war that the International Court of Justice has considered genocidal and for which the International Criminal Court has issued arrest warrants against Israeli officials.[5]

There is nothing shocking or surprising in Roskin's proposition, as all he did was adhere to the principles of Saharanism, which, throughout its history, has always been on the side of colonialism, desertification, racialization, extraction, and the massacre of Indigenous people. Once it is understood within the long lineage of Saharanism's dehumanization of Indigenous inhabitants of arid lands, Roskin's scheme appears rather ordinary because it is, as Israeli historian Yael Zerubavel has already demonstrated, embedded in the instrumental role the desert has played in Zionist imaginaries since the nineteenth century.[6] Hence, "Jewish settlement represented a way to overcome the regressive state of the country," which is another way to say that undeserting the desert, borrowing from European narratives of environmental decline, has been foundational to the Zionist construction of the Jewish homeland.[7] Although there is a profusion of scholarship that addresses the desert as it pertains to Palestine, much of this work has been framed by Orientalism and, more recently, through settler colonialism, both of which cannot account for the desert imaginary that centers on arid lands that occupy thirty-three percent of the Earth's landmass. The ideas that *Desert Imaginations* introduces can help shift the attention to Palestine as a desert and interrogate how Saharanism has been at work in its occupation. This desertifying ideology has been repeated by Donald Trump who, like Roskin, adduces Israel's transformation of Gaza into an uninhabitable space to propose the active emptying of the territory of its residents. Israel desertified Gaza, but Trump, inspired by Saharanism, wants to turn the murdered land into a desertic sea resort.[8]

By furnishing a lexicon and range of concepts that can help reflect on what happens in and to arid lands, *Desert Imaginations* aims to open up space to prioritize a trans-desert approach that captures the myriad political, scientific, and geopolitical enterprises that involve deserts. In December 2020, just a few weeks before the end of his first term, President Trump made a rather stunning announcement in which he handed Western Sahara over to Morocco in exchange for the resumption of diplomatic relations between Morocco and Israel. Western Sahara was annexed by Morocco in 1975 after a national Green March, which mobilized 350,000 unarmed Moroccans to storm the border separating it from Morocco, and since then, de facto administrative authority over the territory devolved to Morocco even though neither the UN nor the majority of world governments recognize the country's sovereignty over this disputed territory, which has had historical ties with Morocco. This annexation led to a war between Morocco and the Algeria-backed independence movement of the Polisario Front from 1975 to 1991, ending when a ceasefire that would lead to a referendum on self-determination was brokered by the UN. The December 2020 announcement, however, is the clearest example of the viability of Saharanism for studying questions of desert people's sovereignty and autonomy. On the one hand, the collusion of American, Israeli, and Moroccan interests resulted in the swapping of recognitions of sovereignty over territories that are considered occupied under international law. On the other hand, this deal sheds light on Morocco's long-standing benefit from the achievements in security and agronomic research that experimental Saharanism has brought to Israel. Israel helped Morocco build its own separation wall in Western Sahara in the 1980s to fend off the Polisario's murderous attacks against the Moroccan army even before it built its own wall in the West Bank in the 2000s. The construction of *al-jidār al-ʿāzil* (the isolation wall) in Western Sahara dashed the Polisario's dreams of winning the war against Morocco, forcing its leaders, and Algeria behind them, to agree to a ceasefire. Although Morocco had a loose sovereignty over broad swaths of both Oriental and Western Sahara, its acceptance of a transactional deal within the Israel-Morocco-US agreement has harmed this legitimacy. Nevertheless, this new stance in Morocco's treatment of this protracted dossier is an indication of the rise of Moroccan Saharanism, which, like its historical precedents, will have no qualms about stripping desert people of their basic rights, including the right to health and self-determination.[9]

Emphasizing the persistence of Saharanism's extractive and exploitive nature does not negate the novel ways in which the forces of counter-Saharanism, as represented in art, jurisprudence, and activism, have engaged with its human and ecological impacts. As I have already discussed some of these ecologically minded interventions in the Saharan and the Arabian deserts in Chapter 5, I am not going to repeat myself here; however, I would like to point out some radical outcomes of desert jurisprudence from Mexico and China. A 2022 exhibit by artist Miguel Fernández de Castro and anthropologist Natalia Mendoza entitled *The Absolute Restoration of All Things* grappled with the legal ramifications of a transformative decision made by the 28th District Unitary Agrarian Court in Mexico in 2014.[10] Their installation revisited the remarkable ruling against the Penmont Mining Company, which, in the three years between 2010 and 2013, illegally operated the Soledad-Dipolos open-pit mine and extracted 236,000 ounces of gold near El Bajío, a cooperatively owned community in the northwest part of the state of Sonora.[11] The extracted gold, which "would take the shape of a 70 × 70 × 70 centimeter cube and would have a value of 436 million dollars,"[12] required a massive enterprise that included digging up and moving 10,833,527 tons of rock. The resolution of a lawsuit originally filed by four community members, known as *ejidatarios*, this milestone court ruling not only required the company to pay restitutions for the gold, but it also contained a remedial dimension that would be impossible to realize.[13] Pursuant to the ruling, Penmont is obligated to "fully restore the ecosystem that prevailed in this place, with its hills, mountains, water, air, flora, and fauna that existed before."[14]

Open-pit extraction sites are open wounds in the belly of the Earth, with companies displacing colossal amounts of natural materials in their search for valuable minerals. The intensive detonation of rocks, use of poisonous chemicals like cyanide and arsenic, and clearing of mountaintops create new topographic realities that disfigure even the most familiar places. Mining disrupts geological time, and no amount of remedial funds or creative architecture, as required by the ruling of Justice Manuel Loya Valverde, will ever succeed in making whole what the mining companies' activities fragmented in their destructive mission. Gonzalo Pimentel, a Chilean anthropologist and archaeologist based in the Atacama Desert, eloquently expressed the truth about the mining industry in deserts, writing that the "voracity and hunger for copper never stops. At the same time, every day the thirst for lithium increases."[15] In light of the mayhem that ensues from this voracity, restorative initiatives have become standard procedure all over the world, with states and societies increasingly aware of the need to clean and repurpose decommissioned mines, particularly sites that are close to urban environments. According to *Quarry Magazine*, "Restoration schemes create opportunities to do something unique and interesting with an area of land, which can meet the policies set by local authorities and also create positive public interest."[16] Accordingly, beyond just eliciting architects' and designers' creative responses to anthropogenic damage, remediation projects are situated at the intersection and coalescence of architectural innovation, landscape design, and environmental awareness. As such, the order for Penmont to restore the landscape and its ecosystem has a holistic connotation, validating community members' rights to reclaim the integrity of their desert environment.[17]

FIGURE 14. The Soledad-Dipolos pit mine in the Sonoran desert, featuring annotative text by Miguel Fernández de Castro and Natalia Mendoza. The text, based on the legal decision against the Penmont mining company in Mexico, signals the limits of law and remediation vis-à-vis the damage of extractive mining at this site. From the exhibition *The Absolute Restoration of All Things*, April 8–July 30, 2022, text labels redrawn for visibility with permission of the artists. Courtesy of Miguel Fernández de Castro and Natalia Mendoza.

However, given the absence of a concrete plan for the execution of the court's decision and Penmont's continued retaliation against the community members who initiated the lawsuit, de Castro and Mendoza's exhibit runs up against the infeasibility of this radical sentence. Embracing this legal oversight nonetheless, *The Absolute Restoration of All Things* drew on this very impossibility to indicate that in the event that it were possible, the total reparation ordered by the court would only foster environmental amnesia. It can even be interpreted as a trap that Saharanism may exploit to make believe that repurposing and redesigning landscapes that testify to brutal attacks on ecosystems can mend the wrongs done to arid lands. The artists took the opposite approach, foregrounding the extent to which the environmental space of the desert was mutilated and questioning the very possibility of making the landscape whole again (Fig. 14). The exhibit provides shocking information about the egregious toll that the production of $436 million worth of gold takes on nature. The short video, playing continuously and echoing in the gallery throughout the duration of the exhibition, submerged visitors in the trenches, the gaping quarries, and the winding roads once taken by heavy-duty trucks in their three-year excavation of the desert. The monstrosity of the aftermath leaves no room for amnesia, for its environmental crime against the people and their land is inscribed in "rocks much older than the dinosaurs."[18] The artists managed in this way to drive a wedge between the law's apparent cure-all solution and the amnesiac reparative projects that are expected to make a fragmented land whole again. Instead of remediations in the form of gardens, visitors are faced with the ugliness of the quarries that attests to the violence done to the desert by modern machinery, pushing them to reconsider any idealistic understandings they might have had about recovering the land's original state.

The immensity of this damage is powerfully expressed by an almost invisible cubical sculpture that now stands as "an anti-monument to the site's dispossession" at the center of the Soledad-Dipolos mine (Fig. 15).[19] Designed by Fernández de Castro and Mendoza and built by the *ejidatarios* who still live at the site, the sculpture represents the volume of all the gold extracted there. Anti-monuments and counter-monuments such as this one have proliferated worldwide to undo and contest dominant narratives that govern the grammar of memory, offering alternatives to the meanings imposed by grand monuments to given events. James Young has written that, in the very specific context of Germany, a counter-monument "functions as a valuable 'counter-index' to the ways time, memory, and current history intersect at any memorial," elaborating that counter-monuments aspire to elicit interaction from viewers.[20] But while urban centers are full of pedestrians who may be pushed to act, how might action be elicited in deserts, particularly as their remoteness has been weaponized by Saharanism's proponents to stifle the voices of their suffering? Even as "the arsenic in the air [of the city Calama in Atacama] daily exceeds more than 200 percent of the allowed European standard," as Pimental notes, "no public health alarm is heard."[21] Further confirming what this book has established regarding Saharanism's negation of any rights that local desert populations might have, Pimental states, "There are no particular actions for civil protection, children, or old people because it is simply not reported."[22] To make things worse, the majority of the population is left in ignorance with no knowledge whatsoever about the "quality of the air they breathe and the water they drink."[23]

Lest I be misconstrued, I hasten to add that the destruction of desert environments, when it elicits public outcry, has in some places resulted in different forms of administrative sanctions, fines, and even prison sentences. A set of

FIGURE 15. The anti-monument as it stands at the Soledad-Dipolos mine. The cube represents the amount of gold Penmont extracted illegally from the mine. From the exhibition *The Absolute Restoration of All Things*, April 8–July 30, 2022. Courtesy of Miguel Fernández de Castro and Natalia Mendoza.

cases against Chinese administrative officials who failed to stop pollution in the Tengger Desert around the time of the Penmont case shows that retributive decisions are not unique to Mexico.[24] The Tengger chemical pollution cases began in 2014 and were settled through mediation in 2017, when eight polluting enterprises agreed to "pay CNY 569 million (USD $82,463,768.10) for the restoration of the contaminated soil and for the prevention of future pollution, and another CNY 6 million (USD $869,565) to a public welfare fund for environmental damage."[25] Although significant in terms of its recognition of pollution in the desert environment, the Tengger case is a far cry from the sweeping decision in Mexico that ordered Penmont to return the extracted gold and restore the ecological desert space to a state that existed prior to the company's harmful extractive activities.

These two cases indicate the need to further explore the intersections between law and other humanistic disciplines as they coalesce to curb Saharanism. They also highlight the fact that, regardless of Saharanism's onslaught on desert environments and their resources, there is a rich life of activism and creative engagement that instantiate nonconventional deserts that do not usually get attention from the media. Confronting proponents of Saharanism has had consequences including murder, as with some of the *ejidatarios* involved in the Penmont case, and imprisonment, like in the case of Swiss Moroccan cardiologist Labbas Sbaï, who was jailed three times between 2006 and 2022. As a Saharan, Sbaï had spent his childhood in the desert oasis of Oum Lâalag before moving the USSR to study medicine and settling in Switzerland, where he worked as a surgeon until he moved back to his hometown in the late 1990s. During his childhood, Sbaï remembers that he "did not dare adventure into the oasis as the vegetation was so dense and the trees were teeming with animals."[26] Nevertheless, between the time of Sbaï's childhood and his definitive return to the oasis, desert wildlife had died out and the oasis needed to be saved. Engaging in his own version of desert ecocare, he opened a natural reservation to provide shelter for both humans and animals that still roam the desert. Since only a holistic approach can save the entire ecosystem, Sbaï has been acting as his community's spokesperson against all types of illegal activities that state agents have fostered in the remote desert.[27] His disregard of the authorities' warnings "to close [his] eyes and be satisfied with doing business," combined with his denunciation of "the smuggling of cigarettes and drugs, and the theft of camels," landed Sbaï in jail in 2006, 2010, and 2022.[28] His legal tribulations in his own desert homeland represent just one facet of the persecution that targets undesirable Saharans who act as conscious stewards of their land and whose actions represent roadblocks that inconvenience the schemes of states, companies, or individuals who implement projects informed by Saharanism.

From activism to music, desert dwellers have grappled with the transformations that changed their environments and their ecosystems. The musical group Daraa Tribes, which emerged from the region of Tagounite in the

Zagora area, has given a macabre image of the changes that swept their desert homeland. Entitled "Draa wash hād al-ḥāla" (Draa what's this deplorable state), one of the band's songs stages a contradiction between the present situation and the past. While the older generation remembers a verdant and oasis-rich rosy land (*wrda fjnān khḍrīn*), the singers' generation see what the song calls "mdbala" (wilt/wilderness).[29] Speaking from the position of today's widespread drought and illness of the palm trees, Draa of the present bears no resemblance to the one that their elders remember. The result is a mnemonic rehabilitation of the desert and a cry against the ravages of climate change brought upon desert spaces like theirs. Most important, however, is the fact that the song undermines any attempt to normalize the desert's death, as Saharanism has done for decades. Daraa Tribes's desert foregrounds a process of change that captures the radical effects man-made climate transformation has had on a concrete location that used to be prosperous.

As demonstrated by these three examples that span Mexico, China, and Morocco, the relevance of the (il)legal extraction of desert resources against the will of their Indigenous stewards serves as a common thread connecting different deserts. As dissimilar as they might seem, the people in these three deserts face the same entrenched Saharanism ideology that is undergirded by military might and a long-standing disempowerment of desert populations. These three cases are not only proof that the arguments I present in *Desert Imaginations* have broader implications, but they also demonstrate that all desert-focused activities and cultural productions—and, by extension, so many of their manifestations in our contemporary lives—require a close monitoring for the influence of Saharanism. As Michel Roux has rightly written, "The Saharan sand has invaded the spheres of our daily life, from the publicity of coffee or perfume to televised reviews of Paris-Dakar [Rally]."[30] This phenomenon extends to an enormous body of literature (both fiction and nonfiction), films, and even commercials that consciously or unconsciously draw on tropes of Saharanism to portray obduracy, heroism, resilience, athleticism, and much more.

Desert Imaginations is also an invitation to identify any aspect of Saharanism in its readers' immediate surroundings. Since both its discursive and practical manifestations have now been defined, it is up to each reader to consider how Saharanism might have informed any aspect, big or small, of their existence and the way they approach deserts, even in the metaphorical sense. It is my hope that every reader who engages with the book will discover the degree to which Saharanism's premises inform their daily imaginaries and soundscapes in both overt and subtle ways. This should lead every reader to undertake an intentional process of unlearning Saharanism and curb its impact on human and nonhuman subjects. This unlearning process should ultimately empower every reader to be a proactive agent of the desert when they gain awareness of the dangers Saharanism represents for sustainability. I will consider *Desert Imaginations* a success if this unlearning helps readers to think about desert life as an equivalent to sea life, albeit in a harsher and drier climate. This desert-ocean connection will help challenge the basic premises of Saharanism and make its devastating impacts more tangible and conceptually imaginable, especially for those who, although unfamiliar with deserts, can mobilize and translate their familiarity with ocean life into forms of sympathy for arid lands regardless of whether they have experienced or seen a real desert or not.

ACKNOWLEDGMENTS

Seven years have passed since I started working on this book project. Throughout this period, I have discussed many of these ideas in my "Saharan Imaginations" seminar, invited lectures, annual meetings, and interdisciplinary conferences and workshops. I also published portions of the project in both academic and public-facing venues to thrust some of my terminology and preliminary findings into the world. Of course, the process of writing and sharing ideas involves many debts to people whose support, friendship, enthusiasm, and intellectual generosity are crucial for the sustenance and completion of any project.

I particularly want to thank friends and colleagues Abdellah Hammoudi, Aomar Boum, Lital Levy, Paul Silverstein, Wendy Belcher, Maati Monjib, Edwige Tamalet Talbayev, Susan Slyomovics, Samia Errazzouki, Joel Lee, Amal Eqeiq, Ezra Feldman, Naïma Hachad, Lama Nassif, Katarzyna Pieprzak, Aly Corey, Sarah Allen, Ben Twagira, Paresh Chandra, Carlos Macías Prieto, Michelle Apostos, Anne Peale, Lisa Conathan, Murad Mumtaz, Ben Connor, Ben Lee Cohen, Brittany Meché, Zakia Salime, Alice Wilson, Miguel Fernández de Castro, Natalia Mendoza, Daniel Mason, Willie Binnie, Hassane Oudadene, Houssaine Hamdoune, Leonardo Lisi, Evelyne Ender, Jane Bennett, and Anne Merril for their support and collegiality. My former students Semra Vignaux, Hamza Woodson, Benjamin Connor, Theo Detweiler, Sama Kreidi, Jacquelin Nordhoff, and Aluna Brogdon, at Williams College, and Olivia Skye Neulight, at Johns Hopkins University, illuminated our seminar discussions with their bright ideas. Over the years, I have had great conversations about desert environments from the Sahara to California with my dear friend Michele Monserati. My partnership with friends and co-conspirators in the Desert Futures Collective, Jill Jarvis and Francisco Eduardo Robles, has been instrumental in reenergizing and starting conversations about deserts across different time zones, even as the COVID-19 pandemic raged globally. My heartfelt thanks go to all the colleagues who responded to our calls for papers and participated in these gatherings whether online or in person. I am also grateful to the reviewers for their terrific and insightful input, which has helped me tremendously to strengthen the final manuscript.

My gratitude also goes to all those who provided venues for me to share this book-in-progress with their wider audiences. Particularly, I want to thank Naghmah Sohrabi for the invitation to give a Crown Seminar at Brandeis University; the organizers of the MESAAS Graduate Student Conference at Columbia University, who invited me to give a keynote address for their annual conference; and the Lecture Committee at Williams College for the opportunity to introduce "Saharanism" as part of the Williams College Lecture Series. In addition to presentations at different professional organizations' annual meetings, I presented portions of this book at invited lectures at Harvard University, University of Pennsylvania, Pennsylvania State University, Johns Hopkins University, and University of Cambridge.

At University of California Press, my heartfelt thanks go to Niels Hooper for his enthusiasm for the project since our initial conversation about it, and to Nora Becker for her expertly steering of the manuscript through production. I also owe my gratitude to Tegan Raleigh for editing a first version of the manuscript and to S. C. Kaplan for lending her unequaled editing skills to the final manuscript. Both Williams College and Johns Hopkins University have provided financial support at different stages of my work on this book. The Dean of Faculty Office at Williams College awarded me generous funding through the Global Initiative Venture Fund for the "Comparative Desert Imaginations: Place, Mobility, and Environment Symposium & Student Workshop," which I organized in 2021. The Dean of the Krieger School of Arts & Sciences at Johns Hopkins University has furnished the funds that allowed me to acquire the rights for images and maps.

Last and not least, I would like to thank my wife, Shaina Adams-El Guabli, and my sons, Ilyas and Naseem, for their patience with me as I worked on this project. I dedicate this book to them with immense recognition of their support.

Although mostly or entirely rewritten, several small portions of the book have appeared in different academic and public-facing venues. The preface is a rewritten version of an article I published in *The Markaz Review*. A section of the introduction and Chapter 3 have been published in *The Architecture Review* and in the special issue of *Expressions maghrébines* I edited on "Experimental Deserts." The epilogue is a rewritten version of my article "Saharanism in the Sonoran," which was published by *The Avery Review*. Chapter 5 is based on "Saharan Gothic: Desert Necrofiction in Maghrebi and Middle Eastern Desert Literature," which appeared in *Middle Eastern Gothics* (Cardiff: University of Wales Press, 2022).

ILLUSTRATIONS

MAPS

FIGURES

NOTES

PREFACE

1. The concept of "sacrifice zones" has been used to talk about the environmental impact of extractive and industrial enterprises during the Cold War, which required sacrificing some areas for the sake of a greater national good. See Steve Lerner, *Sacrifice Zones: The Front Lines of Toxic Chemical Exposure in the United States* (Boston: MIT Press, 2010), 2.

2. Ward Churchill and Winona LaDuke, "Native North America: The Political Economy of Radioactive Colonialism," in *The State of Native America: Genocide, Colonization, and Resistance*, ed. Annette Jaimes (Boston: South End Press, 1992), 241–66.

3. Danielle Endres, "The Rhetoric of Nuclear Colonialism: Rhetorical Exclusion of American Indian Arguments in the Yucca Mountain Nuclear Waste Siting Decision," *Communication and Critical/Cultural Studies* 6, no. 1 (2009): 40.

4. Masen, "Masen: Endless Power for Progress," Masen.ma, accessed May 12, 2024, p. 7, www.masen.ma/sites/default/files/inline-files/MASEN_Brochure_instit_EN_finale.pdf.

5. Zakia Salime, "Life in the Vicinity of Morocco's Noor Solar Energy Project," *Middle East Report* 298 (2021): 22 para., https://merip.org/2021/04/life-in-the-vicinity-of-moroccos-noor-solar-energy-project-2.

6. For technical information about water consumption and Masen's environmental strategy, see Zeina Jokadar and Carlos Ponte, "Ouarzazate Solar Power Complex, Phase 1 Morocco: Specific Environmental and Social Impact Assessment Volume 1," 5 Capitals Environmental and Management Consulting, December 2012, www.masen.ma/sites/default/files/documents_rapport/Masen_NOORoI_SESIA_Volume1_aDfethF%20(1).pdf.

7. "Maḥaṭṭat 'nūr' warzāzāt .. al-ṭāqa al-shamsiyya ʿalā ḥisāb al-māʾ wa-al-filāḥa," *Alyaoum24*, accessed July 20, 2024, https://alyaoum24.com/1343063.html.

8. Patrick Donnelly, "Solar Sacrifice Zones: Who Decides?" *Desert Report*, July 17, 2015, https://desertreport.org/solar-sacrifice-zones-who-decides.

9. Masen, "Masen's Value Chain," YouTube, video, 4:21, accessed February 28, 2024, www.youtube.com/watch?v=HdqN3xX5mAk&ab_channel=Masen.

10. Ibid.

INTRODUCTION

1. See Frank M. Snowden, *Blacks in Antiquity: Ethiopians in the Greco-Roman Experience* (Cambridge, MA: Harvard University Press, 1970), 174–75; Paul Bowles, *The Sheltering Sky* (New York: Paladin, 1949); and André Gide, *L'immoraliste* (Paris: Mercure de France, 1902). Newspapers and scholarship on migration are replete with references to the ways in which CBP and Frontex treat the desert as a dangerous space, making it even harder for migrants to reach the US and Europe.

2. Ḥasan Dawwās, an Algerian student, dedicated a master's thesis to the topic of Saharanism, which he defines as an equivalent of desert Orientalism. Both my definition of Saharanism and the global environmental and ethical ramifications I draw from it are different from Dawwās's use of the term: "Ṣūrat al-mujtama' al-ṣaḥrāwī al-jazā'irī fī al-qarn al-tāsiʿ 'ashar min khilāl kitābāt al-raḥḥāla al-faransiyyīn: Muqāraba susiūthaqāfiyya" (master's thesis, Mentouri University of Constantine, 2008).

3. For a more fleshed out discussion of this program and its impact, see Diana K. Davis, *The Arid Lands: History, Power, Knowledge* (Boston: MIT, 2016), 146–54, and Perrin Selcer, *The Postwar Origins of the Global Environment: How the United Nations Built Spaceship Earth* (New York: Columbia University Press, 2018), 97-132.

4. "Focus on Western Mediterranean Route: Frontex in Spain," *Frontex*, accessed July 12, 2023, https://frontex.europa.eu/media-centre/news/focus/focus-on-western-mediterreanean-route-frontex-in-spain-isGpCE.

5. An impressive body of work has discussed all aspects of the Sahara and other deserts, but there has not been any effort to create a language or a conceptual framework linking these phenomena together. For the Sahara, scholars have examined smuggling, immigration, terrorism, knowledge and trade, and slavery, but each topic (with a few exceptions, of course) is almost confined to the Sahara. Important works include Judith Scheele, *Smugglers and Saints of the Sahara: Regional Connectivity in the Twentieth Century* (Cambridge: Cambridge University Press, 2019); Ghislaine Lydon, *On Trans-Saharan Trails: Islamic Law, Trade Networks, and Cross-Cultural Exchange in Nineteenth-Century Western Africa* (Cambridge: Cambridge University Press, 2009); Jeremy Keenan, *The Dying Sahara: US Imperialism and Terror in Africa* (London: Pluto Press: 2013).

6. Mike Heffernan, "Shifting Sands: The Trans-Saharan Railway," in *Engineering Earth: The Impacts of Megaengineering Projects*, ed. Stanley D. Brunn (New York: Springer, 2011), 617.

7. Brahim El Guabli, "Saharanism in the Sonoran," *The Avery Review*, no. 58 (2022): 22 para., https://averyreview.com/issues/58/saharanism-in-the-sonoran; idem, "Desert Futures Collective: A Conversation with Brahim El Guabli, Jill

Jarvis, and Francisco E. Robles," in *Deserts Are Not Empty*, ed. Samia Henni (New York: Columbia University Press, 2022), 31–35.

8. Edward W. Said, *Orientalism* (New York: Vintage Books, 1978), 150.

9. I agree with Dawwās that "the Sahara is something absolutely different from the Orient" ("Ṣūrat al-mujtamaʿ al-ṣaḥrāwī," n.p.) and that Orientalism has been abusively used to refer to a place that does not necessarily subscribe to its paradigm. Nevertheless, our premises and uses of Saharanism are different in that my intervention is more critical and broader, whereas his is more local and sometimes falls into the trap of the type of Saharanism that I critique.

10. Michel Roux, *Le désert de sable: Le Sahara dans l'imaginaire des français (1900–1994)* (Paris: L'Harmattan, 1996), 14.

11. Said, *Orientalism*, 49 and 19–20.

12. Ibid., 21.

13. Ibn Battuta, *Riḥlat ibn baṭṭuṭa: Tuḥfat al-nuẓẓār fī gharāʾib al-asfār wa ʿajāʾibi al-amṣār* (Beirut: Dār Iḥyāʾ al-ʿUlūm, 1987); Sanmao, *Stories of the Sahara* (London: Bloomsbury, 2019).

14. Reyner Banham, *Scenes in America Deserta* (Salt Lake City: Gibbs M. Smith, 1982), 8.

15. The word *saharien* is one of the most recurrent terms in literature about the Sahara. It is used with a lot of pride and almost connotes the same prestige that *veteran* commands among certain sections of American society today.

16. Jules Toutain has nuanced the uses of this term and the geographies to which it refers. See Jules Toutain, "Le territoire des Musulamii," in *Mémoires de la société nationale des antiques de France* (Paris: C. Klinscksieck, 1898), 58:276.

17. Bernard Simiot, Préaud, André Berthier, and Jean Imberti, "Il faut 'nationaliser' le Sahara," *Hommes et mondes* 62 (September 1951): 550.

18. Ralph Austen, *Trans-Saharan Africa in World History* (New York: Oxford University Press, 2010), 8. For a longer explanation of this racial slur and its origins in ancient Greek literature, see Snowden, *Blacks in Antiquity*, 174–75.

19. Heffernan, "Shifting Sands," 617.

20. Steve Lerner, *Sacrifice Zones: The Front Lines of Toxic Chemical Exposure in the United* States (Boston: MIT Press, 2010), 2.

21. Ibid.

22. Christopher Pollon, *Pitfall: The Race to Mine the World's Most Vulnerable Place* (Berkeley, CA: Greystone Books, 2023), 9.

23. Abd al-Raḥmān al-Saʿdī and Hamāh Allah Wld al-Sālim, eds., *Tārīkh al-sūdān: Kitāb fī tārīkh al-islām wa-al-thaqāfa wa-al-duwwal wa-al-shuʿūb fī ifrīqiyya janūb al-ṣaḥrāʾ wa ghāna wa mālī wa-al-sanghāy* (Beirut: Dār al-Kutub al-ʿIlmiyya, 2012), 124.

24. Mirza H. Alqassab, *Life after Oil: The Survival Predicament of the Gulf Arab States* (Leicestershire: Matador, 2020), 144; see also Christoph Strobel, *The Global Atlantic, 1400 to 1900* (New York: Routledge, 2015).

25. Frank T. Kryza, *The Race for Timbuktu: In Search of Africa's City of Gold* (New York: HarperCollins, 2006), xv–xvi.

26. Strobel, *Global Atlantic*, 30.

27. Boisboissel made these comments in a larger context of analyzing the long process of gaining access to the Sahara from Roman times until its domination by France in his chapter "L'exploration et la pacification du Sahara," in *Le Sahara français*, ed. Jean Charbonneau (Paris: Cahiers Charles de Foucauld, 1955), 133.

28. Leo Africanus, *The History and Description of Africa: And of the Notable Things Therein Contained*, trans. Robert Brown and John Pory (London: Printed for the Hakluyt Society, 1896).

29. I have used the Arabic translation prepared from the French. Haṣan al-Wazzān, *Waṣfu ifrīqiyyā li-al-ḥasan bin muḥammad al-wazzān al-fāsī al-maʿrūf bi-lyon al-ifriqī*, trans. Muhammad Ḥajjī and Muhammad Lakhḍar (Beirut: Dār al-Gharb al-Islāmī, 1983).

30. Ibid., 165.

31. Ibid., 167.

32. Ibid., 165.

33. Ibid.

34. René Caillié, *Journal d'un voyage à Temboctou et à Jenné dans l'Afrique centrale précédé d'observations faites chez les Maures Braknas, les Nalous et d'autres peuples, pendant les années 1824, 1825, 1826, 1827, 1828* (Paris: Imprimerie Royale, 1830).

35. Boisboissel, "L'exploration et la pacification," 134.

36. Journalist Jacques Duquesne draws on the way France celebrated Caillié and others to note, "There existed in France—and only in France—an entire romanticism of the Sahara, which was expressed in literature as well as in the popular songs" (*Histoires vraies: Une vie de journaliste* [Paris: Albin Michel, 2016], 51).

37. Kim Klooster, "The Rise and Transformation of the Atlantic World," in *The Atlantic World: Essays on Slavery, Migration, and Imagination*, ed. Kim Klooster and Alfred Padula (New York: Routledge, 2018).

38. Charles Hansford Adams, *The Narrative of Robert Adams: A Barbary Captive* (New York: Cambridge University Press, 2010), xv.

39. Ibid.

40. Boisboissel does a very good job of tracing these transformations in "L'exploration et la pacification."

41. René Caillié, *Travels through Central Africa to Timbuctoo and across the Great Desert, to Morocco, Performed in the Years 1824–1828*, 2 vols. (London: Henry Colburn and Richard Bentley, 1830), 1:99.

42. Jules Verne, *Les voyageurs du XIXe siècle* (Paris: Bibliothèque d'Éducation et de Récréation, 1880), 12.

43. Ibid.

44. This discourse extended beyond the army and Charles de Foucauld, as I will show later, to include scientists and engineers. See, for instance, A. Fock, "Réponse à M. Émile Broussais—de Paris au Soudan central," in Georges Rolland, *Le transsaharien: Un an après* (Paris: Austin Challamel, 1891), 104.

45. See Chap. 3 for the ways in which ownership of the colonial domain, and the Sahara specifically, was based on the idea that France had been the first to reach some of its areas.

46. Most often this notion of the desert's death and insecurity emerges from the contrast between what it was before and after French occupation. Captain and explorer Louis Voinot wrote, for "a very long time, the Sahara was an unknown land, a mysterious country." See Louis Voinot, "Le transsaharien et le transafricain," *Bulletin de la Société de géographie d'Alger et de l'Afrique du Nord* (First Trimestre 1913), 40.

47. Ibid.

48. See the letter of Lieutenant Colonel Cler in *Campagnes de Crimée, d'Italie, d'Afrique, de Chine et de Syrie, 1849–1862, lettres addressées au Maréchal de Castellane par les Maréchaux Baraguey d'Hilliers et al.*, ed. Esprit Victor Élisabeth Boniface (Paris: Librairies Plon, 1898), 56, and Victor Bernard Derrécagaix, *Le Maréchal Pélissier, duc de Malakoff* (Paris: Librairie Militaire R. Chapelot, 1911), 285–87. The entire population of Zaʿatsha was murdered in 1849. Benjamin Brower provides a vivid description of the gruesome job the French soldiers carried out in this oasis under the command of General Herbillon in *A Desert Named Peace: The Violence of France's Empire in the Algerian Sahara, 1844–1902* (New York: Columbia University Press, 2009), 82–83. See also Julia Clancy-Smith, *Rebel and Saint: Muslim Notables, Populist Protest, Colonial Encounters (Algeria and Tunisia, 1800–1904)* (Berkeley: University of California Press, 1994), 116–17, and Mueni wa Muiu and Guy Martin, *A New Paradigm of the African State: Fundi Wa Afrika* (New York: Palgrave Macmillan, 2009), 69.

49. Eugène Fromentin, *Un été dans le Sahara* (Paris: Librairie Plon, 1856), 113.

50. Ibid., 120.

51. These allegations are mostly conveyed in the Algerian media, but I was unable to find references to them in other contemporaneous sources from the nineteenth century. See Dalila Henache, "Mujahideen Minister: 'French Genocide in Algeria Resembles the Zionist Genocide in Palestine,'" *Echoroukonline*, accessed January 22, 2025, www.echoroukonline.com/mujahideen-minister-french-genocide-in-algeria-resembles-the-zionist-genocide-in-palestine; Hana Saada, "Remembering the Atrocity of Algeria's Laghouat: The 172nd Anniversary of the 1852 Massacre," *dzair-tube.dz*, accessed January 22, 2025, www.dzair-tube.dz/en/remembering-the-atrocity-of-algerias-laghouat-the-172nd-anniversary-of-the-1852-massacre.

52. Fromentin, *Un été*, 129.

53. Sven Lindqvist, *Desert Divers* (London: Granta Books, 2000), 57–58.

54. Ibid., 58.

55. Fromentin also records instances of antisemitism (*Un été*, 129).

56. Valentine Mudimbe, *The Invention of Africa: Gnosis, Philosophy, and the Order of Knowledge* (Bloomington: Indiana University Press, 1988), 15.

57. Henri Duveyrier, *Les Touareg du nord: Exploration du Sahara* (Paris: Challamel Ainé, 1864).

58. Johns David Ragan, *Forgotten Saint-Simonian Travelers in Egypt: Suzanne Voilquin, Ismayl Urbain, Jehan d'Ivary* (Cairo: The American University in Cairo Press, 2025), 37.

59. Dominique Casajus, *Henri Duveyrier: Un saint-simonien au désert* (Paris: Ibis Press, 2007), 139–41.

60. Dominique Casajus has examined the stories of different victims who succumbed in the Tuareg territory after carelessly following in the footsteps of Duveyrier's successful example upon reading his positive assessment of the Tuaregs. See Dominique Casajus, "Henri Duveyrier et le désert des Saint-Simoniens," *Ethnologies comparées* 7 (2004): 5–11.

61. For some of the history about this murder and its mnemonic implications, see John Strachan, "Murder in the Desert: Soldiers, Settlers, and the Flatters Expedition in the Politics and Historical Memory of European Colonial Algeria, 1830-1881," *French History and Civilization* 4 (2011): 210–22.

62. Ernest Mercier, *La France dans le Sahara et au Soudan* (Paris: Ernest Leroux, 1889), 30.

63. Léon Lehureaux, "Les français du Sahara: Les précurseurs," *Les Amis du Sahara: Organe de l'Association "Les Amis du Sahara" Bulletin trimestriel* (April 1932): 9.

64. Ibid.

65. Casajus, "Henri Duveyrier," 6 and 8.

66. Jean-Louis Triaud, *La légende noire de la Sanûsiyya: Une confrérie musulmane saharienne sous le regard français, 1840–1930*, 2 vols. (Paris: Maison des Sciences de l'Homme), 1:2.

67. Even the trans-Saharan train scheme was renounced until the Vichy regime resuscitated it for nationalistic reasons in the 1940s. Aomar Boum and Najib Berber's graphic novel, *Undesirables: A Holocaust Journey to North Africa* (Stanford: Stanford University Press, 2023), recovers parts of this legacy as it pertains to the labor camps in the Sahara.

68. Henri Wolff and Antoine-Auguste Blachère, *Sahara et Soudan: Les régiments de dromadaires* (Paris: Challamel Aîné Éditeur, 1884).

69. Archaeologist André Berthier recycled the same idea when he discusses Rome's division of North Africa and what we can call its "Saharan policy." See Simiot et al., "Il faut 'nationaliser' le Sahara," 550.

70. Austen, *Trans-Saharan Africa in World History*, 11.

71. Wolff and Blachère, *Sahara et Soudan*, 9.

72. Émile Bélime, "Avenir de l'Union française," *Hommes et mondes* 14, no. 58 (1951), 682.

73. Colonel Clément-Célestin d'Eu, *In-Salah et le Tidikelt: Journal des opérations* (Paris: Librairie Militaire R. Chapelot, 1902), 2.

74. Wolff and Blachère, *Sahara et Soudan*, 42, 50.

75. Ibid., 51–53.

76. J. E. H. Boustead, "The Camel Corps of the Sudan Defence Force," *Royal United Services Institution Journal* (1934): 547.

77. Jamal al-Dīn al-Dināṣūrī has highlighted how the establishment of these forces was directed at quashing Saharan people's independence, which they continued to defend until their defeat in 1935. See Raymond Furon, *al-Ṣaḥrāʾ al-kubrā:*

Al-jawānib al-jiūlūjiyya-maṣādir al-tharwa al-maʿdiniyya-istighlāluhā, trans. Jamal al-Dīn al-Dināṣūrī (Cairo: Muʾassasat Sijil al-ʿArab, 1963), 4.

78. Gautier does, however, mention that a colonel named Carbuccia was in charge in 1843 of organizing the first camel-mounted unit in Algeria in his discussion of the likening of the camel's movement to the nauseating effects of the ship on sea waves. Félix Gautier, *La conquête du Sahara: Essai de psychologie politique* (Paris: Armand Colin, 1910), 81.

79. Odie B. Faulk, *The US Camel Corps: An Army Experiment* (Oxford: Oxford University Press, 1976), 16–19; Forrest Bryant Johnson, *The Last Camel Charge: The Untold Story of America's Desert Military Experiment* (New York: Penguin, 2013).

80. Johnson, *Last Camel Charge*, 79.

81. Ibid., 76–77.

82. Ibid., 78–79.

83. Ibid., 82.

84. Ibid.

85. Ibid., 97–98.

86. Philip Jones and Anna Kenny, *Australia's Muslim Cameleers: Pioneers of the Inland, 1860s–1930s* (Kent Town, Australia: Wakefield Press, 2010), 9.

87. Roger Frison-Roche, *La piste oubliée* (Paris: Arthaud, 1950); Roger Frison-Roche, *The Lost Trail of the Sahara: A Novel*, trans. Paul Bowles (New York: Prentice-Hall, 1952).

88. His name is a combination of *beau* (handsome) and *fort* (strong), which further complicates the ramifications of Beaufort's story, particularly in terms of its racial dimensions.

89. Frison-Roche, *Piste oubliée*, 289.

90. Ibid., 261.

91. Ibid., 285.

92. Ibid., 230.

93. Ibid., 288.

94. Philippe Delisle, *Bande dessinée franco-belge et imaginaire colonial: Des années 1930 aux années 1980* (Paris: L'Harmattan, 2016), 38–39. Delisle is very critical of the racializing depiction of Muslims and other colonized people in the works he surveys in this important book.

95. Hergé, *Le crabe aux pinces d'or* (Brussels: Casterman, 1941).

96. Hergé, *Tintin au pays de l'or noir* (Brussels: Casterman, 1950).

97. Pierre Straitur, *Chez les Touareg au litham bleu, grand récit d'aventures vraies* (Paris: Les Éditions Fleurus, 1947).

98. Quoted in Roux, *Désert de sable*, 90.

99. Antoine de Saint-Exupéry, *Terre des hommes* (Paris: Gallimard, 1939); Antoine de Saint-Exupéry, *Le petit prince, avec les dessins de l'auteur* (Paris: Gallimard, 1946).

100. Saint-Exupéry, *Terre des hommes*, 75–76.

101. Paul Rimbault, *Alger 1830–1930: Les grandes figures du centenaire* (Paris: Larose, 1929), 194.

102. Simiot et al., "Il faut 'nationaliser' le Sahara," 541.

103. André Bourgeot, "Sahara: Espace géostratégique et enjeux politiques (Niger)," *Naqd* 3, no. 1 (2014): 154.

104. Patricia Nelson Limerick, *Desert Passages: Encounters with American Deserts* (Albuquerque: University of New Mexico Press, 1985), 165.

105. Ibid., 166.

106. Ibid., 167.

107. Ibid., 168.

108. Ibid.

109. Davis, *The Arid Lands*, 135.

110. George P. Marsh, *Man and Nature or Physical Georgraphy as Modified by Human Action* (New York: Charles Scribner, 1864), 463.

111. Limerick, *Desert Passages*, 171.

112. "Marquis de Morès," National Park Service, updated December 13, 2020, www.nps.gov/thro/learn/historyculture/marquis-de-mores.htm.

113. Richard Dorsey Mohun, "The Scramble for the Upper Nile," *The Century Illustrated Monthly Magazine* 56, no. 1 (1898): 60.

114. Quentin Crewe, *In Search of the Sahara* (London: Michael Joseph, 1983), 30.

115. Davis, *The Arid Lands*, 140.

116. Selcer, *Postwar Origins*, 108–9.

117. Usāmah al-Naḥḥās, *'Imārat al-ṣaḥrā'* (Cairo: Maktabat al-Anjlu al-Miṣrīya, 1986), 2.

118. Jason De León, *The Land of Open Graves: Living and Dying on the Migrant Trail* (Oakland: University of California Press, 2015), 6–8, 16–17.

119. Rémi Carayol and Laurent Gagnol, "Ces murs de sable qui surgissent au Sahara," *Le Monde diplomatique*, accessed January 27, 2025, www.monde-diplomatique.fr/2021/10/CARAYOL/63629.

120. Boum and Berber, *Undesirables*, 99–100.

121. Readers are advised to see the following for further information about these prisons: Susan Slyomovics, *The Performance of Human Rights in Morocco* (Philadelphia: University of Pennsylvania Press, 2005); Brahim El Guabli, *Moroccan Other-Archives: History and Citizenship after State Violence* (New York: Fordham University Press, 2023); Carole Naggar, *Le rouge du sable: Un prisonnier au camp d'Al Kharga en Égypte, 1959–1963* (Paris: L'Harmattan, 2021).

122. Awel Haouati wrote, "The [Islamist] prisoners had in fact been distributed between In Amguel, Reggane, and Oued Namous, sites which were contaminated by radioactivity and the residue of chemical and bacteriological tests inherited from the former colonial power" ("Sahara algérien—Des essais nucléaires aux camps de sûreté," Revue-ballast.fr, June 28, 2017, www.revue-ballast.fr/nucleaire-algerie-camps-dinternement).

123. His two landmark novels in this regard are Abdelrahman Munif, *Sharq al-mutawassiṭ* (Tunis: Dār al-Janūb, 1989), and idem, *al-Ān . . . hunā, aw, sharq al-mutawassiṭ marratan ukhrā* (Beirut: al-Mu'assasa al-'Arabīyya lil-Dirāsat wa-al-Nashr, 1991).

124. Samir Benmalek, "Sur les traces d'André Gide: Séjour d'un écrivain australien en Algérie," *Liberté*, March 26, 2006, www.djazairess.com/fr/liberte/54826.

125. Ibid.

126. Henry de Montherlant, *L'histoire d'amour de la rose de sable* (Paris: Plon, 1954).

127. Brian Edwards, *Morocco Bound: Disorienting America's Maghreb, from Casablanca to the Marrakech Express* (Durham, NC: Duke University Press, 2005), 61–63.

128. Writing in 1923, Sarraut declared that a project that proposed "an overall program of major public works, economic tools and social works" was being discussed by the Committee of Algeria, the Colonies, and the Protectorates in the French parliament. In Sarraut's words, the ratification of the project would likely "give a powerful impetus both to the development of [France's] material wealth and to the human work of civilization pursued by France among its native subjects and protégés." See Albert Sarraut, *La mise en valeur des colonies françaises* (Paris: Payot, 1923), 23.

129. Sony Pictures, "Sahara 1943," dir. Zoltan Korda, YouTube Movies & TV, accessed December 18, 2024, www.youtube.com/watch?v=hHpXK56rsJ8&rco=1.

130. James McDougall and Judith Scheele, *Saharan Frontiers: Space and Mobility in Northwest Africa* (Bloomington: Indiana University Press, 2012), 3.

131. Roslynn D. Haynes, *Seeking the Centre: The Australian Desert in Literature, Art, and Film* (Cambridge: Cambridge University Press, 1999), 67.

132. Bennet Maxwell, "The Emperor of the Sahara," *The Independent*, September 14, 1998, www.independent.co.uk/arts-entertainment/the-emperor-of-the-sahara-1198247.html.

133. Jean-Jacques Bedu, *Moi, empereur du Sahara* (Paris: Albin Michel, 2014), 111.

134. Johnson, *Last Camel Charge*, 77.

135. Jack Mortimer Sheppard, *Sahara Adventure* (London: Jarrolds, 1957), 13.

136. This new discourse is reflected in official statements and also in the writings of French officials whose work focused on the Sahara. See, for instance, Erik Labonne's discussion of the shift in France's view of and approach to the Sahara: "Préface," in Daniel Strasser, *Réalités et promesses sahariennes: Aspects juridiques et économiques de la mise en valeur industrielle du Sahara français* (Paris: Encyclopédie d'Outre-Mer, 1956), 7–10.

137. Ivan Hrbek, "L'Afrique septentrionale et la corne de l'Afrique," in *Histoire générale de l'Afrique,* vol. 8: *L'Afrique depuis 1935*, ed. Ali Mazui and Christophe Wondji (Paris: Éditions UNESCO, 1998), 155. Jean-Michel de Lattre captures the changing strategies around the Sahara in the 1950s in "Sahara, clé de voûte de l'ensemble eurafricain français," *Politique étrangère* 4 (1957): 345–89.

138. Attilio Gaudio, *Le dossier du Sahara occidental* (Paris: Nouvelles Éditions Latines, 1978), 153.

139. Ibid.

140. Marcel Pellenc, "Annexe au procès-verbal de la 1ère séance du 1er décembre 1959," 38, www.senat.fr/rap/1959-1960/i1959_1960_0066_03_23.pdf.

141. Ibid.

142. Pierre Nord, *L'Eurafrique, notre dernière chance* (Paris: Fayard, 1955).

143. Samia Henni, "Oil, Gas, Dust: From the Sahara to Europe," *e-Flux Architecture*, October 2021, www.e-flux.com/architecture/coloniality-infrastructure/410034/oil-gas-dust-from-the-sahara-to-europe.

144. Claude Treyer has discussed how the 1956 Code du pétrolier incentivized foreign companies to enter joint ventures with their French counterparts to exploit Saharan resources. He also drew attention to the fact that this code established a rigid law that the Algerian state inherited after independence. See Claude Treyer, *Sahara 1956–1962* (Paris: Société Les Belles Lettres, 1966), 222.

145. Louis Armand, "Vers un Sahara moderne," *Hommes et mondes* 99 (October 1954): 321.

146. de Lattre, "Sahara, clé de voûte," 349.

147. Armand, "Vers un Sahara moderne," 333.

148. Ibid.

149. André Allix, "Sahara et pétrole 1957," *Revue de géographie de Lyon* 32, no. 4 (1957): 270.

150. de Lattre, "Sahara, clé de voûte," 346.

151. Jacques Soustelle, *Le Sahara d'aujourd'hui et la France de l'an 2000* (Paris: Société Parisienne, 1959), 3.

152. Martin Heidegger, *Country Path Conversations*, trans. Bret W. Davis (Bloomington: Indiana University Press, 2010), 136.

153. Soustelle, *Sahara d'aujourd'hui*, 3.

154. Benjamin Stora, *Les mots de la guerre d'Algérie* (Toulouse: Presses Universitaires du Mirail, 2005), 107.

155. General Charles Ailleret provides important details about the years leading up to nuclear tests and their execution in *L'aventure atomique française* (Paris: Grasset, 1968).

156. Dey Sidi Baba, "Le Sahara de demain," *Perspectives sahariennes* 3 (August 1958): 125.

157. Gaudio, *Dossier du Sahara*, 153.

158. Allal al-Fassi, "Présentation," *Perspectives sahariennes* 1 (June 1958): 4.

159. Abdeljalil, "L'activité économique du Sahara dans le Maghreb," *Perspectives sahariennes* 1 (1958): 22–23.

160. "L'O.C.R.S., dernière base de manœuvre du colonialisme français," *El Moujahid*, June 20, 1960, 133.

161. Ibid.

162. Ibid., 134.

163. "Le Sahara algérien," *El Moujahid*, April 15, 1961, 441–43.

164. Carolyne R. Larson, "Introduction: Tracing the Battle for History," in *The Conquest of the Desert: Argentina's Indigenous Peoples and the Battle for History*, ed. Carolyne R. Larson (Albuquerque: University of New Mexico Press, 2020), 9–10; Allan D. Cooper, *The Geography of Genocide* (Boulder, CO: University Press of America, 2009), 60; W. Dirk Raat, *Lost Worlds of 1863: Relocation and Removal of*

American Indians in the Central Rockies and the Greater Southwest (Hoboken, NJ: John Wiley and Sons, 2021), 117.

165. Paul Josephson, "Industrial Deserts: Industry, Science, and the Destruction of Nature in the Soviet Union," *The Slavonic and East European Review* 85, no. 2 (2007): 295.

166. Brower, *Desert Named Peace*, 213.

167. Ibrahim al-Koni, *al-Waram* (Beirut: al-Muʾassasa al-ʿArabīyya lil-Dirāsāt wa-al-Nashr, 2008).

168. Ibrahim al-Koni, *Nazīf al-ḥajar* (Misrata: al-Dār al-Jamāhīrīya lil-Nashr wa-al-Tawzīʿ wa-al- Iʿlān, 1996).

169. Amitav Ghosh, *The Great Derangement: Climate Change and the Unthinkable* (Chicago: Chicago University Press, 2017), 31.

170. The five volumes are *Mudun al-milḥ: al-Tīh* (Casablanca: al-Markaz al-Thaqāfī al-ʿArabī, 2005); *Mudun al-milḥ: al-Ukhdūd* (Casablanca: al-Markaz al-Thaqāfī al-ʿArabī, 2005), *Mudun al-milḥ: Taqāsīm al-layl wa-al-nahar* (Casablanca: al-Markaz al-Thaqāfī al-ʿArabī, 2005), *Mudun al-milḥ: al-Manbat* (Casablanca: al-Markaz al-Thaqāfī al-ʿArabī, 2005), and *Mudun al-milḥ: Bādiyat al-zulumāt* (Casablanca: al-Markaz al-Thaqāfī al-ʿArabī, 2005).

171. Elisabeth Leuvrey, dir., *At(h)ome* (France: Les Écrans du Large, 2013), DVD.

172. The author of *al-Ṭawāriq ʿabra al- ʿuṣūr* (*The Tuaregs across Time*) indicates that France took its revenge on the Tuaregs for foiling its designs for the Sahara, but he does not elaborate on what this revenge entailed. See al-Shāwī Allalāh al-Bakkāy Amāhīn, *Al-Ṭawāriq ʿabra al- ʿuṣūr* (Benghazi: Dār al-Kutub al-Waṭaniyya, 2000), 155.

173. Ibrahim al-Koni, *Waṭanī ṣaḥrāʾun kubrā* (Beirut: al-Mu'assasa al-ʿArabiyya li-al-Dirāsāt wa-al-Nashr, 2009), 8.

174. Molly Steenson, "The Burning Man Experience: What is Burning Man?," accessed October 13, 2023, https://burningman.org/event/preparation/black-rock-city-guide/first-timers-guide/the-burning-man-experience.

CHAPTER ONE: SPIRITUAL SAHARANISM

1. Pope Francis called attention, among other things, to Foucauld's "human fraternity among the people he served during his life as a simple hermit." See Thaddeus Jones, "De Foucauld: Total Surrender to God and Universal Fraternity," *Vatican News*, May 14, 2022, www.vaticannews.va/en/church/news/2022-05/de-foucauld-example-total-surrender-god-universal-fraternity.html.

2. The long list includes people like Henri Duveyrier, René Caillié, Gordon Laing, Fernand Foureau, and Alexine Tinne, to name just a few. French Historian Jean-Louis Miège has drawn attention to the richness of the clergy's observations about places they lived or traversed. See Jean-Louis Miège, "Les missions protestantes au Maroc 1875–1905," *Hespéris* 1–2 (1955): 153.

3. For a better understanding of the politics of biography and hagiography, see Paul Fournier's richly documented "La biographie de Charles de Foucauld par René Bazin dans les journaux et les revues au début des années 20," in *Charles de Foucauld: Amitiés croisées*, ed. Josette Fournier (Le Coudray-Macouard: Cheminements, 2007), 193–265.

4. André Bourgeot, "Sahara: Espace géostratégique et enjeux politiques (Niger)," *Naqd* 3, no. 1 (2014): 157.

5. For a more detailed discussion of the multitude of complex attitudes vis-à-vis deserts in Christianity and Judaism, see Diana K. Davis, *The Arid Lands: History, Power, Knowledge* (Boston: MIT, 2016), 35–47.

6. Benedicta Ward, *The Desert Fathers: Sayings of the Early Christian Monks* (New York: Penguin, 2003), ix.

7. Ibid.

8. Ibid., x–xi.

9. Ibid., 38.

10. Malek Bennabi, *al-Ẓāhira al-qurʾāniyya*, trans. Abdelṣabūr Shāhin (Beirut: Dār al-Fikr, 2000), 116.

11. Ibid., 117.

12. Muhammad Shahjan al-Nadawi, *al-Siyyāḥa aḥkāmuhā wa ādābuhā fin ḍawʾ al-qānūn wa al-shariʿa: Dirāsa ilmiyya* (Beirut: Dār al-Kutub al-ʿIlmiyya, 2017), 47.

13. Ibid.

14. Ernest Psichari, *Les voix qui crient dans le désert* (Paris: Louis Conard, 1920).

15. Leah Kinberg, "What Is Meant by Zuhd," *Studia Islamica* 61 (1985): 32.

16. Ibid., 35.

17. Ibid.

18. Ibid., 38.

19. In his essay entitled "Meditation on the Temptation of Our Master in the Desert," Foucauld connects the desert with the spirit of Nazareth and Jesus's dedication to worship. See Charles de Foucauld, *Lettres et carnets* (Paris: Éditions du Seuil, 1966), 97–101.

20. Edmund Burke, *The Writings and Speeches of Edmund Burke*, ed. Paul Langford and William Burton Todd, 12 vols. (Oxford: Oxford University Press, 1997), 1:230.

21. Psichari, *Les voix qui crient*, 284.

22. This marks a big shift from what Davis has found in her research about the premodern Christian literature, in which "deserts were not perceived as deforested, ruined landscapes, nor were people blamed or held responsible for their creation." See Davis, *Arid Lands*, 47.

23. Foucauld wrote: "Missionaries like him are very rare. Their role is to prepare the path. . . . There are very few isolated missionaries who act as trailblazers" ("Lettre du bienheureux Charles de Foucauld à René Bazin de l'Académie française, le 29 juillet 1916," *Bulletin du Bureau catholique de presse* 5 [1917], https://archive.org/download/charles-de-foucauld-_-lettre-a-rene-bazin/Charles_de_Foucauld_-_Lettre_a_Rene_Bazin.pdf). In fact, this language indicates that evangelization was

important to Foucauld, but it would not come until the "taming" of the people of the Sahara was completed.

24. Henry de Castries was a well-respected officer, geographer, politician, and explorer in both Algeria and Morocco. His work on Morocco was particularly well received. His main publications include *Agents et voyageurs français au Maroc, 1530–1660* (Paris: Ernest Leroux, 1911), and *Les sources inédites de l'histoire du Maroc de 1530 à 1845* (Paris: Ernest Leroux, 1905).

25. For details about her life, see Hedi Abdel-Jaouad, "Isabelle Eberhardt: Portrait of the Artist as a Young Nomad," *Yale French Studies* 83 (1993): 93–117.

26. He is the author of several books, including *Letters from the Desert* (New York: Orbis Books, 1972).

27. Paul Claudel, "Ma conversion," in *Les témoins du renouveau catholique*, ed. Thomas Mainage (Paris: Gabriel Beauchesne, 1919), 63–64.

28. Berny Sèbe, "Exalting Imperial Grandeur: The French Empire and Its Metropolitan Public," in *European Empires and the People: Popular Responses to Imperialism in France, Britain, the Netherlands, Belgium, Germany, and Italy*, ed. John MacKenzie (Manchester: Manchester University Press, 2011), 20–24.

29. Daniel T. Reff, *Plagues, Priests, and Demons: Sacred Narratives and the Rise of Christianity in the Old World and the New* (Cambridge: Cambridge University Press, 2004), 241.

30. Ibid., 179.

31. María Ruth Noriega Sánchez, *Challenging Realities: Magic Realism in Contemporary American Women's Fiction* (Valencia: Universitat de València, 2002), 149.

32. See David Yetman, *Conflict in Colonial Sonora: Indians, Priests, and Settlers* (Albuquerque: University of New Mexico Press, 2012), 9–28.

33. Ernest Renan's positions vis-à-vis Islam may be representative of the general mood. See Samar Moujaes, "La rencontre entre Renan et l'islam," in *Renan en Orient*, ed. Jean Balcou, Jean Glasser, and Sophie Guermès (Rennes: Presses Universitaires de Rennes, 2022), 213–24, https://doi.org/10.4000/books.pur.160169.

34. For Algeria's place in the politics of secularism, see Rabeh Achi, "1905: Quand l'islam était (déjà) la seconde religion de France," *Multitudes* 59, no. 2 (2015): 45–52.

35. Robert Clarke, "The Idea of Celebrity Colonialism," in *Celebrity Colonialism: Fame, Power, and Representation in Colonial and Postcolonial Cultures*, ed. Robert Clarke (Newcastle upon Tyne: Cambridge Scholars, 2009), 1–10.

36. Berny Sèbe, "Colonial Celebrities in Popular Culture: Heroes of the British and French Empires, 1850–1914," in *Celebrity Colonialism: Fame, Power, and Representation in Colonial and Postcolonial Cultures*, ed. Robert Clarke (Newcastle upon Tyne: Cambridge Scholars, 2009), 40.

37. Patrick Heidsieck, *Le rayonnement de Lyautey* (Paris: Gallimard, 1944), 177.

38. Ibid.

39. Everything she had to say about enslaved Black people was viscerally racist. See Isabelle Eberhardt, *In the Shadow of Islam*, trans. Sharon Bangert (London: Peter Owen, 1993), 45–48, 65–67, 77.

40. The overlaps between Lyautey and Laperrine can be seen in Jean-François Six, *Charles de Foucauld: Sa vie, sa voie* (Paris: Éditions Artège, 2016); Noureddine Belhaddad, "Muqāwamat qabāʾil al-ṣaḥrāʾ li-al-istiʿmār al-faransī-al-isppānī (1912–1934)," in *Al-Ṣaḥrāʾ wa sūs min khilāl al-wathāʾiq wa-al-makhṭuṭāt: al-tawāṣul wa-al-āfāq*, ed. ʿUmar Affā (Rabat: Manshūrāt Kulliyyat al-ʾĀdāb wa-al-ʿUlūm al-Insāniyya, 2002), 128. Dominique Casajus writes, the "Tuareg meet Foucauld for the first time, he was among the soldiers; these same soldiers whose rapid-fire rifles killed more than a hundred of theirs on the plain of Titi in 1902" (Dominique Casajus, *Charles de Foucauld: Moine et savant* [Paris: Éditions du CNRS, 2009], 43). Although Eberhardt was mostly accused of engaging in espionage on behalf of her friend Lyautey, Algerian writer Aboul-Kassem Saadallah also references the accusation by the French administration in Algeria of her being a spy for Germany. See Aboul-Kassem Saadallah, *Tārīkh al-jazāʾir al-thaqāfī aljuzʾ al-rābiʿ 1830–1954* (Beirut: Dār al-Gharb al-Islāmī, 1998), 52.

41. Casajus, *Charles de Foucauld*, 44.

42. In fact, Foucauld said that Laperrine "was the one who gave the Sahara to France despite itself." See René Bazin, *Charles de Foucauld explorateur du Maroc, ermite au Sahara, avec un portrait, un fac-similé d'autographe et une carte-itinéraire* (Paris: Librairie Plon, 1921), 391; and Jean-François Six, *Charles de Foucauld autrement* (Paris: Desclée De Brouwer, 2008). In other versions attributed to influential geographer Félix Gautier, both Laperrine and Foucauld are credited with the conquest of the Sahara. See Bernard Simiot et al., "Il faut 'nationaliser' le Sahara," *Hommes et mondes* 62 (September1951): 541.

43. Charles de Foucauld and Louis Massignon, *L'aventure de l'amour de Dieu: 80 lettres inédites de Charles de Foucauld à Louis Massignon*, ed. Jean François Six (Paris: Le Seuil, 1993). Some of the arguments advanced in this book reveal a gradual disagreement between Foucauld and Laperrine, but it is not certain to what extent the two men discussed this disagreement, particularly because of Foucauld's later letters extolling the security of the Sahara under Laperrine's control.

44. Yan Slobodkin, *The Starving Empire: A History of Famine in France's Colonies* (Ithaca, NY: Cornell University Press, 2023), 35–36.

45. J. Dean O'Donnell, Jr., "Cardinal Charles Lavigerie: The Politics of Getting a Red Hat," *The Catholic Historical Review* 63, no. 2 (1977): 185.

46. Ibid., 187.

47. Bertrand Taithe, "Missionary Militarism? The Armed Brothers of the Sahara and Léopold Joubert in the Congo," in *In God's Empire: French Missionaries and the Modern World*, ed. Owen White and J. P. Daughton (New York: Oxford University Press, 2012), 133.

48. Société contre l'abus du tabac, "Statue du cardinal Lavigerie," *Journal de la Société contre l'abus du tabac* 24 (1900): 80.

49. The emperor intervened to adjudicate the public fight between Marshal Patrice MacMahon and Lavigerie, writing to the latter: "Mr. Archbishop, you have a big task to accomplish—that of moralizing the 200,000 Catholics who are in

Algeria. As for Arabs, leave the General Governor [MacMahon] the task of disciplining them and accustoming them to our domination." See Louis Baunard, *Le cardinal Lavigerie*, 2 vols. (Paris: J. de Gigord, 1922), 1:254.

50. Marcel Emirit, "Le problème de la conversion des musulmans d'Algérie sous le Second Empire: Le conflit entre MacMahon et Lavigerie," *Revue historique* 223, no. 1 (1960): 67.

51. Georges Goyau, "Un grand missionnaire: Le cardinal Lavigerie (1): La vocation missionnaire—Les débuts," *Revue des deux mondes* 26, no. 2 (1925): 326.

52. Emirit, "Problème de la conversion," 66.

53. Louis Barucand, *Un siècle de l'église de France 1800–1900* (Paris: Librairie Ch. Poussielgue, 1902), 453.

54. Joseph W. Peterson, *Sacred Rivals: Catholic Missions and the Making of Islam in Nineteenth-Century France and Algeria* (New York: Oxford University Press, 2022), 141–42.

55. Charles Martial Allemand Lavigerie, *L'armée et la mission de la France en Afrique: Discours prononcé à la cathédrale d'Alger le 25 avril 1875 pour l'inauguration du service religieux dans l'armée d'Afrique par M l'archevêque d'Alger* (Algiers: A. Jourdin, 1875), 28–29, 63.

56. Georges Goyau, "Un grand missionnaire: Le cardinal Lavigerie (2); La résurrection de l'église d'Afrique," *Revue des deux mondes* 26, no. 3 (1925): 604.

57. Ibid., 6.

58. Ibid.

59. Ibid., 9, 11.

60. Ibid., 14.

61. Lavigerie's black-and-white approach manifests in the way he describes the priests who participated in the conquest of Algeria and the way he denigrates Abdel-Kader's staunch resistance to French occupation. While the former embody goodness, the latter represents evil and debased motives.

62. Goyau, "Grand missionnaire 1," 326.

63. Ibid.

64. René Pottier, *Le cardinal Lavigerie apôtre et civilisateur* (Paris: Les Publications Techniques et Artistiques, 1947), 110.

65. Taithe provides an explanation of the politics involved in the military, missionary, and administrative relations in Algeria ("Missionary Militarism," 130). These political divisions even extended to Lavigerie's promotion to cardinalhood. See O'Donnell, "Cardinal Charles Lavigerie," 195.

66. Goyau, "Grand missionnaire 2," 579.

67. Baunard, *Cardinal Lavigerie*, 241–42.

68. Ibid., 532.

69. Lavigerie, *Armée et la mission*, 63.

70. Charles Lavigerie, *Lettre de son éminence le cardinal Lavigerie: À tous les volontaires qui se sont proposés à l'oeuvre antiesclavagiste de France sur l'association des frères armés ou pionniers du Sahara* (Algiers: Adolphe Jourdan, 1891), 6.

71. Goyau, "Grand missionnaire (2)," 608.

72. Charles Martial Allemand Lavigerie, *Lettre de Mgr l'archevêque d'Alger [Lavigerie] à M. le directeur de l'œuvre des écoles d'Orient sur la mission d'Afrique et la création de villages d'Arabes chrétiens en Algérie* (Paris: Bureaux de l'Œuvre des écoles d'Orient, 1876), 11, https://gallica.bnf.fr/ark:/12148/bpt6k57901134.

73. François Ricard, "Les missions d'Afrique des Pères blancs," in *Le tour du monde: Journal des voyages et des voyageurs* (Paris: Librairie Hachette, 1907), 287.

74. Lavigerie quotes this passage from Reclus to convey his point: "Travelers speak vaguely of populations that are not yet converted to Islam and which lived in the mountains of Aougllimiden . . . , but their color is white and marry exclusively amongst themselves." Charles Martial Allemand Lavigerie, *Allocution prononcée le 21 septembre 1890 par S. Em. Le cardinal Lavigerie dans l'église Saint-Sulpice à Paris pour l'ouverture d'un congrès antiesclavagiste* (Paris: À la direction générale de l'œuvre antiesclavagiste, 1890), 91–92.

75. Ibid., 91.

76. Ibid., 95.

77. Ibid., 98.

78. Ibid., 95.

79. Ibid.

80. Ibid.

81. Goyau, "Grand missionnaire (2)," 580; Lavigerie, *Allocution*, 95, 97.

82. It is important to note that Foucauld kept referring to the danger of the Senusiyya until his murder in 1916. See Charles de Foucauld, *Lettres inédites au général Laperrine pacificateur du Sahara* (Paris: La Colombe, 1954).

83. Lavigerie, *Allocution*, 93.

84. Taithe, "Missionary Militarism," 137.

85. William Sharp, "Cardinal Lavigerie's Work in North Africa," *The Atlantic* (August 1894): 214–15.

86. Charles Martial Allemand Lavigerie, *Lettre de Mgr l'archevêque d'Alger à un séminariste de France sur la société des missionnaires d'Alger* (Algiers: Bureau de l'Œuvre des écoles d'Orient, 1878), 14.

87. Ibid., 39, 34; Lavigerie, *Allocution*, 93.

88. Eugène Marin, *Algérie—Sahara—Soudan: Vie, travaux, voyages de Mgr Hacquard des Pères blancs (1860–1901) d'après sa correspondance* (Paris: Berger-Levrault, 1905), 114.

89. Peterson, *Sacred Rivals*, 173.

90. Lavigerie, *Lettre . . . à un séminariste*, 3–4.

91. Peterson, *Sacred Rivals*, 149.

92. Joseph Variot, *Les Pères blancs ou missionnaires d'Alger* (Lille: Desclée, de Brouwer, 1887), 2.

93. Lavigerie, *Lettre . . . à un séminariste*, 30.

94. Ibid., 31.

95. Variot, *Pères blancs*, 6.

96. Œuvre de la propagation de la foi, *Les missions catholiques* 23 (January–December 1891), 328.

97. Ibid.

98. Lavigerie, *Allocution*, 96.

99. Henri Bissuel, *Le Sahara français: Conférence sur les questions sahariennes* (Algiers: Adolphe Jourdan, libraire-éditeur, 1891), 28.

100. Lavigerie, *Lettre . . . à un séminariste*, 40.

101. Ibid., 37–38.

102. Fleuriot de Langle, "Le cardinal Lavigerie," *Revue des deux mondes* (1961): 433.

103. Peterson, *Sacred Rivals*, 143.

104. Taithe, "Missionary Militarism,"132.

105. Pottier, *Cardinal Lavigerie*, 110.

106. Lavigerie, *Lettre . . . à un séminariste*, 4–5; readers can also refer to his long exposé on slavery in different parts of Africa entitled *Lettre de S. É. le cardinal Lavigerie sur l'esclavage africain, à MM. les directeurs de l'Œuvre de la propagation de la foi* (Lyon: Imprimerie Mougin-Rusand, 1888).

107. Ibid., 7.

108. Delina Goxho, "Militarizing the Sahel Won't Make Europe More Secure," *Foreign Policy*, August 5, 2022, https://foreignpolicy.com/2022/08/05/militarizing-sahel-mali-niger-wont-make-europe-more-secure.

109. Lavigerie, *Lettre . . . à un séminariste*, 8.

110. Ibid.

111. Aimé Roche, *Charles de Foucauld* (Lyon: Éditions du Chalet, 1964), 22.

112. Foucauld benefited from the sponsorship of MacCarthy (also written "Mac Carthy" in other sources), who had previously been Henri Duveyrier's mentor and benefactor. MacCarthy was deeply passionate about the desert. Foucauld himself wrote how MacCarthy had given him lessons and advice that helped him in his travels. Foucauld does not seem to have weighed the dangers that his Jewish guide and his coreligionists would have been exposed to had he been caught by the Moroccan authorities.

113. Roche, *Charles de Foucauld*, 22.

114. Charles de Foucauld, *Reconnaissance au Maroc 1883–1884* (Paris: Challamel, 1888).

115. Henri Duveyrier, "Rapport sur le voyage de M. Le Vicomte Charles de Foucauld au Maroc, fait à la Société de géographie de Paris," in Charles de Foucauld, *Reconnaissance au Maroc: Journal de route* (Paris: Société d'Éditions Géographiques, Maritimes et Coloniales, 1939), 21. Foucauld's journey was also the subject of a report for the Société by its General Secretary Charles Maunoir. See Charles Maunoir, "Rapport sur les travaux de la Société de géographie et sur les progrès des sciences géographiques pendant l'année 1884," *Bulletin de la Société de géographie: Rédigé avec le concours de la section de publication par les secrétaires de la commission centrale* (1885): 197–99.

116. Félix Gauthier, *L'Algérie et la métropole* (Paris: Payot, 1920), 134.

117. Marcel Nadeau tells the story of his reburial and how his body was mummified while the corpses of his Muslim companions were entirely eaten away. Using the words of a Muslim soldier who was with Laperrine, Nadeau asserts that Foucauld was "a great marabout." See Marcel Nadeau, ed., *L'expérience de Dieu avec Charles de Foucauld: Introduction et textes choisis par Marcel Nadeau* (Quebec: Éditions Fides, 2004), 40.

118. Ibid., 16–18.

119. Foucauld wrote to MacCarthy, "I was not a believer in God when you met me" and enumerated the blessings of his newfound life as a Trappist in Syria in 1890. Charles de Foucauld, *Charles de Foucauld intime*, ed. Georges Gorrée (Paris: La Colombe, Éditions du Vieux Colombier, 1951), 82.

120. Bazin, *Charles de Foucauld*, 94.

121. Ibid.

122. Paul Lesourd, *La vraie figure du père de Foucauld* (Paris: Ernest Flammarion, 1933), 72.

123. Louis Massignon, *Écrits mémorables*, ed. Christian Jambet et al., 2 vols. (Paris: Robert Laffont, 2009), 1:18.

124. Roche, *Charles de Foucauld*, 42.

125. Charles de Foucauld, *Lettres à Henry de Castries*, ed. Jacques de Dampierre (Paris: Éditions Bernard Grasset, 1938), 86.

126. Ibid., 90.

127. Ibid.

128. Ibid., 90–91.

129. Lavigerie, *Lettre . . . à un séminariste*, 22.

130. Ibid.

131. Ibid., 23.

132. Ibid.

133. Ibid., 35.

134. Charles de Foucauld, *Lettres et carnets* (Paris: Éditions du Seuil, 1966), 36.

135. These French military figures were all, to different degrees, movers and shakers in the colonial system in Algeria and Morocco.

136. Charles Chauvin, *Charles de Foucauld par lui-même et ses héritiers* (Paris: Mediaspaul Éditions, 2010), 66.

137. Foucauld, *Lettres à Henry de Castries*, 113.

138. Foucauld, *Charles de Foucauld intime*, 8.

139. Charles de Foucauld and Abbé Huvelin, *20 ans de correspondance entre Charles de Foucauld et son directeur spiritual (1890–1910)*, ed. Jean-François Six and Brigitte Cuisinier (Paris: Nouvelle Cite, 2010), 300.

140. Ibid., 301.

141. Hugues Didier, "Charles de Foucauld," *Clio*, May 2002, www.clio.fr/bibliotheque/bibliothequeenligne/charles_de_foucauld.php?letter=A.

142. Massignon, *Écrits mémorables*, 2:41

143. Ibid.

144. Casajus, *Charles de Foucauld*, 15.

145. Ibid., 9.

146. Ḥasan Dawwās, "Ṣūrat al-mujtama' al-ṣaḥrāwī al-jazā'irī fī al-qarn al-tāsi' 'ashar min khilāl kitābāt al-raḥḥāla al-faransiyyīn: Muqāraba sūsiūtaqāfiyya" (master's thesis, Mentouri University of Constantine, 2008).

147. Ibid., 28.

148. Ibid., 30.

149. See Suzana Sawyer and Arun Agrawal, "Environmental Orientalisms," *Cultural Critique* 45 (2000): 71–108; and Hamza Hamochene and Katie Sandwell, eds., *Dismantling Green Colonialism: Energy and Climate Justice in the Arab Region* (London: Pluto Press, 2023), 9–10. The emphasis on the "Arab Region" in the title of Hamochene and Sandwell's edited book overshadows the fact that Tamazgha's population is mostly Amazigh. However, the need to conform to the framework of Orientalism must have imposed this framing on the editors.

150. See Alain Messaoudi, *Les arabisants et la France colonial* (Lyon: ENS Éditions, 2015).

151. Michel Roux, *Le désert de sable: Le Sahara dans l'imaginaire des français (1900–1994)* (Paris: L'Harmattan, 1996), 22.

152. Jacques Keryell, "Avant-propos," in *Petits frères de Jésus, Frères au cœur du monde à la suite de Charles de Foucauld: Lettres des fraternités (1960–2002)* (Paris: Éditions Karthala, 2002), 9.

153. He wrote to Laperrine that the other advantage of the new hermitage was to "indicate that we do not have the intention to leave." Foucauld, *Lettres inédites au général*, 144.

154. Foucauld, *Lettres à Henry de Castries*, 113.

155. Ibid., 177.

156. Patrick Heidsieck, *Rayonnement de Lyautey* (Paris: Gallimard, 1944), 201.

157. Foucauld, *Lettres à Henry de Castries*, 192.

158. Michel Carrouges, *Charles de Foucauld: Explorateur mystique* (Paris: Les Éditions du Cerf, 1954), 154.

159. Ibid., 177. One can draw a connection between Lavigerie and Foucauld in this regard. In his instructions to the Brothers of the Sahara, Lavigerie insisted on healthy and sunny housing, but most importantly on simplicity, requiring that the lodging and eating practices should reflect local manners (*Lettre . . . à un séminariste*, 41).

160. Francis Miltoun, *In the Land of Mosques and Minarets* (Boston: Colonial Press, 1908), 225.

161. Eberhardt, *In the Shadow*, 46.

162. Ibid., 48.

163. Ibid., 102.

164. Psichari, *Les voix qui crient*, 284.

165. Ibid., 285.

166. Foucauld, *Lettres inédites*, x.

167. Ibid., 148.

168. Ibid., 30.

169. Ibid.

170. Ibid.

171. Ibid.

172. Anthropologist André Bourgeot has conducted an elaborate analysis in which he situates this plan within its larger historical context. See Bourgeot, "Sahara: Espace géostratégique," 153–92.

173. Foucauld, *Charles de Foucauld intime*, 112.

174. Ibid., 115.

175. Ibid., 116.

176. Ibid., 119.

177. Ibid., 121.

178. Ibid., 122.

179. Ibid.

180. Ibid., 123.

181. Ibid.

182. Ibid., 124.

183. Louis Bertrand has written that "no cloister equals the desert, not only for severing all attachment between you and the world but also for making you feel your dependency while also restoring you to yourself." See Louis Bertrand, "Comment je suis revenu au catholicisme," in *Les témoins du renouveau catholique*, ed. Thomas Mainage (Paris: Gabriel Beauchesne, 1919), 136–37.

184. Florian Pharaon provides a definition of the word *goumier* in *Spahis, tucos et goumiers* (Paris: Challamel Ainé, 1864). Pharaon writes that a *goumier* is "a national guard of the Sahara," adding that he is "simply the independent knight who is mobilized for a short period of time for a given necessity" (ibid., p. 217).

185. Carlo Carretto, *Letters from the Desert*, trans. Rose M. Hancock (Maryknoll, NY: Orbis Books, 2002), xvii.

186. Ibid.

187. Ibid.

188. Ibid.

189. Ibid., 5.

190. Ibid., 11.

191. Ibid., 13.

192. Ibid., 94.

193. Ibid.

194. Ibid., 95.

195. Casajus, *Charles de Foucauld*, 94.

196. Carretto, *Letters*, 80.

197. Ibid., 81.

198. Ibid.

199. Frontex, *Strategic Risk Analysis 2020* (Warsaw: Frontex, 2020), 37, www.frontex.europa.eu/assets/Publications/Risk_Analysis/Risk_Analysis/Strategic_Risk_Analysis_2020.pdf.

200. Ibid., 32.

1. Anne Clermont, "Comment est-on passé de l'ère des utopistes à l'ère des organisateurs?" *La Nef* (January–March 1960): 18.

2. Bernard Simiot, "Il faut 'nationaliser' le Sahara," *Hommes et mondes* 60 (July 1951): 162.

3. Yves de Boisboissel, "L'exploration et la pacification du Sahara," in *Le Sahara français*, edited by Jean Charbonneau (Paris: Cahiers Charles de Foucauld, 1955), 131–60.

4. Clermont, "Comment," 20–23.

5. Perrin Selcer, *The Postwar Origins of the Global Environment: How the United Nations Built Spaceship Earth* (New York: Columbia University Press, 2018), 107.

6. Ibid., 99.

7. Louis Armand, *Le Sahara: L'Afrique et l'Europe, conférence prononcée le vendredi 12 février 1955* (Lyon: publisher unknown, 1955), 6.

8. "Un exposé de M. Max Lejeune sur le fonctionnement du ministère du Sahara," *Le Monde*, June 21, 1957, www.lemonde.fr/archives/article/1957/06/21/un-expose-de-m-max-lejeune-sur-le-fonctionnement-du-ministere-du-sahara_2316339_1819218.html.

9. Clermont, "Comment," 19.

10. Member of Parliament Louis Castex called Labonne "the man who watches over our Sahara" in his discussion of the *combinat* and its important for the French economy. See Louis Castex, "Sahara, terre Promise," *Revue des deux mondes* (July 15, 1953): 210.

11. Commandant Henri Bissuel, an army officer in the Sahara, gave two lectures to his colleagues at the Médéa garrison in which he reflected, among other things, on ways to extract labor and services from local populations. See Henri Bissuel, *Le Sahara français: Conférence sur les questions sahariennes* (Algiers: Adolphe Jourdan, Libraire-Éditeur, 1891).

12. The scholarship on slavery has expanded a great deal in the past few decades; see, among other works, Allan George Barnard Fisher and Humphrey J. Fisher, *Slavery and Muslim Society in Africa: The Institution in Saharan and Sudanic Africa, and the Trans-Saharan Trade* (London: Hurst,1970); and Paul E. Lovejoy, *Transformations in Slavery: A History of Slavery in Africa* (New York: Cambridge University Press, 2011).

13. See Georges R. Manue, "Fondateur de l'Office du Niger: Émile Bélime, le maître de l'eau," *Le Monde*, July 31, 1969.

14. Émile Bélime, "Avenir de l'Union française," *Hommes et mondes* 14, no. 58 (May 1951): 677.

15. Albert Sarraut, *La mise en valeur des colonies françaises, avec onze cartes en noir et en couleurs* (Paris: Payot, 1923).

16. Before Sarraut's book, Maurice Dewavrin and Paul Delibert published *Comment mettre en valeur notre domaine colonial* (Paris: Marcel Rivière, 1920), with an introduction by André Lebon, a former minister of colonies and trade.

17. Charles Louis Abel Tellier, *La conquête pacifique de l'Afrique occidentale par le soleil* (Paris: Librairie Centrales des Sciences Mathématiques, 1890).

18. Pierre Cornet, *Sahara: Terre de demain* (Paris: Nouvelles Éditions Latines, 1956).

19. Edmond Sergent, *Le peuplement humain du Sahara* (Algiers: Institut Pasteur d'Algérie, 1953).

20. See Louis Armand, "Vers un Sahara moderne," *Hommes et mondes* 99 (October 1954): 322.

21. Clermont, "Comment," 18.

22. Boisboissel, "L'exploration et la pacification," 35–39.

23. Henri Duveyrier, *Les Touareg du nord: Exploration du Sahara* (Paris: Challamel Ainé, 1864).

24. Jacques Duquesne, *Histoires vraies: Une vie de journaliste* (Paris: Albin Michel, 2016), 52.

25. See George Demanche, "Occupation d'In Salah," *Revue française de l'étranger et des colonies* 254 (February 1900): 77.

26. A graduate of Saint-Cyr, Flatters fought in the Crimean war in 1853 and received a medal for taking three Russian prisoners, including a captain. After many military successes, he was sent to Laghouat in Algeria in 1876 as a mission chief. His team was composed of six French officers and ten French soldiers, as well as eighty-three *spahis* or Indigenous soldiers. Most of them were killed by the Tuaregs in a location known as Bir-el-Ghamara. See Union coloniale française, *Le domaine colonial français* (Paris: Les Éditions du Cygne, 1929), 323.

27. Benjamin C. Brower, *A Desert Named Peace: The Violence of France's Empire in the Algerian Sahara, 1844–1902* (New York: Columbia University Press, 2009), 199.

28. See Léon Homo, *Nouvelle histoire romaine* (Paris: Librairie Arthème Fayard, 1949), 401–2.

29. Historian Clime Lamming has written a very cogent historical account of the project for this train, explaining the reasons underpinning its undertaking as well as its failure. Lamming calls the project "the most virtual and the most abstract railway in the world; it was the one that made a century of mediatic, political, and oneiric 'buzz' only to leave some forgotten ruins in the sand." ("Le transsaharien: (Mauvais) rêve colonial, ou chance d'une Afrique qui en avait besoin ?" Train Consultant Clive Lamming [blog], July 24, 2019, https://trainconsultant.com/2019/07/24/le-transsaharien-encore-un-mauvais-reve-colonial-ou-peut-etre-la-grande-chance-dune-afrique-qui-en-avait-besoin).

30. See Clément-Célestin d'Eu, *In-Salah et le Tidikelt: Journal des opérations* (Paris: Librairie Militaire R. Chapelot, 1902); Henri Wolff and Antoine-Auguste Blachère, *Sahara et Soudan: Les régiments de dromadaires* (Paris: Challamel Ainé Éditeur, 1884); Brower, *Desert Named Peace.*

31. Boisboissel, "L'exploration et la pacification," 145.

32. Joanna Allan has written about a similar phenomenon in Spanish Sahara. Allan writes, "Colonial research expeditions and networked electrical infrastruc-

ture both served natural resource exploitation. The publications resulting from said expeditions, as well as from pseudoscientific writings and memoirs from military personnel and other colonial actors, shared something else: a major preoccupation with the wind." See Joanna Allan, *Saharan Winds: Energy Systems and Aeolian Imaginaries in Western Sahara* (Morgantown: West Virginia University Press, 2024), 48.

33. Sarraut, *Mise en valeur*, 23.

34. Guy Camille captured the books' impact in his review "La mise en valeur des colonies françaises," *Annales de géographie* 32, no. 177 (1923): 265–71.

35. For a definition of the term "gouverneur des colonies," see Rezzi Nathalie's article "Les gouverneurs français de 1880 a 1914: Essai de typologie," *Outre-mers: Revue d'histoire* 98, nos. 370–371 (2011): 9–19.

36. André Touzet, "Préface," in Albert Sarraut, *La mise en valeur des colonies françaises* (Paris: Payot, 1923), n.p.

37. Ibid.

38. Ibid., 14.

39. Ibid., 38.

40. Ibid., 2.

41. Ibid., 2.

42. Maryinez Lyons, *The Colonial Disease: A Social History of Sleeping Sickness in Northern Zaire, 1900–1940* (Cambridge: Cambridge University Press, 2010), 25.

43. Ibid.

44. Ibid., 28.

45. Maurice Zimmermann, "L'outillage et la mise en valeur du Congo français," *Annales de géographie* 18, no. 97 (1909): 92.

46. Ibid.

47. André Lebon made a similar argument in his introduction to *Comment mettre en valeur votre domaine colonial*. See Dewavrin and Delibert, *Comment mettre en valeur*, 10–11.

48. Sarraut, *Mise en valeur*, 19.

49. Ibid., 20.

50. Ibid., 23.

51. Académie des sciences coloniales, *Annales*, vol. 4 (Paris: Société d'Éditions Géographiques, Maritimes et Coloniales, 1929), 1.

52. Ibid.

53. Ibid., 9.

54. Ibid.

55. Académie des sciences coloniales, *Comptes-rendus des séances: Communications, 1922–1923* (Paris: Société d'Éditions, 1924), 137.

56. Sarraut insisted, "This enrichment of humanity should be achieved and pursued through association and in collaboration with the race that the colonizer governs and which he should increase in human value" (ibid., 132).

57. Pierre Escoube, "Eirik Labonne: Diplomate hors-série," *Revue des deux mondes* (December 1971): 741.

58. Escoube, "Eirik Labonne."

59. Jacques Ellul, *The Technological Society*, trans. John Wilkinson (Paris: Vintage Books, 1964), 249.

60. Maurice Mercier, "Un projet grandiose et constructif: La création d'un territoire autonome saharien français," *Le Sahara français* (Vichy: Cahiers Charles de Foucauld, 1955), 256, 259.

61. Jacques Soustelle, *The Wealth of the Sahara* (New York: The Council on Foreign Affairs, 1959), 9.

62. Émile Bélime, *Gardons l'Afrique*, ed. Jean Charbonneau (Paris: Nouvelles Éditions Latines, 1955), 64–65.

63. Mercier, "Projet grandiose," 259–60.

64. Bélime, "Avenir de l'Union française," 673.

65. Ibid., 676–77.

66. Ibid., 680.

67. Ibid.

68. Bélime compared the production of gold in Siberia to that of South Africa to demonstrate the Sahara's potential (ibid., 680).

69. Ibid., 680.

70. Bélime, *Gardons l'Afrique*, 60, 66.

71. Bélime, "Avenir de l'Union française," 681.

72. Ibid., 680.

73. Ibid., 681.

74. Ibid., 681–82.

75. Simiot, "Il faut 'nationaliser' le Sahara," 162.

76. Ibid.

77. Ibid.

78. Ibid., 163.

79. Ibid., 164.

80. Ibid., 164.

81. Jean Imberti, the founder of the Confédération générale des entreprises du Maroc as well as the Fédération des industries métallurgiques au Maroc, best described how extractive Saharanism conceptualized the desert. For Imberti, "the mineralization of the Sahara" was a fact (Simiot et al., "Il faut 'nationaliser' le Sahara," *Hommes et mondes*, no. 62 [September 1951]: 551). The use of the word "mineralization" is very significant here, as it sums up how the desert was reduced to a source of minerals, at best.

82. Simiot et al., "Il faut 'nationaliser' le Sahara," 437.

83. Ibid.

84. American written media, particularly *Time* and *Foreign Affairs*, dedicated articles to the Sahara's resources in 1956. However, at this time, they were mostly focused on the oil in the Gulf.

85. Bélime, *Gardons l'Afrique*, 62.

86. Simiot et al., "Il faut 'nationaliser' le Sahara," 439.

87. Ibid., 439.

88. Ibid.

89. Ibid., 444. French experts invited France to emulate US undertakings, as was the case in the preface written by General Jean Charbonneau for *Le Sahara français*, ed. Jean Charbonneau (France: Cahiers Charles de Foucauld, 1955), 9.

90. Simiot et al., "Il faut 'nationaliser' le Sahara," 447.

91. Ibid., 544.

92. Ibid., 545.

93. Quoted in Charles-Robert Ageron, "L'Algérie dernière chance de la puissance française: Étude d'un mythe politique (1954–1962)," *Relations internationales* 57 (1989): 123.

94. Ageron complicates this story by revealing the existence of disagreements between the proponents of Saharanism and those who saw in the Sahara a losing affair ("L'Algérie," 124).

95. Robert Capot-Rey, "Le Bureau industriel africain et les recherches minières au Sahara," *Annales de géographie* 64, no. 344 (1955): 296.

96. Louis Armand, "Les techniques à la conquête économique des déserts," in *Le Sahara français*, ed. Jean Charbonneau (Paris: Cahiers Charles de Foucauld, 1955), 277.

97. Allen Edgar Fletcher, *A Wayfarer in North Africa: Tunisia and Algeria* (London: Methuen, 1931), 195.

98. Bélime, *Gardons l'Afrique*, 58.

99. Simiot et al., "Il faut 'nationaliser' le Sahara," 547.

100. Roger Frison-Roche, *Mission Ténéré* (Paris: B. Arthaud, 1960), 21.

101. See Gille Corder, "Faut-il écarter les étrangers de l'exploitation des richesses sahariennes?" in *Le Sahara en questions* (Paris: Julliard, 1960), 51–58; see also in this same volume, "Quels sont les groupes engagés dans la recherche du pétrole au Sahara," 59–70.

102. Bélime, *Gardons l'Afrique*, 71–73.

103. Henri Teissier du Cros, *Louis Armand: Visionnaire de la modernité* (Paris: Éditions Odile Jacob, 1987), 237.

104. Louis Armand, "France et Afrique à l'ère des grandes entreprises," *Hommes et mondes* 120 (1956): 484.

105. Ageron, "L'Algérie," 124.

106. Armand defined the mission of the BIA as "1. Proposing to the government measures of administrative order which the work of prospection necessitates in a first stage; 2. Drawing up the catalogue of the underground riches; 3. Establishing what the Anglophones call the 'technical planning of an industrial complex'" (Armand, "Vers un Sahara moderne," 322).

107. "Ne trahissons pas le Sahara," *Entreprise*, May 1957, 59.

108. Georges Guide, "Le Sahara français," *Hommes et mondes* (April 1956): 56.

109. Mercier, "Projet grandiose et constructif," 258–59.

110. Jean-Michel de Lattre, "Sahara, clé de voute de l'ensemble eurafricain français," *Politique étrangère* 22, no. 4 (1957): 347.

111. Guide discussed many of these issues in "Le Sahara français"; Castex, "Sahara, terre promise," 206.

112. Marc-Robert Thomas, *Sahara et communauté* (Paris: Presses Universitaires de France, 1960), 175.

113. Daniel Strasser, *Réalités et promesses sahariennes: Aspects juridiques et économiques de la mise en valeur industrielle du Sahara français* (Paris: Encyclopédie d'Outre-Mer, 1956), 36.

114. Ibid.

115. Ibid.

116. Michel Biays, "L'avenir économique du Sahara," *Les cahiers économiques* (August-September 1952), 21.

117. Strasser, *Réalités et promesses sahariennes*, 6; Daniel Strasser, *Le Sahara français en 1958* (France: La documentation française, 1958), 20.

118. Guide, "Le Sahara français," 56.

119. Nicolas Bodington, *The Awakening Sahara* (London: Andre Deutsch, 1961), 43.

120. Ibid.

121. Guide, "Le Sahara français," 55; see also Strasser, *Réalités et promesses sahariennes*, 37–43; Thomas, *Sahara et communauté*, 175–78.

122. René Bazin, *Charles de Foucauld: Explorateur du Maroc, ermite au Sahara* (Paris: Librairie Plon, 1921), 288–89.

123. Strasser, *Réalités et promesses sahariennes*, 43.

124. For more details about the history of petrol and French policy in the Sahara, see Samir Salut, "Politique nationale du pétrole, sociétés nationales et 'pétrole franc,'" *Revue historique* 638 (2006): 355–88.

125. Jacques Soustelle, *Le drame algérien et la décadence française: Réponse à Raymond Aron* (Paris: Plon, 1957), 32.

126. Ivan du Jonchay, *L'industrialisation de l'Afrique* (Paris: Payot, 1953), 33.

127. Thomas, *Sahara et communauté*, 178–79.

128. Charles de Gaulle, "Ordonnance n° 45-2563 du 30 octobre 1945 instituant un commissariat à l'énergie atomique," last modified March 18, 2016, www.legifrance.gouv.fr/loda/id/JORFTEXT000000521964/2016-03-18.

129. Soustelle was the minister of the Sahara and deputy minister of atomic energy between 1959 and 1960.

130. Louis Chevalier, "L'industrialisation de l'Afrique du nord," *Population* (1949): 764.

131. "Guy Mollet confirme sa volonté de créer une indissoluble communauté franco-musulmane," *Le Monde*, February 11, 1956.

132. René Pottier, *Histoire du Sahara* (Paris: Nouvelles Éditions Latines, 1947), 306.

133. Ibid.

134. These works resemble each other, highlighting the same questions. See, for instance, Jacques Britsch, *Perspectives sahariennes* (Paris: Charles-Lavauzelle, 1956).

135. Simiot et al., "Il faut 'nationaliser' le Sahara," 551.

136. "Ne trahissons pas le Sahara," 56.

137. Jacques Soustelle, *Le Sahara d'aujourd'hui et la France de l'an 2000* (Paris: Société Parisienne, 1959), 10.

138. Soustelle, *Wealth of the Sahara*, 4.

139. Ibid.

140. Ibid., 4–5.

141. Ibid., 5.

142. Ibid.

143. Ibid., 6.

144. "Jacques Soustelle," *Time* (August 1959), 26.

145. Soustelle, *Le Sahara d'aujourd'hui*, 20.

146. "Jacques Soustelle," 23.

147. Charles-Henri Favrod, *Le poids de l'Afrique* (Paris: Éditions du Seuil, 1958), 18.

148. Armand, "Les techniques à la conquête," 285.

149. Soustelle, *Le Sahara d'aujourd'hui*, 18–19; Soustelle, *Wealth of the Sahara*, 8.

150. Soustelle, *Wealth of the Sahara*, 8.

151. Ibid., 9.

152. Francis Dorrey and Georges Lambert, "Quels problèmes humains se posent dans le Sahara moderne?" *La Nef* (1960): 35–43; Georges Salvy, "Le problème de la main-d'œuvre dans le Sahara de demain," in *Le Sahara français*, ed. Jean Charbonneau (Vichy: Cahiers Charles de Foucauld, 1955), 334–44.

153. Sergent, *Le peuplement humain*, 18, 27, 29.

154. Jeremy Shere, "Frank Shuman's Solar Arabian Dream," *Renewable*, accessed March 1, 2023, https://renewablebook.wordpress.com/chapter-excerpts/350-2.

155. Tellier, *La conquête pacifique*, 66.

156. Ibid.

157. Ibid., 14.

158. Ibid., 84.

159. Marcel Perrot, "Il y a 20 ans . . . Le premier institut universitaire français de l'énergie solaire (I.E.S.U.A)," *Revue internationale d'héliotechnique* (1978), 1, www.musilbrescia.it/minisiti/energia-solare/comples/downloads/PERROT_1_Inizi.pdf.

160. Ibid.

161. Ibid., 2.

162. Ibid., 3.

163. The National Staff, "From Mirage to Reality in 98 years: The Evolution of Solar Power in Egypt," *The National*, September 9, 2010, www.thenationalnews.com/business/energy/from-mirage-to-reality-in-98-years-the-evolution-of-solar-power-in-egypt-1.555752.

164. Ibid.

165. Shere, "Frank Shuman's Solar Arabian Dream."

166. Ibid.

167. Frank Shuman, "Power from Sunshine: A Pioneer Solar Power Plant," *Scientific American* (1911): 291.

168. Ibid., 292.

169. Frank Shuman, "The Solar Engine in Egypt," *Scientific American* (1912): 481.

170. Ibid.

171. Ibid., 292.

172. Frank Shuman, "Feasibility of Utilizing Power from the Sun," *Scientific American* 110, no. 9 (1914): 179.

173. Ibid.

174. Armand, "France et Afrique," 476.

175. Shuman, "Feasibility of Utilizing Power," 179.

176. For a rich history of solar energy, see Geoffrey Jones and Loubna Bouamane, "Power from Sunshine: A Business History of Solar Energy," Working Paper No. 12-105, Harvard Business School, May 25, 2012, www.hbs.edu/ris/Publication%20Files/12-105.pdf.

177. Simiot et al., "Il faut 'nationaliser' le Sahara," 547.

178. Masen, "Masen: Force inépuisable de développement," Masen.ma, accessed July 15, 2023, www.masen.ma/themes/custom/masen/assets/files/Brochure__Fiches_Fr.pdf.

179. Brandon R. Reynolds, "Hot and Bothersome: The Downsides of Desert Solar Projects," *Alta Online*, June 9, 2022, www.altaonline.com/dispatches/a40234357/hot-and-bothersome.

180. US Department of Interior, "Interior Department Advances Three Solar Projects in California, Marking Significant Progress to Develop a Clean Energy Economy," DOI.gov, last modified October 10, 2024, www.doi.gov/pressreleases/interior-department-advances-three-solar-projects-california-marking-significant.

181. Quoted in Reynolds, "Hot and Bothersome," n.p.

182. Barclay Ballard, "The Unexpected Environmental Drawbacks of Concentrated Solar Power Plants," *The New Economy*, June 12, 2019. www.theneweconomy.com/energy/the-unexpected-environmental-drawbacks-of-concentrated-solar-power-plants.

183. "Jacques Soustelle," 29.

184. Ibid., 30.

185. Bernard Simiot, "Le Sahara devant le parlement," *Revue des deux mondes* (January 1957): 166; Clermont "Comment," 24.

186. Louis Armand, "Pourquoi un ensemble industriel au Sahara?" *Revue économique franco-suisse* 33 (1953): 284.

187. Ibid., 281.

188. Ibid., 282.

189. Ibid.

190. Maurice Bourjoul, "Sahara 1956: Mythe et réalités," *Economie et politique* 27 (1956): 61.

191. Bourjoul, "Sahara 1956," 59; du Jonchay, *L'industrialisation*, 187.

192. Armand, "Pourquoi un ensemble industriel," 283–84.

193. Charles Ducarre, "Sahara Test Center," *Flight*, February 13, 1959, 213.

194. Ibid.

195. "Les unités sahariennes: Les centres d'essais," accessed December 20, 2022, www.3emegroupedetransport.com/LESUNITESSAHARIENNESK.htm.

196. Bourjoul, "Sahara 1956," 61.

197. Armand, "Pourquoi un ensemble industriel," 285; Armand, "Vers un Sahara moderne," 323.

198. Armand, "Vers un Sahara moderne," 322.

199. Ibid.

200. Ibid., 333.

201. Armand, "Le Sahara," 7.

202. Guide, "Le Sahara français," 12.

203. Armand, "Pourquoi un ensemble industriel," 285.

204. Armand, "Vers un Sahara moderne," 321.

205. Soustelle, *Sahara d'aujourd'hui*, 20.

206. Michel Roux, *Désert de sable: Le Sahara dans l'imaginaire des français (1900–1994)* (Paris: L'Harmattan, 1996), 113.

CHAPTER THREE: EXPERIMENTAL SAHARANISM

1. Walter T. Swingle, "Date Culture in Southern Morocco," in *Report of the Sixth Annual Date Grower's Institute* (California: Coachella Valley Farmer, 1929), 16–19.

2. Paul B. Popenoe, *Date Growing in the Old World and the New* (Altadena, CA: George Rice, 1905), 261–62.

3. Siham Khoulassa et al., "High-Quality Draft Nuclear and Mitochondrial Genome Sequence of *Fusarium oxysporum f. sp. albedinis* strain 9, the Causal Agent of Bayoud Disease on Date Palm," *Plant Disease* 106, no. 7 (2022): 1974–76; https://doi.org/10.1094/PDIS-01-22-0245-A.

4. Swingle, "Date Culture," 16.

5. Between its appearance in the nineteenth century and the present, Bayoud has killed some twelve million palm trees in Morocco alone. See Nabil Moujaoui, Ednan Hariri, and Mohammed A. Elhoumaizi, "Bayoud and Belaat Diseases of Date Palm (*Phoenix dactylifera* L.) in Figuig Oasis of Morocco," *IOP Conference Series: Earth and Environmental Science* 782, no. 4 (2021): 1.

6. Sarah Seekatz, "America's Arabia: The Date Industry and the Cultivation of Middle Eastern Fantasies in the Deserts of Southern California" (PhD diss., University of California Riverside, 2014), 77–78; Swingle, "Date Culture," 18.

7. Charles C. Colley, "The Desert Shall Blossom: North African Influence on the American Southwest," *Western Historical Quarterly* 14, no. 3 (1983): 279, 286.

8. The complicated story is told in Forrest Bryant Johnson, *The Last Camel Charge: The Untold Story of America's Desert Military Experiment* (New York: Berkley Caliber, 2012).

9. Popenoe talks about his visit to Algeria and his contact with botanist Charles Louis Trabut; see Paul B. Popenoe, "Sahara Desert Plant Life," *The California Garden* 2 (1912): 8.

10. Walter T. Swingle, "Co-Operative Quarantine Date Nurseries," in *Report of the First Date Grower's Institute at Coachella Valley California: February 29th and March 1, 1924* (Coachella, CA: Coachella Valley Farm Center, 1924), 25.

11. "Séance du 13 Novembre 1931," *Bulletin de la société botanique de France* 78, no. 5 (1931): 658.

12. Diana K. Davis, *The Arid Lands: History, Power, Knowledge* (Boston: MIT, 2016), 146.

13. Robert Ito et al., "Proving Grounds: The Desert Holds Its Secrets—Which Is Why It's Been an Ideal Place to Test Out What's Next," *Alta Online*, December 21, 2022, www.altaonline.com/dispatches/a42123566/desert-mysteries-robert-ito-jessica-blough-ed-leibowitz-elizabeth-casillas.

14. General Motors acquired "5,000 acres in Mesa, Arizona. Other major car manufacturers followed suit in the American West, whether in Arizona (Nissan has 4,000 acres in Maricopa; Toyota, 12,000 acres in Wittmann) or California (in the Mojave Desert, Kia has 4,300 acres, and Honda has 2,840 acres)"; ibid.

15. See Mathias Grote, Jiří Janáč, and Darina Martykánová, "Science and Technological Change in Modern History (ca. 1800–1900)," in *The European Experience: A Multi-Perspective History of Modern Europe*, ed. Jan Hansen et al. (Cambridge: Open Book, 2023), 448.

16. Philipp Lehmann, *Desert Edens: Colonial Climate Engineering in the Age of Anxiety* (Princeton, NJ: Princeton University Press, 2022), 10.

17. Terrence R. Fehner and F. G. Gosling, *Origins of the Nevada Test Site* (Washington, DC: US Department of Energy, 2000), 41.

18. Ibid.

19. Henry Fountain, "The Salton Sea, an Accident of History, Faces a New Water Crisis," *New York Times*, February 25, 2023, www.nytimes.com/2023/02/25/climate/salton-sea-colorado-river-drought-crisis.html.

20. Brahim El Guabli, "Saharanism in the Sonoran," *The Avery Review* (2022): 1–11.

21. Lehmann, *Desert Edens*, 40.

22. François Elie Roudaire, *Rapport à M. le ministre de l'instruction publique sur la dernière expédition des chotts: Complément des études relatives au projet de mer intérieure* (Paris: Imprimerie Nationale, 1881), 7–8.

23. M. Henry Chotard, *La mer intérieure du Sahara* (Clermont-Ferrand: Typographie et lithographie G. Mont-Louis, 1876), 3.

24. Ibid., 4.

25. Ernest Hubert Lewis Schwarz, *The Kalahari, or Thirstland Redemption* (Oxford: B.H. Blackwell, 1920), vi.

26. George P. Marsh, *Man and Nature or Physical Georgraphy as Modified by Human Action* (New York: Charles Scribner, 1864), 225–26.

27. It is important to note that French sources foreground the role of Pierre and Marie Curie in this process, whereas American sources emphasize the Anglophone world. See, for instance, F. G. Gosling, *The Manhattan Project: Making the Atomic Bomb* (location unknown: US Government Printing Office, 1999), 1–4.

28. US Nuclear Regulatory Commission, "Backgrounder on Plutonium," NRC.org, last modified January 7, 2021, www.nrc.gov/reading-rm/doc-collections/fact-sheets/plutonium.html.

29. Pierre Billaud discusses the many ways in which Americans indirectly helped the French to advance their march toward a nuclear weapon. Pierre Billaud, *La grande aventure du nucléaire militaire français: Des acteurs témoignent* (Paris: L'Harmattan, 2016), 29–31.

30. Scientist Yves Rocard quotes Charles de Gaulle as having requested access to American nuclear laboratories when the US government offered to help France analyze the atomic cloud of its first bomb. See Yves Rocard, *Mémoires sans concessions* (Paris: Grasset, 1988), 235.

31. Matt Bischoff, *Preparing for Combat Overseas: Patton's Desert Training Center* (Monterey, CA: Lulu.com, 2016), 21.

32. Sarah Seekatz, "Desert Deployment: Southern California's World War II Desert Training Center," *Incendiary Traces*, September 11, 2015, www.incendiary-traces.org/articles/2015/9/11/desert-deployment-southern-californias-world-war-ii-desert-training-center.

33. Ibid. The Defense Technical Information Center also published a 1958 report entitled "Desert Testing of Military Material." Although mostly unreadable, the report helps us make a general sketch of the way the army thinks about deserts.

34. Michael Curtiz, dir., *Casablanca* (Warner Bros., 1943), 102 minutes; Zoltan Korda, dir., *Sahara* (Columbia Pictures, 1943), 97 minutes; Brian T. Edwards, *Morocco Bound: Disorienting America's Maghreb, from Casablanca to the Marrakesh Express* (Durham, NC: Duke University Press, 2005), 61.

35. Edwards, *Morocco Bound*, 61.

36. William Atkins, *The Immeasurable World: A Desert Journey* (New York: Anchor Books, 2018), 12.

37. Steve Walsh, "In Remote Southern California Desert, U.S. Army Tests Advanced Cyber Weapons," NPR, May 31, 2017, www.npr.org/2017/05/31/530929908/in-remote-southern-california-desert-u-s-army-tests-advanced-cyber-weapons.

38. "Mauritania Tests Drones for Desert Locust Combat," BBC, January 10, 2020, www.bbc.com/news/blogs-news-from-elsewhere-51065480.

39. Judith Sunderland, "EU's Drone Is Another Threat to Migrants and Refugees: Frontex Aerial Surveillance Facilitates Return to Abuse in Libya," *Human Rights Watch*, August 1, 2022, www.hrw.org/news/2022/08/01/eus-drone-another-threat-migrants-and-refugees; Zack Campbell, "Swarms of Drones, Piloted by Artificial Intelligence, May Soon Patrol Europe's Borders," *The Intercept*, May 11, 2019, https://theintercept.com/2019/05/11/drones-artificial-intelligence-europe-roborder;

Jasper Jolly, "Airbus to Operate Drones Searching for Migrants Crossing the Mediterranean," *The Guardian*, October 20, 2020, www.theguardian.com/business/2020/oct/20/airbus-to-operate-drones-searching-for-migrants-crossing-the-mediterranean.

40. Odette de Pingandeau, "Poisoned Clouds Over the Lush Oases of Africa," *The Gazette and Daily*, November 16, 1959, 17.

41. Several works come to mind, particularly, Bruno Barrillot, *Les irradiés de la république: Les victimes des essais nucléaires français prennent la parole* (Lyon: Observatoire des armes nucléaires françaises, 2003); Bruno Barrillot, *Les essais nucléaires français 1960–1996: Conséquences sur l'environnement et la santé* (Lyon: Centre de documentation et de recherche sur la paix et les conflits, 1996); Billaud, *Grande aventure.*

42. Rebecca Solnit, *Savage Dreams: A Journey into the Hidden Wars of the American West* (Berkeley: University of California Press, 2014), 5.

43. Ibid.

44. Ito et al., "Proving Grounds."

45. Christopher Nolan, dir., *Oppenheimer* (Universal Pictures, Atlas Entertainment, and Gadget Films, 2023), 180 minutes.

46. Terrence R. Fehner and F.G. Gosling, *Battlefield of the Cold War: The Nevada Test Site, Atmospheric Nuclear Weapons Testing 1951–1963*, vol. 1 (Washington, DC: US Department of Energy, 2006), 10.

47. "Excerpts from Speeches by French and Moroccan Delegates on Sahara Tests," *The New York Times*, November 5, 1959, 4.

48. Jacques Britsch, *Perspective sahariennes* (Paris: Charles-Lavauzelle, 1956), 85.

49. For more information on Ailleret, see Jacques Vallee, *Forbidden Science,* vol. 1; *Journals 1957–1969, a Passion for Discovery* (San Francisco, CA: Lulu.com, 2014), 471.

50. Xavier Liffran has dedicated an article to Ailleret's role in developing the French deterrence creed. See Xavier Liffran, "Redécouvrir Ailleret, 'l'artisan de la force de dissuasion,'" *Revue défense nationale* 807, no. 2 (2020): 41–48.

51. "Man in the News: De Gaulle's Top Soldier; Charles Louis Marcel Ailleret," *The New York Times*, July 30, 1964, 3.

52. Ambassade de France, *France's First Atomic Explosion* (New York: Service de presse et d'information, 1960), 3; Charles Ailleret, *L'aventure atomique française* (Paris: Grasset, 1968), 394–395 ; Captain John A. Berry, "Force de frappe," *Military Review: Professional Journal of the US Army* (November 1967): 70–78.

53. Jacques Chevalier, "Histoire de la DAM," in Pierre Billaud, *La grande aventure du nucléaire militaire français: Des acteurs témoignent* (Paris: L'Harmattan, 2016), 391.

54. Ambassade de France, *France's First Atomic Explosion*, 9.

55. Ailleret, *Aventure atomique*, 226.

56. Ibid.

57. Ibid., 227.

58. Ibid., 228.

59. Ibid., 228; Ambassade de France, *France's First Atomic Explosion*, 25.

60. Ailleret, *Aventure atomique*, 229.

61. Ibid.

62. Ibid.

63. Benjamin Brower, *A Desert Named Peace: The Violence of France's Empire in the Algerian Sahara, 1844–1902* (New York: Columbia University Press, 2009), 200–221.

64. Lehmann gives the examples of Henrik Ibsen and Jules Verne as authors who incorporated Roudaire's story into their literary works (*Desert Edens*, 38–39).

65. *Historique de la compagnie saharienne d'Ouargla* (Paris: Henri Charles-Lavauselle, 1920), 8.

66. Georges Estienne, "Les communications transsahariennes," *Renseignements coloniaux et documents* 2 (1923): 38.

67. Félix Gautier, *Le Sahara avec 4 cartes dans le texte* (Paris: Payot, 1923), 89.

68. Félix Gautier, *Le Sahara vaincu peut-il être dompté? L'aménagement du Sahara*, in Académie des sciences coloniales, *Annales*, vol. 4 (Paris: Société d'Éditions Géographiques, Maritimes et Coloniales, 1929), 27.

69. Ibid., 45.

70. Ibid.

71. Ibid., 101.

72. Lehuraux "founded and chaired the Société amicale des anciens Sahariens, the Rahla, and joined the Institut de recherches sahariennes of which he was appointed as vice president while becoming a member of the Algerian historical society." See "Lehuraux Léon," *Académie des sciences d'outre-mer*, accessed April 21, 2025, https://academieoutremer.fr/academiciens/?aId=799.

73. Léon Lehuraux, "L'automobile au désert," *Les Amis du Sahara* 14 (1935): 12.

74. Ibid., 19.

75. "Séance du 13 Novembre 1931," 658.

76. See Chapter 2 for details about the *mise en valeur*.

77. Jacques Soustelle, *Le Sahara d'aujourd'hui et la France de l'an 2000* (Paris: Société Parisienne, 1959), 5

78. Edmond Sergent, *Le peuplement humain du Sahara* (Algiers: Institut Pasteur d'Algérie, 1953), 9.

79. Ailleret, *Aventure atomique*, 230.

80. Ibid., 232.

81. See Vincent Jauvert's detailed report "Quand la France testait ses armes chimiques en Algérie," *Le nouvel observateur* 1720 (1997): 10–18. For rockets and missiles in the Béchar area, see Charles Ducarre, "Sahara Test Center," *Flight*, February 13, 1959, 213.

82. Ailleret, *Aventure atomique*, 232.

83. Ibid.

84. Ibid., 230.

85. Ibid., 235.

86. Ibid., 236.

87. "Defense of French Nuclear Tests: Jules Moch at the UN," *Ina*, February 13, 1960, https://mediaclip.ina.fr/en/i19021262-defense-of-french-nuclear-tests-jules-moch-at-the-un.html.

88. Ailleret writes about his encounter with Moch at the request of Pierre Guillaumat, who was Ministre des armées in 1959 and had served as the administrator of the CEA from 1951 to 1958. Not without arrogance, Ailleret described how he convinced Moch during their meeting that atomic fallout from the experiments was less dangerous than Moch's chain-smoking. See Ailleret, *Aventure atomique*, 288–89.

89. See Dominique Mongin, *La Direction des applications militaires (CEA/DAM) au cœur de la dissuasion nucléaire française: De l'ère des pionniers au programme simulation* (Paris: CEA/DAM, 2000), 39.

90. Fehner and Gosling, *Battlefield of the Cold War*, 9.

91. Royal Commission into British Nuclear Tests in Australia, *The Report of the Royal Commission into British Nuclear Tests in Australia*, vol. 1 (Canberra: Australian Government Publishing, 1985), 118.

92. Ibid., 108.

93. Jacob G. Warren, "Nuclear Aesthetics against the Colonial Desert," *Third Text* 35, no. 6 (2021): 669. Richard Howit discusses how a variety of activities target lands that belong to Indigenous people, leading to their effective displacement. See Richard Howit, *Rethinking Resource Management Justice, Sustainability, and Indigenous Peoples* (New York: Taylor and Francis, 2002), 31.

94. Royal Commission, *Report of the Royal Commission*, 118.

95. "Excerpts from Speeches," 4.

96. Ibid.

97. Ibid.

98. William Millinship, "Sahara Fall-out Fears," *The Observer*, August 2, 1959, 5.

99. Ambassade de France, *France's First Atomic Explosion*, 3.

100. Trevor Paglen, *Blanks on the Map: The Dark Geography of the Pentagon's Secret World* (New York: New American Library, 2010), 61.

101. Ibid.

102. While much is already known about its nuclear tests, France's ballistic and chemical weapons have received less academic attention, though the B2-Namous base was operational until 1978. See Alice Gorman, "The Archaeology of Space Exploration," *The Sociological Review* 57 (2009): 132–45; J. Bouillet, "L'ère atomique se lève sur les oasis," *Perspectives sahariennes* 4 (1958): 155. Because of the connivence of the Algerian government, this program remained both secret and uncontroversial until *Le nouvel observateur* broke the story in 1999. See Jauvert, "Quand la France testait"; and "Essais chimiques en Algérie," *Dailymotion*, accessed June 16, 2024, www.dailymotion.com/video/xfdvt4.

103. André Bendjebbar, *Histoire secrète de la bombe atomique française* (Paris: Le Cherche Midi Éditeur, 2000), 263.

104. Ailleret, *Aventure atomique*, 10. Retired French general Pierre G. Gallois attended an experiment in 1955 and wrote in his memoirs that he "naturally" submitted a report about the information that he collected, urging France to be

creative with its nuclear strategy to better contribute to the collective defense. See Pierre G. Gallois, *Le sablier du siècle: Mémoires* (Lausanne: L'Age d'Homme, 1999), 344. Tariq Rauf underlines that "French scientists participated in U.S. nuclear testing activities at the Nevada Test Site in 1957 to 1958" ("Viewpoint: French Nuclear Testing: A Fool's Errand," *The Nonproliferation Review* [Fall 1995]: 50).

105. Billaud explains how helpful this visit was to gain time and find testing equipment. See Billaud, *Grande aventure*, 29–31; 405.

106. A. Constandina Titus, *Bombs in the Backyard: Atomic Testing and American Politics* (Las Vegas, NV: University of Las Vegas, 1986), 63.

107. Ailleret, *Aventure atomique*, 321.

108. Ibid., 391.

109. Brahim El Guabli, "Desert Futures Collective: A Conversation with Brahim El Guabli, Jill Jarvis, and Francisco E. Robles," in *Deserts Are Not Empty*, ed. Samia Henni (New York: Columbia University Press, 2022), 34–35.

110. V. K. Krishna Menon, *The Question of French Nuclear Tests in the Sahara: V. K. Krishna Menon's Statement in the United Nations* (New Delhi: Ministry of External Affairs, 1959), 4.

111. Tawia Adamafio, *French Nuclear Tests in the Sahara* (Accra: CPP National Headquarters Bureau of Information and Publicity, 1960), 2, 5.

112. Dexter Masters and Katharine Way, eds., *One World or None* (New York: McGraw-Hill, 1946), 1, 3, 17.

113. Rocard, *Mémoires sans concessions*, 236, 253.

114. The Government of Australia, "International Court of Justice: Application Instituting Proceedings Filed in the Registry of the Court on 9 May 1973, Case Concerning Nuclear Tests (Australia vs France)," *ICJ* (1973), 29, www.icj-cij.org/sites/default/files/case-related/58/13187.pdf.

115. Ibid., 50. See also the Asian-African Legal Consultative Committee, *Report of the Session*, vol. 6 (New Delhi: Secretariat of the Asian-African Legal Consultative Committee, 1964), 96.

116. Ibid., 11.

117. Ibid.

118. See Alfred William Brian Simpson, "Cannibals at Common Law," *The Law School Record* 27 (1981): 3–9.

119. Readers can also check out Brian Simpson's *Cannibalism and Common Law: A Victorian Yachting Tragedy* (Chicago: Chicago University Press, 1984) for the history and legal ramifications of the case.

120. Tim Armstrong, "Slavery, Insurance, and Sacrifice in the Black Atlantic," in *Sea Changes: Historicizing the Ocean*, ed. Bernhard Klein and Gesa Mackenthun (New York: Routledge, 2004), 176.

121. Brower, *Desert Named Peace*, 221.

122. Eugène Fromentin, *Un été dans le Sahara* (Paris: Librairie Plon, 1857), 146–48.

123. Brower, *Desert Named Peace*, 221.

124. "Oscar Temaru: 'De Gaulle est un criminel,'" *Radio1*, February 13, 2017, www.radio1.pf/oscar-temaru-de-gaulle-est-un-criminel.

125. These experiments included surgery, new medicines, and even nutrition. See Ian Mosby, "Administering Colonial Science: Nutrition Research and Human Biomedical Experimentation in Aboriginal Communities and Residential Schools, 1942–1952," *Histoire sociale* 46, no. 1 (2013): 145–72.

126. Vincent Bollenot, "1887. Le code de l'indigénat algérien est généralisé à toutes les colonies françaises," *Encyclopédie d'histoire numérique de l'Europe*, April 16, 2023, https://ehne.fr/fr/eduscol/premi%C3%A8re-g%C3%A9n%C3%A9rale/la-troisi%C3%A8me-r%C3%A9publique-avant-1914-un-r%C3%A9gime-politique-un-empire-colonial/m%C3%A9tropole-et-colonies/1887-le-code-de-l%27indig%C3%A9nat-alg%C3%A9rien-est-g%C3%A9n%C3%A9ralis%C3%A9-%C3%A0-toutes-les-colonies-fran%C3%A7aises.

127. Henri Duveyrier, *Touareg du nord: Exploration du Sahara* (Paris: Challamel Ainé, 1864). For more information about Duveyrier's contribution to the knowledge about the Sahara, see Broc Numa, "Les français face à l'inconnue saharienne: Géographes, explorateurs, ingénieurs (1830–1881)," *Annales de géographie* 96, no. 535 (1987): 314–20. See also Henri Schirmer, "L'exploration du Sahara," *Annales de géographie* 30 (1897): 463–64.

128. Ordinary intertribal pillaging activities were exaggerated to present an imaginary of banditry. Even the Maghrebi editor of the book *La sanglante épopée des Medaganat* wrote that it "recounts the bloody and hectic epic of the Medaganat, successive groups of Saharan ruffians who, between 1860 and 1885, sowed death, terror and desolation among oasis populations of the ksars." Alfred Le Châtelier, *La sanglante épopée des Medaganat*, ed. Abderrahmane Rahbani (Algiers: Éditions Grand-Alger Livres, 2007), 5.

129. Ailleret, *Aventure atomique*, 327.

130. Antoine Schwere, "Auprès de ma bombe," in Pierre Billaud, *La grande aventure du nucléaire militaire français: Des acteurs témoignent* (Paris: L'Harmattan, 2016), 122.

131. Ibid., 155.

132. Bendjebbar, *Histoire secrète*, 270.

133. Muriam Haleh Davis, *Markets of Civilization: Islam and Racial Capitalism in Algeria* (Durham, NC: Duke University Press, 2022), 7.

134. Muḥammad Saʿīd al-Qashshāṭ, *Jihād al-lībiyyīn ḍidda faransā fī al-ṣaḥrāʾ al-kubrā 1854–1988* (Beirut: Dār al-Qamāṭī, 1989), 195.

135. Mériem Khellas, *L'Afrique de Berliet: La pénétration automobile au Sahara* (Paris: L'Harmattan, 2022), 56.

136. Henri J. Hugot, ed., *Missions Berliet: Ténéré-Tchad* (Paris: Arts et Métiers Graphiques, 1962), 9.

137. Khellas, *Afrique de Berliet*, 110.

138. Ibid., 111.

139. Ibid., 124.

140. Mike Ryan, "1922 Citroën Kegresse Auto-Chenille," October 7, 2020, www.justcars.com.au/news-and-reviews/feature-1922-citro-n-kegresse-auto-chenille/886163.

141. Roger Frison-Roche, *Mission Ténéré* (Paris: B. Arthaud, 1960), 22.

142. Louis Castex, "Sahara, terre promise," *Revue des deux mondes* (July 15, 1953): 203.

143. Ibid., 202.

144. Hugot, *Missions Berliet*, 21.

145. Frison-Roche, *Mission Ténéré*, 23.

146. Ibid., 27.

147. Ibid., 21–22; Foureau's own book about this mission, *Documents scientifiques de la Mission saharienne* (Paris: Publication de la Société de Géographie, 1905), is worth consulting. See also "Review: The Results of the Foureau-Lamy Mission," *The Geographical Journal* 28, no. 3 (1906): 280–83.

148. Hugot, *Missions Berliet*; Frison-Roche, *Mission Ténéré*.

149. Hugot, *Missions Berliet*, 10.

150. Ibid.

151. al-Markaz al-Waṭanī li-al-Dirāsāt wa-al-Baḥth fī al-Ḥaraka al-Waṭaniyya wa Thawrat Awwal Nuvambr 1954, *al-Tajārib al-nawawiyya al-faransiyya fī al-jazā'ir: Dirāsāt wa buḥūth wa shahādāt* (Algiers: al-Markaz al-Waṭanī li-al-Dirāsāt wa-al-Baḥth fī al-Ḥaraka al-Waṭaniyya wa Thawrat Awwal Nuvambr 1954, 2000).

152. Ibid., 5.

153. International Atomic Energy Agency, *Conditions at the Former French Nuclear Test Sites in Algeria: Preliminary Assessment and Recommendations* (Vienna: International Atomic Energy Agency, 2005), 1–2.

154. al-Markaz al-Waṭanī, *al-Tajārib al-nawawiyya*, 15–42; *al-Tafjīrāt al-nawawiyya al-faransīyya fī al-ṣaḥrā' al-jazā'irīyya* (Adrar: Manshūrāt Jāmi'at Aḥmad Draia, 2020), 2.

155. Schwere, "Auprès de ma bombe," 122.

156. al-Markaz al-Waṭanī, *al-Tajārib al-nawawiyya*, 28.

157. Remus Prăvălie, "Nuclear Weapons Tests and Environmental Consequences: A Global Perspective," *Ambio* 43, no. 6 (2014): 738.

158. *al-Tafjīrāt al-nawawiyya*, 14.

159. al-Qashshāṭ, *Jihādu al-lībiyyīn*, 195.

160. Meriem Khālidī and Sanīsna Faḍīla, "al-talawwuth al-ish'ā'ī al-nawawī wa atharuhu 'alā al-bī''a fī minṭaqt al-rraqān," in *al-Tafjīrāt al-nawawiyya al-faransīyya fī al-ṣaḥrā' al-jazā'irīyya* (Adrar: Manshūrāt Jāmi'at Aḥmad Draia, 2020), 80.

161. Ibid., 81.

162. Jacques Ellul, *The Technological Society*, trans. John Wilkinson (Paris: Vintage Books, 1964), 106–7.

163. Ibid.

164. Danielle Endres, *Nuclear Decolonization: Indigenous Resistance to High-Level Nuclear Waste* (Columbus: The Ohio State University Press, 2023), ix.

165. Christine Chanton, the daughter of one of the survivors, has written a study about some of the tests' impact on French veterans. See Christine Chanton, *Les vétérans des essais nucléaires français au Sahara* (Paris: L'Harmattan, 2006).

CHAPTER FOUR: SEXUAL SAHARANISM

1. André Gide, *Si le grain ne meurt* (Paris: Éditions de la Nouvelle Revue Française, 1924), 119.

2. Ibid.

3. Ibid., 128–29.

4. Ibid., 73.

5. Samir Benmalek, "Sur les traces d'André Gide: Séjour d'un écrivain australien en Algérie," *Liberté*, March 26, 2006, www.djazairess.com/fr/liberte/54826.

6. Benmalek commented on Dessaix's justification of Gide's pedophilia by writing that he "could have had the moderation of this other biographer who acknowledges: 'his [Gide's] sexual practices on the Maghreb's little boys would doubtlessly not be accepted today.' And it matters less that this biographer had not stayed in Algeria." Ibid.

7. Haytham Guesmi, "Reckoning with Foucault's Sexual Abuse of Boys in Tunisia," *Al Jazeera*, April 16, 2024, www.aljazeera.com/opinions/2021/4/16/reckoning-with-foucaults-sexual-abuse-of-boys-in-tunisia.

8. Ibid.

9. John Weightman, "André Gide and the Homosexual Debate," *The American Scholar* 59, no. 4 (1990): 592.

10. See Michel Foucault, "Of Other Spaces," trans. Jay Miskowiec, *Diacritics* 16, no. 1 (1986): 22–27.

11. Al-Ṭayyib Būderbala, "Ṣurāt al-jazā'ir fī al-riwāya al-faransiyya," *Majallat 'Ulūm al-Lugha al-'Arabiyya wa-Ādābuhā* 2, no. 2 (2010): 8.

12. Joseph Massad, *Desiring Arabs* (Chicago: Chicago University Press, 2007), 336.

13. See Jonathan Kemp, *Homotopia? Gay Identity, Sameness, and the Politics of Desire* (Santa Barbara, CA: Punctum Books, 2015), 15.

14. Weightman, "André Gide," 592.

15. Geoff Nicholson, *Day Trips to the Desert: A Sort of Travel Book* (London: Sceptre, 1993), 16.

16. See Julia Clancy-Smith, "Islam, Gender, and Identities in the Making of French Algeria, 1830–1962," in *Domesticating the Empire: Race, Gender, and Family Life in French and Dutch Colonialism*, ed. Julia Clancy-Smith and Frances Gouda (Charlottesville: University Press of Virginia, 1998), 154–74.

17. Hector France's *Musk, Hashish, and Blood* (New York: Avon, 1951) is an important example. In Clancy-Smith's own words, this book contributed to the legitimization of "the illicit sex for a prurient European audience" ("Islam, Gender, and Identities," 157–58).

18. Mohammed Thabet, *Nisā' al-ʿālam kamā ra'aytuhunna* (Cairo: Hindawi Foundation, 1917), 112.

19. Clancy-Smith, "Islam, Gender, and Identities," 155.

20. Steven T. Jones, *The Tribes of Burning Man: How an Experimental City in the Desert is Shaping the New American Counterculture* (San Francisco, CA: Consortium of Collective Consciousness, 2011), 187.

21. Ibid., 16.

22. Ibid.

23. Brian Doherty notes, "At burning man, it is almost certain no one would call the cops on you. However, they might well attract a cruising officer's attention by gathering around or even cheering you on" (*This Is Burning Man: Oil, Gas, and Crime* [New York: Little Brown, 2007]); see also Rick Ruddell, *The Dark Side of the Boomtown* (New York: Palgrave, 2017), 31.

24. Michael Brodeur and Banning Liebscher, *Revival Culture: Prepare for the Next Great Awakening* (Bloomington, IN: Baker, 2012), 135.

25. Zygmunt Bauman, "From Pilgrims to Tourists, or a Short History of Identity," in *Questions of Cultural Identity*, ed. Stuart Hall and Paul du Gay (London: Sage, 1996), 20.

26. Edmond Jabès, *The Book of Margins*, trans. Rosemarie Waldrop (Chicago: Chicago University Press, 1997), xvi.

27. Bauman, "From Pilgrims to Tourists," 20–21.

28. Ibid., 21.

29. Doreen Massey, *For Space* (London: Sage, 2008), 173; Caren Kaplan, *Questions of Travel: Postmodern Discourses of Displacement* (Durham, NC: Duke University Press, 1996), 66.

30. Kaplan, *Questions of Travel*, 66.

31. Ibid.

32. Gilles Deleuze and Félix Guattari, *A Thousand Plateaus: Capitalism and Schizophrenia*, trans. Brian Massumi (Minneapolis: University of Minnesota Press, 1987), 251.

33. Guattari's Saharanism can also be seen in his proposal of a "machinic ecology," which is his version of human environmental engineering: Félix Guattari, *Three Ecologies*, trans. Ian Pindar and Paul Sutton (New Brunswick, NJ: Athlone Press, 2000), 66. However, as it pertains to the desert, this machinic ecology rests on colonial ideas of making deserts bloom again by "bring[ing] vegetation back to the Sahara." Ibid.

34. Kaplan, *Questions of Travel*, 66.

35. Joyce E. Salisbury, "When Sex Stopped Being a Social Disease," in *Medieval Sexuality: A Casebook*, ed. April Harper and Caroline Proctor (New York: Routledge, 2008), 47.

36. Ibid., 54.

37. Ibid.

38. Muḥammad al-Sheikh Birābiḥ, "Namādhij min muqāwamāt Awlād Nāyl li-al-tawssuʿ al-faransī fī al-hiḍāb al-wusṭā (1849–1854)," *Qaḍāyā Tārikhiyya* 3, no. 1

(2018): 148. Several Algerian scholars have attended to the religious and social origins of this struggle, which contributed significantly to the "popular resistances" against the French in the nineteenth century. See, for example, Al-Ṭayyib al-Bāz, "al-Muqāwamāt al-shaʿbiyya al-maḥalliyya li-awlād nāyl wa-mawqifuhā min muqāwamat al-amīr ʿabd al-qādir: Mūsa al-darqāwī namūdhajan," *Majllat Ḥaqāʾiq al-Dirāsāt al-Nafsiyya wa-al-Ijtimāʿiyya* 3, no. 10 (2018): 390.

39. al-Bāz, "al-Muqāwamāt al-shaʿbiyya," 390.

40. Lebbaz Taieb and Abderrahmane Guenchouba, "La résistance des Ouled Nail après 1847 selon les écrits d'Arnaud, interprète militaire dans La Revue Africaine," *Dirassat wa Abhath: The Arabic Journal of Human and Social Sciences* 13, no. 2 (2021): 152.

41. Guy de Maupassant, *Au soleil* (Paris: Louis Conard, 1908), 61.

42. Benjamin Brower, *A Desert Named Peace: The Violence of France's Empire in the Algerian Sahara, 1844–1902* (New York: Columbia University Press, 2009), 104–5.

43. Ibid., 115–17.

44. Thabet, *Nisāʾ al-ʿālam*, 112.

45. Ibid.

46. Eugène Fromentin, *Un été dans le Sahara* (Paris: La Librairie Plon, 1857), 33.

47. Ibid., 37.

48. Ibid.

49. Guy de Maupassant, *Les carnets de voyage: Édition critique et annotée par Gérard Delaisement* (Paris: Rive Droite, 2006), 165; 442.

50. Théophile Gauthier, *Voyage en Algérie: Présentation de Denise Brahimi* (Paris: La Boite à Document, 1989), 156–57.

51. Patrick Aurousseau, "Le regard porté sur les prostituées en Algérie, un modèle de domination occidental? L'exemple de l'apparition des 'Ouled-Naïl' chez Fromentin, Maupassant et Gide," *Viattica* 5 (2018): 2.

52. Malek Alloula, *The Colonial Harem*, trans. Myrna Godzich and Wlad Godzich (Minneapolis: University of Minnesota Press, 1986), 54.

53. Marnia Lazreg, *The Eloquence of Silence: Algerian Women in Question* (New York: Routledge, 2014), 31.

54. For a full biography and a list of his achievements, see Alfred Rambaud, "Un pionnier d'Afrique: Émile Masqueray," *Revue politique et littéraire* 6 (February 9, 1895): 162–68.

55. Émile Masqueray, *Souvenirs et visions d'Afrique* (Paris: E. Dentu, éditeur, 1894), 81.

56. Ibid., 80.

57. Ibid., 83.

58. Ibid., 95–96.

59. Ibid., 30.

60. Ibid., 31.

61. Barbara Wright, *Eugène Fromentin: A Life in Art and Letters* (Bern: Peter Lang, 2000), 254.

62. Lazreg, *Eloquence of Silence*, 32

63. Barkahoum Ferhati, "La danseuse prostituée dite 'Ouled Naïl,' entre mythe et réalité (1830–1962): Des rapports sociaux et des pratiques concrètes," *Clio* 17 (2003): 101–13, https://doi.org/10.4000/clio.584.

64. Lazreg, *Eloquence of Silence*, 32.

65. Ibid.

66. Robert Hérisson, *Avec le père de Foucauld et le Général Laperrine: Carnets d'un saharien 1909–1911* (Paris: Librairie Plon, 1937), 2.

67. Sven Lindqvist, *Desert Divers* (London: Granta Books, 2000), 123.

68. Ibid.

69. Clancy-Smith, "Islam, Gender, and Identities," 158.

70. Edgar Fletcher Allen, *A Wayfarer in North Africa: Tunisia and Algeria* (London: Methuen, 1931), 152.

71. Ibid., 154.

72. Ibid., 155. Algerian anthropologist Barkahoum Ferhati has shown that the colonial administration avoided the closure of brothels mandated by law in 1845 so as to accommodate tourists and the military in the Sahara. See Ferhati, "Danseuse prostituée dite 'Ouled Naïl.'"

73. Fletcher Allen, *Wayfarer in North Africa*, 160.

74. Ibid., 158.

75. See Floyd Gibbons, "Algeria's Charm Lies in Oriental Air of Mystery," *French Colonial Digest* (June 1924): 147, 149, 154, 157; Floyd Gibbons, "Algeria's Charm Lies in Oriental Air of Mystery," *French Colonial Digest* (July 1924): 171, 173, 178.

76. Alexander Powell, "Sirens of the Sands," *The Metropolitan Magazine* 36, no. 1 (1912): 23.

77. Ibid.

78. William Dickson Boyce, *Illustrated Africa: North, Tropical, South* (New York: Rand McNally, 1925), 101.

79. Ibid., 108.

80. Jack Mortimer Sheppard, *Sahara Adventure* (London: Jarrods, 1957), 176.

81. Ibid., 177.

82. Christopher Sawyer-Laucanno, *An Invisible Spectator: A Biography of Paul Bowles* (New York: Grove, 1989), 143.

83. Ibid.

84. Pierre Bonardi, *Ouled-Naïl et méharistes* (Paris: Les Éditions de France, 1936), 17.

85. Maupassant, *Au soleil*, 69.

86. Robert Dessaix, *Arabesques: A Tale of Double Lives* (Sydney: Pan Macmillan, 2009), 200.

87. Sheppard, *Sahara Adventure*, 176.

88. Maupassant, *Au soleil*, 64.

89. Ibid., 65.

90. Melville William Hilton-Simpson, *Algiers and Beyond* (New York: D. Appleton, 1907), 132.

91. Fletcher Allen, *Wayfarer in North Africa*, 160.

92. Sheppard, *Sahara Adventure*, 176.

93. Lindqvist, *Desert Divers*, 123.

94. Jessica Jacobs, *Sex, Tourism, and the Postcolonial Encounter: Landscapes of Longing in Egypt* (New York: Ashgate, 2010)

95. Ibid., xii, 50–67.

96. Ibid., 57.

97. Ibid.

98. Ibid., 59.

99. Corinne Cauvin Verner, "Le tourisme sexuel vu du Sahara marocain: Une économie de razzia?" *L'Année du Maghreb* 6 (2010): 47–77, http://journals.openedition.org/anneemaghreb/807.

100. Ibid., para. 28.

101. Lindqvist, *Desert Divers*, 124–25.

102. Maupassant, *Au soleil*, 70.

103. Ibid., 71.

104. Todd Shepard, *Sex, France, and Arab Men* (Chicago: Chicago University Press, 2017), 4–5.

105. Maupassant, *Au soleil*, 71.

106. Ibid.

107. Ibid.

108. Hanan al-Shaykh, *Misk al-ghazāl: Riwāyah* (Beirut: Dār al-Adāb, 1988).

109. Massad, *Desiring Arabs*, 340.

110. Lindqvist, *Desert Divers*, 125.

111. André Gide, *The Immoralist*, trans. Richard Howard (New York: Vintage International, 1996), 37.

112. Ibid., 38.

113. Ibid., 49.

114. Ibid., 150.

115. Ibid., 160–61.

116. Ibid., 146.

117. Ibid., 161.

118. Ibid., 110.

119. Ibid., 105.

120. Guy Dugas, "André Gide en Algérie: Les écrivains d'Algérie face à la morale gidienne," *Bulletin des Amis d'André Gide* 22, no. 102 (1994): 249–68.

121. Ibid., 252.

122. Gide, *Si le grain*, 51.

123. Ibid., 70.

124. Ibid., 72–73.

125. Ibid., 54.

126. Ibid.

127. Ibid., 139.

128. Ibid.

129. Weightman, "André Gide," 592.

130. Martin Halliwell, *Transatlantic Modernism: Moral Dilemmas in Modernist Fiction* (Edinburgh: Edinburgh University Press, 2006), 56.

131. Frederick Grubb, "On the Frontier: The Art of André Gide," *Theology* 62, no. 465 (1959): 100.

132. Ibid., 101.

133. Samih Murkus, *Kalām al-ʿilm fī al-ḥubb wa-al-jins* (Cairo: Markaz al-Maḥrūṣa li-al-Nashr wa-al-Khadamāt al-Ṣaḥafiyya wa-al-Maʿlūmāt, 2021), 110.

134. Antony Copley, *Sexual Moralities in France, 1780–1980: New Ideas on the Family, Divorce, and Homosexuality; An Essay on Moral Change* (New York: Routledge, 1989), 161–71.

135. Jonathan Dollimore, *Sexual Dissidence: Augustine to Wilde, Freud to Foucault* (Oxford: Clarendon Press, 1991), 11.

136. Ibid., 1.

137. Ibid., 13.

138. Copley also discusses Wilde's influence on Gide (*Sexual Moralities in France*, 161–62).

139. Dollimore, *Sexual Dissidence*, 12.

140. Dessaix, *Arabesques*, 11.

141. Ibid., 36.

142. Colm Tóibín, "Love in a Dark Time," *London Review of Books*, April 19, 2001, www.lrb.co.uk/the-paper/v23/n08/colm-toibin/love-in-a-dark-time.

143. Ibid.

144. Būderbala, "Ṣurāt al-jazāʾir," 11.

145. Farid Laroussi, *Postcolonial Counterpoint: Orientalism, France, and the Maghreb* (Toronto: University of Toronto Press, 2016), 102.

146. Caroline Framke, "Westworld's Boring Orgy Reminds Us that Joyless Sex Has Become HBO's Specialty," *Vox*, October 31, 2016, www.vox.com/culture/2016/10/31/13477222/westworld-orgy-contrapasso.

147. Bill Keveney, "Evan Rachel Wood: How the Uprising of Oppressed *Westworld* Androids Mirrors Me Too Movement," *USA Today*, May 26, 2018, www.usatoday.com/story/life/tv/2018/03/26/evan-rachel-wood-how-uprising-oppressed-westworld-androids-mirrors-me-too-movement/446953002.

148. Ibid.

149. Jason Lee, *Sex Robots: The Future of Desire* (Cham: Palgrave Macmillan, 2017), 6.

150. Alex Goody and Antonia Mackay, *Reading Westworld* (Cham: Palgrave Macmillan, 2019). Good and Mackay make some important distinctions by drawing on Kate Devlin's book *Turned On: Science, Sex, and Robots* (London: Bloomsbury, 2018) and particularly her definition of automata as "machines that give the appearance of being self-powered and self-driven working independently . . . in fact, they are mechanistic, performing repetitive pre-set actions that might seem self-selected but are merely automated" (p. 46).

151. Goody and Mackay, *Reading Westworld*, 3.

152. Ibid.

153. Ibid.

154. Rebecca Solnit, "A Broken Idea of Sex Is Flourishing: Blame Capitalism," *The Guardian*, May 12, 2018, www.theguardian.com/commentisfree/2018/may/12/sex-capitalism-incel-movement-misogyny-feminism.

155. Ibid., 9.

156. Josh Wigler, "Inside *Westworld*'s 'Epic' Orgy Scene," *The Hollywood Reporter*, October 30, 2016, www.hollywoodreporter.com/tv/tv-news/westworld-orgy-scene-explained-942103.

157. Ibid.

158. Liz Shannon Miller, "*Westworld* Review: 'Contrapasso' Searches for Purpose in between the Orgies," *Indiewire*, October 30, 2016, www.indiewire.com/criticism/shows/westworld-review-season-1-episode-5-contrapasso-orgy-recap-spoilers-1201741702.

159. Ibid.

160. Emily Witt, *Future Sex* (New York: Farrar, Straus and Giroux, 2016), 173.

161. Ibid., 177.

162. Ibid.

163. "What Is Burning Man? The 10 Principles of Burning Man," Burningman.org, accessed May 15, 2024, https://burningman.org/about/10-principles.

164. Ibid.

165. Ibid.

166. Ibid.

167. Jones, *Tribes of Burning Man*, 189.

168. Barry Taylor, *Sex, God, and Rock 'n' Roll: Catastrophes, Epiphanies, and Sacred Anarchies* (Minneapolis, MN: Fortress Press, 2020), 53.

169. Ibid.

170. Jones, *Tribes of Burning Man*, 189.

171. Witt, *Future Sex*, 189.

172. Ibid., 188–89.

CHAPTER FIVE: "UNITY OF CREATURES"

1. One need only refer to the prolific literature about "atoms for peace" and all the different ways in which these endeavors were marketed for the general audiences.

2. Vanda Felbab-Brown, "The Wall: The Real Cost of a Barrier between the United States and Mexico," Brookings.edu, August 2017, brookings.edu/articles/the-wall-the-real-costs-of-a-barrier-between-the-united-states-and-mexico; Luis Alberto Urrea, *The Devil's Highway: A True Story* (New York: Back Bay Books, 2004); Jason De León, *The Land of Open Graves Living and Dying on the Migrant Trail* (Oakland: University of California Press, 2015).

3. France is particularly guilty in this regard. See Direction des applications militaires, *La Direction des applications militaires (CEA/DAM) au cœur de la dissuasion nucléaire française: De l'ère des pionniers au programme Simulation*, CEA/DAM (2025), www.cea.fr/presse/Documents/actualites/direction-applications-militaires-cea-dissuasion-nucleaire-france.pdf.

4. See Chap. 4 for more details about the critique of the romanticized uses of nomadism in theoretical works.

5. Ivan Southall, *Woomera* (Sydney: Agnus and Robertson, 1962), 3.

6. Readers interested in this history should refer to Bruno Barrillot's extensive work. See Bruno Barrillot, *Les déchets nucléaires militaires français* (Lyon: Centre de documentation et de recherche sur la paix, 1994); *Les essais nucléaires français 1960–1996: Conséquences sur l'environnement et la santé* (Lyon: Centre de documentation et de recherche sur la paix et les conflits, 1996); *L'héritage de la bombe: Sahara, Polynésie (1960–2002), les faits, les personnels, les populations* (Lyon: Centre de documentation et de recherche sur la paix et les conflits, 2002); *Les irradiés de la république: Les victimes des essais nucléaires français prennent la parole* (Lyon: Observatoire des armes nucléaires françaises, 2003); and *Le complexe nucléaire: Des liens entre l'atome civil et l'atome militaire* (Lyon: Centre de documentation et de recherche sur la paix et les conflits, 2005).

7. Abdelrahman Munif, *Mudun al-milḥ* (Beirut: al-Muʾassasa al-ʿArabīyya lil-Dirāsāt wa-al-Nashr, 1985), translated by Peter Theroux as *Cities of Salt* (New York: Vintage International, 1989); Ibrahim al-Koni, *Nazīf al-ḥajar* (Limassol: Tāsīlī li-al-Nashr wa-al-Iʿlām, 1992), translated by May Jayyusi and Christopher Tingley as *The Bleeding of the Stone* (Northampton, MA: Interlink Books, 2013). While I have read the Arabic originals of both, I reference the English versions of these books in this chapter.

8. Serpil Oppermann and Serenella Iovino, eds., "Introduction," in *Environmental Humanities: Voices from the Anthropocene* (New York: Rowman and Littlefield, 2017), 5.

9. Ibrahim al-Koni, *Waṭanī ṣaḥrāʾ kubrā: Ḥiwārāt* (Beirut: al-Muʾassasa al-ʿArabīyya lil-Dirāsāt wa-al-Nashr, 2009), 8, 233. It also appears recurrently throughout his interviews, particularly in Ibrahim al-Koni, "Abḥathu ʿan al-usṭūra li-takhliqanī," *Aletihad*, March 6, 2008, www.aletihad.ae/article/10700/2008/%D8%A5%D8%A8%D8%B1%D8%A7%D9%87%D9%8A%D9%85-%D8%A7%D9%84%D9%83%D9%88%D9%86%D9%8A:-%D8%A3%D8%A8%D8%AD%D8%AB-%D8%B9%D9%86-%D8%A7%D9%84%D8%A3%D8%B3%D8%B7%D9%88%D8%B1%D8%A9-%D9%84%D9%83%D9%8A-%D8%AA%D8%AE%D9%84%D9%82%D9%86%D9%8A; and Sāmī Klaib, "Ibrahīm al-kūnī . . . takrīm al-gharb wa tajāhul al-ʿarab," *Al Jazeera*, June 29, 2009, www.aljazeera.net/programs/privatevisit/2009/6/29/%D8%A5%D8%A8%D8%B1%D8%A7%D9%87%D9%8A%D9%85-%D8%A7%D9%84%D9%83%D9%88%D9%86%D9%8A-%D8%AA%D9%83%D8%B1%D9%8A%D9%85-%D8%A7%D9%84%D8%BA%D8%B1%D8%A8-%D9%88%D8%AA%D8%AC%D8%A7%D9%87%D9%84.

10. Abdelrahman Munif, cited in Iskandar Ḥabash, *al-Qirāʾa wa-al-nisyān: Al-khurūj min mudun al-milḥ* (London: Ṭawā li-al-Thaqāfa wa-al-Nashr wa-al-Iʿlām, 2015), 32.

11. Al-Koni blurs the distinction between fiction and reality, writing that they "overlap and exchange roles in a dialectical relationship" (*Waṭanī ṣaḥrāʾ kubrā*, 227–28). Munif, by contrast, retains the distinction between fiction and nonfiction, but he attributes to the novel the ability to provide "a true and faithful reading of reality that carries a share of dreams and desires in order to achieve a better reality, a less miserable life" (Ḥabash, *al-Qirāʾa wa-al-nisyān*, 27).

12. Omar Al Ansari, *Ṭabīb tinbuktū* (Beirut: al-Mu'assasa al-ʿArabīyya lil-Dirāsāt wa-al-Nashr, 2011); Hocine Hacene, *Le Sahara dans l'enfer des essais nucléaires français: Un crime sans fin* (Algiers: Houma Éditions, 2018). All translations from Arabic and French are mine unless otherwise noted.

13. Federation of Nigeria, *Nuclear Tests in the Sahara: Report by the Joint United Kingdom-Nigerian Scientific Committee on the Monitoring of Radioactivity 9* (Lagos: Federal Government Printer, 1960), 8.

14. M. Gast, "Inîker, Enîker," *Encyclopédie berbère* 24 (2001): 3760–62, http://journals.openedition.org/encyclopedieberbere/1578.

15. Barrillot, *L'héritage de la bombe*, 24–25.

16. Some of the works that engage with these questions include Ibn Khaldun, *The Muqaddimah: An Introduction to History*, trans. Franz Rosenthal (Princeton, NJ: Princeton University Press, 2005); Mondher Kilani, *La construction de la mémoire: Le lignage et la sainteté dans l'oasis d'El Ksar* (Geneva: Éditions Labor et Fides, 1992); Ghislaine Lydon, "A Thirst for Knowledge: Arabic Literacy, Writing Paper, and Saharan Bibliophiles in the Southwestern Sahara," in *The Trans-Saharan Book Trade: Manuscript Culture, Arabic Literacy, and Intellectual History in Muslim Africa*, ed. Graziano Krätli and Ghislaine Lydon (Leiden: Brill, 2011), 35–72.

17. See, for instance, Joanna Allan, *Saharan Winds: Energy Systems and Aeolian Imaginaries in Western Sahara* (Morgantown: West Virginia University Press, 2024), and Alice Wilson, *Afterlives of Revolution: Everyday Counterhistories in Southern Oman* (Stanford, CA: Stanford University Press, 2023).

18. See Natalia Mendoza's work about mining on the Mexican side of the Sonora, "Depoliticizing Conflict in Sonora, Mexico: (Il)legality, Territory and the Continuum of Violence," *European Review of Latin American and Caribbean Studies* 112 (2021): 117–36. For a discussion of Tuareg resistance and the impact of geopolitics, extending from intelligence services to armed Islamist groups, see Hélène Claudot-Hawad, "La 'Question touarègue': Quels enjeux?" in *La guerre au Mali: Comprendre la crise au Sahel et au Sahara; Enjeux et zones d'ombre*, ed. Michel Galy (Paris: La Découverte, 2013), 125–47.

19. Ḥabash, *al-Qirāʾa wa-al-nisyān*, 56.

20. Morgan Ndlovu has delineated how Western-centric epistemic views tend to dismiss Indigenous knowledge as obsolete. See Morgan Ndlovu, "Why Indigenous Knowledges in the 21st Century? A Decolonial Turn," *Yesterday & Today* 11 (2014): 85.

21. Balqīs al-Anṣārī, "Mā bayna al-wujūd wa-al-ʿadam: Baytun fī al-dunyā, baytun fī al-ḥanīn," *Mana*, March 7, 2024, https://mana.net/al-koni.

22. Clifford Geertz, *The Interpretation of Cultures* (New York: Basic Books, 1973), 3–30.

23. Geoff Nicholson, *Day Trips to the Desert: A Sort of Travel Book* (London: Sceptre, 1993), 23.

24. al-Konī, *Waṭanī ṣaḥrāʾ kubrā*, 231.

25. Ibrahim al-Koni, "Talbīs al-namaṭ: al-ṣaḥrāʾu namūdhajan," *Sky News Arabia*, September 10, 2023, www.skynewsarabia.com/blog/1651820-%D8%AA%D9%84%D8%A8%D9%8A%D8%B3-%D8%A7%D9%84%D9%86%D9%91%D9%85%D8%B7-%D8%A7%D9%84%D8%B5%D8%AD%D8%B1%D8%A7%D8%A1-%D9%86%D9%85%D9%88%D8%B0%D8%AC%D8%A7%D9%8B.

26. al-Koni, "Talbīs al-namaṭ."

27. al-Koni, *Waṭanī ṣaḥrāʾ kubrā*, 8, 233; al-Koni, "Abḥathu ʿan al-usṭūra li-takhluqanī"; Klaib, "Ibrahīm al-kūnī."

28. ʿAbdulghānī al-Nablusī, *Iyḍāḥu al-maqṣūd min waḥdat al-wujūd*, ed. ʿIzza Khaḍra (Damascus: Maṭbaʿat al-ʿIlm, 1969).

29. IPCC, *Climate Change 2022: Impacts, Adaptation, and Vulnerability; Contribution of Working Group II to the Sixth Assessment Report of the Intergovernmental Panel on Climate Change* (New York: Cambridge University Press, 2022), 13.

30. Ibid., 9.

31. Ibid., 238, 263, 272, 615.

32. al-Koni, "Abḥathu ʿan al-usṭūra li-takhluqanī."

33. Ibid.

34. Environmental studies scholars Oppermann and Iovino speak of the need for "new theoretical models of environmentality that coalesce human and nonhuman ecologies" (*Environmental Humanities*, 1), while Matsuoka and Sorenson have argued for the need for both reason and emotion in order "to work against violence, exploitation, marginalization, and dominance over other animals" (Atsuko Matsuoka and John Sorenson, eds., *Critical Animal Studies: Towards Trans-Species Social Justice* [London: Rowman and Littlefield, 2018], 4).

35. Anna L. Tsing, *The Mushroom at the End of the World: On the Possibility of Life in Capitalist Ruins* (Princeton, NJ: Princeton University Press, 2015), 28.

36. Al-Koni, *Bleeding*, 39.

37. Arthur J. Arberry, *The Koran Interpreted* (London: George Allen and Unwin, 1955), 132.

38. Ibid., 89.

39. Ibid.

40. Ibid., 88.

41. Ibid.

42. Lisa Kröger, "Panic, Paranoia, and Pathos: Ecocriticism in the Eighteenth-Century Gothic Novel," in *EcoGothic*, ed. Andrew Smith and William Hughes (Manchester: Manchester University Press, 2013), 22.

43. al-Koni, *Bleeding*, 89.

44. Félix Gautier, *Le Sahara: Avec 4 cartes dans le texte* (Paris: Payot, 1923), 23. The *méharistes* were the native camel-mounted units, which Laperrine established to police the Sahara; see the Introduction.

45. Military physician Robert Hérisson mentions about ten instances of hunting gazelles during his journey from Biskra to the Hoggar. See Robert Hérisson, *Avec le père de Foucauld et le Général Laperrine: Carnets d'un saharien 1909–1911* (Paris: Librairie Plon, 1937).

46. Fernand Foureau, *Documents scientifiques de la Mission saharienne* (Paris: Publication de la Société de Géographie, 1905), 16, 21–22.

47. Gabriele Volpato and Patricia Howard, "The Material and Cultural Recovery of Camels and Camel Husbandry among Sahrawi Refugees of Western Sahara," *Pastoralism* 4, no. 7 (2014): 1–3; Félix Gautier has provided many useful details about camels in *La conquête du Sahara: Essai de psychologie politique* (Paris: Armand Colin, 1910), 99–100.

48. al-Koni, *Bleeding*, 134.

49. Ibid., 8.

50. al-Konī, *Waṭanī ṣaḥrā' kubrā*, 8.

51. Ibid.

52. Both *anhī* (the lost book) and *nāmūs* appear together in al-Koni's fiction and nonfiction. See, for instance, Ibrahim al-Koni, *Wāw al-Ṣughrā* (Beirut: al-Mu'assasa al- ʿArabīyya lil-Dirāsāt wal-Nashr, 1997), 168.

53. Klaib, "Ibrahīm al-kūnī."

54. Hamid Ait Slimane, "Tanezrouft," in *Le Tanezrouft* (Paris: Mon petit éditeur, 2011), 27–34.

55. Ḥabash, *al-Qirā'a wa-al-nisyān*, 52–55; Abdelrahman Munif, *Bayna al-thaqāfa wa-al-siyyāsa* (Beirut: al-Markaz al-Thaqāfī al-ʿArabī li-al-Nashr wa-al-Tawzīʿ, 2007), 241–42.

56. "Limādhā intaqamat al-suʿūdiyya min kātib riwāyat 'mudun al-milḥ'?" *Al Jazeera*, April 21, 2019, www.aljazeera.net/programs/outside-the-text/2019/4/21/%D9%84%D9%85%D8%A7%D8%B0%D8%A7-%D8%A7%D9%86%D8%AA%D9%82%D9%85%D8%AA-%D8%A7%D9%84%D8%B3%D8%B9%D9%88%D8%AF%D9%8A%D8%A9-%D9%85%D9%86-%D9%83%D8%A7%D8%AA%D8%A8-%D8%B1%D9%88%D8%A7%D9%8A%D8%A9.

57. Ibid.

58. Stacey Balkan and Swaralipi Nandi, eds., *Oil Fictions: World Literature and our Contemporary Petrosphere* (University Park: Pennsylvania State University Press, 2021), 2.

59. "Limādhā intaqamat al-suʿūdiyya min kātib riwāyat 'mudun al-milḥ'?"

60. In his interviews with Lebanese journalist Iskandar Ḥabash, Munif explained: "All my family is there [Saudi Arabia], and I am the only who lives outside the Arabian Peninsula. There is affinity, nostalgia, the natural right. . . . I feel that there are things that need to be completed. However, I previously worked in a political framework which led to the withdrawal of my passport and caused issues" (Ḥabash, *al-Qirā'a wa-al-nisyān*, 53).

61. Paul Silverstein has conducted ethnographic work in Goulmima, in the Ghéris Valley in the governorate of Errachidia, and shown how this desert area played a crucial role in achieving some of fundamental goals of the Amazigh Cultural Movement (ACM). The way the activism of the members of Tilelli Association, which was located in the desert periphery, influenced the entirety of the ACM, which was mostly situated in the center of the country, is reminiscent of Ibn Khaldun's argument in which he associated sociopolitical and cultural renewal with the desert. See Paul Silverstein, "The Racial Politics of the Amazigh Revival in North Africa and beyond," POMEPS.org, accessed July 24, 2024, https://pomeps.org/the-racial-politics-of-the-amazigh-revival-in-north-africa-and-beyond.

62. Ḥabash, *al-Qirāʾa wa-al-nisyān*, 32.

63. Robert Nixon, *Slow Violence and the Environmentalism of the Poor* (Cambridge, MA: Harvard University Press, 2011), 89.

64. Graeme Macdonald, "Oil and World Literature," *American Book Review* 33, no. 3 (2012): 7.

65. Abdelrahman Munif, *Mudun al-milḥ: Bādiyat al-zulumāt* (Casablanca: al-Markaz al-Thaqāfī al-ʿArabī, 2005), 205.

66. Munif, *Bayna al-thaqāfa*, 118.

67. Roger Allen, *The Arabic Literary Heritage* (Cambridge: Cambridge University Press, 2005), 309.

68. Munif, *Cities of Salt*, 1.

69. The emir naively (or cunningly) declares to the elders who lodge a complaint against the unwanted presence of the Americans: "People of Wadi al-Uyoun, you will be among the richest and the happiest of mankind, as if God saw none but you"; ibid., 85.

70. Ibid., 135.

71. Ibid., 121.

72. Ibid., 122.

73. Ibid, 106.

74. Ibid., 106.

75. Ibid.

76. Ibid., 110.

77. Nixon, *Slow Violence*, 69.

78. Munif, *Bayna al-thaqāfa*, 113.

79. See Office of the Historian, "The 1928 Red Line Agreement," History.state.gov., accessed April 24, 2025, https://history.state.gov/milestones/1921-1936/red-line; see also Anthony Sampson, *The Seven Sisters: The Great Oil Companies and the World They Shaped* (New York: Viking Press, 1975).

80. Allen, *Arabic Literary Heritage*, 309; Nixon, *Slow Violence*, 68–102.

81. Munif, *Cities of Salt*, 91.

82. Ibid., 91.

83. Ḥabash, *al-Qirāʾa wa-al-nisyān*, 55.

84. Ibid., 55–56.

85. Nixon, *Slow Violence*, 85.

86. Byron Glennis, "Introduction," in *Globalgothic*, ed. Byron Glennis (Manchester: Manchester University Press, 2013), 1–10.

87. Ibid., 199.

88. Ibid., 201.

89. Ibid., 206.

90. Ibid., 295.

91. Frantz Fanon, *Les damnés de la terre* (Paris: La Découverte, 2002), 42–43. Omar AlShehabi has demonstrated that since the discovery of oil in Bahrain in 1933, petromodernity has brought cars and residential compounds to the Gulf. AlShehabi emphasizes the racializing nature of the comfortable gated compounds where white workers lived vs. the simpler, less developed spaces dedicated to Arab workers. See Omar AlShehabi, "al-Bīyʾa wa mudun al-khalīj al-nafṭiyya," in *al-Bīyʾa fī al-khalīj*, ed. Hamad al-Reyes, Safia Ajlan, and Omar AlShehabi (Kuwait: Markaz al-Khalīj li-Siyāsāt al-Tanmiyya, 2021), 28–29.

92. Dori M. Laub, "An Event without a Witness: Truth, Testimony, and Survival," in *Testimony: Crises of Witnessing in Literature, Psychoanalysis, and History*, ed. Shoshana Felman and Dori Laub (New York: Routledge, 1992), 79.

93. Munif, *Cities of Salt*, 131.

94. Ibid.

95. Language is one the facets that Munif has examined in his discussion of the absence of cultural integration of guest workers into the Gulf. See Munif, *Bayna al-thaqāfa*, 112–13.

96. Ibid., 112.

97. AlShehabi, "al-Bīyʾa wa mudun al-khalīj al-nafṭiyya," 19–20.

98. Munif, *Bayna al-thaqāfa*, 114.

99. Ibid., 115.

100. Ibid.

101. Ibid.

102. Ibid.

103. al-Koni, *Waṭanī ṣaḥrāʾ kubrā*, 9–10.

104. Munif, *Bayna al-thaqāfa*, 120.

105. Ibid.

106. Hamad al-Reyes, Safia Ajlan, and Omar AlShehabi, eds., *al-Bīyʾa fī al-khalīj* (Kuwait: Markaz al-Khalīj li-Siyāsāt al-Tanmiyya, 2021).

107. Omar AlShehabi, "Taṣdīr al-tharwa wa-ightirāb al-insān: Tārīkh al-khalal al-intājī fī buldān al-khalīj al-ʿarabiyya," *al-Mustaqbal al-ʿArabī* 475 (2018): 13.

108. Ibid., 17.

109. See, among others, Henry Grabar, "Line in the Sand, Head in the Clouds," *Slate*, August 1, 2022, https://slate.com/business/2022/08/neom-renderings-cliches-mbs.html; Edwin Heathcote, "Saudi's Neom Is Dystopia Portrayed as Utopia," *Financial Times*, August 1, 2022, www.ft.com/content/04fcb9d4-5907-45b0-9388-f84b34bc4bea; Erin Cunningham, "Saudi Crown Prince Wants You Talking about His 'City of the Future,'" *The Washington Post*, July 29, 2022, www.washingtonpost.com/world/2022/07/28/neom-te-line-city-saudi-arabia-mbs-khashoggi-europe;

and Bill Chappell, "A 105-Mile-Long City Will Snake through the Saudi Desert: Is That a Good Idea?" NPR, July 26, 2022, www.npr.org/2022/07/26/1113670047/saudi-arabia-new-city-the-mirror-line-desert.

110. Mariam Nihal, "The Line in Neom Is 'the Greatest Real Estate Challenge that Humans Have Faced,'" *National News*, August 17, 2022, www.thenationalnews.com/gulf-news/2022/08/17/the-line-in-neom-is-the-greatest-property-challenge-that-humans-have-faced.

111. Dania Akkad, "Neom: Saudi Arabia Sentences Tribesmen to Death for Resisting Displacement," *Middle East Eye*, October 7, 2022, www.middleeasteye.net/news/neom-saudi-arabia-sentences-tribesmen-death-resisting-displacement.

112. Ali Dogan, "Saudi Arabia's Neom Diplomacy," Carnegie Endowment for International Peace, March 3, 2021, https://carnegieendowment.org/sada/83975.

113. Kingdom of Saudi Arabia, "The Story of Transformation," Vision2030, accessed January 24, 2025, www.vision2030.gov.sa/en/explore/story-of-transformation.

114. Of the many international news outlets that covered Neom's construction, Grabar's "Line in the Sand" was particularly critical. However, the ecological desert itself as an object of transformation has been mostly absent from these articles. MBS evinces a strong understanding of tropes informed by Saharanism in stating that the "LINE will tackle the challenges facing humanity in urban life today and will shine a light on alternative ways to live" (Mohammed Bin Salman, "HRH Crown Prince Mohammed Bin Salman Announces Designs for THE LINE, the City of the Future in Neom," Neom, accessed January 27, 2025, www.neom.com/en-us/newsroom/hrh-announces-theline-designs). In other words, the desert is presented as a hypermodern refuge for those disillusioned with Euro-America. See Naama Riba, "Neom and the Line: Saudi Arabia's Futuristic City Already Belongs in the Past," *Haaretz*, August 2, 2022, www.haaretz.com/middle-east-news/2022-08-02/ty-article-magazine/.premium/neom-and-the-line-saudi-arabias-futuristic-city-already-belongs-in-the-past/00000182-53b8-d2c3-a5a3-57f802a30000.

115. Kingdom of Saudi Arabia, "Environment and Nature," Vision2030, accessed June 14, 2024, www.vision2030.gov.sa/en/progress/environment-nature. When I rechecked this information in January 2025, the page has disappeared. However, readers can find this information here: Kingdom of Saudi Arabia, "SGI Target: Reduce Carbon Emissions by 278 mtpa by 2030," Saudi Green Initiative, accessed January 26, 2025, www.sgi.gov.sa/about-sgi/sgi-targets/reduce-carbon-emissions.

116. Kingdom of Saudi Arabia, "Environment and Nature."

117. Munif, *Bayna al-thaqāfa*, 116.

118. Robert Mogielnicki, "Neom Is Becoming a Destination of Destinations," The Arab Gulf States Institute in Washington, January 26, 2024, https://agsiw.org/neom-is-becoming-a-destination-of-destinations.

119. AlArabiya, "al-Amīr muḥammad bin salman: Al-Sharq al-awsaṭ sayakūn ūrūppā al-jadīda," *YouTube*, October 24, 2018, video, 1:27, www.youtube.com/watch?v=wZxDddQ8isg.

120. Alqst for Human Rights documents the countless ways in which Saudi authorities violated Indigenous people's rights in order to clear the lands for

construction. See Alqst for Human Rights, *The Dark Side of Neom: Expropriation, Expulsion, and Prosecution of the Region's Inhabitants*, February 2023, https://alqst.org/uploads/the-dark-side-of-neom-expropriation-expulsion-and-prosecution-en.pdf.-en.pdf.

121. "al-Ḥwīṭāt .. sukkan aṣliyyūn sāhamū bi-ta'sīs al-sa'ūdiyya fabanat 'neom' 'alā ashlā'ihim," *Alestiklal*, 2023, www.alestiklal.net/ar/article/dep-news-1663890731.

122. Dania Akkad and Rayhan Uddin, "Neom: Saudi Arabia Jails Tribesmen for 50 Years for Rejecting Displacement," *Middle East Eye*, September 13, 2022, www.middleeasteye.net/news/saudi-arabia-neom-tribesmen-imprisoned-rejecting-displacement.

123. Alqst for Human Rights et al., "Open Letter from NGOs Calling on Companies Involved in Saudi Arabia's NEOM Project to Condemn Human Rights Violations Accompanying It," *Alqst*, June 2, 2020, www.alqst.org/ar/posts/431.

124. Adam Greenfield, "All Those Complicit in Neom's Design and Construction Are Already Destroyers of Worlds," *Dezeen*, November 2, 2022, www.dezeen.com/2022/11/02/neom-the-line-saudi-arabia-architects-opinion.

125. Martin Chulov, "'Night of the Beating': Details Emerge of Riyadh Ritz-Carlton Purge," *The Guardian*, November 19, 2020, www.theguardian.com/world/2020/nov/19/saudi-accounts-emerge-of-ritz-carlton-night-of-the-beating.

126. "Saudi Arabia: Corruption Crackdown 'Ends with $106bn Recovered,'" *Al Jazeera*, January 31, 2019, www.aljazeera.com/news/2019/1/31/saudi-arabia-corruption-crackdown-ends-with-106bn-recovered.

127. Chulov, "Night of the Beating."

128. Mark Beeson, "The Coming of Environmental Authoritarianism," *Environmental Politics* 19, no. 2 (2010): 276–94.

129. Christian Bataille, "Rapport n°179—L'évaluation de la recherche sur la gestion des déchets nucléaires à haute activité—Tome II: Les déchets militaires," *Office parlementaire d'évaluation des choix scientifiques et technologiques*, 1997–98, www.senat.fr/rap/097-179/097-179_mono.html.

130. "61 Years Later, Algerians Still Suffer from France's Atomic Legacy," *TRT-World*, 2021, www.trtworld.com/magazine/61-years-later-algerians-still-suffer-from-france-s-atomic-legacy-44187.

131. Ahmed Boussaid, "Ihtimāmātu al-farnsiyyīna bistikshāfi iqlīm tanzrūft 1900–1962," *Mjallat al-Sāwra li-al-Dirāsāt al-Insāniyya wa-al-Ijtimā'iyya* 2, no. 8 (2022): 116.

132. The names of these bombs are Agate (1961), Béryl (1962), Émeraude (1963), Améthyste (1963), Rubis (1963), Opale (1964), Topaze (1964), Turquoise (1964), Saphir (1965), Jade (1965), Corindon (1965), Tourmaline (1965), and Grenat (1966). See Christian Bataille and Henri Revol, "Rapport sur les incidences environnementales et sanitaires des essais nucléaires effectués par la France entre 1960 et 1996 et éléments de comparaison avec les essaies des autres puissances nucléaires," Senat.fr, accessed April 24, 2025, www.senat.fr/rap/r01-207/r01-2071.pdf.

133. See Barrillot, *Les irradiés*, 18–112.

134. al-Markaz al-Waṭanī li-al-Dirāsāt wa-al-Baḥth, *al-Tajārib al-nawawiyya al-faransiyya fī al-jazāʾir: Dirāsāt wa buḥūth wa shahadat* (Algiers: al-Markaz al-Waṭanī li-al-Dirāsāt wa-al-Baḥth fī al-Ḥaraka al-Waṭaniyya wa Thawrat Awwal Nuvambr 1954, 2000), 32–39; Jean-Claude Amiard, *Military Nuclear Accidents: Environmental, Ecological, Health, and Socio-Economic Consequences* (Newark, NJ: John Wiley, 2019), 103.

135. See Chap. 3 and Danielle Endres, "The Rhetoric of Nuclear Colonialism: Rhetorical Exclusion of American Indian Arguments in the Yucca Mountain Nuclear Waste Siting Decision," *Communication and Critical/Cultural Studies* 6, no. 1 (2009): 39–60.

136. Barrillot, *L'héritage de la bombe*, 35.

137. Sūrī Imān and Bin Sahla Thānī Bin Ali, "al-Tajārib al-nawawiyya al-faransiyya fī al-jazāʾir wa-āthāruha ʿalā al-bīyʾa," *Majallat al-Ḥaqūq wa-al-ʿUlūm al-Insāniyya* 15, no. 1 (2022): 372.

138. Brahim El Guabli, "Entretien avec Hawad: 'Nous sommes des cadavres, et pire, des cadavres invisibles,'" *Expressions maghrébines* 23, no. 1 (2024): 112.

139. Some examples of this rich and amply available scholarship in Arabic include Lakhḍar Shʿshʿiyya, "Al-Asās al-qānūnī al-dawlī li-mas'ūliyyat faransā ʿan tajāribiha al-nawawiyya fī al-jazāʾir (dirāsat li-taḥdīd al-qawāʿid al-mawḍūʿiyya wa-al-ijrāʾiyya fī al-qānūn al-dawlī li-muṭalabat faransā bi-al-taʿwīḍ)," *Majallat al-Wāḥāt li-al-Buḥūt wa-al-Dirāsāt* 7, no. 2 (2014): 356–66; Musṭafā Kamāl Mnāyf, "al-Tajārib al-nawawiyya al-faransiyya fī al-jazāʾir fī ẓill aḥkām al-qānūn al-dawlī" (master's thesis, University of Tiaret, 2019), http://dspace.univ-tiaret.dz/bitstream/123456789/1096/1/TH.M.DRO.AR.2019.26.pdf; Muḥammad al-Mahdī Bakrāwī and Inṣāf Bin ʿImrān, "al-Buʿd al-qānūnī li-al-āthār al-ṣiḥịhhiya wa-al-bīyʾiyya li-al-tajārib al-nawawiyya al-faransiyya fī al-ṣaḥrāʾ al-jazāʾiriyya min manẓūr al-qānūn al-dawlī al-insānī," *Darātir al-Siyyāsa wa-al-Qānūn* 8 (2013): 18–28; Nāṣir Bilbukhārī, "al-Tajārib al-nawawiyya al-fanransiyya fī rqqān," *Majallat al-Badr* 2, no. 2 (2010): 22–24; Ibrāhīm Yāma and Yamīna Bilbālī, "al-Āthār al-bīyʾiyya al-nātija ʿan al-tajārib al-nawawiyya al-faransiyya fī al-jazāʾir 'rqqān unmūdhajan,'" *Majallat al-Bayān li-al-Dirāsāt al-Qānūniyya wa-al-Siyyāsiyya* 2, no. 1 (2017): 27–35.

140. "Le document choc sur la bombe A en Algérie," *Le Parisien*, February 14, 2014, www.leparisien.fr/archives/le-document-choc-sur-la-bombe-a-en-algerie-14-02-2014-3588699.php.

141. Brahim El Guabli, *Moroccan Other-Archives: History and Citizenship after State Violence* (New York: Fordham University Press, 2023).

142. Hacene, *Le Sahara dans l'enfer*, 82.

143. Abdelfatah Belaroussi, "al-Āthār al-ṣiḥḥiyya li-al-jarāʾim al-nawawiyya al-faransiyya fī rqqān," *Majallat Āfāq ʿIlimiyya* 14, no. 1 (2022): 210, 219–20.

144. Abdelkadhem Aboudi, "al-Tajārib al-nawawiyya al-faransiyya wa-makhāṭir al-talawwuth al-ishʿāʿī ʿalā al-ṣiḥḥa wa-al-bīyʾa fī al-madā al-qarīb wa-al-baʿīd," *al-Maṣādir* 1, no. 1 (1999): 250–314.

145. Jeremey Keenan, *Sahara Man: Travelling with the Tuareg* (London: J. Murray, 2001), 71.

146. Ibid.

147. "61 Years Later."

148. An important reference in this regard is Jean-Marie Collin and Patrice Bouveret's report *The Waste from French Nuclear Tests in Algeria, Radioactivity under the Sand: Analysis with Regard to the Treaty on the Prohibition of Nuclear Weapons* (Berlin: Heinrich Böll Foundation, 2020).

149. Aḥmad al-Madīnī, "'Umar al-anṣārȳ *Ṭabīb tinbuktū*: Yudāwī al-ṭawāriq bibalsam al-riwāya," *Alquds*, January 11, 2012, www.alquds.co.uk/%D8%B9%D9%85%D8%B1-%D8%A7%D9%84%D8%A3%D9%86%D8%B5%D8%A7%D8%B1%D9%8A-%D8%B7%D8%A8%D9%8A%D8%A8-%D8%AA%D9%86%D8%A8%D9%83%D8%AA%D9%88-%D9%8A%D8%AF%D8%A7%D9%88%D9%8A-%D8%A7%D9%84%D8%B7%D9%88%D8%A7.

150. Philippe Lefevre Witier, "Disappearing Human Ecosystems," in *Environmental Management in Practice: Managing the Ecosystem*, vol. 3, ed. Bhaskar Nath, Dimitri Devuyst, Luc Hens, Paul Compton (New York: Routledge, 1999), 257–58.

151. Al Ansari, *Ṭabīb tinbuktū*, 118.

152. Leuvrey and Bruno Hadji's documentary *At(h)ome* contains statements from a couple of these workers.

153. Charles Ailleret, *L'aventure atomique française* (Paris: Grasset, 1958), 229–30.

154. Al Ansari, *Ṭabīb tinbuktū*, 85.

155. See Bataille, "Rapport n° 179."

156. See Joan Tilouine, "Algérie: Itinéraire d'un nuage radioactive," *Jeune Afrique*, March 5, 2014, www.jeuneafrique.com/134334/politique/alg-rie-itin-raire-d-un-nuage-radioactif.

157. Sūrī and Bin ʿAlī, "al-Tajārib al-nawawiyya," 377.

158. Hacene, *Le Sahara dans l'enfer*, 78–79.

159. René Pottier, *Laperrine conquérant pacifique du Sahara* (Paris: Nouvelles Éditions Latines, 1943), 148.

160. Al Ansari, *Ṭabīb tinbuktū*, 86.

161. Sophie Courageot, "Les poussières de sable du Sahara étaient porteuses de Césium-137, résidu d'anciens essais nucléaires français," *France Info*, February 26, 2021, https://france3-regions.francetvinfo.fr/bourgogne-franche-comte/jura/les-poussieres-de-sable-du-sahara-etaient-porteuses-de-cesium-137-residu-d-anciens-essais-nucleaires-francais-1973641.html.

162. Sumiyya Lwāfī, "al-Tajārib al-nawawiyya al-faranisyya fī al-ṣaḥrāʾ al-jazāʾiriyya 1960–1966 tafjīrāt rqqān unmūdhajan," *Al-Majalla al-Maghāribiyya li-al-Dirāsāt al-Tārīkhiyya wa-al-Ijtimāʿiyya* 13, no. 1 (2021): 45; Būzīdī Waḥīd, "al-Tajārib al-nawawiyya al-faransiyya fī al-ṣaḥrāʾ al-jazāʾiriyya min khilāl al-ṣaḥafa al-faransiyya: Tafjīrāt 13 fivriyi 1960 unmūdhajan," *Al-Sāwra li-al-Dirāsāt al-Insāniyya wa-al-Ijtimāʿiyya* 8, no. 2 (2022): 18.

163. Barrillot, *L'héritage de la bombe*, 29, and Barrillot, *Les essais nucléaires français*, 43.

164. Hacene, *Le Sahara dans l'enfer*, 74.

165. Ibid., 82.

166. Ibid., 79.

167. Ibid., 57.

168. Ibid., 81.

169. "Sahara: Des déchets radioactifs français enfouis sous le sable," *Franceinfo*, December 4, 2020, www.francetvinfo.fr/monde/afrique/algerie/sahara-des-dechets-radioactifs-francais-enfouis-sous-le-sable_4207387.html.

170. Hacene Hachemi, "al-Tajārib al-nawawiyya al-faransiyya fi-al-jazāʾir wa-qānūn mūrīn bayna rafʿ al-ḥaraj al-siyyāsī wa-taḥqīq al-iʿtirāf bi-al-dhākira," *Majallat al-Nāqid li-al-Dirāsāt al-Siyyāsiyya* 7, no. 2 (2023), 346.

171. *Al Jazeera* also adduces a total of fifty-seven experiments, including seventeen nuclear tests, that France carried out in the Sahara between 1960 and 1966. See "Mādhā tukhfī al-ṣaḥrāʾ? Jarāʾim al-tajārib al-nawawiyya al-faransiyya fī ṣaḥrāʾ al-jazāʾir," *Al Jazeera*, June 16, 2023, www.aljazeera.net/midan/eye/2023/6/16/%D8%B4%D8%A7%D9%87%D8%AF-%D9%85%D8%A7%D8%B0%D8%A7-%D8%AA%D9%8F%D8%AE%D9%81%D9%8A-%D8%A7%D9%84%D8%B5%D8%AD%D8%B1%D8%A7%D8%A1%D8%9F-%D8%AC%D8%B1%D8%A7%D8%A6%D9%85.

172. Abdelaziz Rājiʿī and Nawī Bin Mabrūk, "al-Tajārib al-nawawiyya al-faransiya bi-al-ṣaḥrāʾ al-jazāʾiriyya fī mīyzān al-qānūn al-dawlī al-insānī 1960–1966," *Majallat al-Ustādh al-Bāḥith li-al-Dirāsāt al-Qānūniyya wa-al-Siyyāsiyya* 5, no. 1 (2020): 1008.

173. Ibid.

174. Saʿdī Baziyyān, *Jarāʾim faransā fī al-jazāʾir min al-jinirāl būjū ilā al-jinirāl usārīs* (Algiers: Dār Huma, 2005), 9.

175. Hacene, *Le Sahara dans l'enfer*, 79.

176. Leuvrey, *At(h)ome.*

177. Rābiḥī Faḍīla, "al-Tajārib al-nawawiyya al-faransiyya fī al-ṣaḥrāʾ al-jazāʾiriyya 1960–1966 wa-inʿikāsātuha" (master's thesis, University of Biskra, 2013), 64, http://archives.univ-biskra.dz/bitstream/123456789/3363/1/71.pdf.

178. Ibid., 55.

179. Ibid.

180. Muṣṭfā Shakīrī, "al-Koni: al-Ṣaḥrāʾ al-kubrā maskūna bi-al-ḥurriyya . . . wa-ightirāb al-waṭan ʿuzlatun wujūdiyya," *Hespress*, May 2, 2022, www.hespress.com/%D8%A7%D9%84%D9%83%D9%88%D9%86%D9%8A-%D8%A7%D9%84%D8%B5%D8%AD%D8%B1%D8%A7%D8%A1-%D8%A7%D9%84%D9%83%D8%A8%D8%B1%D9%89-%D9%85%D8%B3%D9%83%D9%88%D9%86%D8%A9-%D8%A8%D8%A7%D9%84%D8%AD%D8%B1%D9%8A%D8%A9-979778.html.

EPILOGUE

1. Joel Roskin, "Why Moving to the Sinai Peninsula Is the Solution for Gaza's Palestinians," *The Jerusalem Post*, December 25, 2023, www.jpost.com/opinion/article-779510.

2. Ibid.

3. Ibid.

4. Ibid.

5. International Court of Justice, "Application of the Convention on the Prevention and Punishment of the Crime of Genocide in the Gaza Strip (South Africa v. Israel)," *International Court of Justice*, January 26, 2024, www.icj-cij.org/sites/default/files/case-related/192/192-20240126-sum-01-00-en.pdf; Office of the Prosecutor, "Statement of ICC Prosecutor Karim A.A. Khan KC on the Issuance of Arrest Warrants in the Situation in the State of Palestine," *International Criminal Court*, November 21, 2024, www.icc-cpi.int/news/statement-icc-prosecutor-karim-aa-khan-kc-issuance-arrest-warrants-situation-state-palestine.

6. Yael Zerubavel, *Desert in the Promised Land* (Stanford, CA: Stanford University Press, 2022).

7. Ibid., 23–27.

8. Dave Lawler and Barak Ravid, "Trump Claims U.S. Will 'Take Over' Gaza and Turn It into New 'Riviera,'" *Axios*, February 4, 2025, www.axios.com/2025/02/05/trump-gaza-takeover-palestinians-israel.

9. Ersela Kripa, Francesco Marullo, and Stephen Mueller, "In Conversation with Gonzalo Pimentel," *Journal of Architectural Education* 77, no. 2 (2023): 429, https://doi.org/10.1080/10464883.2023.2233389.

10. Miguel Fernández de Castro and Natalia Mendoza, *The Absolute Restoration of All Things*, Storefront for Art and Architecture, 2022, video installation and sculpture, https://storefront.nyc/program/the-absolute-restoration-of-all-things.

11. This ruling was preceded by sixty-seven other court decisions that had outcomes in favor of the *ejidos* (the plaintiffs) that were not executed. The 2014 ruling, the main focus of the exhibition, draws on a precedent (188/2009) in which Penmont was defeated, and the judge used the same language of restoration. This 2009 ruling canceled the company's permits, thus paving the way for establishing the illegality of its excavations between 2010 and 2013, which is reflected in the landmark 2014 decision. Javiera Martinez and Holly Jones, "The Struggle of a Community in Sonora against the Grupo Fresnillo Mining Company in Mexico," *London Mining Network*, March 3, 2022, https://londonminingnetwork.org/2022/03/struggle-in-sonora-against-fresnillo. For more details about the history of *ejidos* since their reestablishment by the Mexican Revolution in 1917, see Clara Eugenia Salazar Cruz, "La privatisation des terres collectives agraires dans l'agglomération de Mexico: L'impact des réformes de 1992 sur l'expansion urbaine et la régularisation des lots urbains," *Revue tiers monde* 206, no. 2 (2011): 95–114.

12. Fernández de Castro and Mendoza, *Absolute Restoration of All Things*.

13. El Bajío v. Minera Penmont, unpublished source XP 188-2009 Resolutivos Sentencia Y Auto 19 ENE 2014, Art. 6 of the ruling issued by Justice Manuel Loya Valverde.

14. Fernández de Castro and Mendoza, *Absolute Restoration of All Things*. In addition to restoring the ecosystem to its original state, the ruling required Penmont to purge it of all contaminating elements caused directly or indirectly by the com-

pany. See also Tribunal Unitario Agrario Distrito Veintiocho, Expediente: 188/2009, Hermosillo, Sonora (Mex), 3.

15. Kripa, Marullo, and Mueller, "Conversation with Gonzalo Pimentel," 429.

16. "Getting Creative in Quarry Restoration Design," *Quarry Magazine*, January 2, 2007, www.quarrymagazine.com/2007/01/02/getting-creative-in-quarry-restoration-design.

17. I use the terms "community members" and "community" instead of "Indigenous" solely as more representative terminology of the complex makeup of this society that includes Indigenous and peasant elements. Readers can refer to Natalia Mendoza, "Depoliticizing Conflict in Sonora, Mexico: (Il)legality, Territory, and the Continuum of Violence," *European Review of Latin American and Caribbean Studies* 112 (2021): 117–36.

18. Luz Cecilia Andrade Reyes, "El Bajío: El ejido de Sonora que resiste contra la mina de oro de Baillères," *Corriente Alterna*, January 11, 2022, https://corrientealterna.unam.mx/territorios/el-bajio-el-ejido-de-sonora-que-resiste-contra-la-mina-de-oro-de-bailleres.

19. De Castro and Mendoza, *Absolute Restoration of All Things.*

20. James Young, "The Counter-Monument: Memory against Itself in Germany Today," *Critical Inquiry* 18, no. 2 (1992): 277–81.

21. Kripa, Marullo, and Mueller, "Conversation with Gonzalo Pimentel," 429.

22. Ibid.

23. Ibid.

24. Chen Jie, "Death of the Desert," *China Dialogue*, July 14, 2015, https://chinadialogue.net/en/pollution/8015-death-of-the-desert.

25. "Untreated Waste Water Dumped by Chemical Plants into Tengger Desert, Inner Mongolia-Ningxia-Gansu, China," *Global Atlas of Environmental Justice*, last modified May 2, 2022, https://ejatlas.org/print/1-untreated-waste-water-dumped-by-chemical-plants-in-tengger-desert-inner-mongoliachina.

26. Ian Hamel, "Labbas Sbaï, le chirurgien suisse qui voulait faire reverdir le désert marocain," *Swissinfo*, June 27, 2022, www.swissinfo.ch/fre/economie/labbas-sba%c3%af-le-chirurgien-suisse-qui-voulait-faire-reverdir-le-d%c3%a9sert-marocain/47688324.

27. Ibid.

28. Ibid.

29. Daraa Tribes, "Daraa Tribes Perform Arabic Music at Liverpool Arab Arts Festival," posted September 9, 2020, by Liverpool Arab Arts Festival, YouTube, 4 min., 58 sec., www.youtube.com/watch?v = yFcvbp2rsbU&t = 607s.

30. Michel Roux, *Le désert de sable: Le Sahara dans l'imaginaire des français (1900–1994)* (Paris: L'Harmattan, 1996), 7.

BIBLIOGRAPHY

Abdeljalil. "L'activité économique du Sahara dans le Maghreb." *Perspectives sahariennes* 1 (1958): 22–23.

Abdel-Jaouad, Hedi. "Isabelle Eberhardt: Portrait of the Artist as a Young Nomad." *Yale French Studies* 93 (1993): 93–117.

Aboudi, Abdelkadhem. "al-Tajārib al-nawawiyya al-faransiyya wa-makhāṭir al-talawwuth al-ish'ā'ī 'alā al-ṣiḥḥa wa-al-bīy'a fī al-madā al-qarīb wa-al-ba'īd." *Al-Maṣādir* 1, no. 1 (1999): 250–314.

Académie des sciences coloniales. *Annales*. Vol. 4. Paris: Société d'Éditions Géographiques, Maritimes et Coloniales, 1929.

———. *Comptes-rendus des séances: Communications, 1922–1923*. Paris: Société d'Éditions Géographiques, Maritimes et Coloniales, 1924.

Académie des sciences d'outre-mer. "Lehuraux Léon." https://academieoutremer.fr/academiciens/?aId=799.

Achi, Rabeh. "1905: Quand l'islam était (déjà) la seconde religion de France." *Multitudes* 59, no. 2 (2015): 45–52.

Adamafio, Tawia. *French Nuclear Tests in the Sahara*. Accra: CPP National Headquarters Bureau of Information and Publicity, 1960.

Adams, Charles Hansford. *The Narrative of Robert Adams: A Barbary Captive*. New York: Cambridge University Press, 2010.

Africanus, Leo. *The History and Description of Africa: And of the Notable Things Therein Contained*. Translated by Robert Brown and John Pory. London: Printed for the Hakluyt Society, 1896.

Ageron, Charles-Robert. "L'Algérie dernière chance de la puissance française: Étude d'un mythe politique (1954–1962)." *Relations internationales* 57 (1989): 113–39.

Ailleret, Charles. *L'aventure atomique française*. Paris: Grasset, 1958.

Akkad, Dania. "Neom: Saudi Arabia Sentences Tribesmen to Death for Resisting Displacement." *Middle East Eye*, October 7, 2022. www.middleeasteye.net/news/neom-saudi-arabia-sentences-tribesmen-death-resisting-displacement.

Akkad, Dania, and Rayhan Uddin. "Neom: Saudi Arabia Jails Tribesmen for 50 Years for Rejecting Displacement." *Middle East Eye*, September 13, 2022. www

.middleeasteye.net/news/saudi-arabia-neom-tribesmen-imprisoned-rejecting-displacement.

Al Ansari, Omar. *Ṭabīb tinbuktū*. Beirut: al-Mu'assasah al-ʿArabīyya lil-Dirāsāt wa-al-Nashr, 2011.

AlArabiya. "al-Amīr muḥammad bin salman: Al-Sharq al-awsaṭ sayakūn ūrūppā al-jadīda." *YouTube*, October 24, 2018, video, 1:27. www.youtube.com/watch?v=wZxDddQ8isg.

Alestiklal. "al-Ḥwīṭāt..sukkan aṣliyyūn sāhamū bi-ta'sīs al-sa'ūdiyya fabanat 'neom' ʿalā ashlā'ihim." 2023. www.alestiklal.net/ar/article/dep-news-1663890731.

Allan, Joanna. *Saharan Winds: Energy Systems and Aeolian Imaginaries in Western Sahara*. Morgantown: West Virginia University Press, 2024.

Allen, Roger. *The Arabic Literary Heritage*. Cambridge: Cambridge University Press, 2005.

Allix, André. "Sahara et pétrole 1957." *Revue de géographie de Lyon* 32, no. 4 (1957): 269–76.

Alloula, Malek. *The Colonial Harem*. Translated by Myrna Godzich and Wlad Godzich. Minneapolis: University of Minnesota Press, 1986.

Alqassab. Mirza H. *Life after Oil: The Survival Predicament of the Gulf Arab States*. Leicestershire: Matador, 2020.

Alqst for Human Rights. "The Dark Side of Neom: Expropriation, Expulsion, and Prosecution of the Region's Inhabitants." *Alqst*, February 2023, https://alqst.org/uploads/the-dark-side-of-neom-expropriation-expulsion-and-prosecution-en.pdf.

Alqst for Human Rights, et al. "Open Letter from NGOs Calling on Companies Involved in Saudi Arabia's NEOM Project to Condemn Human Rights Violations Accompanying It." Alqst, June 2, 2020. www.alqst.org/ar/posts/431.

AlShehabi, Omar. "al-Bīy'a wa mudun al-khalīj al-nafṭiyya." In *Al-Bīy'a fī al-khalīj*, edited by Hamad al-Reyes, Safia Ajlan, and Omar AlShehabi, 16–51. Kuwait: Markaz al-Khalīj li-Siyāsāt al-Tanmiyya, 2021.

———. "Taṣdīr al-tharwa wa-ightirāb al-insān: Tārīkh al-khalal al-intājī fī buldān al-khalīj al- ʿarabiyya." *Al-Mustaqbal al-ʿArabī* 475 (2018): 11–28.

Alyaoum24. "Maḥaṭṭat 'nūr' warzāzāt .. al-ṭāqa al-shamsiyya ʿalā ḥisāb al-mā' wa-al-filāḥa." https://alyaoum24.com/1343063.html.

Amāhīn al-Shāwī, Allalāh al-Bakkāy. *al-Ṭawāriq ʿabra al-ʿuṣūr*. Benghazi: Dār al-Kutub al-Waṭaniyya, 2000.

Ambassade de France. *France's First Atomic Explosion*. New York: Service de presse et d'information, 1960.

Amiard, Jean-Claude. *Military Nuclear Accidents: Environmental, Ecological, Health, and Socio-Economic Consequences*. Newark: John Wiley, 2019.

Les Amis du Sahara. *Les Amis du Sahara: Organe de l'association 'Les Amis du Sahara': Bulletin trimestriel*, 1932.

Andrade Reyes, Luz Cecilia. "El Bajío: El Ejido de Sonora que resiste contra la mina de oro de Baillères." *Corriente Alterna*, January 11, 2022. https://corrientealterna

.unam.mx/territorios/el-bajio-el-ejido-de-sonora-que-resiste-contra-la-mina-de-oro-de-bailleres.

Anṣārī, Balqīs al-. "Mā bayna al-wujūd wa-al-ʿadam: Baytun fī al-dunyā, baytun fī al-ḥanīn." *Mana*, March 7, 2024. https://mana.net/al-koni.

Arberry, Arthur. *The Koran Interpreted*. London: George Allen and Unwin, 1955.

Armand, Louis. "France et Afrique à l'ère des grandes entreprises." *Hommes et mondes* 120 (July 1956): 475–85.

———. "Pourquoi un ensemble industriel au Sahara?" *Revue économique franco-suisse* 33 (1953): 281–85.

———. *Le Sahara: L'Afrique et l'Europe, conférence prononcée le vendredi 12 février 1955*. Lyon: publisher unknown, 1955.

———. "Les techniques à la conquête économique des déserts." In *Le Sahara français*, edited by Jean Charbonneau, 274–87. Paris: Cahiers Charles de Foucauld, 1955.

———. "Vers un Sahara moderne." *Hommes et mondes* 99 (October 1954): 321–33.

Armstrong, Tim. "Slavery, Insurance, and Sacrifice in the Black Atlantic." In *Sea Changes: Historicizing the Ocean*, edited by Bernhard Klein and Gesa Mackenthun, 167–85. New York: Routledge, 2004.

Asian-African Legal Consultative Committee. *Report of the Session*. Vol. 6. New Delhi: Secretariat of the Asian-African Legal Consultative Committee, 1964.

Atkins, William. *The Immeasurable World: A Desert Journey*. New York: Anchor Books, 2018.

Aurousseau, Patrick. "Le regard porté sur les prostituées en Algérie, un modèle de domination occidental? L'exemple de l'apparition des 'Ouled-Naïl' chez Fromentin, Maupassant et Gide." *Viattica* 5 (2018): 2–16.

Austen, Ralph. *Trans-Saharan Africa in World History*. New York: Oxford University Press, 2010.

Bakrāwī, Muḥammad al-Mahdī, and Bin ʿImrān Inṣāf, "al-Buʿd al-qānūnī li-al-āthār al-ṣiḥiḥhiya wa-al-bīyʾiyya li-al-tajārib al-nawawiyya al-faransiyya fī al-ṣaḥrāʾ al-jazāʾiriyya min manẓūr al-qānūn al-dawlī al-insānī." *Darātir al-Siyyāsa wa-al-Qānūn* 8 (2013): 18–28.

Balkan, Stacey, and Swaralipi Nandi, eds. *Oil Fictions: World Literature and Our Contemporary Petrosphere*. University Park: Pennsylvania State University Press, 2021.

Ballard, Barclay. "The Unexpected Environmental Drawbacks of Concentrated Solar Power Plants." *The New Economy*, June 12, 2019. www.theneweconomy.com/energy/the-unexpected-environmental-drawbacks-of-concentrated-solar-power-plants.

Banham, Reyner. *Scenes in America Deserta*. Salt Lake City: Gibbs M. Smith, 1982.

Barrillot, Bruno. *Le complexe nucléair: Des liens entre l'atome civil et l'atome militaire*. Lyon: Centre de documentation et de recherche sur la paix et les conflits, 2005.

———. *Les déchets nucléaires militaires français*. Lyon: Centre de documentation et de recherche sur la paix, 1994.

———. *Les essais nucléaires français 1960–1996: Conséquences sur l'environnement et la santé*. Lyon: Centre de documentation et de recherche sur la paix et les conflits, 1996.
———. *Les irradiés de la république: Les victimes des essais nucléaires français prennent la parole*. Lyon: Observatoire des armes nucléaires françaises, 2003.
Barucand, Louis. *Un siècle de l'église de France 1800–1900*. Paris: Librairie Ch. Poussielgue, 1902.
Bataille, Christian. "Rapport n°179—L'évaluation de la recherche sur la gestion des déchets nucléaires à haute activité—Tome II: Les déchets militaires." Office parlementaire d'évaluation des choix scientifiques et technologiques, 1997–98. www.senat.fr/rap/o97-179/o97-179_mono.html.
Bataille, Christian, and Henri Revol. "Rapport sur les incidences environnementales et sanitaires des essais nucléaires effectués par la France entre 1960 et 1996 et éléments de comparaison avec les essaies des autres puissances nucléaires." Office parlementaire d'évaluation des choix scientifiques et technologiques, 2001–2. www.senat.fr/rap/r01-207/r01-2071.pdf.
Bauman, Zygmunt. "From Pilgrims to Tourists, or a Short History of Identity." In *Questions of Cultural Identity*, edited by Stuart Hall and Paul du Gay, 18–36. London: Sage, 1996.
Baunard, Louis. *Le cardinal Lavigerie*. 2 vols. Paris: J. de Gigord, 1922.
Bāz, al-Ṭayyib al-. "al-Muqāwamāt al-shaʿbiyya al-maḥalliyya li-awlād nāyl wa-mawqifuhā min muqāwamat al-amīr ʿabd al-qādir: Mūsa al-darqāwī namūdhajan." *Majllat Ḥaqāʾiq al-Dirāsāt al-Nafsiyya wa-al-Ijtimāʿiyya* 3, no. 10 (2018): 388–94.
Bazin, René. *Charles de Foucauld: Explorateur du Maroc, ermite au Sahara*. Paris: Librairie Plon, 1921.
Baziyyān, Saʿdī. *Jarāʾim faransā fī al-jazāʾir min al-jinirāl būjū ilā al-jinirāl usārīs*. Algiers: Dār Huma, 2005.
BBC. "Mauritania Tests Drones for Desert Locust Combat." January 10, 2020. www.bbc.com/news/blogs-news-from-elsewhere-51065480.
Bedu, Jean-Jacques. *Moi, empereur du Sahara*. Paris: Albin Michel, 2014.
Beeson, Mark. "The Coming of Environmental Authoritarianism." *Environmental Politics* 19, no. 2 (2010): 276–94.
Belaroussi, Abdelfatah. "al-Āthār al-ṣiḥḥiyya li-al-jarāʾim al-nawawiyya al-faransiyya fī rqqān." *Majallat Āfāq ʿIlimiyya* 14, no. 1 (2022): 208–25.
Belhaddad, Noureddine. "Muqāwamat qabāʾil al-ṣaḥrāʾ li-al-istiʿmār al-faransī-al-isppānī (1912–1934)." In *Al-Ṣaḥrāʾ wa sūs min khilāl al-wathāʾiq wa-al-makhṭuṭāt: al-tawāṣul wa-al-ʾāfāq*, edited by ʿUmar Affā, 123–37. Rabat: Manshūrāt Kulliyyat al-ʾĀdāb wa-al-ʿUlūm al-Insāniyya, 2002.
Bélime, Émile. "Avenir de l'Union française." *Hommes et mondes* 14, no. 58 (May 1951): 672–88.
———. *Gardons l'Afrique*. Paris: Nouvelles Éditions Latines, 1955.
Bendjebbar, André. *Histoire secrète de la bombe atomique française*. Paris: Le Cherche Midi Éditeur, 2000.

Benmalek, Samir. "Sur les traces d'André Gide: Séjour d'un écrivain australien en Algérie." *Liberté*, March 26, 2006. www.djazairess.com/fr/liberte/54826.

Bennabi , Malek. *al-Ẓāhira al-qurʾāniyya*. Translated by Abdelṣabūr Shāhin. Beirut: Dār al-Fikr, 2000.

Berry, John A. "Force de frappe." *Military Review: Professional Journal of the US Army* (November 1967): 70–78.

Bertrand, Louis. "Comment je suis revenu au catholicisme." In *Les témoins du renouveau catholique*, edited by Thomas Mainage, 119–54. Paris: Gabriel Beauchesne, 1919.

Biays, Michel. "L'avenir économique du Sahara." *Les cahiers économiques* (August–September 1952): 16–26.

Bilbukhārī, Nāṣir. "al-Tajārib al-nawawiyya al-fanransiyya fī rqqān." *Majallat al-Badr* 2, no. 2 (2010): 22–24.

Billaud, Pierre. *La grande aventure du nucléaire militaire français: Des acteurs témoignent*. Paris: L'Harmattan, 2016.

Bin Salman, Mohammed. "HRH Crown Prince Mohammed bin Salman Announces Designs for THE LINE, the City of the Future in Neom." Neom, July 25, 2022. www.neom.com/en-us/newsroom/hrh-announces-theline-designs.

Birābiḥ, Muḥammad al-Sheikh. "Namādhij min muqāwamāt Awlād Nāyl li-al-tawssuʿ al-faransī fī al-hiḍāb al-wusṭā (1849–1854)." *Qaḍāyā Tārikhiyya* 3, no. 1 (2018): 147–66.

Bischoff, Matt. *Preparing for Combat Overseas: Patton's Desert Training Center*. Monterey, CA: Lulu.com, 2016.

Bissuel, Henri. *Le Sahara français: Conférence sur les questions sahariennes*. Algiers: Adolphe Jourdan, libraire-éditeur, 1891.

Bodington, Nicolas. *The Awakening Sahara*. London: Andre Deutsch, 1961.

Boisboissel, Yves de. "L'exploration et la pacification du Sahara." In *Le Sahara français*, edited by Jean Charbonneau, 131–60. Paris: Cahiers Charles de Foucauld, 1955.

Bollenot, Vincent. "1887. Le code de l'indigénat algérien est généralisé à toutes les colonies françaises." *Encyclopédie d'histoire numérique de l'Europe*, April 16, 2023. https://ehne.fr/fr/eduscol/premi%C3%A8re-g%C3%A9n%C3%A9rale/la-troisi%C3%A8me-r%C3%A9publique-avant-1914-un-r%C3%A9gime-politique-un-empire-colonial/m%C3%A9tropole-et-colonies/1887-le-code-de-l%27indig%C3%A9nat-alg%C3%A9rien-est-g%C3%A9n%C3%A9ralis%C3%A9-%C3%A0-toutes-les-colonies-fran%C3%A7aises.

Bonardi, Pierre. *Ouled-Naïl et méharistes*. Paris: Les Éditions de France, 1936.

Boniface, Esprit Victor Élisabeth, comte de Castellane, ed. *Campagnes de Crimée, d'Italie, d'Afrique, de Chine et de Syrie, 1849–1862, lettres addressées au Maréchal de Castellane par les Maréchaux Baraguey d'Hilliers et al.* Paris: Librairies Plon, 1898.

Bouillet, J. "L'ère atomique se lève sur les oasis." *Perspectives sahariennes* 4 (1958): 155–57.

Boum, Aomar, and Berber Najib. *Undesirables: A Holocaust Journey to North Africa*. Stanford, CA: Stanford University Press, 2023.

Bourgeot, André. "Sahara: Espace géostratégique et enjeux politiques (Niger)." *Naqd* 3, no. 1 (2014): 153–92.
Bourjoul, Maurice. "Sahara 1956: Mythe et réalités." *Economie et politique* 27 (1956): 55–68.
Boussaid, Ahmed. "Ihtimāmātu al-farnsiyyīna bistikshāfi iqlīm tanzrūft 1900–1962." *Mjallat al-Sāwra li-al-Dirāsāt al-Insāniyya wa-al-Ijtimāʿiyya* 2, no. 8 (2022): 113–37.
Boustead, J. E. H. "The Camel Corps of the Sudan Defence Force." *Royal United Services Institution Journal* (1934): 547–57.
Bowles, Paul. *The Sheltering Sky*. New York: Paladin, 1949.
Boyce, William D. *Illustrated Africa: North, Tropical, South*. New York: Rand, McNally, 1925.
Britsch, Jacques. *Perspectives sahariennes*. Paris: Charles-Lavauzelle, 1956.
Brodeur, Michael, and Banning Liebscher. *Revival Culture: Prepare for the Next Great Awakening*. Bloomington, IN: Baker, 2012.
Brower, Benjamin. *A Desert Named Peace: The Violence of France's Empire in the Algerian Sahara, 1844–1902*. New York: Columbia University Press, 2009.
Būderbala, al-Ṭayyib. "Ṣurāt al-jazāʾir fī al-riwāya al-faransiyya." *Majallat ʿUlūm al-Lugha al-ʿArabiyya wa-Ādābuhā* 2, no. 2 (2010): 6–19.
Bulletin de la Société Botanique de France. "Séance du 13 novembre 1931." *Bulletin de la Société Botanique de France* 78, no. 5 (1931): 657–59.
Burke, Edmund. *The Writings and Speeches of Edmund Burke*. Vol. 1. Edited by Paul Langford and William Burton Todd. Oxford: Oxford University Press, 1997.
Burning Man Project. "The 10 Principles of Burning Man." https://burningman.org/about/10-principles.
Caillié, René. *Journal d'un voyage à Temboctou et à Jenné dans l'Afrique centrale précédé d'observations faites chez les Maures Braknas, les Nalous et d'autres peuples; pendant les années 1824, 1825, 1826, 1827, 1828*. Paris: Imprimerie Royale, 1830.
———. *Travels through Central Africa to Timbuctoo and across the Great Desert, to Morocco, Performed in the Years 1824–1828*. Vol. 1. London: Henry Colburn and Richard Bentley, 1830.
Camille, Guy. "La mise en valeur des colonies françaises." *Annales de géographie* 32, no. 177 (1923): 265–71.
Campbell, Zack. "Swarms of Drones, Piloted by Artificial Intelligence, May Soon Patrol Europe's Borders." *The Intercept*, May 11, 2019. https://theintercept.com/2019/05/11/drones-artificial-intelligence-europe-roborder.
Capot-Rey, Robert. "Le Bureau industriel africain et les recherches minières au Sahara." *Annales de géographie* 64, no. 344 (1955): 296–97.
Carayol, Rémi, and Gagnol, Laurent. "Ces murs de sable qui surgissent au Sahara." *Le Monde diplomatique*, October 2021. www.monde-diplomatique.fr/2021/10/CARAYOL/63629.
Carretto, Carlo. *Letters from the Desert*. New York: Orbis Books, 1972.
———. *Letters from the Desert*. Translated by Rose M. Hancock. Maryknoll, NY: Orbis Books, 2002.

Carrouges, Michel. *Charles de Foucauld: Explorateur mystique.* Paris: Les éditions du Cerf, 1954.
Casajus, Dominique. *Charles de Foucauld: Moine et savant.* Paris: Éditions du CNRS, 2009.
———. "Henri Duveyrier et le désert des Saint-Simoniens." *Ethnologies comparées* 7 (2004): 5–11.
———. *Henri Duveyrier: Un saint-simonien au désert.* Paris: Ibis Press, 2007.
Castex, Louis. "Sahara, terre promise." *Revue des deux mondes* (July 15, 1953): 201–13.
Castries, Henry de. *Agents et voyageurs français au Maroc, 1530–1660.* Paris: Ernest Leroux, 1911.
———. *Les sources inédites de l'histoire du Maroc de 1530 à 1845.* Paris: Ernest Leroux, 1905.
Cauvin Verner, Corinne. "Le tourisme sexuel vu du Sahara marocain: Une économie de razzia?" *L'année du Maghreb* 6 (2010): 47–77. http://journals.openedition.org/anneemaghreb/807.
Chanton, Christine. *Les vétérans des essais nucléaires français au Sahara.* Paris: L'Harmattan, 2006.
Chappell, Bill. "A 105-Mile-Long City Will Snake through the Saudi Desert: Is That a Good Idea?" NPR, July 26, 2022. www.npr.org/2022/07/26/1113670047/saudi-arabia-new-city-the-mirror-line-desert.
Charbonneau, Jean, ed. *Le Sahara français.* France: Cahiers Charles de Foucauld, 1955.
Chauvin, Charles. *Charles de Foucauld par lui-même et ses héritiers.* Paris: Mediaspaul Éditions, 2010.
Chevalier, Jacques. "Histoire de la DAM." In Pierre Billaud, *La grande aventure du nucléaire militaire français: Des acteurs témoignent*, 387–403. Paris: L'Harmattan, 2016.
Chevalier, Louis, "L'industrialisation de l'Afrique du nord." *Population* (1949): 763–65.
Chotard, Henry. *La mer intérieure du Sahara.* Clermont-Ferrand: Typographie et lithographie G. Mont-Louis, 1876.
Chulov, Martin. "'Night of the Beating': Details Emerge of Riyadh Ritz-Carlton Purge." *The Guardian*, November 19, 2020. www.theguardian.com/world/2020/nov/19/saudi-accounts-emerge-of-ritz-carlton-night-of-the-beating.
Churchill, Ward, and Winona LaDuke. "Native North America: The Political Economy of Radioactive Colonialism." In *The State of Native America: Genocide, Colonization, and Resistance*, edited by Annette Jaimes, 241–66. Boston, MA: South End Press, 1992.
Clancy-Smith, Julia. "Islam, Gender, and Identities in the Making of French Algeria, 1830–1962." In *Domesticating the Empire: Race, Gender, and Family Life in French and Dutch Colonialism*, edited by Julia Clancy-Smith and Frances Gouda, 154–74. Charlottesville: University Press of Virginia, 1998.
———. *Rebel and Saint: Muslim Notables, Populist Protest, Colonial Encounters (Algeria and Tunisia, 1800–1904).* Berkeley: University of California Press, 1994.

Clarke, Robert. "The Idea of Celebrity Colonialism." In *Celebrity Colonialism: Fame, Power, and Representation in Colonial and Postcolonial Cultures*, edited by Robert Clarke, 1–10. Newcastle upon Tyne: Cambridge Scholars, 2009.

Claudel, Paul. "Ma Conversion." In *Les témoins du renouveau catholique*, edited by Thomas Mainage, 63–71. Paris: Gabriel Beauchesne, 1919.

Claudot-Hawad, Hélène. "La 'Question touarègue': Quels enjeux?" In *La guerre au Mali: Comprendre la crise au Sahel et au Sahara; Enjeux et zones d'ombre*, edited by Michel Galy, 125–47. Paris: La Découverte, 2013.

Clermont, Anne. "Comment est-on passé de l'ère des utopistes à l'ère des organisateurs?" *La Nef* (January–March 1960):17-24.

Colley, Charles C. "The Desert Shall Blossom: North African Influence on the American Southwest." *Western Historical Quarterly* 14, no. 3 (1983): 277–90.

Collin, Jean-Marie, and Patrice Bouveret. *The Waste from French Nuclear Tests in Algeria, Radioactivity under the Sand: Analysis with Regard to the Treaty on the Prohibition of Nuclear Weapons*. Berlin: Heinrich Böll Foundation, 2020.

Cooper, Allan D. *The Geography of Genocide*. Boulder, CO: University Press of America, 2009.

Copley, Antony. *Sexual Moralities in France, 1780–1980: New Ideas on the Family, Divorce, and Homosexuality; An Essay on Moral Change*. New York: Routledge, 1989.

Corder, Gille. "Faut-il écarter les étranger de l'exploitation des richesses sahariennes?" In *Le Sahara en questions*, 51–58. Paris: Julliard, 1960.

Cornet, Pierre. *Sahara: Terre de demain*. Paris: Nouvelles Éditions Latines, 1956.

Courageot, Sophie. "Les poussières de sable du Sahara étaient porteuses de Césium-137, résidu d'anciens essais nucléaires français." *France Info*, last modified February 28, 2021. https://france3-regions.francetvinfo.fr/bourgogne-franche-comte/jura/les-poussieres-de-sable-du-sahara-etaient-porteuses-de-cesium-137-residu-d-anciens-essais-nucleaires-francais-1973641.html.

Crewe, Quentin. *In Search of the Sahara*. London: Michael Joseph, 1983.

Cunningham, Erin. "Saudi Crown Prince Wants You Talking about His 'City of the Future.'" *The Washington Post*, July 28, 2022. www.washingtonpost.com/world/2022/07/28/neom-te-line-city-saudi-arabia-mbs-khashoggi-europe.

Curtiz, Michael, dir. *Casablanca*. Warner Bros., 1943. 102 minutes.

Dailymotion. "Essais chimiques en Algérie." Posted October 25, 2010. www.dailymotion.com/video/xfdvt4.

Daraa Tribes. "Daraa Tribes Perform Arabic Music at Liverpool Arab Arts Festival." Posted September 9, 2020, by Liverpool Arab Arts Festival. *YouTube*, 4 min., 58 sec. www.youtube.com/watch?v=yFcvbp2rsbU&t=607s.

Davis, Diana K. *The Arid Lands: History, Power, Knowledge*. Boston: MIT, 2016.

Davis, Muriam Haleh. *Markets of Civilization: Islam and Racial Capitalism in Algeria*. Durham, NC: Duke University Press, 2022.

Dawwās, Ḥasan. "Ṣūrat al-mujtamaʿ al-ṣaḥrāwī al-jazāʾirī fī al-qarn al-tāsiʿ ʿashar min khilāl kitābāt al-raḥḥāla al-faransiyyīn: Muqāraba sūsiūtaqāfiyya." Master's thesis, Mentouri University of Constantine, 2008.

De León, Jason. *The Land of Open Graves: Living and Dying on the Migrant Trail.* Oakland: University of California Press, 2015.

Deleuze, Gilles, and Félix Guattari. *A Thousand Plateaus: Capitalism and Schizophrenia.* Translated by Brian Massumi. Minneapolis: University of Minnesota Press, 1987.

Delisle, Philippe. *Bande dessinée franco-belge et imaginaire colonial: Des années 1930 aux années 1980.* Paris: L'Harmattan, 2016.

Demanche, George. "Occupation d'In Salah." *Revue française de l'étranger et des colonies* 254 (1900): 69–78.

Derrécagaix, Victor Bernard. *Le Maréchal Pélissier, duc de Malakoff.* Paris: Librairie Militaire R. Chapelot, 1911.

Dessaix, Robert. *Arabesques: A Tale of Double Lives.* Sydney: Pan Macmillan, 2009.

d'Eu, Clément-Célestin. *In-Salah et le Tidikelt: Journal des opérations.* Paris: Librairie Militaire R. Chapelot, 1902.

Devlin, Kate. *Turned On: Science, Sex, and Robots.* London: Bloomsbury, 2018.

Dewavrin, Maurice, and Paul Delibert. *Comment mettre en valeur notre domaine colonial.* Paris: Marcel Rivière, 1920.

Didier, Hugues. "Charles de Foucauld." *Clio,* May 2002. www.clio.fr/bibliotheque/bibliothequeenligne/charles_de_foucauld.php?letter=A.

Direction des applications militaires. *La Direction des applications militaires (CEA/DAM): Au coeur de la dissuasion nucléaire française.* CEA/DAM, 2025. www.cea.fr/presse/Documents/actualites/direction-applications-militaires-cea-dissuasion-nucleaire-france.pdf.

Dogan, Ali. "Saudi Arabia's Neom Diplomacy." Carnegie Endowment for International Peace, March 3, 2021. https://carnegieendowment.org/sada/83975.

Doherty, Brian. *This is Burning Man: Oil, Gas, and Crime.* New York: Little Brown, 2007.

Dollimore, Jonathan. *Sexual Dissidence: Augustine to Wilde, Freud to Foucault.* Oxford: Clarendon Press, 1991.

Donnelly, Patrick. "Solar Sacrifice Zones: Who Decides?" *Desert Report,* July 17, 2015. https://desertreport.org/solar-sacrifice-zones-who-decides.

Dorrey, Francis, and Georges Lambert. "Quels problèmes humains se posent dans le Sahara moderne?" *La Nef* (1960): 35–43.

Dorsey Mohun, Richard. "The Scramble for the Upper Nile." *The Century Illustrated Monthly Magazine* 56, no. 1 (1898): 59–61.

Ducarre, Charles. "Sahara Test Center." *Flight,* February 13, 1959.

Dugas, Guy. "André Gide en Algérie: Les écrivains d'Algérie face à la morale gidienne." *Bulletin des Amis d'André Gide* 22, no. 102 (1994): 249–68.

Duquesne, Jacques. *Histoires vraies: Une vie de journaliste.* Paris: Albin Michel, 2016.

Duveyrier, Henri. "Rapport sur le voyage de M. le Vicomte Charles de Foucauld au Maroc, fait à la Société de géographie de Paris." In Charles de Foucauld, *Reconnaissance au Maroc: Journal de route,* 11–21. Paris: Société d'Éditions Géographiques, Maritimes et Coloniales, 1939.

———. *Les Touareg du nord: Exploration du Sahara*. Paris: Challamel Ainé, 1864.

Eberhardt, Isabelle. *In the Shadow of Islam*. Translated by Sharon Bangert. London: Peter Owen, 1993.

Edwards, Brian. *Morocco Bound: Disorienting America's Maghreb, from Casablanca to the Marrakesh Express*. Durham, NC: Duke University Press, 2005.

El Guabli, Brahim. "Desert Futures Collective: A Conversation with Brahim El Guabli, Jill Jarvis, and Francisco E. Robles." In *Deserts Are Not Empty*, edited by Samia Henni, 25–48. New York: Columbia University Press, 2022.

———. "Entretien avec Hawad: 'Nous sommes des cadavres, et pire, des cadavres invisibles.'" *Expressions maghrébines* 23, no. 1 (2024): 107–16.

———. *Moroccan Other-Archives: History and Citizenship after State Violence*. New York: Fordham University Press, 2023.

———. "Saharanism in the Sonoran." *The Avery Review* 58 (2022): 1–11.

Ellul, Jacques. *The Technological Society*. Translated by John Wilkinson. Paris: Vintage Books, 1964.

Emirit, Marcel. "Le problème de la conversion des musulmans d'Algérie sous le Second Empire: Le conflit entre MacMahon et Lavigerie." *Revue historique* 223, no. 1 (1960): 63–84.

Endres, Danielle. *Nuclear Decolonization: Indigenous Resistance to High-Level Nuclear Waste*. Columbus: The Ohio State University Press, 2023.

———. "The Rhetoric of Nuclear Colonialism: Rhetorical Exclusion of American Indian Arguments in the Yucca Mountain Nuclear Waste Siting Decision." *Communication and Critical/Cultural Studies* 6, no. 1 (2009): 39–60.

Entreprise. "Ne trahissons pas le Sahara." May 1957.

Escoube, Pierre. "Eirik Labonne: Diplomate hors-série." *Revue des deux mondes* (1971): 739–41.

Estienne, Georges. "Les communications transsahariennes." *Renseignements coloniaux et documents* 2 (1923): 37–42.

Faḍīla, Rābiḥī. "al-Tajārib al-nawawiyya al-faransiyya fī al-ṣaḥrāʾ al-jazāʾiriyya 1960–1966 wa-inʿikāsātuha." Master's thesis, University of Biskra, 2013. http://archives.univ-biskra.dz/bitstream/123456789/3363/1/71.pdf.

Fanon, Frantz. *Les damnés de la terre*. Paris: La Découverte, 2002.

Fassi, Allal al-. "Presentation." *Perspectives sahariennes* 1 (June 1958): 4.

Faulk, Odie B. *The US Camel Corps: An Army Experiment*. Oxford: Oxford University Press, 1976.

Favrod, Charles-Henri. *Le poids de l'Afrique*. Paris: Éditions du Seuil, 1958.

Federation of Nigeria. *Nuclear Tests in the Sahara: Report by the Joint United Kingdom–Nigerian Scientific Committee on the Monitoring of Radioactivity 9*. Lagos: Federal Government Printer, 1960.

Fehner, Terrence R., and F. G. Gosling. *Battlefield of the Cold War: The Nevada Test Site, Atmospheric Nuclear Weapons Testing 1951–1963*. Vol. 1. Washington, DC: US Department of Energy, 2006.

———. *Origins of the Nevada Test Site*. Washington, DC: US Department of Energy, 2000.

Felbab-Brown, Vanda. "The Wall: The Real Cost of a Barrier between the United States and Mexico." Brookings.edu, August 2017. www.brookings.edu/articles/the-wall-the-real-costs-of-a-barrier-between-the-united-states-and-mexico.

Ferhati, Barkahoum. "La danseuse prostituée dite 'Ouled Naïl,' entre mythe et réalité (1830–1962): Des rapports sociaux et des pratiques concrètes." *Clio* 17 (2003): 101–13. https://doi.org/10.4000/clio.584.

Fernández de Castro, Miguel, and Natalia Mendoza. *The Absolute Restoration of All Things*. Storefront for Art and Architecture, 2022. Video installation and sculpture. https://storefront.nyc/program/the-absolute-restoration-of-all-things.

Fisher Allan, George Barnard, and Humphrey J. Fisher. *Slavery and Muslim Society in Africa: The Institution in Saharan and Sudanic Africa, and the Trans-Saharan Trade*. London: Hurst, 1970.

Fletcher Allen, Edgar. *A Wayfarer in North Africa: Tunisia and Algeria*. Methuen, 1931.

Fock, A. "Réponse à M. Émile Broussais—de Paris au Soudan central." In Georges Rolland, *Le transsaharien: Un an après*, 101–27. Paris: Austin Challamel, 1891.

Foucauld, Charles de. *Charles de Foucauld intime*. Edited by Georges Gorrée. Paris: La Colombe, Éditions du Vieux Colombier, 1951.

———. "Lettre du bienheureux Charles de Foucauld à René Bazin de l'Académie française, le 29 juillet 1916." *Bulletin du Bureau catholique de presse* 5 (1917). https://archive.org/download/charles-de-foucauld-_-lettre-a-rene-bazin/Charles_de_Foucauld_-_Lettre_a_Rene_Bazin.pdf.

———. *Lettres à Henry de Castries*. Edited by Jacques de Dampierre. Paris: Éditions Bernard Grasset, 1938.

———. *Lettres et carnets*. Paris: Éditions du Seuil, 1966.

———. *Reconnaissance au Maroc, 1883–1884*. Paris: Challamel, 1888.

Foucauld, Charles de, and Abbé Huvelin. *Charles de Foucauld—Abbé Huvelin: 20 ans de correspondance entre Charles de Foucauld et son directeur spiritual (1890–1910)*. Edited by Jean-François Six and Brigitte Cuisinier. Paris: Nouvelle Cite, 2010.

Foucauld, Charles de, and Henri Laperrine. *Lettres inédites au général Laperrine pacificateur du Sahara*. Paris: La Colombe, 1954.

Foucauld, Charles de, and Louis Massignon. *L'aventure de l'amour de Dieu: 80 lettres inédites de Charles de Foucauld à Louis Massignon*. Edited by Jean François Six. Paris: Le Seuil, 1993.

Foucault, Michel. "Of Other Spaces." Translated by Jay Miskowiec. *Diacritics* 16, no. 1 (1986): 22–27.

Fountain, Henry. "The Salton Sea, an Accident of History, Faces a New Water Crisis." *The New York Times*, February 25, 2023. www.nytimes.com/2023/02/25/climate/salton-sea-colorado-river-drought-crisis.html.

Foureau, Fernand. *Documents scientifiques de la Mission saharienne*. Paris: Publication de la Société de Géographie, 1905.

Fournier, Paul. "La biographie de Charles de Foucauld par René Bazin dans les journaux et les revues au début des années 20." In *Charles de Foucauld: Amitiés croisées*, edited by Josette Fournier, 193–65. Le Coudray-Macouard: Cheminements, 2007.

Framke, Caroline. "Westworld's Boring Orgy Reminds Us that Joyless Sex Has Become HBO's Specialty." *Vox*, October 31, 2016. www.vox.com/culture/2016/10/31/13477222/westworld-orgy-contrapasso.

France, Hector. *Musk, Hashish, and Blood*. New York: Avon, 1951.

Franceinfo. "Sahara: Des déchets radioactifs français enfouis sous le sable." December 4, 2020. www.francetvinfo.fr/monde/afrique/algerie/sahara-des-dechets-radioactifs-francais-enfouis-sous-le-sable_4207387.html.

Frison-Roche, Roger. *The Lost Trail of the Sahara: A Novel*. Translated by Paul Bowles. New York: Prentice-Hall, 1952.

———. *Mission Ténéré*. Paris: B. Arthaud, 1960.

———. *La piste oubliée*. Paris: Arthaud, 1950.

Fromentin, Eugène. *Un été dans le Sahara*. Paris: Librairie Plon, 1857.

Frontex. "Focus on Western Mediterranean route: Frontex in Spain." Accessed July 12, 2023. https://frontex.europa.eu/media-centre/news/focus/focus-on-western-mediterreanean-route-frontex-in-spain-isGpCE.

———. *Strategic Risk Analysis 2020*. Warsaw: Frontex, 2020. www.frontex.europa.eu/assets/Publications/Risk_Analysis/Risk_Analysis/Strategic_Risk_Analysis_2020.pdf.

Furon, Raymond. *al-Ṣaḥrāʾ al-kubrā: Al-jawānib al-jiūlūjiyya-maṣādir al-tharwa al-maʿdiniyya-istighlāluhā*. Translated by Jamal al-Dīn al-Dināṣūrī. Cairo: Muʾassasat Sijil al-ʿArab, 1963.

Gallois, Pierre. *Le sablier du siècle: Mémoires*. Lausanne: L'Age d'Homme, 1999.

Gast, M. "Inîker, Enîker." *Encyclopédie berbère* 24 (2001): 3760–62. http://journals.openedition.org/encyclopedieberbere/1578.

Gaudio, Attilio. *Le dossier du Sahara occidental*. Paris: Nouvelles Éditions Latines, 1978.

Gauthier, Théophile. *Voyage en Algérie: Présentation de Denise Brahimi*. Paris: La Boite à Document, 1989.

Gautier, Félix. *L'Algérie et la métropole*. Paris: Payot, 1920.

———. *La conquête du Sahara: Essai de psychologie politique*. Paris: Armand Colin, 1910.

———. *Le Sahara: Avec 4 cartes dans le texte*. Paris: Payot, 1923.

———. *Le Sahara vaincu peut-il être dompté? L'aménagement du Sahara*. In Académie des sciences coloniales, *Annales*. Vol. 4. Paris: Société d'Éditions Géographiques, Maritimes et Coloniales, 1929.

Geertz, Clifford. *The Interpretation of Cultures*. New York: Basic Books, 1973.

The Geographical Journal. "Review: The Results of the Foureau-Lamy Mission." *The Geographical Journal* 28, no. 3 (1906): 280–83.

Ghosh, Amitav. *The Great Derangement: Climate Change and the Unthinkable*. Chicago: Chicago University Press, 2017.

Gibbons, Floyd. "Algeria's Charm Lies in Oriental Air of Mystery." *French Colonial Digest* (1924): 147, 149, 154, 157, 173, 178.

Gide, André. *The Immoralist*. Translated by Richard Howard. New York: Vintage International, 1996.

———. *L'immoraliste*. Paris: Mercure de France, 1902.

———. *Si le grain ne meurt*. Paris: Éditions de la Nouvelle Revue Française, 1924.

Glennis, Byron. "Introduction." In *Globalgothic*, edited by Byron Glennis, 1–10. Manchester: Manchester University Press, 2013.

Global Atlas of Environmental Justice. "Untreated Waste Water Dumped by Chemical Plants into Tengger Desert, Inner Mongolia-Ningxia-Gansu, China." Last modified May 2, 2022. https://ejatlas.org/print/1-untreated-waste-water-dumped-by-chemical-plants-in-tengger-desert-inner-mongoliachina.

Goody, Alex, and Antonia Mackay. *Reading Westworld*. Cham: Palgrave Macmillan, 2019.

Gorman, Alice. "The Archaeology of Space Exploration." *The Sociological Review* 57 (2009): 132–45.

Gosling, F. G. *The Manhattan Project: Making the Atomic Bomb*. Location unknown: US Government Printing Office, 1999.

Government of Australia. "International Court of Justice: Application Instituting Proceedings Filed in the Registry of the Court on 9 May 1973, Case Concerning Nuclear Tests (Australia vs France)." ICJ, 1973. www.icj-cij.org/sites/default/files/case-related/58/13187.pdf.

Goxho, Delina. "Militarizing the Sahel Won't Make Europe More Secure." *Foreign Policy*, August 5, 2022. https://foreignpolicy.com/2022/08/05/militarizing-sahel-mali-niger-wont-make-europe-more-secure.

Goyau, Georges. "Un grand missionnaire: Le cardinal Lavigerie (1): La vocation missionnaire—Les débuts." *Revue des deux mondes* 26, no. 2 (1925): 310–43.

———. "Un grand missionnaire: Le cardinal Lavigerie (2): La résurrection de l'église d'Afrique." *Revue des deux mondes* 26, no. 3 (1925): 579–609.

Grabar, Henry. "Line in the Sand, Head in the Clouds." *Slate*, August 1, 2022. https://slate.com/business/2022/08/neom-renderings-cliches-mbs.html.

Greenfield, Adam. "All Those Complicit in Neom's Design and Construction Are Already Destroyers of Worlds." *Dezeen*, November 2, 2022. www.dezeen.com/2022/11/02/neom-the-line-saudi-arabia-architects-opinion.

Grote, Mathias, Jiří Janáč, and Darina Martykánová. "Science and Technological Change in Modern History (ca. 1800–1900)." In *The European Experience: A Multi-Perspective History of Modern Europe*, edited by Jan Hansen, Jochen Hung, Jaroslav Ira, Judit Klement, Sylvain Lesage, Juan Luis Simal, and Andrew Tompkins, 441–50. Cambridge: Open Book, 2023.

Grubb, Frederick. "On the Frontier: The Art of André Gide." *Theology* 62, no. 465 (1959): 100–105.

Guattari, Félix. *Three Ecologies*. Translated by Ian Pindar and Paul Sutton. New Brunswick, NJ: Athlone Press, 2000.

Guesmi, Haytham. "Reckoning with Foucault's Sexual Abuse of Boys in Tunisia." *Al Jazeera*, April 16, 2021. www.aljazeera.com/opinions/2021/4/16/reckoning-with-foucaults-sexual-abuse-of-boys-in-tunisia.

Guide, Georges. "Le Sahara français." *Hommes et mondes* 117 (April 1956): 53–61.

Ḥabash, Iskandar. *al-Qirāʾa wa-al-nisyān: Al-khurūj min mudun al-milḥ*. London: Ṭawā li-al-Thaqāfa wa-al-Nashr wa-al-Iʿlām, 2015.

Hacene, Hocine. *Le Sahara dans l'enfer des essais nucléaires français: Un crime sans fin*. Algiers: Houma Éditions, 2018.

Hachemi, Hacene. "al-Tajārib al-nawawiyya al-faransiyya fi-al-jazāʾir wa-qānūn mūrīn bayna rafʿ al-ḥaraj al-siyyāsī wa-taḥqīq al-iʿtirāf bi-al-dhākira." *Majallat al-Nāqid li-al-Dirāsāt al-Siyyāsiyya* 7, no. 2 (2023): 336–61.

Halliwell, Martin. *Transatlantic Modernism: Moral Dilemmas in Modernist Fiction*. Edinburgh: Edinburgh University Press, 2006.

Hamel, Ian. "Labbas Sbaï, le chirurgien suisse qui voulait faire reverdir le désert marocain." *Swissinfo*, June 27, 2022. www.swissinfo.ch/fre/economie/labbas-sba%c3%af-le-chirurgien-suisse-qui-voulait-faire-reverdir-le-d%c3%a9sert-marocain/47688324.

Hamochene, Hamza, and Sandwell Katie, eds. *Dismantling Green Colonialism: Energy and Climate Justice in the Arab Region*. London: Pluto, 2023.

Haouati, Awel. "Sahara algérien—Des essais nucléaires aux camps de sûreté." *Revue-ballast.fr*, June 28, 2017. www.revue-ballast.fr/nucleaire-algerie-camps-dinternement.

Haynes, Roslynn D. *Seeking the Centre: The Australian Desert in Literature, Art, and Film*. Cambridge: Cambridge University Press, 1999.

Heathcote, Edwin. "Saudi's Neom Is Dystopia Portrayed as Utopia." *Financial Times*, August 1, 2022. www.ft.com/content/04fcb9d4-5907-45b0-9388-f84b34bc4bea.

Heffernan, Mike. "Shifting Sands: The Trans-Saharan Railway." In *Engineering Earth: The Impacts of Megaengineering Projects*, edited by Stanley D. Brunn, 617–26. New York: Springer, 2011.

Heidegger, Martin. *Country Path Conversations*. Translated by Bret W. Davis. Bloomington: Indiana University Press, 2010.

Heidsieck, Patrick. *Le rayonnement de Lyautey*. Paris: Gallimard, 1944.

Henache, Dalila. "Mujahideen Minister: 'French Genocide in Algeria Resembles the Zionist Genocide in Palestine.'" *Echoroukonline*, December 4, 2023. www.echoroukonline.com/mujahideen-minister-french-genocide-in-algeria-resembles-the-zionist-genocide-in-palestine.

Henni, Samia. "Oil, Gas, Dust: From the Sahara to Europe." *e-Flux Architecture*, October 2021. www.e-flux.com/architecture/coloniality-infrastructure/410034/oil-gas-dust-from-the-sahara-to-europe.

Hergé. *Le crabe aux pinces d'or*. Brussels: Casterman, 1941.

———. *Tintin au pays de l'or noir*. Brussels: Casterman, 1950.

Hérisson, Robert. *Avec le père de Foucauld et le Général Laperrine: Carnets d'un saharien 1909–1911*. Paris: Librairie Plon, 1937.

Hilton-Simpson, Melville William. *Algiers and Beyond.* New York: D. Appleton, 1907.
Historique de la compagnie saharienne d'Ouargla. Paris: Henri Charles-Lavauselle, 1920.
Homo, Léon. *Nouvelle histoire romaine.* Paris: Librairie Arthème Fayard, 1949.
Howit, Richard. *Rethinking Resource Management Justice, Sustainability, and Indigenous Peoples.* New York: Taylor and Francis, 2002.
Hrbek, Ivan. "L'Afrique septentrionale et la corne de l'Afrique." In *Histoire générale de l'Afrique.* Vol. 8, *L'Afrique depuis 1935*, edited by Ali Mazui and Christophe Wondji, 127–60. Paris: Editions UNESCO, 1998.
Hugot, Henri J., ed. *Missions Berliet: Ténéré-Tchad.* Paris: Arts et Métiers Graphiques, 1962.
Ibn Battuta. *Riḥlat ibn baṭṭuṭa: Tuḥfat al-nuẓẓār fī gharāʾib al-asfār wa ʿajāʾibi al-amṣār.* Beirut: Dār Iḥyā al-ʿUlūm, 1987.
Ibn Khaldun. *The Muqaddimah: An Introduction to History.* Translated by Franz Rosenthal. Princeton, NJ: Princeton University Press, 2005.
Imān, Sūrī, and Bin Sahla Thānī Bin Ali. "al-Tajārib al-nawawiyya al-faransiyya fī al-jazāʾir wa-āthāruha ʿalā al-bīyʾa." *Majallat al-Ḥaqūq wa-al-ʿUlūm al-Insāniyya* 15, no. 1 (2022): 369–86.
Ina. "Defense of French Nuclear Tests: Jules Moch at the UN." February 13, 1960. https://mediaclip.ina.fr/en/i19021262-defense-of-french-nuclear-tests-jules-moch-at-the-un.html.
International Atomic Energy Agency. *Conditions at the Former French Nuclear Test Sites in Algeria: Preliminary Assessment and Recommendations.* Vienna: International Atomic Energy Agency, 2005.
International Court of Justice. "Application of the Convention on the Prevention and Punishment of the Crime of Genocide in the Gaza Strip (South Africa v. Israel)." *International Court of Justice*, January 26, 2024. www.icj-cij.org/sites/default/files/case-related/192/192-20240126-sum-01-00-en.pdf.
IPCC. *Climate Change 2022: Impacts, Adaptation, v Vulnerability: Contribution of Working Group II to the Sixth Assessment Report of the Intergovernmental Panel on Climate Change.* New York: Cambridge University Press, 2022.
Ito, Robert, Ed Leibowitz, Elizabeth Casillas, and Jessica Blough. "Proving Grounds: The Desert Holds Its Secrets—Which Is Why It's Been an Ideal Place to Test Out What's Next." *Alta Online*, December 21, 2022. www.altaonline.com/dispatches/a42123566/desert-mysteries-robert-ito-jessica-blough-ed-leibowitz-elizabeth-casillas.
Jabès, Edmond. *The Book of Margins.* Translated by Rosemarie Waldrop. Chicago: Chicago University Press, 1997.
Jacobs, Jessica. *Sex, Tourism, and the Postcolonial Encounter: Landscapes of Longing in Egypt.* New York: Ashgate, 2010.
Jauvert, Vincent. "Quand la France testait ses armes chimiques en Algérie." *Le nouvel observateur* 1720 (1997): 10–18.
Al Jazeera. "Limādhā intaqamat al-suʿūdiyya min kātib riwāyat 'mudun al-milḥ'?" April 21, 2019. www.aljazeera.net/programs/outside-the-text/2019/4/21/%D9%8

4%D9%85%D8%A7%D8%B0%D8%A7-%D8%A7%D9%86%D8%AA%D9%82%D9%85%D8%AA-%D8%A7%D9%84%D8%B3%D8%B9%D9%88%D8%AF%D9%8A%D8%A9-%D9%85%D9%86-%D9%83%D8%A7%D8%AA%D8%A8-%D8%B1%D9%88%D8%A7%D9%8A%D8%A9.

———. "Mādhā tukhfī al-ṣaḥrā'? Jarā'im al-tajārib al-nawawiyya al-faransiyya fī ṣaḥrā' al-jazā'ir." June 16, 2023. www.aljazeera.net/midan/eye/2023/6/16/%D8%B4%D8%A7%D9%87%D8%AF-%D9%85%D8%A7%D8%B0%D8%A7-%D8%AA%D9%8F%D8%AE%D9%81%D9%8A-%D8%A7%D9%84%D8%B5%D8%AD%D8%B1%D8%A7%D8%A1%D8%9F-%D8%AC%D8%B1%D8%A7%D8%A6%D9%85.

———. "Saudi Arabia: Corruption Crackdown 'Ends with $106bn Recovered.'" January 31, 2019. www.aljazeera.com/news/2019/1/31/saudi-arabia-corruption-crackdown-ends-with-106bn-recovered.

Jie, Chen. "Death of the Desert." *China Dialogue*, July 14, 2015. https://chinadialogue.net/en/pollution/8015-death-of-the-desert.

Johnson, Forrest Bryant. *The Last Camel Charge: The Untold Story of America's Desert Military Experiment*. New York: Berkley Caliber, 2012.

Jokadar, Zeina, and Carlos Ponte. "Ouarzazate Solar Power Complex, Phase 1 Morocco: Specific Environmental and Social Impact Assessment Volume 1." 5 Capitals Environmental and Management Consulting, December 2012. www.masen.ma/sites/default/files/documents_rapport/Masen_NOORoI_SESIA_Volume1_aDfethF%20(1).pdf.

Jolly, Jasper. "Airbus to Operate Drones Searching for Migrants Crossing the Mediterranean." *The Guardian*, October 20, 2020. www.theguardian.com/business/2020/oct/20/airbus-to-operate-drones-searching-for-migrants-crossing-the-mediterranean.

Jonchay, Ivan du. *L'industrialisation de l'Afrique*. Paris: Payot,1953.

Jones, Geoffrey, and Loubna Bouamane. "Power from Sunshine: A Business History of Solar Energy." HBS Working Paper Series, 2012. www.hbs.edu/ris/Publication%20Files/12-105.pdf.

Jones, Philip, and Anna Kenny. *Australia's Muslim Cameleers: Pioneers of the Inland, 1860s–1930s*. Kent Town, Australia: Wakefield Press, 2010.

Jones, Steven T. *The Tribes of Burning Man: How an Experimental City in the Desert Is Shaping the New American Counterculture*. San Francisco, CA: Consortium of Collective Consciousness, 2011.

Jones, Thaddeus. "De Foucauld: Total Surrender to God and Universal Fraternity." *Vatican News*, May 14, 2022. www.vaticannews.va/en/church/news/2022-05/de-foucauld-example-total-surrender-god-universal-fraternity.html.

Josephson, Paul. "Industrial Deserts: Industry, Science, and the Destruction of Nature in the Soviet Union." *The Slavonic and East European Review* 85, no. 2 (2007): 294–32.

Journal du 3ème Groupe de Transport. "Les Unités sahariennes: Les centres d'essais." www.3emegroupedetransport.com/LESUNITESSAHARIENNESK.htm.

Kaplan, Caren. *Questions of Travel: Postmodern Discourses of Displacement.* Durham, NC: Duke University Press, 1996.
Keenan, Jeremey. *The Dying Sahara: US Imperialism and Terror in Africa.* London: Pluto Press, 2013.
———. *Sahara Man: Travelling with the Tuareg.* London: J. Murray, 2001.
Kemp, Jonathan. *Homotopia? Gay Identity, Sameness, and the Politics of Desire.* Santa Barbara, CA: Punctum Books, 2015.
Keryell, Jacques. "Avant-propos." In *Petits frères de Jésus: Frères au cœur du monde à la suite de Charles de Foucauld; Lettres des fraternités (1960–2002)*, 7–11. Paris: Éditions Karthala, 2002.
Keveney, Bill. "Evan Rachel Wood: How the Uprising of Oppressed *Westworld* Androids Mirrors Me Too Movement." *USA Today*, March 26, 2018. www.usatoday.com/story/life/tv/2018/03/26/evan-rachel-wood-how-uprising-oppressed-westworld-androids-mirrors-me-too-movement/446953002.
Khālidī, Meriem, and Sanīsna Faḍīla. "al-Talawwuth al-ishʿāʿī al-nawawī wa atharuhu ʿalā al-bīyʾa fī minṭaqt al-rraqān." In *al-Tafjīrāt al-nawawiyya al-faransīyya fī al-ṣaḥrāʾ al-jazāʾirīyya*, 70–85. Adrar: Manshūrāt Jāmiʿat Aḥmad Drāya, 2020.
Khellas, Mériem. *L'Afrique de Berliet: La pénétration automobile au Sahara.* Paris: L'Harmattan, 2022.
Khoulassa, Siham, et al. "High-Quality Draft Nuclear and Mitochondrial Genome Sequence of *Fusarium oxysporum* f. sp. *albedinis* strain 9, the Causal Agent of Bayoud Disease on Date Palm." *Plant Disease* 106, no. 7 (2022): 1974–76. https://doi.org/10.1094/PDIS-01-22-0245-A.
Kilani, Mondher. *La construction de la mémoire: Le lignage et la sainteté dans l'oasis d'El Ksar.* Geneva: Éditions Labor et Fides, 1992.
Kinberg, Leah. "What Is Meant by Zuhd." *Studia Islamica* 61 (1985): 27–44.
Kingdom of Saudi Arabia. "SGI Target: Reduce Carbon Emissions by 278 mtpa by 2030." Saudi Green Initiative. www.sgi.gov.sa/about-sgi/sgi-targets/reduce-carbon-emissions.
———. "The Story of Transformation." Vision2030. www.vision2030.gov.sa/en/explore/story-of-transformation.
Klaib, Sāmī. "Ibrahīm al-kūnī . . . takrīm al-gharb wa tajāhul al- ʿarab." *Al Jazeera*, June 29, 2009. www.aljazeera.net/programs/privatevisit/2009/6/29/%D8%A5%D8%A8%D8%B1%D8%A7%D9%87%D9%8A%D9%85-%D8%A7%D9%84%D9%83%D9%88%D9%86%D9%8A-%D8%AA%D9%83%D8%B1%D9%8A%D9%85-%D8%A7%D9%84%D8%BA%D8%B1%D8%A8-%D9%88%D8%AA%D8%AC%D8%A7%D9%87%D9%84.
Klooster, Kim. "The Rise and Transformation of the Atlantic World." In *The Atlantic World: Essays on Slavery, Migration, and Imagination*, edited by Kim Klooster and Alfred Padula, 1–42. New York: Routledge, 2018.
Koni, Ibrahim al-. "Abḥathu ʿan al-usṭūra li-takhliqanī." *Aletihad*, March 6, 2008. www.aletihad.ae/article/10700/2008/%D8%A5%D8%A8%D8%B1%D8%-%A7%D9%87%D9%8A%D9%85-%D8%A7%D9%84%D9%83%D9%88%D9%8

6%D9%8A:-%D8%A3%D8%A8%D8%AD%D8%AB-%D8%B9%D9%86-%D8%A7%D9%84%D8%A3%D8%B3%D8%B7%D9%88%D8%B1%D8%A9-%D9%84%D9%83%D9%8A-%D8%AA%D8%AE%D9%84%D9%82%D9%86%D9%8A.
———. *The Bleeding of the Stone*. Translated by May Jayyusi and Christopher Tingley. Northampton, MA: Interlink Books, 2013.
———. *Nazīf al-ḥajar*. Limassol: Tāsīlī li- al-Nashr wa-al-Iʿlām, 1992.
———. *Nazīf al-ḥajar*. Misrata: al-Dār al-Jamāhīrīyah lil-Nashr wa-al-Tawzīʿ wa-al-Iʿlān, 1996.
———. "Talbīs al-namaṭ: al-ṣaḥrāʾu namūdhajan." *Sky News Arabia*, September 10, 2023. www.skynewsarabia.com/blog/1651820-%D8%AA%D9%84%D8%A8%D9%8A%D8%B3-%D8%A7%D9%84%D9%86%D9%91%D9%85%D8%B7-%D8%A7%D9%84%D8%B5%D8%AD%D8%B1%D8%A7%D8%A1-%D9%86%D9%85%D9%88%D8%B0%D8%AC%D8%A7%D9%8B.
———. *al-Waram*. Beirut: al-Muʾassasa al-ʿArabīyya lil-Dirāsāt wa-al-Nashr, 2008.
———. *Waṭanī saḥrāʾ kubrā*. Beirut: al-Muʾassasa al-ʿArabīyya lil-Dirāsāt wa-al-Nashr, 2009.
———. *Wāw al-Ṣughrā*. Beirut: al-Muʾassasa al-ʿArabīyya lil-Dirāsāt wa-al-Nashr, 1997.
Korda, Zoltan, dir. *Sahara*. Columbia Pictures, 1943. 97 minutes.
Kripa, Ersela, Francesco Marullo, and Stephen Mueller. "In Conversation with Gonzalo Pimentel." *Journal of Architectural Education* 77, no. 2 (2023): 427–35. https://doi.org/10.1080/10464883.2023.2233389.
Kröger, Lisa. "Panic, Paranoia, and Pathos: Ecocriticism in the Eighteenth-Century Gothic Novel." In *EcoGothic*, edited by Andrew Smith and William Hughes, 15–27. Manchester: Manchester University Press, 2013.
Kryza, Frank. *The Race for Timbuktu: In Search of Arica's City of Gold*. New York: HarperCollins, 2006.
Labonne, Erik. "Préface." In Daniel Strasser, *Réalités et promesses sahariennes: Aspects juridiques et économiques de la mise en valeur industrielle du Sahara français*, 7–10. Paris: Encyclopédie d'Outre-Mer, 1956.
Lamming, Clive. "Le transsaharien: (Mauvais) rêve colonial, ou chance d'une Afrique qui en avait besoin?" Train Consultant Clive Lamming (blog), July 24, 2019. https://trainconsultant.com/2019/07/24/le-transsaharien-encore-un-mauvais-reve-colonial-ou-peut-etre-la-grande-chance-dune-afrique-qui-en-avait-besoin.
Langle, Fleuriot de. "Le cardinal Lavigerie." *Revue des deux mondes* (1961): 428–39.
Laroussi, Farid. *Postcolonial Counterpoint: Orientalism, France, and the Maghreb*. Toronto: University of Toronto Press, 2016.
Larson, Carolyne R. "Introduction: Tracing the Battle for History." *The Conquest of the Desert: Argentina's Indigenous Peoples and the Battle for History*, ed. Carolyne R. Larson, 1–16. Albuquerque: University of New Mexico Press, 2020.
Lattre, Jean-Michel de. "Sahara, clé de voûte de l'ensemble eurafricain français." *Politique étrangère* 22, no. 4 (1957): 345–89.

Laub, Dori. "An Event without a Witness: Truth, Testimony, and Survival." In *Testimony: Crises of Witnessing in Literature, Psychoanalysis, and History*, edited by Shoshana Felman and Dori Laub, 75–92. New York: Routledge, 1992.

Lavigerie, Charles Martial Allemand. *Allocution prononcée le 21 septembre 1890 par S. Em. le cardinal Lavigerie dans l'église Saint-Sulpice à Paris pour l'ouverture d'un congrès antiesclavagiste*. Paris: À la direction générale de l'œuvre antiesclavagiste, 1890.

———. *L'armée et la mission de la France en Afrique: Discours prononcé à la cathédrale d'Alger le 25 avril 1875 pour l'inauguration du service religieux dans l'armée d'Afrique par M l'archevêque d'Alger*. Algiers: A. Jourdin, 1875.

———. *Lettre de Mgr l'archevêque d'Alger [Lavigerie] à M. le directeur de l'œuvre des écoles d'Orient sur la mission d'Afrique et la création de villages d'Arabes chrétiens en Algérie*. Paris: Bureaux de l'œuvre des écoles d'Orient, 1876.

———. *Lettre de Mgr L'archevêque d'Alger à un séminariste de France sur la société des missionnaires d'Alger*. Algiers: Bureau de l'œuvre des écoles d'Orient, 1878.

———. *Lettre de S. É. le cardinal Lavigerie sur l'esclavage africain, à MM. les directeurs de l'Œuvre de la propagation de la foi*. Lyon: Imprimerie Mougin-Rusand, 1888.

———. *Lettre de Son Éminence le cardinal Lavigerie: À tous les volontaires qui se sont proposés à l'oeuvre antiesclavagiste de France sur l'association des frères armés ou pionniers du Sahara*. Algiers: Adolphe Jourdan, 1891.

Lawler, Dave, and Barak Ravid. "Trump Claims U.S. Will 'Take Over' Gaza and Turn It Into New 'Riviera.'" *Axios*, February 4, 2025. www.axios.com/2025/02/05/trump-gaza-takeover-palestinians-israel.

Lazreg, Marnia. *The Eloquence of Silence: Algerian Women in Question*. New York: Routledge, 2014.

Le Châtelier, Alfred. *La sanglante épopée des Medaganat*, edited by Abderrahmane Rebahi. Algiers: Éditions Grand-Alger-Livres, 2007.

Lee, Jason. *Sex Robots: The Future of Desire*. Cham: Palgrave Macmillan, 2017.

Lefevre Witier, Philippe. "Disappearing Human Ecosystems." In *Environmental Management in Practice*. Vol. 3, *Managing the Ecosystem,* edited by Bhaskar Nath, Dimitri Devuyst, Luc Hens, Paul Compton, 251–66. New York: Routledge, 1999.

Lehmann, Philipp. *Desert Edens: Colonial Climate Engineering in the Age of Anxiety*. Princeton, NJ: Princeton University Press, 2022.

Lehuraux, Léon. "L'automobile au désert." *Les Amis du Sahara* 14 (1935): 7–39.

———. "Les français du Sahara: Les précurseurs." *Les Amis du Sahara: Organe de l' Association "Les Amis du Sahara" Bulletin trimestriel* (April 1932): 6–20.

Lerner, Steve. *Sacrifice Zones: The Front Lines of Toxic Chemical Exposure in the United States*. Boston: MIT Press, 2010.

Lesourd, Paul. *La vraie figure du père de Foucauld*. Paris: Ernest Flammarion, 1933.

Leuvrey, Elisabeth, dir. *At(h)ome*. Les Écrans du Large, 2013. DVD.

Liffran, Xavier. "Redécouvrir Ailleret, 'l'artisan de la force de dissuasion.'" *Revue défense nationale* 807, no. 2 (2020): 41–48.

Limerick, Patricia Nelson. *Desert Passages: Encounters with American Deserts*. Albuquerque: University of New Mexico Press, 1985

Lindqvist, Sven. *Desert Divers*. London: Granta Books, 2000.
Lovejoy, Paul E. *Transformations in Slavery: A History of Slavery in Africa*. New York: Cambridge University Press, 2011.
Lwāfī, Sumiyya. "al-Tajārib al-nawawiyya al-faranisyya fī al-ṣaḥrā' al-jazā'iriyya 1960–1966 tafjīrāt rqqān unmūdhajan." *Al-Majalla al-Maghāribiyya li-al-Dirāsāt al-Tārīkhiyya wa-al-Ijtimā'iyya* 13, no. 1 (2021): 40–54.
Lydon, Ghislaine. "A Thirst for Knowledge: Arabic Literacy, Writing Paper, and Saharan Bibliophiles in the Southwestern Sahar." In *The Trans-Saharan Book Trade: Manuscript Culture, Arabic Literacy, and Intellectual History in Muslim Africa*, edited by Graziano Krätli and Ghislaine Lydon, 35–72. Leiden: Brill, 2011.
———. *On Trans-Saharan Trails: Islamic Law, Trade Networks, and Cross-Cultural Exchange in Nineteenth-Century Western Africa*. Cambridge: Cambridge University Press, 2009.
Lyons, Maryinez. *The Colonial Disease: A Social History of Sleeping Sickness in Northern Zaire, 1900–1940*. Cambridge: Cambridge University Press, 2010.
Macdonald, Graeme. "Oil and World Literature." *American Book Review* 33, no. 3 (2012): 7 and 31.
Madīnī, Aḥmad al-. "'Umar al-anṣārȳ 'ṭabīb tinbuktū': Yudāwī al-ṭawāriq bibalsam al-riwāya," *Alquds*, January 11, 2012. www.alquds.co.uk/%D8%B9%D9%85%D8%B1-%D8%A7%D9%84%D8%A3%D9%86%D8%B5%D8%A7%D8%B1%D9%8A-%D8%B7%D8%A8%D9%8A%D8%A8-%D8%AA%D9%86%D8%A8%D9%83%D8%AA%D9%88-%D9%8A%D8%AF%D8%A7%D9%88%D9%8A-%D8%A7%D9%84%D8%B7%D9%88%D8%A7.
Manue, Georges R. "Fondateur de l'Office du Niger: Émile Bélime, le maître de l'eau." *Le Monde*, July 31, 1969.
Marin, Eugène. *Algérie—Sahara—Soudan: Vie, travaux, voyages de Mgr Hacquard des Pères blancs (1860–1901) d'après sa correspondance*. Paris: Berger-Levrault, 1905.
al-Markaz al-Waṭanī li-al-Dirāsāt wa-al-Baḥth fī al-Ḥaraka al-Waṭaniyya wa Thawrat Awwal Nuvambr 1954. *al-Tajārib al-nawawiyya al-faransiyya fī al-jazā'ir: Dirāsāt wa buḥūth wa shahadat*. Algiers: al-Markaz al-Waṭanī li-al-Dirāsāt wa-al-Baḥth fī al-Ḥaraka al-Waṭaniyya wa Thawrat Awwal Nuvambr 1954, 2000.
Marsh, George P. *Man and Nature or Physical Georgraphy as Modified by Human Action*. New York: Charles Scribner, 1864.
Martinez, Javiera, and Holly Jones. "The Struggle of a Community in Sonora against the Grupo Fresnillo Mining Company in Mexico." London Mining Network, March 3, 2022. https://londonminingnetwork.org/2022/03/struggle-in-sonora-against-fresnillo.
Masen. *Masen: Endless Power for Progress*. www.masen.ma/sites/default/files/inline-files/MASEN_Brochure_instit_EN_finale.pdf.
———. "Masen: Force inépuisable de développement." www.masen.ma/themes/custom/masen/assets/files/Brochure__Fiches_Fr.pdf.
———. "Masen's Value Chain." *YouTube*, video, 4:21. www.youtube.com/watch?v=HdqN3xX5mAk&ab_channel=Masen.

Masqueray, Émile. *Souvenirs et visions d'Afrique*. Paris: E. Dentu, éditeur, 1894.
Massad, Joseph. *Desiring Arabs*. Chicago: Chicago University Press, 2007.
Massey, Doreen. *For Space*. London: Sage, 2008.
Massignon, Louis. *Écrits mémorables*. Edited by Christian Jambet, François Angelier, François L'Yvonnet, and Ayada Souâd. 2 vols. Paris: Robert Laffont, 2009.
Masters, Dexter, and Katharine Way, eds. *One World or None*. New York: McGraw-Hill, 1946.
Matsuoka, Atsuko, and John Sorenson, eds. *Critical Animal Studies: Towards Trans-Species Social Justice*. London: Rowman and Littlefield, 2018.
Maunoir, Charles. "Rapport sur les travaux de la Société de géographie et sur les progrès des sciences géographiques pendant l'année 1884." *Bulletin de la Société de géographie: Rédigé avec le concours de la section de publication par les secrétaires de la commission central* (1885): 197–99.
Maupassant, Guy de. *Au soleil*. Paris: Louis Conard, 1908.
———. *Les carnets de voyage: Édition critique et annotée par Gérard Delaisement*. Paris: Rive Droite, 2006.
Maxwell, Bennet. "The Emperor of the Sahara." *The Independent*, September 14, 1998. www.independent.co.uk/arts-entertainment/the-emperor-of-the-sahara-1198247.html.
McDougall, James, and Judith Scheele. *Saharan Frontiers: Space and Mobility in Northwest Africa*. Bloomington: Indiana University Press, 2012.
Mendoza, Natalia. "Depoliticizing Conflict in Sonora, Mexico: (Il)legality, Territory, and the Continuum of Violence." *European Review of Latin American and Caribbean Studies* 112 (2021): 117–36.
Menon, V. K. Krishna. *The Question of French Nuclear Tests in the Sahara: V. K. Krishna Menon's Statement in the United Nations*. New Delhi: Ministry of External Affairs, 1959.
Mercier, Ernest. *La France dans le Sahara et au Soudan*. Paris: Ernest Leroux, 1889.
Mercier, Maurice. "Un projet grandiose et constructif: La création d'un territoire autonome saharien français." In *Le Sahara français*, edited by Jean Charbonneau, 253–63. Vichy: Cahiers Charles de Foucauld, 1955.
Messaoudi, Alain. *Les arabisants et la France colonial*. Lyon: ENS Éditions, 2015.
Miège, Jean-Louis. "Les missions protestantes au Maroc 1875–1905." *Hespéris* 1–2 (1955): 153–92.
Miller, Liz Shannon. "*Westworld* Review: 'Contrapasso' Searches for Purpose in between the Orgies." *Indiewire*, October 30, 2016. www.indiewire.com/criticism/shows/westworld-review-season-1-episode-5-contrapasso-orgy-recap-spoilers-1201741702.
Millinship, William. "Sahara Fall-out Fears." *The Observer*, August 2, 1959.
Miltoun, Francis. *In the Land of Mosques and Minarets*. Boston: Colonial Press, 1908.
Mnāyf, Musṭafā Kamāl. "al-Tajārib al-nawawiyya al-faransiyya fī al-jazā'ir fī ẓill aḥkām al-qānūn al-dawlī." Master's thesis, Ibn Khaldun University of Tiaret,

2019. http://dspace.univ-tiaret.dz/bitstream/123456789/1096/1/TH.M.DRO.AR.2019.26.pdf.
Mogielnicki, Robert. "Neom Is Becoming a Destination of Destinations." The Arab Gulf Institute in Washington, January 26, 2024. https://agsiw.org/neom-is-becoming-a-destination-of-destinations.
Le Monde. "Guy Mollet confirme sa volonté de créer une indissoluble communauté franco-musulmane." February 11, 1956.
———. "Un exposé de M. Max Lejeune sur le fonctionnement du ministère du Sahara." June 21, 1957. www.lemonde.fr/archives/article/1957/06/21/un-expose-de-m-max-lejeune-sur-le-fonctionnement-du-ministere-du-sahara_2316339_1819218.html..
Mongin, Dominique. *La Direction des applications militaires (CEA/DAM) au cœur de la dissuasion nucléaire française: De l'ère des pionniers au programme Simulation*. Paris: CEA/DAM, 2000.
Montherlant, Henry de. *L'histoire d'amour de la rose de sable*. Paris: Plon, 1954.
Mosby, Ian. "Administering Colonial Science: Nutrition Research and Human Biomedical Experimentation in Aboriginal Communities and Residential Schools, 1942–1952." *Histoire sociale* 46, no. 1 (2013): 145–72.
Moujaes, Samar. "La rencontre entre Renan et l'islam." In *Renan en Orient*, edited by Jean Balcou, Jean Glasser, and Sophie Guermès, 213–24. Rennes: Presses Universitaires de Rennes, 2022. https://doi.org/10.4000/books.pur.160169.
El Moujahid. "L'O.C.R.S., dernière base de manœuvre du colonialisme français." June 20, 1960.
———. "Le Sahara algérien." April 15, 1961.
Moujaoui, Nabil, Ednan Hariri, and Mohammed A. Elhoumaizi. "Bayoud and Belaat Diseases of Date Palm (*Phoenix dactylifera* L.) in Figuig Oasis of Morocco." *IOP Conference Series: Earth and Environmental Science* 782, no. 4 (2021): 1–7.
Mudimbe, Valentine. *The Invention of Africa: Gnosis, Philosophy, and the Order of Knowledge*. Bloomington: Indiana University Press, 1988.
Munif, Abdelrahman. *al-Ān . . . hunā, aw, sharq al-mutawassiṭ marratan ukhrā*. Beirut: al-Mu'assasa al-ʿArabīyya lil-Dirāsat wa-al-Nashr, 1991.
———. *Bayna al-thaqāfa wa-al-siyyāsa*. Beirut: al-Markaz al-Thaqāfī al-ʿArabī li-al-Nashr wa-al-Tawzīʿ, 2007.
———. *Cities of Salt*. Translated by Peter Theroux. New York: Vintage International, 1989.
———. *Mudun al-milḥ*. Beirut: al-Mu'assasa al-ʿArabīyya lil-Dirāsat wa-al-Nashr, 1985.
———. *Mudun al-milḥ: al-Manbat*. Casablanca: al-Markaz al-Thaqāfī al-ʿArabī, 2005.
———. *Mudun al-milḥ: al-Tīh*. Casablanca: al-Markaz al-Thaqāfī al-ʿArabī, 2005.
———. *Mudun al-milḥ: al-Ukhdūd*. Casablanca: al-Markaz al-Thaqāfī al-ʿArabī, 2005.
———. *Mudun al-milḥ: Bādiyat al-zulumāt*. Casablanca: al-Markaz al-Thaqāfī al-ʿArabī, 2005.

———. *Mudun al-milḥ: Taqāsīm al-layl wa-al-nahar*. Casablanca: al-Markaz al-Thaqāfī al-ʿArabī, 2005.
———. *Sharq al-mutawassiṭ*. Tunis: Dār al-Janūb, 1989.
Murkus, Samih. *Kalām al-ʿilm fī al-ḥubb wa-al-jins*. Cairo: Markaz al-Maḥrūṣa li-al-Nashr wa-al-Khadamāt al-ṣaḥafiyya wa-al-Maʿlūmāt, 2021.
Nablusī, ʿAbdulghānī al-. *Iyḍāḥu al-maqṣūd min waḥdat al-wujūd*. Edited by ʿIzza Khaḍra. Damascus: Maṭbaʿat al-ʿIlm, 1969.
Nadawi, Muhammad Shahjan al-. *al-Siyyāḥa aḥkāmuhā wa ādābuhā fin ḍawʾ al-qānūn wa al-shariʿa: Dirāsa ʿilmiyya*. Beirut: Dār al-Kutub al-ʿIlmiyya, 2017.
Nadeau, Marcel, ed. *L'expérience de Dieu avec Charles de Foucauld*. Quebec: Éditions Fides, 2004.
Naggar, Carole. *Le rouge du sable: Un prisonnier au camp d'Al Kharga en Égypte, 1959–1963*. Paris: L'Harmattan, 2021.
Naḥḥās, Usāmah al-. *ʿImārat al-ṣaḥrāʾ*. Cairo: Maktabat al-Anjlu al-Miṣrīyya, 1986.
National Park Service. "Marquis de Morès." Last modified December 13, 2020. www.nps.gov/thro/learn/historyculture/marquis-de-mores.htm.
National Staff. "From Mirage to Reality in 98 Years: The Evolution of Solar Power in Egypt." *The National*, September 9, 2010. www.thenationalnews.com/business/energy/from-mirage-to-reality-in-98-years-the-evolution-of-solar-power-in-egypt-1.555752.
Ndlovu, Morgan. "Why Indigenous Knowledges in the 21st Century? A Decolonial Turn." *Yesterday & Today* 11 (2014): 84–98.
New York Times. "Excerpts from Speeches by French and Moroccan Delegates on Sahara Tests." November 5, 1959.
———. "Man in the News: De Gaulle's Top Soldier; Charles Louis Marcel Ailleret." July 30, 1964.
Nicholson, Geoff. *Day Trips to the Desert: A Sort of Travel Book*. London: Sceptre, 1993.
Nihal, Mariam. "The Line in Neom Is 'the Greatest Real Estate Challenge that Humans Have Faced.'" *National News*, August 17, 2022. www.thenationalnews.com/gulf-news/2022/08/17/the-line-in-neom-is-the-greatest-property-challenge-that-humans-have-faced.
Nixon, Robert. *Slow Violence and the Environmentalism of the Poor*. Cambridge: Harvard University Press, 2011.
Nolan, Christopher, dir. *Oppenheimer*. Universal Pictures, Atlas Entertainment, and Gadget Films, 2023. 180 minutes.
Nord, Pierre. *L'Eurafrique, notre dernière chance*. Paris: Fayard, 1955.
Noriega Sánchez, María Ruth. *Challenging Realities: Magic Realism in Contemporary American Women's Fiction*. Valencia: Universitat de València, 2002.
Numa, Broc. "Les français face à l'inconnue saharienne: Géographes, explorateurs, ingénieurs (1830–1881)." *Annales de géographie* 96, no. 535 (1987): 302–38.
O'Donnell, J. Dean, Jr. "Cardinal Charles Lavigerie: The Politics of Getting a Red Hat." *The Catholic Historical Review* 63, no. 2 (1977): 185–203.

Œuvre de la Propagation de la foi. *Les missions catholiques* 23 (January–December 1891).
Office of the Historian. "The 1928 Red Line Agreement." History.state.gov. https://history.state.gov/milestones/1921-1936/red-line.
Office of the Prosecutor. "Statement of ICC Prosecutor Karim A. A. Khan KC on the Issuance of Arrest Warrants in the Situation in the State of Palestine." International Criminal Court, November 21, 2024. www.icc-cpi.int/news/statement-icc-prosecutor-karim-aa-khan-kc-issuance-arrest-warrants-situation-state-palestine.
Oppermann, Serpil, and Iovino Serenella, eds. *Environmental Humanities: Voices from the Anthropocene*. Lanham, MD: Rowman & Littlefield, 2017.
Paglen, Trevor. *Blanks on the Map: The Dark Geography of the Pentagon's Secret World*. New York: New American Library, 2010.
Le Parisien. "Le document choc sur la bombe A en Algérie." *Le Parisien*, February 14, 2014. www.leparisien.fr/archives/le-document-choc-sur-la-bombe-a-en-algerie-14-02-2014-3588699.php.
Pellenc, Marcel. "Annexe au procès-verbal de la 1ère séance du 1er décembre 1959." www.senat.fr/rap/1959-1960/i1959_1960_0066_03_23.pdf.
Perrot, Marcel. "Il y a 20 ans . . . Le premier institut universitaire francais de l'energie solaire (I.E.S.U.A)." *Revue internationale d'héliotechnique* (1978): 1–7. www.musilbrescia.it/minisiti/energia-solare/comples/downloads/PERROT_1_Inizi.pdf.
Peterson, Joseph W. *Sacred Rivals: Catholic Missions and the Making of Islam in Nineteenth-Century France and Algeria*. New York: Oxford University Press, 2022.
Pharaon, Florian. *Spahis, turcos et goumiers*. Paris: Challamel Ainé, 1864.
Pingandeau, Odette de. "Poisoned Clouds Over the Lush Oases of Africa." *The Gazette and Daily*, November 16, 1959.
Pollon, Christopher. *Pitfall: The Race to Mine the World's Most Vulnerable Place*. Berkeley, CA: Greystone Books, 2023.
Popenoe, Paul B. *Date Growing in the Old World and the New*. Altadena, CA: George Rice, 1905.
———. "Sahara Desert Plant Life." *The California Garden* 2 (1912): 8–10.
Pottier, René. *Le cardinal Lavigerie apôtre et civilisateur*. Paris: Les Publications Techniques et Artistiques, 1947.
———. *Histoire du Sahara*. Paris: Nouvelles Éditions Latines, 1947.
———. *Laperrine conquérant pacifique du Sahara*. Paris: Nouvelles Éditions Latines, 1943.
Powell, Alexander. "Sirens of the Sands." *The Metropolitan Magazine* 36, no. 1 (1912): 22–24, 59.
Prăvălie, Remus. "Nuclear Weapons Tests and Environmental Consequences: A Global Perspective." *Ambio* 43, no. 6 (2014): 729–44.
Psichari, Ernest. *Les voix qui crient dans le désert*. Paris: Louis Conard, 1920.
Qashshāt, Muḥammad Saʿīd al-. *Jihād al-lībiyyīn ḍidda faransā fī al-saḥrāʾ al-kubrā 1854–1988*. Beirut: Dār al-Qamāṭī, 1989.

Quarry Magazine. "Getting Creative in Quarry Restoration Design." January 2, 2007. www.quarrymagazine.com/2007/01/02/getting-creative-in-quarry-restoration-design.

"Quels sont les groupes engagés dans la recherche du pétrole au Sahara." In *Le Sahara en questions*, 59–70. Paris: Julliard, 1960.

Raat, W. Dirk. *Lost Worlds of 1863: Relocation and Removal of American Indians in the Central Rockies and the Greater Southwest*. Hoboken, NJ: John Wiley, 2021.

Radio 1. "Oscar Temaru: 'De Gaulle est un criminel.'" February 13, 2017. www.radio1.pf/oscar-temaru-de-gaulle-est-un-criminel.

Ragan, Johns David. *Forgotten Saint-Simonian Travelers in Egypt: Suzanne Voilquin, Ismayl Urbain, Jehan d'Ivary*. Cairo: The American University in Cairo Press, 2025.

Rājiʿī, Abdelaziz, and Nawī Bin Mabrūk. "al-Tajārib al-nawawiyya al-faransiya bi-al-ṣaḥrāʾ al-jazāʾiriyya fī mīyzān al-qānūn al-dawlī al-insānī 1960–1966." *Majallat al-Ustādh al-Bāḥith li-al-Dirāsāt al-Qānūniyya wa-al-Siyyāsiyya* 5, no. 1 (2020): 1002–25.

Rambaud, Alfred. "Un pionnier d'Afrique: Émile Masqueray." *Revue politique et littéraire* 6 (February 9, 1895): 162–68.

Rauf, Tariq. "Viewpoint: French Nuclear Testing; A Fool's Errand." *The Nonproliferation Review* (Fall 1995): 49–57.

Reff, Daniel. *Plagues, Priests, and Demons: Sacred Narratives and the Rise of Christianity in the Old World and the New*. Cambridge: Cambridge University Press, 2004.

Reyes, Hamad al-, Safia Ajlan, and Omar AlShehabi, eds. *al-Bīyʿa fī al-khalīj*. Kuwait: Markaz al-Khalīj li-Siyāsāt al-Tanmiyya, 2021.

Reynolds, Brandon R. "Hot and Bothersome: The Downsides of Desert Solar Projects." *Alta Online*, June 9, 2022. www.altaonline.com/dispatches/a40234357/hot-and-bothersome.

Rezzi, Nathalie. "Les gouverneurs français de 1880 à 1914: Essai de typologie." *Outre-mers: Revue d'histoire* 98, nos. 370–371 (2011): 9–19.

Riba, Naama. "Neom and the Line: Saudi Arabia's Futuristic City Already Belongs in the Past." *Haaretz*, August 2, 2022. www.haaretz.com/middle-east-news/2022-08-02/ty-article-magazine/.premium/neom-and-the-line-saudi-arabias-futuristic-city-already-belongs-in-the-past/00000182-53b8-d2c3-a5a3-57f802a30000.

Ricard, François. "Les Missions d'Afrique des Pères blancs." In *Le tour du monde: Journal des voyages et des voyageurs*, 277–88. Paris: Librairie Hachette, 1907.

Rimbault, Paul. *Alger 1830–1930: Les grandes figures du centenaire*. Paris: Larose, 1929.

Rocard, Yves. *Mémoires sans concessions*. Paris: Grasset, 1988.

Roche, Aimé. *Charles de Foucauld*. Lyon: Éditions du Chalet, 1964.

Roskin, Joel. "Why Moving to the Sinai Peninsula Is the Solution for Gaza's Palestinians." *The Jerusalem Post*, December 25, 2023. www.jpost.com/opinion/article-779510.

Roudaire, François Elie. *Rapport à M. le ministre de l'Instruction publique sur la dernière expédition des chotts: Complément des études relatives au projet de mer intérieure.* Paris: Imprimerie Nationale, 1881.

Roux, Michel. *Le désert de sable: Le Sahara dans l'imaginaire des français (1900–1994).* Paris: L'Harmattan, 1996.

Royal Commission into British Nuclear Tests in Australia. *The Report of the Royal Commission into British Nuclear Tests in Australia.* Vol. 1. Canberra: Australian Government Publishing, 1985.

Ruddell, Rick. *The Dark Side of the Boomtown.* New York: Palgrave, 2017.

Ryan, Mike. "1922 Citroën Kegresse Auto-chenille." October 7, 2020. www.justcars.com.au/news-and-reviews/feature-1922-citro-n-kegresse-auto-chenille/886163.

Saada, Hana. "Remembering the Atrocity of Algeria's Laghouat: The 172nd Anniversary of the 1852 Massacre." *dzair-tube.dz*, December 4, 2024, www.dzair-tube.dz/en/remembering-the-atrocity-of-algerias-laghouat-the-172nd-anniversary-of-the-1852-massacre.

Saadallah, Aboul-Kassem. *Tārīkh al-jazāʾir al-thaqāfī aljuzʾ al-rābiʿ 1830–1954.* Beirut: Dār al-Gharb al-Islāmī, 1998.

Saʿdī, Abd al-Raḥmān al-, and Hamāh Allah Wld al-Sālim, eds. *Tārīkh al-sūdān: Kitāb fī tārīkh al-islām wa-al-thaqāfa wa-al-duwwal wa-al-shuʿūb fī ifrīqiyya janūb al-ṣaḥrāʾ wa ghāna wa mālī wa-al-sanghāy.* Beirut: Dār al-Kutub al-ʿIlmiyya, 2012.

Said, Edward. *Orientalism.* New York: Vintage Books, 1978.

Saint-Exupéry, Antoine de. *Le petit prince, avec les dessins de l'auteur.* Paris: Gallimard, 1946.

———. *Terre des hommes.* Paris: Gallimard, 1939.

Salazar Cruz, Clara Eugenia. "La privatisation des terres collectives agraires dans l'agglomération de Mexico: L'impact des réformes de 1992 sur l'expansion urbaine et la régularisation des lots urbains." *Revue tiers monde* 206, no. 2 (2011): 95–114.

Salime, Zakia. "Life in the Vicinity of Morocco's Noor Solar Energy Project." *Middle East Report* 298 (2021): 22 para. https://merip.org/2021/04/life-in-the-vicinity-of-moroccos-noor-solar-energy-project-2.

Salisbury, Joyce E., "When Sex Stopped Being a Social Disease." In *Medieval Sexuality: A Casebook*, edited by April Harper and Caroline Proctor, 46–58. New York: Routledge, 2008.

Salut, Samir. "Politique nationale du pétrole, sociétés nationales et 'pétrole franc.'" *Revue historique* 638 (2006): 355–88.

Salvy, Georges. "Le problème de la main-d'œuvre dans le Sahara de demain." In *Le Sahara français*, edited by Jean Charbonneau, 334–44. Vichy: Cahiers Charles de Foucauld, 1955.

Sampson, Anthony. *The Seven Sisters: The Great Oil Companies and the World They Shaped.* New York: Viking Press, 1975.

Sanmao. *Stories of the Sahara.* London: Bloomsbury, 2019.

Sarraut, Albert. *La mise en valeur des colonies françaises, avec onze cartes en noir et en couleurs.* Paris: Payot, 1923.

Sawyer, Suzana, and Agrawal Arun. "Environmental Orientalisms." *Cultural Critique* 45 (2000): 71–108.
Sawyer-Laucanno, Christopher. *An Invisible Spectator: A Biography of Paul Bowles.* New York: Grove, 1989.
Scheele, Judith. *Smugglers and Saints of the Sahara: Regional Connectivity in the Twentieth Century.* Cambridge: Cambridge University Press, 2019.
Schirmer, Henri. "L'exploration du Sahara." *Annales de géographie* 30 (1897): 461–64.
Schwarz, Ernest Hubert Lewis. *The Kalahari, or Thirstland Redemption.* Oxford: B. H. Blackwell, 1920.
Schwere, Antoine. "Auprès de ma bombe." In Pierre Baillaud, *La grande aventure du nucléaire militaire français: Des acteurs témoignent,* 109–88. Paris: L'Harmattan, 2016.
Sèbe, Berny. "Colonial Celebrities in Popular Culture: Heroes of the British and French Empires, 1850–1914." In *Celebrity Colonialism: Fame, Power, and Representation in Colonial and Postcolonial Cultures,* edited by Robert Clarke, 37–54. Newcastle upon Tyne: Cambridge Scholars, 2009.
———. "Exalting Imperial Grandeur: The French Empire and Its Metropolitan Public." In *European Empires and the People: Popular Responses to Imperialism in France, Britain, the Netherlands, Belgium, Germany, and Italy,* edited by John MacKenzie, 19–56. Manchester: Manchester University Press, 2011.
Seekatz, Sarah. "America's Arabia: The Date Industry and the Cultivation of Middle Eastern Fantasies in the Deserts of Southern California." PhD diss., University of California Riverside, 2014.
———. "Desert Deployment: Southern California's World War II Desert Training Center." *Incendiary Traces,* September 11, 2015. www.incendiarytraces.org/articles/2015/9/11/desert-deployment-southern-californias-world-war-ii-desert-training-center.Selcer, Perrin. *The Postwar Origins of the Global Environment: How the United Nations Built Spaceship Earth.* New York: Columbia University Press, 2018.
Sergent, Edmond. *Le peuplement humain du Sahara.* Algiers: Institut Pasteur d'Algérie, 1953.
Shakīrī, Muṣṭfā. "al-Koni: Al-Ṣaḥrā' al-kubrā maskūna bi-al-ḥurriyya . . . wa-ightirāb al-waṭan 'uzlatun wujūdiyya." *Hespress,* May 2, 2022. www.hespress.com /%D8%A7%D9%84%D9%83%D9%88%D9%86%D9%8A-%D8%A7%D9%84% D8%B5%D8%AD%D8%B1%D8%A7%D8%A1-%D8%A7%D9%84% D9%83% D8%A8%D8%B1%D9%89-%D9%85%D8%B3%D9%83%D9%88% D9%86% D8%A9-%D8%A8%D8%A7%D9%84%D8%AD%D8%B1%D9%8A% D8%A9-979778.html.
Sharp, William. "Cardinal Lavigerie's Work in North Africa." *The Atlantic* (August 1894): 214–27.
Shaykh, Hanan al-. *Misk al-ghazāl: Riwāyah.* Beirut: Dār al-Adāb. 1988.
Shere, Jeremy. "Frank Shuman's Solar Arabian Dream." *Renewable.* https://renewablebook.wordpress.com/chapter-excerpts/350-2.

Shepard, Todd. *Sex, France, and Arab Men*. Chicago: Chicago University Press, 2017.

Sheppard, Jack Mortimer. *Sahara Adventure*. London: Jarrods, 1957.

Sh'sh'iyya, Lakhḍar. "al-Asās al-qānūnī al-dawlī li-mas'ūliyyat faransā 'an tajāribiha al-nawawiyya fī al-jazā'ir (dirāsat li-taḥdīd al-qawā'id al-mawḍū'iyya wa-al-ijrā'iyya fī al-qānūn al-dawlī li-muṭalabat faransā bi-al-ta'wīḍ)." *Majallat al-Wāḥāt li-al-Buḥūt wa-al-Dirāsāt* 7, no. 2 (2014): 356–66.

Shuman, Frank. "Feasibility of Utilizing Power From the Sun." *Scientific American* (1914): 179.

———. "Power from Sunshine: A Pioneer Solar Power Plant." *Scientific American* (1911): 291–92.

———. "The Solar Engine in Egypt." *Scientific American* (1912): 481.

Sidi Baba, Dey. "Le Sahara de demain." *Perspectives sahariennes* 3 (1958): 121–28.

Silverstein, Paul. "The Racial Politics of the Amazigh Revival in North Africa and Beyond." POMEPS.org. https://pomeps.org/the-racial-politics-of-the-amazigh-revival-in-north-africa-and-beyond.

Simiot, Bernard. "Il faut 'nationaliser' le Sahara." *Hommes et mondes* 60 (July 1951): 161–64.

———. "Le Sahara devant le parlement," *Revue des deux mondes* (January 1957): 163–69.

Simiot, Bernard, Préaud, André Berthier, and Jean Imberti. "Il faut 'nationaliser' le Sahara." *Hommes et mondes* 62 (September 1951): 530–53.

Simiot, Bernard, Général Catroux, Gustave L.-S. Mercier, C. Maitre-Devallon, and André Reymond. "Il faut 'nationaliser' le Sahara." *Hommes et mondes* 61 (August 1951): 436–53.

Simpson, Alfred William Brian. *Cannibalism and Common Law: A Victorian Yachting Tragedy*. Chicago: Chicago University Press, 1984.

———. "Cannibals at Common Law." *The Law School Record* 27 (1981): 3–9.

Six, Jean-François. *Charles de Foucauld autrement*. Paris: Desclée De Brouwer, 2008.

———. *Charles de Foucauld: Sa vie, sa voie*. Paris: Éditions Artège, 2016.

Slimane, Hamid Ait. *Le Tanezrouft*. Paris: Mon petit éditeur, 2011.

Slobodkin, Yan. *The Starving Empire: A History of Famine in France's Colonies*. Ithaca, NY: Cornell University Press, 2023.

Slyomovics, Susan. *The Performance of Human Rights in Morocco*. Philadelphia: University of Pennsylvania Press, 2005.

Snowden, Frank. *Blacks in Antiquity: Ethiopians in the Greco-Roman Experience*. Cambridge, MA: Harvard University Press, 1970.

Société contre l'abus du tabac. "Statue du cardinal Lavigerie." *Journal de la Société contre l'abus du tabac* 24 (1900): 79–80.

Solnit, Rebecca. "A Broken Idea of Sex Is Flourishing: Blame Capitalism." *The Guardian*, May 12, 2018. www.theguardian.com/commentisfree/2018/may/12/sex-capitalism-incel-movement-misogyny-feminism.

———. *Savage Dreams: A Journey into the Hidden Wars of the American West*. Berkeley: University of California Press, 2014.

Sony Pictures. "Sahara 1943." YouTube Movies & TV, video, 97:41 minutes. www.youtube.com/watch?v=hHpXK56rsJ8&rco=1.
Soustelle, Jacques. *Le drame algérien et la décadence française: Réponse à Raymond Aron*. Paris: Plon, 1957.
———. *Le Sahara d'aujourd'hui et la France de l'an 2000*. Paris: Société Parisienne, 1959.
———. *The Wealth of the Sahara*. New York: The Council on Foreign Affairs, 1959.
Southall, Ivan. *Woomera*. Sydney: Agnus and Robertson, 1962.
Steenson, Molly. "The Burning Man Experience: What Is Burning Man?" https://burningman.org/event/preparation/black-rock-city-guide/first-timers-Boisguide/the-burning-man-experience.
Stora, Benjamin. *Les mots de la guerre d'Algérie*. Toulouse: Presses Universitaires du Mirail, 2005.
Strachan, John. "Murder in the Desert: Soldiers, Settlers, and the Flatters Expedition in the Politics and Historical Memory of European Colonial Algeria, 1830–1881." *French History and Civilization* 4 (2011): 210–22.
Straitur, Pierre. *Chez les Touareg au litham bleu, grand récit d'aventures vraies*. Paris: Les Éditions Fleurus, 1947.
Strasser, Daniel. *Réalités et promesses sahariennes: Aspects juridiques et économiques de la mise en valeur industrielle du Sahara français*. Paris: Encyclopédie d'Outre-Mer, 1956.
———. *Le Sahara français en 1958*. France: La documentation française, 1958.
Strobel, Christoph. *The Global Atlantic, 1400 to 1900*. New York: Routledge, 2015.
Sunderland, Judith. "EU's Drone Is Another Threat to Migrants and Refugees: Frontex Aerial Surveillance Facilitates Return to Abuse in Libya." *Human Rights Watch*, August 1, 2022. www.hrw.org/news/2022/08/01/eus-drone-another-threat-migrants-and-refugees.
Swingle, Walter T. "Co-Operative Quarantine Date Nurseries." In *Report of the First Date Grower's Institute at Coachella Valley California: February 29th and March 1, 1924*, 25–26. Coachella, CA: Coachella Valley Farm Center, 1924.
———. "Date Culture in Southern Morocco." In *Report of the Six Annual Date Grower's Institute*, 16–19. California: Coachella Valley Farmer, 1929.
al-Tafjīrāt al-nawawiyya al-faransīyya fī al-ṣaḥrāʾ al-jazāʾirīyya. Adrar: Manshūrāt Jāmiʿat Aḥmad Draia, 2020.
Taieb, Lebbaz, and Abderrahmane Guenchouba. "La résistance des Ouled Nail après 1847 selon les écrits d'Arnaud, interprète militaire dans *La Revue Africaine*." *Dirassat wa Abhath: The Arabic Journal of Human and Social Sciences* 13, no. 2 (2021): 150–59.
Taithe, Bertrand. "Missionary Militarism? The Armed Brothers of the Sahara and Léopold Joubert in the Congo." In *In God's Empire: French Missionaries and the Modern World*, edited by Owen White and J. P. Daughton, 129–50. New York: Oxford University Press, 2012.
Taylor, Barry. *Sex, God, and Rock 'n' Roll: Catastrophes, Epiphanies, and Sacred Anarchies*. Minneapolis: Fortress Press, 2020.

Teissier du Cros, Henri. *Louis Armand: Visionnaire de la modernité.* Paris: Éditions Odile Jacob, 1987.

Tellier, Charles Louis Abel. *La conquête pacifique de l'Afrique occidentale par le soleil.* Paris: Librairie Centrales des Sciences Mathématiques, 1890.

Thabet, Mohammed. *Nisā' al-ʿālam kamā raʾaytuhunna.* Cairo: Hindawi Foundation, 1917.

Thomas, Marc-Robert. *Sahara et communauté.* Paris: Presses Universitaires de France, 1960.

Tilouine, Joan. "Algérie: Itinéraire d'un nuage radioactive." *Jeune Afrique,* March 5, 2014. www.jeuneafrique.com/134334/politique/alg-rie-itin-raire-d-un-nuage-radioactif.

Time. "Jacques Soustelle." August 17, 1959.

Titus, A. Constandina. *Bombs in the Backyard: Atomic Testing and American Politics.* Las Vegas, NV: University of Las Vegas, 1986.

Tóibín, Colm. "Love in a Dark Time." *London Review of Books,* April 19, 2001. www.lrb.co.uk/the-paper/v23/n08/colm-toibin/love-in-a-dark-time.

Toutain, Jules. "Le territoire des Musulamii." In *Mémoires de la société nationale des antiques de France* 58:271–94. Paris: C. Klinscksieck, 1898.

Touzet, André. "Préface." In Albert Sarraut, *La mise en valeur des colonies françaises.* Paris: Payot, 1923.

Treyer, Claude. *Sahara 1956–1962.* Paris: Société Les Belles Lettres, 1966.

Triaud, Jean-Louis. *La légende noire de la Sanûsiyya: Une confrérie musulmane saharienne sous le regard français, 1840–1930.* Vol. 1. Paris: Maison des Sciences de l'Homme.

TRTWorld. "61 Years Later, Algerians Still Suffer From France's Atomic Legacy." 2021. www.trtworld.com/magazine/61-years-later-algerians-still-suffer-from-france-s-atomic-legacy-44187.

Tsing, Anna. *The Mushroom at the End of the World: On the Possibility of Life in Capitalist Ruins.* Princeton, NJ: Princeton University Press, 2015.

Union coloniale française. *Le domaine colonial français.* Paris: Les Éditions du Cygne, 1929.

Urrea, Luis Alberto. *The Devil's Highway: A True Story.* New York: Back Bay Books, 2004.

US Department of Energy. *Battlefield of the Cold War: The Nevada Test Site, Atmospheric Nuclear Weapons Testing, 1951–1963.* Washington, DC: US Department of Energy, 2006.

US Department of Interior. "Interior Department Advances Three Solar Projects in California, Marking Significant Progress to Develop a Clean Energy Economy." DOI.gov, last modified October 10, 2024. www.doi.gov/pressreleases/interior-department-advances-three-solar-projects-california-marking-significant.

US Nuclear Regulatory Commission. "Backgrounder on Plutonium." NRC.org, last modified January 7, 2021. www.nrc.gov/reading-rm/doc-collections/fact-sheets/plutonium.html.

Vallee Jacques. *Forbidden Science.* Vol. 1, *Journals 1957–1969, a Passion for Discovery.* California: Lulu.com, 2014.
Variot, Joseph. *Les Pères blancs ou missionnaires d'Alger.* Lille: Desclée, de Brouwer, 1887.
Verne, Jules. *Les voyageurs du XIXe siècle.* Paris: Bibliothèque d'Éducation et de Recréation, 1880.
Vision 2030. "Environment and Nature." www.vision2030.gov.sa/en/progress/environment-nature.
Voinot, Louis. "Le transsaharien et le transafricain." *Bulletin de la Société de géographie d'Alger et de l'Afrique du Nord* (First Trimestre 1913): 39–107.
Volpato, Gabriele, and Patricia Howard. "The Material and Cultural Recovery of Camels and Camel Husbandry among Sahrawi Refugees of Western Sahara." *Pastoralism* 4, no. 7 (2014): 1–23.
Waḥīd, Būzīdī. "al-Tajārib al-nawawiyya al-faransiyya fī al-ṣaḥrā' al-jazā'iriyya min khilāl al-ṣaḥafa al-faransiyya: Tafjīrāt 13 fivriyi 1960 unmūdhajan." *Al-Sāwra li-al-Dirāsāt al-Insāniyya wa-al-Ijtimā'iyya* 8, no. 2 (2022): 12–29.
Walsh, Steve. "In Remote Southern California Desert, US Army Tests Advanced Cyber Weapons." *NPR*, May 31, 2017. www.npr.org/2017/05/31/530929908/in-remote-southern-california-desert-u-s-army-tests-advanced-cyber-weapons.
wa Muiuand, Mueni, and Guy Martin. *A New Paradigm of the African State: Fundi Wa Afrika.* New York: Palgrave Macmillan, 2009.
Ward, Benedicta. *The Desert Fathers: Sayings of the Early Christian Monks.* New York: Penguin, 2003.
Warren, Jacob G. "Nuclear Aesthetics against the Colonial Desert." *Third Text* 35, no. 6 (2021): 667–88.
Wazzān, Haṣan al-. *Waṣfu ifrīqiyyā li-al-ḥasan bin muḥammad al-wazzān al-fāsī al-ma'rūf bi-lyon al-ifriqī.* Translated by Muhammad Ḥajjī and Muhammad Lakhḍar. Beirut: Dār al-Gharb al-Islāmī, 1983.
Weightman, John. "André Gide and the Homosexual Debate." *The American Scholar* 59, no. 4 (1990): 591–601.
Wigler, Josh. "Inside *Westworld*'s 'Epic' Orgy Scene." *The Hollywood Reporter*, October 30, 2016. www.hollywoodreporter.com/tv/tv-news/westworld-orgy-scene-explained-942103.
Wilson, Alice. *Afterlives of Revolution: Everyday Counterhistories in Southern Oman.* Stanford: Stanford University Press, 2023.
———. *Sovereignty in Exile: A Saharan Liberation Movement Governs.* Philadelphia: University of Pennsylvania Press, 2016.
Witt, Emily. *Future Sex.* New York: Farrar, Straus and Giroux, 2016.
Wolff, Henri, and Antoine-Auguste Blachère. *Sahara et Soudan: Les régiments de dromadaires.* Paris: Challamel Ainé Éditeur, 1884.
Wright, Barbara. *Eugène Fromentin: A Life in Art and Letters.* Bern: Peter Lang, 2000.
Yāma, Ibrāhīm, and Yamīna Bilbālī. "al-Āthār al-bīy'iyya al-nātija 'an al-tajārib al-nawawiyya al-faransiyya fī al-jazā'ir 'rqqān unmūdhajan.'" *Majallat al-Bayān li-al-Dirāsāt al-Qānūniyya wa-al-Siyyāsiyya* 2, no. 1 (2017): 27–35.

Yetman, David. *Conflict in Colonial Sonora: Indians, Priests, and Settlers*. Albuquerque: University of New Mexico Press, 2012.

Young, James. "The Counter-Monument: Memory against Itself in Germany Today." *Critical Inquiry* 18, no. 2 (1992): 267–96.

Zerubavel, Yael. *Desert in the Promised Land*. Stanford, CA: Stanford University Press, 2022.

Zimmermann, Maurice. "L'outillage et la mise en valeur du Congo français." *Annales de géographie* 18, no. 97 (1909): 90–92.

INDEX

Duveyrier, Henri, 10–11, 49, 70, 123, 218n60, 223n2, 229n112
Duquesne, Jacques, 216n36

Eberhardt, Isabelle, xv, 36, 37, 38, 55–56, 226n40
ecocare, xvi, 194–95; Indigenous perspectives, 166–68, 187–91, 258n20; and nuclear testing, 186–94; and oil capitalism, 175–82, 183–86; unity of creatures (*waḥdat al-kāʾināt*), 166, 169–75
Edwards, Brian, 104
El Cherif, Bahmaoui, 128
Ellul, Jacques, 75, 128
Endres, Danielle, x, 129
Entreprise, 86
Escoube, Pierre, 75
Estienne, Georges, 110
experimental Saharanism, xv, 23, 46, 99–108, 246n102; agriculture, 99–100; environmental engineering, 46, 102–3, 182–83; military training, 104–5; nuclear testing, 26, 103–4, 105–6, 107–24, 127–30, 186–94, 192–94; racism and, 100, 122–24; solar energy, 90–92; technological testing, 100–101, 124–26; transnational dynamics of, 99–100, 101–4, 107–8, 113–14, 117
extractive Saharanism, xv, 24–26, 66–69, 171–72, 222n144; botanical resources, 99–100; French administration of the Sahara, 69, 75–85, 94–97; French *mise en valeur*, 71–75, 79, 88; and human labor, 68–69, 85–86, 87–89; oil, 28, 29–30, 67, 69, 75, 77, 80–81, 85, 87, 88, 175–82, 183–86; solar energy, ix–xiii, 89–94; transnational dynamics of, 76, 79–81, 87, 88*fig.*, 93, 94–95, 117, 237n89

Fairchild, David, 100
Fanon, Frantz, 180
Fassi, Allal al-, 27
Faulk, Odie, 13
Faure, Edgar, 83
Fehner, Terrence, 102
Felbab-Brown, Vanda, 164
Fernández de Castro, Miguel: *The Absolute Restoration of All Things*, 201, 203–4, 205*fig.*
Flatters, Paul, 11, 30, 55, 67, 70, 123, 234n26
FLN (Algerian National Liberation Front), 27
Foucauld, Charles de, 37, 61–64, 85, 216n44, 223n1, 224nn19,23, 226n40, 228n82, 229n112, 229n115, 230nn117,119, 231n159; and colonialist martyrology, 11, 15–16; cultural networks of, 33–34, 48–49, 52–54, 65; and François-Henry Laperrine, 38, 39*fig.*, 40*fig.*, 52, 56–57, 59, 226nn42–43, 231n153; militarism of, 56–59; and spiritual Saharanism, xv, 32–33, 36, 48–54, 59; and universal brotherhood, 44, 54–56. *See also* spiritual Saharanism
Foucault, Michel, 132
Foureau, Fernand, 223n2
Fournier, Paul, 224n3
Francis (pope), 32, 223n1
French Colonial Digest, 145
Frison-Roche, Roger, 13–14, 80, 126; *La piste oubliée du désert*, 50
Fromentin, Eugène, 9–10, 140; *Un été dans le Sahara*, 121
Frontex (European Border and Coast Guard Agency), 1, 2, 65, 214n1

Gagnol, Laurent, 18
Gardet, Louis, 61
Gaulle, Charles de, 108, 243n30
Gautier, Félix, 49, 74, 110, 172, 219n78, 226n40, 260n47
Gautier, Théophile: *Voyage en Algérie*, 140
Gaza, xvi, 199–200
Gerboise bleue, 113, 118, 120, 122, 127, 129, 186, 190, 191*fig.*
Ghosh, Amitav, 29
Gide, André, xvi, 1, 131–33, 146, 160; *L'immoraliste*, 20–21, 132, 133, 149–52, 153–54; same-sex pedophilia, 149–56; *Si le grain ne meurt*, 131, 149, 152. *See also* sexual Saharanism
Goody, Alex, 158, 255n150
Gorrée, Georges, 52, 57
Gosling, F. G., 102

63–64, 65; racism, 54–56, 65; versus other desert spiritualities, 34–36, 64. *See also* Foucauld, Charles de; Lavigerie, Charles Martial Allemand
Star Wars, 1, 2
Straiteur, Pierre, 15
Staoueli, Henri de, 52
Stora, Benjamin, 25
Strassmann, Fritz, 103
Strobel, Christoph, 6
Sturt, Charles, 22
Suez Canal, 101, 102
Sūrī, Imān, 190
SW (Special Weapons), 108–9
Swingle, Walter, 99–100

Taithe, Bertrand, 39, 44, 227n65
Tanezrouft (Algeria), 109–12, 114, 115, 186
Taylor, Barry, 161
Tellier, Charles, 69, 89–90, 92
Temaru, Oscar, 122
Thabet, Mohammed, 135, 139
Time, 87, 88*fig.*, 94, 236n84
Tinne, Alexine, 223n2
Tintin, 14
Titus, A. Constandina, 117
Treyer, Claude, 222n144
Trump, Donald, 200
Tsing, Anna, 170
ṭṭāqa, x–xii
Tuaregs, 13–14, 29, 80, 148, 170, 189, 218n60, 223n172; and Charles de Foucauld, 16, 52, 55, 56, 58, 63, 64; defeat by French, 48, 191; killing of Lieutenant Flatters, 11, 30, 55, 70, 123, 234n26; missionary killings, 43, 46; and nuclear racism, 30, 123, 187; territorial resistance of, 11, 48, 110, 123, 168, 189; writers, 29, 166, 187, 193
Turner, George, 145

UNESCO, 1, 2; Arid Zone Program, 2, 67, 100
Union française, 82–83, 96
Urrea, Luis Alberto, 164

Verner, Corinne Cauvin, 148

waḥdat al-kāʾināt. *See* ecocare: unity of creatures (*waḥdat al-kāʾināt*)
Walker, William Ernest, 23
Warren, Jacob, 114
Wazzān, Haṣan al- (Leo Africanus), 1, 6–7
Weightman, John, 153
Westworld, xvi, 157–59, 163
White Army (Frères armés ou pionniers du Sahara), 44–45
White Fathers (Pères blancs), 43–44, 45, 46, 51
Wilde, Oscar, xvi, 131–32, 150, 154–55, 160
Witt, Emily, 160, 161–62
Wolff, Henri, 11–12
Wright, Barbara, 142

Young, James, 204

Zimmerman, Maurice, 73
ZOIA (Zone d'organisation industrielle africaine), 81–84
Zone 42, 115

Founded in 1893,
UNIVERSITY OF CALIFORNIA PRESS
publishes bold, progressive books and journals on topics in the arts, humanities, social sciences, and natural sciences—with a focus on social justice issues—that inspire thought and action among readers worldwide.

The UC PRESS FOUNDATION
raises funds to uphold the press's vital role as an independent, nonprofit publisher, and receives philanthropic support from a wide range of individuals and institutions—and from committed readers like you. To learn more, visit ucpress.edu/supportus.